Strategic Management and Economics in Health Care

Michael Chletsos • Anna Saiti

Strategic Management and Economics in Health Care

Springer

Michael Chletsos
University of Piraeus
Piraeus, Greece

Anna Saiti
Harokopio University
Athens, Greece

ISBN 978-3-030-35369-8 ISBN 978-3-030-35370-4 (eBook)
https://doi.org/10.1007/978-3-030-35370-4

This Springer imprint is published by the registered company Springer Nature Switzerland AG
The registered company address is: Gewerbestrasse 11, 6330 Cham, Switzerland

To Marina, Marios, and Valya

Preface

It is well known that health care is one of the fundamental sectors necessary for the social and economic development of a country. In practice, this means that a country cannot effectively address far-reaching social and economic problems without providing qualitative healthcare services to its citizens. Moreover, a healthcare system cannot become more effective without improvements in its structure and organization. A hospital is the basic and most significant healthcare unit within the healthcare system. Hence, the application of management and economic analysis principles would result in the smoother and more effective functioning of hospitals.

The challenge is for hospitals to have organizational and functional organs that reflect the standards and innovations of their external environment. The rapid changes in the global social and economic environment, together with re-alignments in the internal environment of healthcare units (such as developments in information technology and new working methods), call for a more strategic approach. Strategic management addresses the challenge of how any organization or enterprise, public or private, profit or nonprofit, can not only survive the current demands of a competitive market but also establish the foundations for successful performance in the future. Certainly, it is not enough for a healthcare unit to rest on current successes since certain conditions are required for that success to be sustained. Strategic management can provide hospitals with a comprehensive and sustainable way of handling organizational and managerial matters by establishing rational connections between many factors and parameters.

Economic analysis also helps the healthcare sector to be more effective since it is not just "common sense" or "presentiment" but constitutes economic thinking that facilitates decision making through the process of economic analysis and economic thought. Thus an analysis of, for example, how material resources could be better managed would yield recommendations for enhancing the health unit's performance.

Since this book offers significant managerial and economic knowledge on hospitals, it can be of value not only to employees of healthcare organizations and students but also to any professional practitioner in other fields of, or on the fringes of, the public sector (such as municipalities, regional authorities, and district authorities) as well as the private sector. This book brings together knowledge and thinking in the realms of scientific management and economics, thus making it a valuable tool for explaining complicated managerial and economic problems and for facilitating decision-making processes.

The uniqueness of this book lies in the fact that it bridges management and economic sciences—two complementary sciences that feed the process of making rational decisions. Such knowledge may not be easily found in a single book on health care or indeed on any other sector. This complementarity in management and economics, together with the way the information has been laid out in this book, will help the reader not only comprehend and analyze real problems but most importantly make rational decisions that will significantly improve an organization's performance. Key points conclude each chapter to ensure understanding of the main themes covered.

This book covers all the basic issues of strategic management and economic analysis which are necessary elements for the smooth functioning of the most essential healthcare unit, namely, the hospital. Its content has been arranged into the following chapters:

- Chapter 1 refers to the basic concepts of strategic management and analyzes its key elements.
- Chapter 2 analyzes in depth the environment (both internal and external) within which healthcare units (including hospitals) function.
- Chapter 3 focuses on the process of strategic management and investigates the shaping and the implementation of healthcare units' strategies.
- Chapter 4 analyzes strategic planning in the healthcare sector and presents strategic planning models.
- Chapter 5 discusses the strategic changes in the healthcare sector and analyzes in depth the process of a strategic change.
- Chapter 6 addresses TQM (total quality management) in the healthcare sector and analyzes in depth the implementation of TQM in healthcare units.
- Chapter 7 presents and analyzes the organizational forms of hospitals, the different types of hospital ownership, and the role of the government in the healthcare system when different types of hospitals coexist.
- Chapter 8 discusses in an analytical way the economics of hospitals.
- Chapter 9 examines the hospital as a supplier of healthcare services.
- Chapter 10 addresses the nature of hospitals' financing and analyzes their means of financing.
- Chapter 11 addresses the efficiency and economic performance of hospitals.

Piraeus, Greece Michael Chletsos
Athens, Greece Anna Saiti

Acknowledgements

We would like to deeply thank our family members for their continued support and encouragement. We would also like to express our sincere thanks to Mr Henry Scott and Mrs Gillian Karamani for their inputs and ideas in helping shape this book into its current form.

Contents

Chapter 1
Basic Dimensions of Strategic Management

Key Chapter Concepts

- All organizations (and hospitals) survive because they have a perspective. Hence, organizations should not be indifferent to the events happening in their broader environment, but rather they should adopt a proactive approach which facilitates a more direct confrontation of those events.
- Organizations need to plan and anticipate the future so as to establish a special position in the environment. For this to happen, organizations need to have a mission and a vision. This means they need to see clearly "what they are doing," "where they are going," and "what they want to become." All these need to be communicated in an efficient way to the organizational members.
- Environmental standards in the external environment of an organization are changing rapidly. Therefore, organizations (hospitals included) need to formulate a strategy if they are to avoid any threats and risks and sustain a positive and competitive position within the environment.
- Managers/leaders may align their organization to their strategy, while indeed the strategy should be aligned with the organizational culture.
- Strategy is the basic prerequisite for anticipating the future, while policy provides the predefined framework and formulates actions for the organization's smooth operation. Both are needed for successful performance.

1.1 What Is Mission?

Whether an organization is private, nonprofit, or public (e.g., a hospital, an educational institution, or a firm), it has the ultimate purpose of surviving. To continue its survival, it needs to address certain existential questions, namely, "what we are doing?" and "what is our mission?" (Drucker, 1974, p. 61, cited by David & David, 2017, pp. 160–161). The mission is an organization's reason for being. Therefore, the mission of an organization indicates "a basic function or duty" and sets a basis

M. Chletsos, A. Saiti, *Strategic Management and Economics in Health Care*,
https://doi.org/10.1007/978-3-030-35370-4_1

for the development of an organizational strategy as it clarifies the practical function of the organization in order to achieve a superior performance (David & David, 2015; Koontz & Weihrich, 2010; Saitis & Saiti, 2018; Whitehead, 2002).

We may note that in this book, despite any distinction in the relevant literature, we are going to use the terms "mission" and "purpose" interchangeably (Cady, Wheeler, DeWolf, & Brodke, 2011; Hill, Jones, & Schilling, 2015; Mullins, 2010; Papoulias, 2002; Sidhu, 2003; Zavlanos, 2003). Therefore, for example, the mission (or the purpose) of a hospital unit also corresponds to the services it offers, which must satisfy the needs of patients. Furthermore, the mission (or the purpose) of a hospital is to provide effective care to the community.

The mission (or the purpose) of an organization should be carefully and clearly formulated, indicating the true targets and the actual improvement of the organization, be understood by all the organizational stakeholders concerning the challenges and the importance of the mission, include "a sense of strong vision," and focus on the "emotional involvement of staff members" (Campbell & Yeung, 1991, pp. 17–18).

The mission should be communicated to organizational members directly, as should the organizational strategy for achieving a superior organizational performance. An organization's mission is communicated through the formulation of a mission statement which serves as a communication channel—a two-way process of information flow regarding an organization's strategic choices and directions between managers and staff members. The mission statement should create a climate of mutual, real, motivating, inspirational, and clear understanding of the organization's purpose and activities (Cady et al., 2011; Čuić, 2013; Falsey, 1989; Huff, Floyd, Sherman, & Terjesen, 2009; Lynch, 2006; Stemler & Bebell, 1999; Verma, 2009). The mission statement is not just a simple transmission of information about the organization but it is a process (depending on the content) that influences either positively or negatively the thoughts, views, and behavior of an organization's members and consequently their performance.

Hence, managers should not write statements without considering and understanding the organization's alignment, but they should focus on more meaningful statements that contain two-way communication about the internal and external organizational environment and strong motives for the development of the team spirit among the organizational members (Cady et al., 2011). In other words, they should distinguish "organizational effectiveness" from "organizational actions."

Therefore, the mission of an organization is a general determination which is very crucial. And this is because, through the mission, goals and activities are clarified and the strategies and policies of the organization are outlined. Due to its great importance, during the development of a mission's declaration, the organization's management must take into consideration three basic elements (Fagiano, 1995; Hill, Jones, and Schilling, 2015; Kanellopoulos, 1995; Kaplan & Norton, 1996; Rarick & Vitton, 1995; Verma, 2009), namely, the history of the organization, the distinguished abilities of the organization (i.e., the things the organization performs well at), and its environment, which we will address in the second chapter of this book.

1.2 What Is Vision?

1.2.1 Aim and Meaning

In the relevant literature, it is often mentioned that each social organization, regardless of its type of activity, must have vision, since vision expresses the expectations and dreams of the organization's members about its future. An organization's vision expresses its desired results, it should be in accordance with the organization's values and culture, and it should be inspirational and go beyond the ordinary. It is the basis for the expectations created regarding the organization's future. Vision "is the ability to see the bigger picture and to take the long term view" (Whitehead, 2002, cited by Mullins, 2010, p. 392). The term "vision" is considered as "the description of ideals and organizational goals" (Spanos, 1993, p. 57), "the dream of the future we wish to create for our group. Vision is not what we are, but what we want to become. Creating vision is the essential act of leadership" (David & David, 2015, p. 171; Matejka, Kurke, & Gregory, 1993, p. 34), "the values that shapes its culture" (Curran & Totten, 2010, p. 116), " a picture of what the firm wants to be and, in broad terms, what it wants to ultimately achieve" (Hitt, Ireland, & Hoskisson, 2017, p. 18), and "an expectation, a hope, a dream about an ideal future, better than the present and anticipated by the people" (Bouradas, 2005, p. 88). For example, the vision of a hospital unit might be its future status as a "quality hospital," striving for excellence.

Based on the above definitions, we can see that vision moves an organization's mission forward, since "it is addressed to the mind and heart of the organization's people" (Bouradas, 2001, p. 53). In the case of a hospital unit, accepting a specific vision has the potential to become a spiritual and sentimental challenge because the members of the hospital community must answer to basic questions such as:

- Which ideals do we want to achieve?
- What would that mean about us?
- Do we have to make sacrifices during the year to make the vision a reality?
- Will we be able to respond if we have to act differently?

From the answers to the above questions, we can infer whether or not (a) a vision is feasible, that is, whether it derives from a clear and rational perception of the organization's function, or if it is just a "chimera" or a good intention, and (b) the majority of the team's members are making additional sacrifices for a better future. The vision should imply a united effort since it can lead to changes in behavior and certainly influence performance. For this reason, the development of effort enhancement, enthusiasm, and optimization should be integral elements of a vision (Matejka et al., 1993; Ricci, 2011). Therefore, in order to improve an organization's functionality, a feasible vision serves three basic purposes (Kotter, 2012):

First, to clarify the general direction of change (e.g., of working methods) since most of the time the organization's members disagree on new methods for conducting work. The weakness of taking decisions can be overcome when it is explained that the suggested way of working is actually better than the current one. Moreover, a clearer direction may lead to a simplification of procedures and, by extension, to a reduction in human efforts and costs.

Second, to incite the members of the organization to take actions toward a definite direction, even if the initial steps are painful at a personal level. However, a feasible vision acknowledges that sacrifices are necessary while making it clear that these sacrifices will benefit and cause a level of personal satisfaction higher than the present one.

Last but not least, to help coordinate different person's actions in an efficient way, since administrators and managers comprehend what they must do, without the organizational members requesting any clarification which sometimes hinders unanimous support or causes conflicts, and in a way they can work autonomously.

From the above analysis, we may conclude that a good and feasible vision is crucial for the decisions and attitudes of a team's members as it "attracts and incites people to the implementation of ideal major breakthroughs, giving meaning to everyday life" (Bouradas, 2001, p. 53).

1.2.2 Vision Transmission

The formulation and propagation of the vision to all members of the organization is a basic duty of the senior management, since the specific goals and activities for attaining these goals are formulated and coordinated according to the vision. However, it is not sufficient just to formulate and propagate the vision because, as it is argued (Bouradas, 2005), "the vision must be communicated to people in order to understand and embrace it. To apprehend the distinctive image of a better future and to see their own improved position in the better anticipated future of the business. Needless to say, the communication of the vision cannot be done with frames on the walls and luxurious bows. That must be accomplished through interpersonal communication, so that the employees can be convinced about the honesty, commitment and the passion of the senior management for this issue, except for the acknowledgement of the vision" (p. 89). In other words, in order for a vision to be effective, it must be simple, understandable, and transmitted convincingly, since these features help an organization's members' actions to be addressed, aligned, and inspired. Nonetheless, with an unclear vision, it is difficult to lead an organization's members to take correct and proper decisions, and the greatest, insignificant decisions may create intense conflicts, consume energy, and destroy members' moral. Or, as Kotter (2012) put it distinctively, "You are going to confront problems when you cannot describe within five minutes the vision that constitutes the motivation of an initiative for changes, so as to get a reaction showing that you understand and care" (p. 8). It is true, though, that the success or failure of the vision's transmission depends on many unknown factors such as how it will be transferred or how it will be perceived by the recipient. However, four basic steps provide useful guidelines for communicating the vision:

- Focus on both the qualitative and quantitative elements of a vision. The basic elements for the effective transmission of a vision are clarity, inclusiveness, and honesty.
- Consider the conditions under which the recipients (stakeholders) will receive the vision's message such as how, when, and where it will be transferred.
- Promote two-way communication. In order for the manager to be certain that the vision is understood by the members, he should give them the opportunity to freely express their views. Certainly, this action needs to be linked with "practical methods" for a climate of cooperation and mutual understanding to be created.
- Have a good understanding of the role of informal communication. This means that effective communication channels are established within an organization when managers use the informal organizing so as to complete the communication channels of the formal organization. Hence, it is essential that the upper hierarchical levels of an organization are in touch with the lower levels so as to capture any misunderstanding in the vision's transmission.

1.2.3 Characteristics of an Effective Vision

From the above, it becomes evident that the actual power of a vision is unleashed when most implicated parties in the organization comprehend its goals and direction. To make this happen, a vision must be effective, i.e., it needs to incorporate all the elements required for the goals to be achieved. According to Kotter (2012), an effective vision has the following characteristics:

- It is understandable, clearly describing a future image of the organization.
- It is feasible, consisting of realistic goals.
- It is clear enough, indicating in an unambiguous way the direction of the decisions that needs to be taken.
- It is flexible, leaving room for individual initiatives and future actions as circumstances change.
- It can be transmitted, i.e., easily explained, within short amount of time.

1.2.4 Development of Leaders/Managers Toward the Creation and Transmission of a Vision

At first we have to notice that scientists' views diverge regarding the nature of leadership capability. The smooth and efficient function of an organization and hence a hospital presupposes that harmonious cooperation between leaders and staff members is assured. In order for this to happen, a leader should create effective communication channels with his/her staff members. Here, communication channels are intended to mean that staff members should be kept informed of what is happening in the organization (hospital) and about the plans and future actions of the organization. On one hand, there are those who claim that leadership capability is acquired (Skoulas, 1983, p. 83, Williams & Johnson, 2004)—you are not born a leader but you become one. Consequently, this capability can be obtained. Also, the art of leading is not static but dynamic. The leadership's function is based on principals and mechanistic standards that constantly change. A leader must adjust to, and be familiar with, habits, cultural traditions, systems of values, and society's expectations. On the other hand, there are researchers such as Professor Zaleznik who support the view that "leadership cannot be taught" (Zaleznik, 1977). This view can be valid for persons who are qualified with leadership abilities and in conjunction with interacting variables (such as followers' goals, occasional activities) (Brown, 1981; Kourtis, 1977). A failure in the communication within an organization (a hospital) could lead to misunderstanding, agitation, and strong feelings of disappointment. Consequently, the role of the leader in the communication flow is crucially important.

If we take into consideration (a) the theory that "leadership is much more than technique" (Northouse, 2012; Zaleznik, 1977) that it is more than a combination of talent and capabilities (insight, boldness, concern, persuasion, etc.) which someone must have and (b) the fact that most people in leading positions are not born leaders, we can accept the opinion that "skill and foresight that an efficient leader should have, can be obtained through education and experience" (Williams & Johnson, 2004; Zavlanos, 1998, p. 294).

By applying the above thoughts to hospitals, we may claim that the development of hospital leaders' leadership capabilities is not accomplished after a seminar lasting just a few days or weeks or through the attendance of a bachelor or master's program in a health unit's management. Indeed, more education could actually help managers to a degree. The exploitation of the organization's (hospital's) workplace is also required, since the workplace and its environment are fundamentally significant factors in the ongoing development of leadership abilities (Kotter, 2012; Saitis & Saiti, 2018).

But how can that happen in a hospital unit? A leader's responsibility is not confined to ensuring that the necessary conditions for the smooth operation of a hospital are in place. A good leader must take care of the staff member's development simultaneously as a trainer. He/she must transmit to his/her collaborators the required knowledge and capabilities so that they can perform their work effectively.

For example, the doctor that starts practicing with a vast amount of knowledge and some practical experience, it is certain that he will need management support due to the complexity and frequent changes in the medical field, if they are to respond to their duties in a successful and efficient way.

In reality, a hospital manager should, on a daily basis, support all staff members through encouragement and guidance and by ensuring a working environment that allows them to improve themselves, that is, behaving toward them as though they are better at their work than they really are. This enhances the personnel's confidence and by extension increases the likelihood of reaching an exceptional performance.

Since an individual does willingly what is really in their personal interest, a hospital manager should stimulate his/her colleague's interest in their duties. Or as characteristically is said, "most people are satisfied and incited from their work, when through it, evolve their knowledge, abilities and personality. Human development boosts confidence and contributes essentially to professional evolvement and progress, and it satisfies the needs of integration and self-esteem" (Bouradas, 2005, p. 296).

Hence, a question arises: what are the basic points around which the education of staff members must revolve? Even though development is a personal issue (depending on one's learning ability, their motivations, and personality), the development of employees in a hospital unit is strongly affected by the manager. This kind of development program must include at least the following elements.

Developing a Sense of Responsibility

Taking as granted that people (hospital staff members included) (a) are responsible for their actions, so awakening a sense of responsibility is a common feeling, which can drive employees to greater achievements, and (b) are more interested in a duty, as they feel more capable of completing it, then the manager must properly train his/her subordinates about the way they practice their duties and how to encourage and guide them so they discover on their own the best way to reach the most satisfying outcome. In a sense, the manager provides a framework for freedom of initiative to his/her staff members by creating the feeling that they can make a valuable contribution using their own set of abilities. In order for a manager to enhance the sense of responsibility, he/she needs to assign responsibilities to the employees. Many managers consider it difficult to assign responsibilities to trainers as they feel that they are overburdening their personnel or that they are not sure that the work will be done properly. Some may even agree with McGregor's theory X, which assumes that most employees are truants and do not want to take over responsibilities. Undoubtedly, when we assign duties/responsibilities to inexperienced individuals for the first time, we will definitely discover that they will need more than the usual estimated time that we would have needed for those duties than if we had carried out the task on our own. In line with what has been done, we can support that managers should share responsibility with their staff members, since assignment contributes to the development of skills and abilities.

Developing a Sense of Solidarity

The sense of solidarity among the members of a typical organization (and for a hospital unit) is a basic characteristic of an efficient organization since actions do not have consequences just for those who carried them out, but they have repercussions for the entire organization. For this reason, as the sense of solidarity increases, the degree of personnel's responsibility increases as well. Based on this perception, the manager should know how to develop the feeling of mutual support among his/her staff members. Of course, it is not easy for a manager to achieve perfect harmony among the employees, because they are different persons with varying attitudes, perceptions, aspirations, and behaviors in the working environment. Despite the difficulties, a manager can confront unpleasant situations (jealousy, competition, creation of "cliques"), if he/she can preserve coordinated collaboration with all hospital personnel. Moreover, we must not forget that each staff member easily examines and judges everything from his point of view without taking into account the group's needs. An individual usually sees what bothers or impedes him/her from carrying out their work. To conclude, the hospital manager's duty is to give to his staff members the potential to understand that the effective operation of the hospital unit must lean on collective effort and all employees must harmoniously work for the accomplishment of their hospital's common goals.

Development of Work's Excellence

The transmission of knowledge and experience to the correct use of available job tools is a characteristic example in this direction.

Development of Work Execution Planning

The manager ought to teach his staff members that before starting a task, they must consider the way of completing it. Through this technique, they will be in the position to know what they want to do, and in what way, in a predetermined time frame. Finally, we notice that the nontypical form of personnel's education from the hospital unit's manager is a voluntary activity, the success of which depends on the will of both sides: managers and employees.

1.3 Objective or Aim[1]

1.3.1 Different Approaches to Meanings

After defining "mission" and "vision," there follows an urgent need to design individual objectives. Objectives are the horizon toward the collective activity of a team's efforts. An actual effective activity can exist when the organization's

[1] In the relevant literature (Cady et al., 2011; Georges, Efthimiadou, & Tsytos, 1998; Mullins, 2010; Sarsentis, 1996, p. 20; Zevgaridis, 1983, p. 20), there is a distinction between objective purposes and aims. The objective purpose or general goal is perceived as a subjective prearranged desired state that cannot be evaluated accurately by third parties. However, "objective" also has a special quantitative or qualitative concept. It is about a countable description of a desired result

members know what to do. We observe that the aim of an organization (and hence a hospital) is not related to its objectives. The objective of a hospital should be stable and could be to provide qualitative health-care services and medical care to all social groups while advancing medical research so as to promote medical treatments. On the contrary, aims are specific but changing expressions of purpose at each moment, taking into consideration the existing changes (financial, social, technological) in the hospital's environment.

Depending on the time horizon, aims are distinguished in the short term (1 year long), the middle term (2–4 years), and the long term (5 years and over).

Irrespective of time length, aims aspire to create a situation as a result of a collaborative action. They pursue changes that take the organization closer to its destination—changes which, once achieved, can become stepping-stones to new aims. These objectives are specific and changing expressions of the purpose at every moment in time.

1.3.2 Categories of Aims

A hospital unit, as a structured organization, has aims which should be completed through certain procedures. In other words, a hospital's survival can be attributed to the transformation of general pursuits and matters of health, which are institutionalized through specific and achievable goals. Of course, the aims of hospital organizations have been a point of reference for many researchers (such as Ginter, Duncan, and Swayne (2018), Hoy and Miskel (1987), Longest and Darr (2014), Paisey (1992), and Schulz and Johnson (1990)), and so far there is no commonly accepted list of categories for these goals. For the purposes of this book, we may adopt Alan Paisey's view (1992), according to which three categories of aims must be taken into account by the organizations (and thus by hospitals):

- *Personal aims* that are formulated by health personnel and patients. These goals specify changes that people desire for themselves, working circumstances and employment terms.
- *Hospital aims*, which refer to structural changes and which individuals aspire to separately. There are changes in individuals' behavior that contain changes in knowledge, skills, and habits. Hospital aims are mainly to do with changes in the provision of health-care services.
- *Aims of resources* that primarily refer to material resources which the employee needs in order for their task to become feasible. However, if the word "resources" is defined "as anything at the hospital's disposal to achieve its goals," then the

within a given time and certain financial constraints. Since (a) many writers such as Koontz, O'Donnell, and Weihrich (1980) use these terms interchangeably and (b) in everyday life we do not make the above distinction uniformly, the terms "objective purposes and aims" will be used interchangeably in this book.

aim of resources can refer to structural changes in terms of human resources and material resources that are or could be available to the hospital so as to satisfy individual and hospital aims.

Given that a hospital's goals are many and material resources are limited, the hospital management should prioritize the kind of treatments that patients should have taken as both inpatients and outpatients. As hospital goals need to be set in line with the resources available, the pursuit of sensationalist performance statistics should be avoided so as not to stretch the human resources to breaking point.

1.3.3 Strategy for Creating Aims

The way that aims are created has exceptional meaning. That is valid for the hospital aims and the resource aims as well.

But who is responsible for forming these aims? According to Paisey (1992), there are two strategies for an organization (and hence a hospital) to formulate goals: the "downward" (top-down) strategy is imperative, because it is formulated by a person or a small group collectively, and the "upward" (bottom-up) strategy, where hospital goals are underlined by the needs of health system (i.e., its users—the patients). This strategy considers each one's interests and expresses goals in coordination with the hospital members' goals.

Even though both strategies have advantages and drawbacks, we think that in a democratic society the hospital aims should follow the upward formulation method, while resource aims must be defined by the central administration which funds the system. However, the efficient flow of information depends on the formulation of an organizational structure for the health-care system. In strictly centralized health-care systems, however, hospital aims are not formulated by the internal environment and by the widely accepted views of society, but instead by the central authorities (administration). Regardless of the type of health-care system and management structure (whether strictly hierarchical or flat), if the system follows an organization-enabling structure, the upward formulation method will be facilitated within hospitals and the strategic intentions will be communicated to the organizational members in an efficient and effective way that establishes the basis for improved performance.

1.4 What Is Strategy?

1.4.1 Aims and Meaning

Many researchers have converged on the conclusion that the term "strategy" has its roots in the strictly hierarchical sector of the armed forces and consists of a strategic plan devised to gain a competitive advantage by putting the enemy in a difficult position and thus weaken them so as to win the war (Bruce & Langdon, 2001; Georgopoulos, 2006; Papadakis, 2007; Saitis & Saiti, 2018; Whipp, 1998).

Although "strategy" is sometimes used in the traditional military sense and nowadays implies a kind of competition, it is used even more to reflect the broader general ideas of an organization's operation. In particular, a strategy establishes as a rule a general program of action and resources' apposition for the achievement of certain aims. The formulation of a strategy involves organizational changes that give value to the organization (Boyd, 1991; Hughes & Beatty, 2005; Kaplan & Norton, 1996; Koontz et al., 1980; Kukalis, 1991). It is related with long-term performance since it is based on long-term targets and determines the position of an organization within its environment.

1.4.2 But What Is Strategy?

According to Dubrin (1997), the word "strategy" is defined as the "organization's program or the apprehension program for the achievement of mission and aims in its environment" (p. 133). The strategy is a collective program of what the organization wants to be (Boyd, 1991; Silbiger, 1993); it is a guide that makes the actions of an organization's members more visible to managers and at the same time allows managers to ensure the suitability of these actions (Boyd, 1991; Koontz & Weihrich, 2010; Salaman & Storey, 2005).

The term "strategy" (Anthony, 1965) is also viewed as a "procedure followed to take decisions for the objective purposes of the organization, for changes on these objective purposes, for the resources used in the achievement of objective purposes and for the policies that will govern acquisition, use and disposal of these resources" (p. 24).

There are writers who define this specific term as an action plan (which depicts the direction of the organization in the competitive environment" (Zavlanos, 1998, p. 126) and as a dynamic means which "contains the aims and plans of the organization and an action program for the achievement of these goals and plans in this competitive environment" (Kanellopoulos, 1995, p. 86). It examines not only the organization's aims but also the means of existence and the general direction of the organization which is based on the examination and analysis of differences between the organization's position and its competitors (Goldstein & Pfeifer, 1993; Hill et al., 2015; Hitt et al., 2017; Kaplan & Norton, 1996; Melcher & Kerzner, 1988). Therefore, it is a process that, through operational activities (a sequence of steps), an organization attempts to achieve its aims and objectives.

Based on the above definitions, it is evident that strategy is not just a group of rules or programmed directions, but it is rather a full and integrated plan which an organization should implement so as to respond to its mission and reach its vision. It also determines the levels of targeted performance (Salaman & Storey, 2005, p. 104). It is a declaration of intentions which determine what we want to become in the future.

1.4.3 Thus, a Question Arises: Why Is Strategy Planning Important for Modern Organizations?

First, we should emphasize the fact that strategy is an important and integral part of each organization regardless of the size or type of activity that develops within the organizational environment. This is due to the fact that the environment in which an organization finds itself is becoming ever more complicated and changeable. Therefore, a strategy is a continuous process whereby an organization's current data is analyzed to determine its future direction. In other words, strategy helps toward (and indeed enhances) an organization's effective and superior performance. Among the basic roles of strategy that contribute to the success of an organization are (Papadakis, 2007, pp. 34–37):

- *Gives an organization direction* since strategy determines the long-term plans and targets to be implemented.
- *Supports homogenous decision-making* since the decisions for the achievement of targets lean toward a clear and acceptable strategy agreed by all stakeholders.
- *Coordinates all the members' activities*, since the collective action is based on programmed actions.
- *Helps reduce the impact of uncertainties in the external environment* since, through a strategy, it is much easier for a manager to identify and distinguish an opportunity from a threat. For this reason, a strategy is absolutely necessary in times of intense changes.
- *Gives a sustainable competitive advantage to the organization* since it allows the successful and harmonic connection between the external environment and the organization's internal capabilities.

Based on the above, we may support the view that a strategy ensures that the daily decisions are in accordance with the long-term targets of an organization. On the contrary, the lack of a strategy increases the likelihood that current decisions will have a negative impact on the future outcomes of the organization. Furthermore, a strategy is an important tool for an organization to interact with its environment, but most of all, it harmonizes the direction of organizational members' efforts as they cooperate in order to achieve the organization's goals (Bruce & Langdon, 2000; Georgopoulos, 2006; Hart, 1992; Kaplan & Norton, 1996). It should be noted that strategy does not determine exactly how the targets will be achieved because this can be clarified by the implementation of support programs.

1.4.4 Characteristics of an Effective Strategy

In the previous subsection, we mentioned that strategy can be a complete plan, applied by the organization to correspond to its mission and to reach its vision. In order for this plan to attribute to the success of an organization (a hospital), it must consist of these elements:

- Contain simple and long-term purposes
- For the competitive environment of the organization to have been fully understood
- For an objective assessment of resources (human and material) of the organization to have been carried out and the content, duration, adjustment process, and changing conditions to have been clarified
- For a formulated strategy to be implemented efficiently and transparently through a capable and steady management
- To ensure there is support for innovation through a proactive approach
- For members' staff actions to be well coordinated since the implementation of any strategic plan is based on a number of interrelated actions

1.4.5 Ways of Avoiding Bad Strategies

It is generally accepted that in times of financial crisis, such as the one we are going through, every incorrect decision, every wrong choice made by the administration of the public or private institutions may have dramatic repercussions, both for the present and for the future of specific organizations. This acceptance leads us to the following question.

1.4.6 What Should a Leading Manager Do to Avoid Defective Strategies?

In the daily and weekly press, we often read texts about wrong choices received by skilled leading managers of large organizations. In particular, it mentions that distinguished leading managers of organizations (with enough experience and correct information) succumb to terrible mistakes and make wrong choices that ultimately lead to strategic mistakes. Of course, strategic mistakes derive from many factors such as the precaution mechanisms, a leader's specific character, and the procedure by which a decision is received and implemented. However, in the case of a defective strategy, the issue should not be a fear of failure but how a leading manager can learn from their mistakes. In close relation to this problem, this long-term research showed that half of the organizational defaults could be avoided if in the entire strategy development process a "Devil's advocate" was present to evaluate things that could be done differently (Damoulianou, 2011; Mullins, 2010; Olson & Simerson, 2015; Schermerhorn, Hunt, & Osborn, 2002). In an ideal world, there would be an independent person (or a group of people) that is/are completely neutral, i.e., they would not personally benefit in any way from the outcome and the strategy planning process. The challenge would then be to compose a report for the leadership of the organization, outlining what is missing from the strategy planning process. For this reason, this specific person would have the right to pose questions to the manager responsible for strategy design, such as:

- Is this strategy feasible?
- Have you taken into consideration all the dissenter's requests?
- Have you objectively mapped out the strengths and weaknesses of the organization?

In this way, it would help leading members to gain a fuller picture of members' sentiments that incorporates all feedback (both positive and negative) through upward communication (Saitis & Saiti, 2018). Or, as it was characteristically put by Goleman (2001), "people who exhibit the *Communication* competence are effective in the give-and-take of emotional information, deal with difficult issues straightforwardly, listen well and welcome sharing information fully, and foster open communication and stay receptive to bad news as well as good" (p. 37).

Finally, we notice that the role of the "Devil's advocate" is not to investigate the leading managers who are responsible for planning strategies. Instead, their role is to investigate facts and not the feelings and intuitions that accompany them. Thus, for this reason, persons who come to rushed conclusions should be avoided.

1.5 Elements of Policy

1.5.1 Meaning

For the objectives and purposes of an organization to become a reality, its administration ought to take certain decisions that dictate a certain strategy and define ways of implementing it. On one hand, these decisions must be compatible with the strategy's content and programs. On the other hand, they must be coordinated and have cohesion. Meaningful policies can cover this necessity (Bouradas, 2001).

For Koontz et al. (1980), "policies were identified as guides to thinking in decision making. They assume that when decisions are made, these will fall within certain boundaries. Policies do not require action, but are intended to guide managers in their decisions commitments when they do make decisions" (p. 274). It is general declarations or perceptions guiding or defining the course of thoughts and energies when taking decisions (Koontz et al., 1980, p. 164). Based on this perception, "policy" defines an area in which a decision is going to be taken and ensures that the decision will be consistent with the organization's goals. According to another view (Dubrin, 1997), the term "policy" is considered as a general guideline that must be followed for the organization's decision-making and activities. Some writers converged on the conclusion that the term "policy" in fact refers to "documented guidelines that make the company's strategy specific" (Papoulias, 2002, p. 135) and includes "guidelines, rules, and procedures established to support efforts to achieve stated objectives and are guides to decision making and address repetitive or recurring situations" (David & David, 2015, p. 46). For others, policies constitute "general directions of activity in which objective purposes are joined" (Sarsentis, 1996, p. 21) and also "general and unstable directives that make it easier for managers to make decisions, allowing them to use their judgment in specific restrictions" (Kanellopoulos, 1995, p. 82).

From the abovementioned definitions, it is evident that researchers in science administration do not agree on a commonly accepted definition of the term "policy." However, we may perceive "policy" to be either "a general declaration" and "a general guideline" or a "documented directive" and "general activity directive," which is nothing more than the administrative mechanism which sets the framework for decision-making in relation to the objectives of the organization (hospital).

1.5.2 Approaches to the Term "Policy"

Even though policies are designed to be consistent with strategic plans, they do leave room for interpretation by the competent single member or collective administrative body. There lies a critical point in the application of policies, since their interpretation by managers may possibly lead to directives that take the organization away from its goals. To illustrate the point, we will mention an example of policy and how this can be interpreted.

Example of a policy: "When you choose the leading manager in the field of health care, take into consideration only the candidates who are administratively capable or promising to become administratively capable with good personal character and are distinct for their social offer."

The members of the Selection Committee who will be called to apply the above policy must answer the following questions:

- What do we mean by the term "administratively capable"?
- How can we evaluate the "administrative ability" of each candidate manager?
- What do we mean when we say that a candidate must have "good personal character?"
- What does "promising to be administratively capable" mean?
- What can we include in the meaning "social offer of the candidate"?

The above example not only shows the degree of difficulty in the interpretation of a policy but also proves why in many cases its implementation is administratively rather difficult.

1.5.3 Difficulties in Understanding the Term "Policy"

According to what was previously mentioned, the term "policy" is most commonly regarded as a predefined frame in which managers must take decisions for issues concerning the organization's operation. However, because the above term can be an object of misunderstanding, we consider it appropriate to mention two examples from a hospital environment in order to better comprehend the term "policy."

Example 1 *Employment of medical personnel.*

"No doctor of secondary care is allowed to have a private practice while being a hospital employee."

Example 2 *Granting permission to participate in a conference, postgraduate course, or research study.*

"Every manager (Clinic or Hospital) or Science Council can grant hospital staff permission for participating in a Conference, Postgraduate course or Research study as long as it suffices to meet scientific reasons and the proper functioning of the hospital is not disturbed."

By granting a hospital's medical staff the permission to participate in a conference, master's course, or research study, the scope of a manager's personal judgment remains fairly broad and that is why this case counts as a policy. On the contrary, a doctor's employment policy does not leave any freedom for a manager's personal judgment so it counts as a rule. By saying "rule," we mean a certain course of action that must be followed by all members of the organization. It is a certain type of expression that is used to inform someone what they must or must not do. For example, the phrase "the use of mobile phones during class is forbidden," which expresses a specific way of behavior, is a rule (Kanellopoulos, 1995). Therefore, rules allow organizations to put their employees in positions of responsibility, so they cannot act differently.

In conclusion, policies do not require action but do provide leading managers at all administration levels with the right to act in accordance with their judgment. Otherwise, if an instruction does not require a manager's personal judgment during the decision-making process, then it is a rule.

1.5.4 Is "Strategy" Different from "Policy"?

According to Koontz et al. (1980), "strategies and policies have a close relationship with each other" (p. 274). The abovementioned researchers claim that strategies express a general command of action and a development of effort and resources for the achievement of essential objectives. A strategy concerns the direction toward which human and material resources will be used in order to maximize the possibility of achieving a chosen goal. Policies, however, are thought's guiders during decision-making. Hence, the essence of a policy allows an administrative manager to act according to his/her judgment. Furthermore, while policies do not demand action, their purpose is to guide administrative managers in their commitments when they take decisions.

Some policies and strategies that give a consolidated direction to the entire organization can essentially be coextensive. However, we can make a logical distinction of these meanings by saying that policies guide leading managers' thoughts during decision-making while strategies are the decisions that an organization has made to commit certain resources in order to fulfil a particular goal (Koontz et al., 1980).

1.5.5 Policy Sources

Policies can be discerned into many categories (Koontz et al., 1980), among which are the following:

- "Authentic or created" policies deriving from the free will of the pertinent leading managers of the organization. The so-called policies basically come with the organization's aims and are usually the creations of the superior management of the specific organization (Koontz et al., 1980). We say "usually" because the opinion that "all policies" are designated by the superior leading managers of the organization is not absolutely correct. Of course, the higher the position of a leader in the organization's administrative structure, the more important is their role in policy-making. And the highest leadership has a leading role in defining the general policies of an organization, which is rational, since the purpose of policies is to guide decision-making from managers of subordinate hierarchical levels. Nevertheless, even if staff members' managers must apply the policies defined by their superiors, they still have the ability to determine policies themselves so as to guide their collaborators (Koontz et al., 1980; Mullins, 2010).
- "Mandatory or imposed" policies which are asserted by external factors such as government, trade unions, and various social teams (e.g., political parties, faith institutions, etc.) either in the form of direct provisions or through collective negotiations or with some other activities of various social actors that can form or dictate the policy of any organization, whether public or private.

1.5.6 Factors for Effective Policy Implementation

In order to become effective and efficient, a policy must ensure certain conditions are met, among which are the following:

- To serve a specific aim of the organization
- To be explained to, and analyzed by, the organization's members involved in its application in a conceivable way so that each member learns what to do, as well as how and when to complete it
- For a communication network to exist so that the manager responsible for the policy's application can be constantly informed about the course of its implementation and the results
- To have the flexibility to adjust to every future change in an organization's internal and external environment

- To be achievable, that is, for the decisions of leading managers (and, by extension, the designation of aims) not to exceed the organization's abilities

1.6 What Is a Program?

The outcomes of the programming process are the programs, which are directly connected to the implementation of a specific task. Or, as Allen (1958) put it, the program gives a "gradual approach to the achievement of objective purposes" (p. 34). Referring to programs, Koontz et al. (1980) further inform us that a "complex amount of aims, policies, procedures, rules, duties' assignment, needed actions, sources to be used and other elements mandatory for the implementation of a given action are usually corroborated by the necessary funds and operation's budgets" (p. 168).

Based on the above, we could say that programs of action refer to a sequence of steps which, if interrupted, can prevent its objective purposes from being achieved, especially when some elements (political procedures, budgets, etc.) are lacking in some way (e.g., integrity, quantity, quality).

A program is a significant tool for the organization (hospital) since it is the operational function of the organization's strategy. It focuses mainly on guiding the lower levels in the organization's structure and therefore aligns all staff members to the organization's strategy (Kaplan & Norton, 1996; Longest & Darr, 2014). Indeed, the execution and the realization of a strategy is not easy as it should be linked to changes in contextual factors (Kaplan & Norton, 1996; Kukalis, 1991). Besides, a strategy without implementation and execution is not a strategy but merely an intention. Therefore, a program should be carefully designed, have continuity, and include all the necessary details such as time frame in order to better reflect the environmental complexity. And although the degree of influence of environmental complexity and uncertainty on strategic choices depends, among other things, on the perceived sensitivity of managers to the organization's environment (both internal and external), a program remains a crucial and necessary tool for the execution of the organization's strategy.

With particular reference to the health-care sector, planning and programming are even more important because hospitals have a societal orientation, public accountability, responsibility, and a crucial role within a community—aspects that are very much under the spotlight in emergency situations such as an earthquake or the outbreak of an epidemic. The planning and programming of a hospital's actions reaffirm the provision of health-care services on a continuous basis as they align all employees to the achievement of targets and thus help hospitals to best serve the community, no matter the circumstances. Indeed, a hospital's program coordinates all the departments and units, assigns roles and responsibilities among staff members, and links all levels of the hierarchy to the execution of the strategy. Within this framework, hospitals ensure the commitment of the upper levels of leadership to the realization of its strategy while, through this mobilization, the cooperation of the hospitals' human resources is enhanced. Thus, hospitals are better able to meet the challenges of social accountability, trust, efficiency, and effectiveness.

References

Allen, L. (1958). *Management and organization*. New York: McGraw Hill.

Anthony, N. B. (1965). *Planning and control system: A. framework for analysis*. Boston: Division of Research, Harvard Business School.

Bouradas, D. (2001). *Management*. Athens, Greece: Benou Publications. (in Greek).

Bouradas, D. (2005). *Leadership*. Athens, Greece: Kritiki Publishing. (in Greek).

Boyd, B. K. (1991). Strategic planning and financial performance: a meta analytic review. *Journal of Management Review, 28*(4), 353–363.

Brown, J. (1981). *The social psychology of industry*. New York: Penguin Books.

Bruce, A., & Langdon, K. (2000). *Strategic thinking*. New York: DK Essential Managers.

Bruce, A., & Langdon, K. (2001). *Strategic design*. Athens, Greece: Ellinika Grammata Publishing (in Greek).

Cady, S. H., Wheeler, J. V., DeWolf, J., & Brodke, M. (2011). Mission, vision and values: what do they say ? *Organization Development Journal, 29*(1), 63–78.

Campbell, A., & Yeung, S. (1991). Creating a sense of mission. *Long Range Planning, 24*(4), 10–20.

Čuić, T. A. (2013). Defining strategy using vision and mission statements of croatian organizations in times of crisis. In: *The 6th international conference "The changing economic landscape: issues, implications and policy options" May 30–June 1, Economic Research Special Issue 2013*, pp. 331–342

Curran, C. R., & Totten, M. K. (2010). Mission, strategy and stakeholders. *Nursing Economics, 28*(2), 116–118.

Damoulianou, Ch. (2011). Brainstorming is neglected and adopted its pilot. *Kathimerini, Greek newspaper* 2 February 2011, p. 10 (in Greek).

David, F. R., & David, F. R. (2015). Strategic management: a competitive advantage approach. In *Concepts and cases* (16th ed.). England: Pearson.

David, F. R., & David, F. R. (2017). Strategic management: a competitive advantage approach. *Concepts and cases* (16th ed.). England: Pearson Education Limited.

Drucker, P. (1974). *Management: Tasks, responsibilities, and practices*. New York: Harper & Row.

Dubrin, A. J. (1997). *Essentials of management* (14th ed.). UK: South Western College Publishing.

Fagiano, D. (1995). Value is as value does. *Management Review, 84*(7), 5.

Falsey, T. A. (1989). *Corporate philosophies and Mission statements: A survey and guide for corporate communicators and management*. New York: Quorum Books.

Georges, D. P., Efthimiadou, A., & Tsytos, D. (1998). *Practical orientation in modern management*. Athens, Greece: Ellinika Grammata Publications. (in Greek).

Georgopoulos, N. (2006). *Strategic management*. Athens, Greece: Benou Publishing. (in Greek).

Ginter, P. M., Duncan, W. J., & Swayne, L. G. (2018). *The strategic management of health care organizations* (8th ed.). Hoboken, NJ: Wiley.

Goldstein, L., & Pfeifer, T. (1993). *Applied strategic planning*. New York: McGraw-Hill Inc.

Goleman, D. (2001). An EI based theory of performance. In G. Cherniss & D. Goleman (Eds.), *The emotionally intelligent workplace* (pp. 27–44). San Francisco: Jossey Bass.

Hallinger, P., & Heck, R. (2004). Understanding the contribution of leadership to school improvement. In M. Wallace & L. Paulson (Eds.), *Learning to read critically in educational leadership and management* (pp. 215–235). London: SAGE Publication.

Hart, S. L. (1992). An integrative framework for strategy-making processes. *Academy of Management Review, 17*(2), 327–351.
Hill, W. L., Jones, G. R., & Schilling, M. A. (2015). *Strategic management theory* (11th ed.). Cengage Learning: Boston, MA.
Hitt, M. A., Ireland, R. D., & Hoskisson, R. E. (2017). Strategic management. Competitiveness and globalization. In *Concepts and cases* (12th ed.). Boston, MA, Cengage Learning.
Hoy, W., & Miskel, C. (1987). Educational administration: Theory research and practice. In *New York*. Lane Akers.
Huff, A. S., Floyd, S. W., Sherman, H. D., & Terjesen, S. (2009). *Strategic management, logic and action*. New York: Wiley.
Hughes, R. L., & Beatty, K. C. (2005). *Becoming a strategic leader*. San Francisco: Jossey Bass.
Kanellopoulos, C. (1995). *Management—Effective administration*. Athens, Greece: Kanellopoulos Publications. (in Greek).
Kaplan, R. S., & Norton, D. P. (1996). *Using the balanced scorecard as a strategic management system* (pp. 37–48). Harvard Business Review.
Koontz, H., O'Donnell, C., & Weihrich, H. (1980). *Management* (7th ed.). London: McGraw Hill International Book Company.
Koontz, H., & Weihrich, H. (2010). *Essentials of management: An international perspective*. New Delhi: McGraw Hill.
Kotter, J. P. (2012). *Leading change*. Boston, MA: Harvard Business Review Process.
Kourtis, K. E. (1977). *The theory and the practice of modern administration Athens*. Greece: Kourtis Publications. (in Greek).
Kukalis, S. (1991). Determinants of strategic planning systems in large organizations: A contingency approach. *Journal of Management Review, 28*(2), 143–160.
Longest, B. B., & Darr, K. (2014). *Managing health services: Organizations and systems* (6th ed.). Baltimore, MD: Health Profession Press.
Lynch, R. (2006). *Corporate strategy* (4th ed.). England, UK: Prentice Hall.
Matejka, K., Kurke, L. B., & Gregory, B. (1993). Mission impossible? Designing a great mission statement to ignite your plans. *Management Decision, 31*(4), 34–37.
Melcher, B., & Kerzner, H. (1988). *Strategic planning: Development and implementation*. Blue Ridge Summit PA: Tab Books.
Mullins, L. J. (2010). *Management and organisational behavior* (9th ed.). London: Prentice Hall.
Northouse, P. G. (2012). *Leadership. Theory and practice* (6th ed.). Thousand Oaks, CA: Sage Publication.
Olson, A. K., & Simerson, B. K. (2015). *Leading with strategic thinking*. Hoboken, NJ: Wiley.
Paisey, A. (1992). *Organization and management in schools* (2nd ed.). London: Longman.
Papadakis, V. (2007). *Business strategy. Greek and international experience* (Vol. A). Athens, Greece: Benou Publishing. (in Greek).
Papoulias, D. (2002). *Business strategic management & change management*. Athens, Greece: Kastanioti Publishing. (in Greek).
Rarick, C. A., & Vitton, J. (1995). Corporate strategy: Mission statement make cents. *Journal of Business Strategy, 16*(1), 11–12.
Ricci, F.A. (2011). Managing the organizational vision, mission and planning: Five steps toward a successful leadership strategy. In: *Paper presented in The Chair Academy 20th Annual International Leadership Conference, Strategic Leadership, Dallas, Texas March 24*, p. 7.
Saitis, C., & Saiti, A. (2018). *Initiation of educators into educational management secrets*. New York: Springer.
Salaman, G. & Storey, J. (2005). Achieving 'Fit': Managers' theories of how to manage innovation. In Salaman, G., Storey, J. and Billsberry, J. (Eds,) Strategic human resource management: Theory and practice. A reader, (pp. 91–115), London: Sage Publications
Sarsentis, V. (1996). *Strategy and business policy*. Piraeus, Greece: Stamoulis Publishing. (in Greek).
Schermerhorn, J. R., Hunt, J. G., & Osborn, R. N. (2002). *Organizational behaviour* (7th ed.). Hoboken, NJ: Wiley.

Schulz, R., & Johnson, A. C. (1990). *Management of hospitals and health services. Strategic issues and performance* (3rd ed.). Beard Books.
Sidhu, J. (2003). Mission statements: Is it time to shelve them? *European Management Journal, 21*(4), 439–446.
Silbiger, S. (1993). *The ten day MBA: A step by step guide to mastering the skills taught in America's top business schools*. London, UK: Piatkus.
Skoulas, N. (1983). *The human nature of management*. Athens, Greece: Livanis Publications. (in Greek).
Spanos, A. (1993). *Total quality*. Athens, Greece: Galaios. (in Greek).
Stemler, S., & Bebell, D. (1999). An empirical approach to understanding and analyzing the mission statements of selected educational institutions. In: Paper presented at the Annual Meeting of the New England Educational Research Organization (NEERO) (Portsmouth, New Hampshire, April 9, 1999).
Verma, H. V. (2009). Mission statements: A study of intent and influence. *Journal of Services Research, 9*(2), 153–172.
Whipp R. (1998). Creative deconstruction: Strategy and organisations. In: Paper presented the ESRC seminar series, Redefining Educational Management, Cardiff.
Whitehead, M. (2002). Everyone's a leader now. *Supply Management, 7*(4), 22–24.
Williams, K., & Johnson, B. (2004). *Introducing management: A development guide*. Great Britain: Planta Tree.
Zaleznik, A. (1977). Managers and leaders: Are they different? Harvard Business Review, Classic, pdf file 16 pages. https://hbr.org/2004/01/managers-and-leaders-are-they-different
Zavlanos, M. (1998). *Management*. Athens, Greece: Ellin Publishing. (in Greek).
Zavlanos, M. (2003). *Total quality in education*. Athens, Greece: Stamouli Publishing. (in Greek).
Zevgaridis, S. (1983). *Organization and administration. Vol. D*, Thessaloniki, Greece: Kiriakidis Publishing (in Greek).

Chapter 2
Environment and Health-Care Units

Key Chapter Concepts

- The effective functionality of modern organizations is judged by their ability to respond directly to the continuous and rapid changes in their internal and external environment.
- Health-care targets and material resources need to be aligned realistically. In other words, targets should not be set that exceed either human or system capacities for whatever reason (e.g., to impress financers, etc.). Effectiveness depends on the abilities of the managerial mechanism that programs, organizes, and coordinates all hospital actions.
- Organizational culture indicates the way in which activities are carried out in the organization and thus influences the work done by its members. The type of an organization's dominant culture seems to be determined by the degree to which the elements of one type prevail over other types of culture. The shaping of a positive culture in a health-care unit it is not simply a matter of stating some values or principles in the form of interventions and wishes.
- A strong/positive culture can bestow great benefits upon organizations (hospitals included) that enable them to preserve and develop such a culture if it exists or to create it if it is absent.
- A health-care unit should be open to society in general so as to develop and cultivate between them a cooperation with mutual respect and a common target for treating civilians in terms of high-quality health-care services.

2.1 Environmental Dependency of Health-Care Units

As we may see further in this book, health-care units (and hospitals) are open systems and have a continuous interdependence and interaction with their operating environment. The word "system" embraces a number of elements and relations that

M. Chletsos, A. Saiti, *Strategic Management and Economics in Health Care*,
https://doi.org/10.1007/978-3-030-35370-4_2

exist between them (Papoulias, 2002, p. 4) and includes basic components such as inputs, outputs, feedback, limits, and processes (Hoy & Miskel, 1996).

The perception of a system's results is of particular significance when implementing strategies/programs because it drives an organization's leaders to seek out significant external influences/threats and to create units that will be ready to respond effectively to the trials presented by the outside world (Borenstein, Badamgarav, Henning, Gano, & Weingarten, 2004; Boyne, 2003; Papoulias, 2002). With particular reference to the health-care system, the environmental influences, which are numerous and varied (e.g., technological, economic, etc.), transfer various tensions in the external environment through a feedback mechanism that affects significant elements of the system such as the structure, the people, the duties, and their inter-relations within health-care organizations (hospitals). For example, changes that are provoked in the economic field shape new social structures that shape new interests which lead to conflict among social groups. Within this framework, through its political activities, the State introduces reforms which inevitably prompt counterreforms (Michopoulos, 1998; Saiti, 2013) or, as Bouzakis (1994) implied, reforms in social fields such as health care and education have a close and direct relation with the economic, political, ideological, cultural, and educational fields of power (p. 30).

Thus, the complexity of the relations and organizational transactions with the external environment is being recognized as one of the most crucial problems since the variety of social, economic, and technological transfers determine the extent to which a hospital can function effectively. Therefore, when the central administration of the health-care sector sets its strategies, it should analyze not only the external but also the internal environment of the hospital units in order to identify more accurately the true capacity of these units.

This analysis aims to identify which of those variables are a strength of the hospital and which are a weakness. At this point it should be mentioned that a variable can be characterized as a strength when it constitutes an element of improvement in the services provided by a particular hospital. Ensuring the availability of essential tools such as medical monitors and patient records may be considered as examples in this regard. On the contrary, a variable can be characterized as a weakness when a strategy cannot be implemented or it is undesirable. A shortage of resources and a high turnover of both medical and nursing staff are among the potential obstacles to the smooth and effective functioning of a hospital and hence can be characterized as a weakness.

In summary, we support the view that, in order to avoid the negative influence of any weakness, it is absolutely necessary for the central administration to carry out a careful and detailed analysis of both the external and the internal environment, while the second step in the environmental analysis is to determine those actions that may be performed better and hence improve the efficiency of the hospital's operation. Although it is very complex and difficult to analyze an organization's environment, Hoy and Miskel (1996) suggested there are three general, but at the same time useful, dimensions which require special scrutiny by the central administrators:

1. The degree of uncertainty. The greater the complication and instability of the environmental conditions lead to a greater uncertainty in hospital operations.
2. The extent of the organizational ethos (the degree to which the environment is organized and structured) is another variable for consideration since the environment generates substantial limitations and consequently demands compliance and commitment.
3. The extent of resource scarcity, since scarcity generates competition with other social organizations for the same resources.

No doubt, these environmental dimensions not only threaten the smooth and effective performance of hospitals but also bring to the surface the necessity for strategic programs to be developed in the health-care sector. It should be mentioned that, out of all types of health-care units, the most important one is the hospital since it has the closest two-way influence and interaction with the health-care system. For this reason, in the following sections, we will make special reference to, and give more emphasis to, hospitals.

2.2 Studying Health-Care Units/Hospitals

2.2.1 What Is a Hospital?

A hospital is an organized social unit that could be public or private (nonprofit or profit) which derives from the human need for cooperation and the feeling of security among people that live in society. But what is a hospital?

From the relevant literature, it is clear that there is no single widely accepted definition of the term "hospital." The difficulty in determining the meaning arises from the fact that a hospital is a complicated and dynamic entity which is impossible to describe precisely and to define comprehensively.

The American Hospital Association (AHA) defines a hospital as "a health care facility that has an organized medical and professional staff, inpatient beds available 24 h a day and the primary function of providing inpatient medical, nursing and other health care services for surgical and non-surgical conditions and usually provides some outpatient services, especially emergency care" (Abdelhak and Hanken, 2016, p. 726). Within the same framework, the World Health Organization (WHO) defines hospitals as "health care institutions that have organized medical and other professional staff and inpatients facilities, and deliver services 24 h, 7 days per week" (www.who.int/hospital/en/).

Abdelhak and Hanken (2016, p. 4) define a hospital as a health-care unit that provides health-care services to patients, including health-care organizations (and clinics) and health-care professionals. Abel-Smith (1976); Chletsos (2011); Hosking (2004); Ifantopoulos (2006); Li, Benton, and Leong (2002); and Snook (2004) define hospitals as health-care units that provide health-care services (inpatient and outpatient services). However, while their operation, organization, type, and development have undergone tremendous change over time, one thing is certain: a continuous effort is being made to improve the quality of their services and to make them accessible to all citizens. Indeed, Feldstein (1977) claimed that any changes occurring in health-care services are mainly due to changes in, and the growth of, public and private insurance in health-care systems. Furthermore, Douglas and Ryman (2003), McKee and Healy (2002), and Noether (1988) mentioned that changes in the population trend and developments in technology and pharmaceutical research have forced hospitals to be more competitive mainly in terms of providing better quality services while limiting or even reducing their cost so as to improve the efficiency of their operation and consequently attract more patients.

Indeed, in recent years hospitals have increasingly been adopting management techniques that will give them the flexibility to improve the quality of the health-care services they provide. Significantly, in the same period patients have become more demanding as they become better informed through the rapid explosion of information made available on the Internet regarding the quality of medical care. For this reason, hospital policies are becoming more patient-focused so as to raise their level of satisfaction, offer more qualitative services, and hence gain more patients in an increasingly competitive hospital sector. As a result of this rapid increase of hospital competition, over the last 5 years the main goals of hospitals have been to attract more patients, reduce costs, and improve the efficiency of their operation in order to ensure their sustainability.

In addition, as the main contributor to public well-being in terms of the population's health, hospitals are continuously under pressure from the political arena to meet the increasing and more diverse demands for health care while at the same time striving to absorb and implement advances in knowledge and technology.

There are different types of hospitals in terms of ownership which can be broadly classified according to their main source of funding. If a hospital receives most of its funding from the public purse, then it is governmental and it is governed by elected officials. If not, then it is a nongovernmental organization. This can be (a) private, if it is funded by investors whereby it is governed either by an individual partnership or a corporation, or (b) nonprofit whereby the owners and hence the main source of funding come from the church or unions such as community hospitals.

Clearly, none of the above definitions/categories provide a comprehensive definition of a hospital and certainly do not capture the objective of this entity in its entirety. On the contrary, each specific scientific analysis can only represent a one-sided view of a multifaceted reality. A hospital's multifaceted nature can be attributed to its perception by different sciences (e.g., psychology, economics, etc.). However, as each scientific discipline conducts its own research on hospitals, they each deal with a certain category of problems from a different perspective.

In the case of vague objectives such as the definition of a hospital or the analysis of a research method, we may observe that the research is based exclusively on the researcher's expectation and interpretation. It is therefore rational for many researchers to see the same research object from many different perspectives and to define the research object differently. Besides, the phenomena of a hospital and each activity taken within its internal environment can be expressed from multidimensional perspectives so

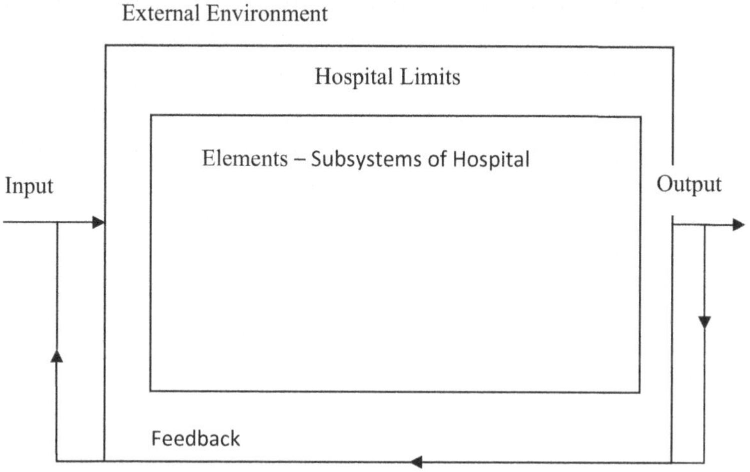

Fig. 2.1 Presents a hospital as an open system and its functions

it would be completely impossible to fully cover the object's meaning. No matter how researchers define the term "hospital," in practice it seems that hospitals act within a social context for the achievement of its aims and express their actions in a collective way. Within this framework, according to the systemic view, a hospital is an open system because it exists and functions within a broader environment (which consists of other systems of various scales that influence and are influenced by it).

During the communication process with the external environment, a hospital accepts inputs from it (e.g., patients) by executing the function of entrance. It then transforms them into the internal environment by executing the process of transformation or processing and provides the output process (product or service) by executing the process of output (Fig. 2.1).

According to the above figure, a hospital consists of many elements/subsystems that are in continuous interdependence and interaction. However, the aims and needs of a subsystem are often in conflict with the aims and needs of other subsystems. Hence, if we consider a medical doctor as a subsystem of the hospital (system), we may expand the study in the investigation of arguments and conflicts that may derive from the conflict between personal and organizational aims. Thus, the existence of these subsystems causes the complexity of the hospital as a health-care unit which in turn prevents it from functioning in a steady state.

2.2.2 Hospital Aims

The targets of hospitals are a reference point for many scientists. However, there is no accepted ranking/prioritization of these targets. For the purpose of this book, our preference will lean toward the view of Becker and Sloan (1985), Hanlon (2001),

Marchinko and Hetico (2013), Mullins (2010), Paisey (1992), and Perry, Staudenmayer, and Votta (1994) according to which organizations and hence hospitals generally consider three main groups of targets:

- Personal targets—those which derive from the health-care workforce or the patients. These targets consider changes which people desire for themselves such as working conditions and terms of employment.
- Health-care targets—which refer to changes of structures and strive to be fulfilled by the human subsystems (medical personnel, patients, etc.). They are changes that occur in behavior: changes in knowledge, abilities, and habits. Health-care targets tend to be adjusted to keep pace with the changes in patients' behavior/demands.
- Targets for resources—these refer to the material substructure which is necessary to facilitate the work of health-care personnel in order for health-care services to not only exist but meet the needs of the patients. Certainly if we define the word "resources" as anything available in a hospital in order to achieve its aims, then hospital targets can be considered to refer to changes in the structures of both the human and the material resources which are or could be available in hospitals for satisfying personal and hospital targets.

Since the health-care targets are many while the material resources are limited, the management of hospitals should aim to prioritize those resources in a way that optimizes the efficient and effective provision of quality health-care services to patients. Clearly, health-care targets and material resources need to be aligned realistically. In other words, targets should not be set that exceed either human or system capacities for whatever reason (e.g., to impress financers, etc.).

2.2.3 Hospital Functions

In a hospital, as in every social organization, we may define certain functions such as groups of actions that are interrelated and directed toward the achievement of a certain project (Arah, Klazinga, Delnoij, Ten Asbroek, & Custers, 2003; Becker & Sloan, 1985; Blair, Nix, Payne, Rotarious, & Whitehead, 2004; Scott & Davis, 2016; Yasin, Alavi, Kunt, & Zimmerer, 2004). We may mention that there are many controversial views about the distinction of the organization's functions. This contradiction could be attributed to the fact that there is no organization that has the same structure, function, targets, working conditions, culture, etc. as another one, even if they are in the same sector.

With particular reference to the functioning of hospitals, we may distinguish three groups, namely (Cuellar & Gertler, 2006; Li et al., 2002; McConnell, Chang, Maddox, Wholey, & Lindrooth, 2014; Swayne, Duncan, & Ginter, 2006; Tomasik, 2013), the function of services which is related to a specialized workforce and the provision of services (in health care), the function of choice which is related to the delegation of health-care services, and the function of legalization which is related to the political organization of the society.

Based on the type of jobs (mainly medical) that are carried out in a hospital, we may identify two further groups of functions: productive functions which are related to the efficient and effective provision of health-care services and assistant functions which are related to the managerial functions.

According to some researchers, a hospital has three functions, namely:

- A socializing function through which a hospital maintains and promotes the sociocultural system whereby it adjusts its provisions to the values, rules, etc. of the social environment
- A choice function according to which the provision of health-care services is related to their assessment and their effective and efficient provision
- A security function which is related to the family and the economy, in as much as the hospital provides its staff with job security

Indeed, hospital leaderships design such policies so as to satisfy patients' needs, to cover as much as possible from the large variety of qualitative health care and reduce any inefficiency in their operations. For this reason the basic dimensions of hospital management focus on the following (Arah et al., 2003; Hosking, 2004; McConnell et al., 2014; Snook, 2004):

- Study the hospital environment carefully so as to have the best possible picture and to determine the targets.
- Develop the actions that should be taken to closely monitor their performance.
- Weigh up the possibilities and focus on the quality of their operations.
- Ensure staff are motivated so as to boost the job satisfaction of the health-care providers.

In summary, in each hospital there are a number of related actions executed by people who are specialized. The goal of these actions is to achieve the hospital's targets.

2.2.4 Conditions for Effective Hospital Performance

As we have already mentioned, a hospital is a social organization or a social system that consists of a number of functional elements, each of which executes a particular job, all co-functioning and interrelated for the achievement of certain targets. For the realization of those targets, a hospital should function in an effective way.

But what is an effective hospital? First we may emphasize that hospitals work in a very complicated environment with many internal and external factors and, as a consequence, it is difficult to determine common targets. Furthermore, a hospital is not just an organization where the social dynamic is being developed but is also an institution with an orientation toward continuous assessment. It is an orientation that pervades every aspect of the health-care system (Papanaum, 1995, p. 40).

In other words, effectiveness in the field of health-care management is a complicated term since there are no defined criteria, such as the types of conditions treated, etc., that can capture the full complexity of hospitals (Guzzo & Dickson, 1996; Snook, 2004) nor can some of the key targets of hospitals be calculated. Moreover, from relevant research in recent decades (Arah et al., 2003; Blair et al., 2004; Boyne, 2003; Counte & Meurer, 2001; Hit & Middlemist, 1979; Lezotte, 1992; Mamouz, Rousseau, & Hudon, 2016; etc.) regarding the effectiveness of hospitals, there is no specific theory which can explain what it is that distinguishes an effective hospital from an ineffective one. However, no one can deny the view that, in order for an organization to be sustainable, it has to be effective. And in order for this to happen, a given organization (such as a hospital) should satisfy certain criteria of performance (Argyris, 1957; Likert, 1961). Within this framework, we may consider that a hospital is effective if the observed results of its actions succeed or attain its initial targets (Arah et al., 2003; Boyne, 2003; Campbell, 1977; Gilley, Dixon, & Gilley, 2008; Guzzo & Dickson, 1996; Perry et al., 1994) or, as Mortimore and Whitty (2001), Ouston (2003), Stoll (2003), and Stoll and Myers (1998) suggested, that an effective organization and hence hospital is one which provides a level of health-care services that exceeds expectations.

This raises a question: What are the factors that characterize a hospital as effective?

Although there is no simple combination of factors that can produce an effective hospital, many researchers have recognized certain common procedures and characteristics of the most effective organizations and those that have been improved. Indeed, many researchers have converged on a list of factors/keys of effectiveness (Counte & Meurer, 2001; Hit & Middlemist, 1979; Sammons, Hilliman, & Mortimore, 1995; Yasin et al., 2004). While these keys are neither exhaustive nor necessarily independent of each other, they can offer a useful summary of the most common factors that have been found to be associated with the effective performance and operation of organizations (Borenstein et al., 2004; Boyne, 2003; Guzzo & Dickson, 1996; Scott & Davis, 2016; Yasin et al., 2004).

Despite the difficulties in explaining the term "effective hospital," we consider it useful to refer to some of the factors that may contribute to the effective performance of a hospital. These factors are:

- Leadership. The chief executive managers of a hospital, apart from their bureaucratic role, are there to inspire the health-care workforce by example of their own work ethic and establish an appropriate climate in which all their human resources can flourish. Moreover, they are responsible for strategic planning, for setting the hospital's policy, and for determining the general guidelines by which staff should carry out their duties in order to achieve the hospital's targets and fulfill its vision. Indeed, the hospital leadership is responsible for planning and determining guidelines that aim to ensure the organization will meet continuously changing demands and adapt seamlessly to any changes in the internal and external environment in a sustainable manner.

- Structure and organization of the health-care services. All procedures of the health-care services should be clear and express the targets and the expectations of the hospital.
- Stability of the health-care workforce. A high turnover of health-care staff inhibits the cohesion, knowledge exchange, and continuity of the workforce. This is a negative influence on their morale and consequently on their performance. Moreover, regular changes in health-care personnel present the leadership of the hospital with a major problem as they confound their plans for the implementation of creative actions.
- Organization support. An effective hospital needs comfortable spaces for the residence of the patients, functional buildings, and modern labs. Moreover, it needs a capable medical and nursing force as well as administrative staff. While all these alone cannot secure the qualitative provision of health-care services, the lack of them certainly contributes to a hospital's ineffectiveness.
- Communication. Effective communication among hospital staff and patients can contribute significantly in an effective way to the achievement of a hospital's goals.
- Positive climate. In a hospital with a positive climate, the emphasis is on the appraisal of health-care staff (rather than their punishment) and on an efficient communication between staff and patients. All these are a positive influence on achieving targets and boost a hospital's performance.

It should be mentioned though that the above factors and many others have organizational meaning (and hence are significant) only when there is a connection between them which is based on the values and the principles prescribed by the hospital leadership. This means that effectiveness depends on the abilities of the managerial mechanism that programs, organizes, and coordinates all hospital actions.

2.3 Meaning and Content of the Environment

In the previous section, we mentioned that a hospital is an open system, i.e., the organization cannot survive without an exchange of information with the wider system in which it belongs. Hence, a hospital is a subsystem of a wider system, while each element of a hospital is also a subsystem of it. For example, the people who are staff members of a hospital can each be considered to be a subsystem of it. Moreover, we may accept the view that the performance of a system depends not only on its subsystems but also on the capacity of the wider system in which it belongs. This means that the performance of a doctor might change when employed in another organization. Furthermore, even the efficiency of a hospital can be affected when significant numbers of staff move on. In general, when a hospital is "better" than another one, this tends to be because the one with the more efficient performance has more appropriate working conditions.

So what is the difference between two chief executive managers in two different hospitals where one is considered to be more efficient than the other one? The efficient manager is the one who can perceive the meaning of the wider environment within which the hospital is functioning. The chief executive managers in a hospital may often think that they are simply performing a bureaucratic or directorial role, but if they understood that no organization is independent of the environment in which it operates, then their hospital would be more efficient. Due to this significance, the leadership of a hospital should carefully examine the wider environment of the hospital in order to be able to better understand the organization's context. For effective hospital management, it is necessary for the manager to be able position the hospital in society's value chain.

But what do we understand by "environment"?

First, we should underline the fact that the term "environment," like many other terms in organizational science, is a meaning that cannot be fully defined. And this is because of the contradiction among scientists in the systemic theory regarding the elements that combine to make up the environment of a social organization (Hoy & Miskel, 1996, p. 204). "The environment of an organization is anything that can be outside its limits…" (Bolman & Deal, 1984, p. 44; Robey, 1982, p. 121) and anything that does not belong in the system (Scott, 1981, p. 165). Since these definitions are without any practical meaning, the study of an environment should be limited to an examination of the environmental elements that are interrelated with an organization. In the particular case of a hospital, it is not necessary to write down all those physical and social factors that operate outside its limits. However, the study of environmental forces that influence its function one way or another is crucial. The basic sectors of a hospital's environment are presented in Table 2.1.

Table 2.1 illustrates the wide variety of factors that influence both the structure and the functioning of a hospital and determine its efficiency. These factors can be grouped into three categories:

- Those inside the hospital (internal environment)
- Those outside the hospital which have a direct relation with the function of the hospital (special environment)
- Those outside the hospital which have an indirect influence on the hospital functioning (external environment)

Indeed, a hospital is in a continuous process of exchanging information and energies with its external environment. Moreover, it is clear that hospital leaders have a complicated role to perform and that a crucial factor is the continuous need for information, mainly on organizational and functional issues at all levels (local,

Table 2.1 Basic system functions of a hospital's environment

Hospital system functions	Internal environment (human factor, building, etc.) which determines the limits of a hospital
	Special environment
	External environment

national, international). Consequently, health-care management should carefully examine the environment of hospitals in order to better understand their capacity to serve society. In the relevant literature (Guzzo & Dickson, 1996; Hoy & Miskel, 1996; Payne, 1991; Scott & Davis, 2016; Thomas, 1974), researchers usually converged in their interpretation of the terms "internal environment" and "external environment." This perhaps underlines the fact that the factors encountered in a social organization, in their process of survival, stem out from the efforts of other organizations (subsystems, supersystems) to survive and develop. These conflicting factors between organizations (systems) need to be carefully examined by managerial science.

2.4 The Internal Environment of Health-Care Organizations (Hospitals)

The internal environment of a health-care organization, as in every type of organization, consists of specific factors (elements) which, one way or another, influence the organization's functioning, behavior, and effectiveness. Hence, it is necessary to analyze in detail the specific environment of health-care organizations so as to be able to estimate their strengths and weaknesses and consequently to determine those actions which will contribute to an improved functionality. For instance, one strategy for success may be to gain a good knowledge of the procurement procedures of local medical suppliers so as to ensure the unit has an adequate supply of the resources necessary to effectively provide health-care services.

Although many health-care units may function in the same district or region, there might be differences between them in terms of the quality of the health-care services they provide. Why? Simply because each unit has a certain set of strengths and weaknesses which influence its effectiveness. In order for the managers to formulate rational and effective strategies, they should analyze not only the external but also the internal environment of the health-care unit (hereafter referred to as "hospital") so as to determine the strategy which will help to overcome any weaknesses and improve the quality of the unit's health-care provision. The internal factors that need to be analyzed and that will either empower or hinder a proposed strategy are structure, location, culture, and resources.

2.4.1 *Structure*

Structure is the way in which a hospital is organized "in terms of the flow of communication, power and work" (Child, 1972; Georgopoulos, 2006; Levine & White, 1961; Scott & Davis, 2016). In other words, an organization's structure is a system of working relations, accountability, and power within which all working functions of the organization are implemented and each position in the health-care unit is linked with defined duties, rules, and an expected framework of behavior (Carter, 1971; Child, 1972; Michopoulos, 1998; Ouinn, 1980; Schneeweiss, 1998).

By focusing our attention on hospital management, we may notice that the term refers to a specific area (or function) of a hospital for which a manager has the power to execute certain activities. The effective functioning of a hospital forces the need for a manager to be present since the implementation of an organization's aims demands, among other things, a capable leadership that can coordinate all the factors that play a role in the hospital and thus continuously shape and maintain a favorable working environment. The manager of a hospital also serves the purpose of helping his/her colleagues to properly understand the hospital's expectations and policies.

Among other expectations of leadership, the basic and most important one is to ensure the greatest possible staff performance for the achievement of the hospital's goals. For this reason, we may support the view that the role of a hospital manager is very important, one which is heavily dependent on their duties and the position they hold in the hospital's hierarchy. Such a role has a strong communicative function as the manager plays a central role between the upper levels of the health-care system and the staff members. Each program of health-care policy created centrally and directed from the top of the hierarchical pyramid to all hospitals is "filtered" through the hospital's management. How well it gets implemented depends on how it is presented to staff, and this depends on the psychological approach and the abilities of the manager. Hence, the degree of success in bringing about a positive change in the health-care system, and more specifically in achieving the hospital's aims, depends on the appropriate selection of managers. Indeed, in a well-organized hospital the manager/leader's most important role is the management of human resources. Moreover, no matter how well and rationally planned the communication and structural system is, it cannot achieve its expected outcome without appointing appropriate people in the managerial positions.

A leader should have a vision and be able to coordinate their staff to achieve common goals. Furthermore, a manager should function as a positive example for staff members who are easily influenced by his/her behavior. In general, it is essential to encourage the willing contribution of others in order to get a task implemented, with the higher aim of increasing the hospital's effectiveness. As the focal point for sending and receiving messages within a hospital, it is the manager/leader's responsibility to create a climate conducive to communication, to encourage his/her colleagues to show their understanding, to express their opinions freely, and to offer feedback. If they receive a complaint, they should examine the issue carefully, keep themselves continually informed about the matter, recognize possible wrong behavior, and end up with an action plan. Moreover, if they are confronted with a conflict, they need to investigate the case carefully and in depth, identify the roots of the conflict, and propose a solution that would be mutually agreeable to both sides. As a mentor, the manager/leader needs to establish a strong cooperation with the staff of the hospital, developing friendly and sincere relations so that they will be able to help and guide them in all difficult situations. Finally, as a motivator of his/her staff members, the manager/leader should apply the incentives that the hospital can offer and combine them with his/her communication skills in order to motivate the staff toward an improved performance. By recognizing and acknowledging the efforts of their staff members, the manager/leader can create an appropriate motivational climate that will ensure their commitment and thus help meet the hospital's higher goals.

2.4.2 *The Location*

The location of a hospital's facility is often influenced by external factors such as the transportation network that serves the medical personnel, political and social patterns, the financial and social circumstances of an area, etc. Even the location of the city in which the hospital operates plays a role since, as we have already mentioned, financial, social, and other factors have an impact on its operation. For example, natural factors such as cold, heat, noise, etc. may have a negative influence on personnel's health and by extension on their performance. In other words, both the neighborhood of the hospital and the demographic composition of the region's population are of great significance. For instance, if a hospital is located in a working class neighborhood or where the majority of occupants are migrants, then it may face issues (such as patients with inadequate health insurance, language barriers, etc.) which another hospital located in a better and socially more homogeneous area would not have to deal with.

2.4.3 *An Organization's Culture*

Meaning and Content

It is generally accepted that the effective function of modern organizations is judged by their ability to respond directly to the continuous and rapid changes in their environment. For this reason, modern organizations tend to prefer lean organization structures, since they more readily facilitate the delegation of responsibilities to the lower levels of the organization's hierarchy. Therefore, "front line" managers who are more aware of the organization's actual operational situation are able to make decisions more responsibly and swiftly, in comparison to those decisions taken (for the same issue) by the senior hierarchical levels.

Although lean structures contribute to speedier decision-making, however, it is not a panacea for enhancing an organization's effectiveness, simply because the culture of the organization may be a hindrance (Williams & Johnson, 2004). A member of a public or private organization, at every administrative level, constitutes an integral part of the organization's culture. Therefore, it is of considerable importance for each manager to thoroughly know the organization in which he/she works, not only from an operational viewpoint but also to better understand the fundamental values, perceptions, and beliefs on which the specific organization is based.

But what do we mean by an organization's "culture"? First, we must emphasize that the various interpretations of "culture" bring about confusion and difficulties regarding the perception of the term (Daskalakis, 2009; Grint, 2005; Hofstede, 1980; Koen, 2005). There is no commonly accepted definition of culture from an anthropological point of view. On the contrary, we find many controversial definitions. There should not be any surprise in the fact that there are multiple definitions for the culture of an organization. For instance, researchers such as Schein (2010, pp. 7–10) and Taylor (1911) define an organization's culture as a "standard model with underlying assumptions which have been found, discovered or developed from a specific group of people as they learn to confront problems that occur during their adjustment to the external environment and their internal execution and which have functioned well enough during their implementation, so that they can be considered valid and therefore be taught to the new team members as the proper way to perceive, think and feel these kinds of problems" and as "a wholeness that encompasses knowledge, beliefs, art, ethics, justice, customs and all other skills and controversies that an individual obtains as a society member" (Kontis, 1994, p. 236). From these definitions it appears that culture is an outcome of learning through a team experience and has a meaning only for a specific social group. Thus, an individual is not born with a form of culture. He does not have any ideas, thoughts, habits, and patterns of behavior, meaning that culture is a concept that is learned during an individual's lifetime and through interaction with other people. Consequently, the learning and transmission of culture, through language, are its main characteristics. That is why anthropologists consider learning about culture to be equivalent to the process of socializing (Hickson, Hinings, McMillan, & Schwitter, 1974; Koen, 2005; Koulougliotis, 1992; Trompenaars & Hampden-Turner, 1999).

Some other researchers such as Bouradas (2001) and Georgopoulos (2006) consider culture as "a system of common values, beliefs, basic acknowledgements, meanings and non-formal rules which, as a common reference framework of collective, cognitive programming, connects people by defining how they think and behave, what they do, how they do it and why" (p. 544) and as "a sum of beliefs, expectations and values which are common to the members of an organization (business), making it unique. It creates behavioral rules and clarifies the accepted behavior of all staff members, from the leading managers to the employees at the operating level of the managerial hierarchy" (p. 144). In some way, culture gives the organization its sense of identity, that is, "this is who we are… this is what we do… this is the reason of our existence" (Georgopoulos, 2006; Hofstede, 1980).

There are those who see culture as "a plan of beliefs and anticipations shared by the organizational members" which produces "rules which in a dynamic way shape the behavior of people and groups in the organization" (Schwartz & Davis, 1981, p. 33) and as "the ideology of the organization" which contains a number of items (e.g., values, perceptions) and distinguish it from other organizations (Mintzberg, 1979, 1983; Mintzberg, Lampel, Quinn, & Ghoshal, 2003).

Reflecting on the above definitions, we may say that culture:

- Has a wide concept, its boundaries are almost undefined, and is used in a variety of ways. Due to the multiple associations that the term has, many researchers appear to use it interchangeably with terms such as "education," "intellectual cultivation," and "cultural center," among others.
- Is present in the organization's environment through the activities of individuals.
- Is cultivated only where there are people, i.e., it has a social context. This feature shows that culture is not inherent but is a result of learning. It is taught to an individual throughout their lifetime and through their interaction with other people.
- Influences the behavior of a social team's (the organization's) members through types or patterns imposed and encouraged by the social system.

Hence, culture indicates the way in which activities are carried out in the organization and thus influences the work done by its members. It is claimed that the way in which the work is completed is a result of certain special characteristics of the organization (Beyer & Trice, 1987; Deal & Kennedy, 1982; Hofstede, 1980; Peters & Waterman, 1982; Schermerhorn, Hunt, & Osborn, 2002; Williams & Johnson, 2004), such as:

- *The history*, since an organization's own philosophical tendencies were undoubtedly established at the time the organization was founded, and these characterize it. For example, in the case of a hospital founded 150 years ago, its "founding fathers" would have set out a process by which the hospital's leadership makes decisions and would have put the appropriate structures in place so as to ensure that those decisions could be implemented effectively.
- *The size*, since small organizations face different administrative challenges compared to bigger ones. In a small hospital, the supervisors may adopt centralized management methods simply because they have a small number of staff members. On the other hand, managers of big hospitals with a large number of staff members have the luxury of delegating responsibilities to members of the hospital community.
- *The agent*, since public organizations (hospitals, schools) normally focus their attention on the assurance of legal rights and on the fair use of resources to show accountability to the taxpaying citizens. In contrast, the management of private organizations has greater freedom in decision-making and in the use of resources.
- *The purpose*, since the foundation of specific organizations is interweaved with the production of goods or the provision of services, which have the characteristics of routine and repetition. For instance, if we consider a simple artisanship of shoe production, there is no scope for creativity at the production plant. But, if we consider the activities of a research center, clearly its success is based on the creative thinking of its members. In these cases, there is great importance in the level of freedom regarding "the way things happen in the organization" for the achievement of specific goals.

Culture of Health-Care Units

A formal organization such as a hospital has, without doubt, specific characteristics that secure a special position in the competitive environment and at the same time constitute its culture.

According to Anthopoulou (1999, p. 26), "a culture is the climate and the atmosphere of an organization." In other words, it is a combination of some external elements that affect the needs and the provisions of a hospital or health-care unit (e.g., rooms for patients) and other external elements related with the human relations and emotions (such as the sense of satisfaction).

The culture of health-care units may be defined as a result of attitudes, values, behaviors, and practices which are dominant in a health-care unit (Matsagouras, 2000, p. 172). Hence, as the values and perceptions that constitute a health-care unit's culture become clearer, then the stronger is the dominant culture that determines the orientation, ethics, interpersonal relations, values, etc. of the organization members.

The culture of a health-care unit does not have a standard form. It is continually restructuring and reshaping through the interventions and interactions of the organization members, as they interact with the local community and as the influences of everyday life take effect. It is a self-perpetuating cycle of interventions between the existing health-care unit's culture and its members (Kontakos, 2009, p. 82).

Based on the above, and given that culture is the driving force behind procedures, changes, and the implementation of innovative actions (Chrispeels, 1992; Fan, 2000; Hofstede, 1980; Koen, 2005; Mullins, 2010), it is evident that the development of a "healthy" culture is an absolute necessity.

Types of Culture/Subculture in an Organization

As we mentioned above, culture is developed only in social groups. In practice, this means that each social team has its own culture and not only does different things but also sees things differently. In this sense, there is no "common" reality that all people experience in the same way. Thus, it explains why persons of different social teams (Child, 1972; Denison, 1990; Koulougliotis, 1992; Sackman, 2011; Schein, 2010):

- Find it difficult to comprehend each other
- Have different perceptions of the same reality
- Tend to evaluate the behavior of other people in terms of their own culture

At a national level, this phenomenon constitutes the national culture which, according to Hofstede (1980), Grint (2005), Mullins (2010), Pheysey (1993), and Schein (2010), can be distinguished into the following four types:

- *Avoidance of uncertainty*. In this type of culture, it is clear what is permitted and what is not. Basic elements of this type of culture are legality, class, and clarity.

- *Individualization*. In this culture, competition and the tendency for independence prevail.
- *Distance based on validity*. A basic feature of this culture is respect for the senior managers in society, who are accepted by others and are acknowledged to have the right to power.
- *An emphasis on "women's" values*. Women's values are the key features here: friendship, collaboration, partnership, etc. (Kantas, 1995, p. 75).

By transferring the above thoughts to the level of an organization (hospital, business), we may see that researchers such as Charles Handy (1981) and others (Bouradas, 2001; Cardador & Rupp, 2011; Denison, 1990; Hofstede, 1980; Panagiotopoulou, 1997; Sackman, 2011; Williams & Johnson, 2004) described four types of culture in an organization and gave them symbolic names of ancient Greek gods.

The Culture of Power (Zeus) This type of culture expresses elements of a bossy and centralized leader. Thus, when superior managers confront a problem, they take quick decisions, based either on their long-term experience or on their instinct. For organizations with a power culture to be successful, it is essential for their leader to be powerful and capable. This is particularly true for small organizations.

The Culture of Role (Apollo) This type of culture is the opposite of the power culture, and we can see it mainly in large organizations characterized by bureaucracy. In these organizations, rationalism and legality in the actions and decisions of superior managers prevail. Furthermore, the impersonal bureaucratic process guarantees standardization and stability. We have to notice that the culture of role has an advantage in the decision-making process based on a rational framework of rules. However, this type of culture has drawbacks, as such organizations tend to have difficulty in responding quickly to changes imposed by their external environment.

The Culture of Work (Athena) This model of culture is noticeable in organizations with a tendency for creativity and innovative thought. People working in an organization with this model tend to respect each other's knowledge, experiences, and ability for generating new ideas for the successful completion of a given task. The power of these people comes from their contribution to the results achieved. The basic characteristics of this model are meritocracy, team work, and creativity. It therefore functions positively in environments of radical change because its fundamental benefit is the discovery of multiple solutions for each separate problem. However, it has its drawbacks: it is difficult to maintain control since the hierarchical structure of organization is not being implemented.

The Culture of Individualism (Dionysos) This type of culture is based on the promotion of independence and individualism. Here, organizations serve the needs of their members, allowing them to act according to their personal aims. People of this category do not easily accept hierarchies or show much respect for others, and when they work in teams, they aspire for more independence and flexibility.

According to Handy (1981), no one model of organizational culture is better than the others, since each one has its own advantages and disadvantages. So, the secret of success is to ensure that each organizational culture has a functional mixture that reflects the organization's size, stage of development, and the circumstances of the organization's external environment. In the real world, a "mixture" often means that a dominating culture of an organization "borrows" elements from other cultures. For example, an organization based on the power culture can, as it grows, borrow the control elements of efficiency from the role culture. Also, for an organization of the role culture to better adapt to radical changes, it can create a responsible work team by adopting methods from the work culture (Williams & Johnson, 2004).

In conclusion, the type of an organization's dominant culture seems to be determined by the degree to which the elements of one type prevail over other types of culture.

Subculture and Its Significance

Different cultures do not only exist among national societies but also in a social team (organization). The individual forms of culture appearing in a social organization (e.g., hospital, school, company) are called subcultures (Beyer & Trice, 1987; Daskalakis, 2009; Osborn & Baughn, 1994; Schermerhorn et al., 2002). According to Martin and Siehl (1983), there are three kinds of subculture appearing in an organization:

- *The increasing subculture*, which will support and significantly boost the basic values of the dominating culture
- *The rectangular subculture*, in which its members simultaneously acknowledge the basic values of the dominating culture and other different values which are not conflicting with those of the dominating culture
- *The non-culture*, including values which contradict some of the basic values of the organization (Kantas, 1995, p. 87)

Nevertheless, if the above types of subculture coexist to varying degrees, then it is possible for problems to arise in the organization since each of these subcultures significantly influences the attitudes and behaviors of the organization's members. However, these problems can be addressed. For example, in a non-culture it is possible to "effect some useful functions for the dominating culture by showing the limits between an acceptable and unacceptable behavior and by providing a safe shelter for the development of renewing ideas" (Martin & Siehl, 1983, p. 63; Kantas, 1995, p. 97). It should be noted that the organization's administration needs to intervene in a timely manner in cases where non-culture exceeds the organization's limits of undesirable behavior, that is, when it contains values in direct contradiction to some of the fundamental values of the organization.

Significance of Organizational Culture

It has already been mentioned that organizational culture indicates the way in which things happen in the organization. Thus, it formulates the general behavior of the organization's members. According to Beyer and Trice (1987), Bouradas (2005), Hickson et al. (1974), Hofstede (1980), Iordanoglu (2008), Mintzberg et al. (2003), Osborn and Baughn (1994), and Schermerhorn et al. (2002), a strong, united, and appropriate culture can:

- *Affect the ability of an organization to establish a strategic direction* and, by extension, to gain the most benefit from a strategy's implementation. For instance, a strategy of change in the health-care sector will never achieve sustained success if it is not supported by a culture of creativity and the discovery of new ideas.
- *Support or prevent change.* In the case of an organization with a positive culture, its staff members are proud of their work because they participate in the constant refinement of procedures, and they feel free to achieve their goals and gain job satisfaction when procedures are completed. They are also open to change, and they trust themselves and can work autonomously without any supervision. In an excellent working environment, the expectation is for performance to reach high levels. High performance begins when the person is committed to team work, strives for perfection, and embraces change in the organization. On the contrary, when the culture of the organization is negative, its members waste their time on contradictions and noncreative activities. In addition, these members can be characterized by their low morale, a resistance to change and improvement, a reluctance to make the effort to implement the project at hand, and low cohesion. In a negative working environment, changes do not happen easily and the "partner issues" provoke negativity and often lead to the psychological distancing of members from the employing organization.
- *Assure the appropriate attitudes and behaviors of the organizational members,* since a strong culture implies a strong sense of social discipline among its members.
- *Lead the organization members in a common direction.* It removes uncertainty, since a united and strong culture helps the organizational members toward a common aim, through collaboration and coordination.

Summarizing the above, we can claim that a strong/positive culture can bestow great benefits upon organizations (hospitals included) that enable them to preserve and develop such a culture if it exists or to create it if it is absent (Beyer & Trice, 1987; Hofstede, 1980; Papoulias, 2002; Schermerhorn et al., 2002). Of course, the popularity of the term "organizational culture" is, to a great extent, due to the number of additional books referring to successful business cooperatives. The underlying message from all these analyses is that efficient organizations have powerful and special cultures and that the basic role of a managerial leadership is to establish organizational culture.

When referring to "strong and special cultures," we mean that effective organizations:

- *Respond directly* to the challenges of the environment and avoid wasting much time on programming and analyzing.
- *Are distinguished* for excellent interpersonal relationships and respect among administrators and employees. In the internal operations of a hospital unit, there are common values, expectations, etc. which connect the members of the specific unit with each other.
- *Encourage their members* to submit ideas and take initiatives.
- *Share the same fundamental values.*
- *Have lean structures*, which enhance interactive communication between managers and employees and encourage the decentralization of power and responsibility to the lower hierarchical levels of the organization (Hickson et al., 1974; Iordanoglu, 2008; Mullins, 2010; Peters & Waterman, 1982; Trompenaars & Hampden-Turner, 1999).

By concentrating our interest on hospitals and having in mind that health contributes significantly to the social, cultural, and financial development of a country, a change in the mission, aims, strategies, or policies might fail if it is not compatible with the accepted culture of the hospital. Since this culture functions as a mechanism of cohesion and communication between members and incites the organizational members to common objectives, we can support the view that, particularly in a centralized system, the central management ought to show an awareness of the hospital's culture and then proceed to improve its circumstances if it wants to acquire strategic command, that is, to ensure the successful implementation of health policies.

Creating a Positive Culture in a Hospital or Health-Care Unit

It is generally accepted that a social organization (and hence a hospital or a health-care unit) presents a general atmosphere that determines the reactions of its members toward the whole. Indeed, those who have worked in different organizations, whether public or private, quickly realize that they each present a different working environment which can either be pleasant and creative or depressing and repellent. As Halpin (1966, p. 31) mentioned, in an organization such as a hospital, you may see employees working pleasantly and in harmony and this happy atmosphere is transferred to the patients, in another you may sense an atmosphere of dissatisfaction, and in a third you may detect a false setup that tries to hide its real state of affairs. Based on the above, we may support the view that the environment of a hospital or health-care unit constitutes its unique character and it is the element which differentiates the organization from other units, even if the remaining characteristics are the same.

Hence, a health-care unit that functions within a positive working environment creates a good reputation for that particular unit and quickly draws the attention of the community. Moreover, it creates and enhances commitment and devotion to the well-being of employees, and, as a result, the mood of the employees becomes more conducive to contributing new ideas and knowledge and consequently the quality of the health-care services provided is raised. The greater commitment of the staff members within a positive working environment establishes the feeling of trust between them and the manager, and hence both enjoy a more rewarding cooperation.

So what factors contribute to a positive culture in a hospital/health-care unit?

The field of health care is rather unique since it is a large yet relatively unnoticed part of society, though it serves all citizens and covers their health-care needs. Units in this field require managers who can manage with sensitivity and compassion. Through their leadership role, they have the biggest influence upon, and are ultimately responsible for, shaping a positive environment for their health-care unit (Beyer & Trice, 1987; Bouradas, 2005; Hickson et al., 1974; Iordanoglu, 2008; Mintzberg et al., 2003; Mullins, 2010; Peters & Waterman, 1982; Schermerhorn et al., 2002; Trompenaars & Hampden-Turner, 1999). While there are a variety of activities that shape this role, a manager's first priority is to manage the cooperation they have with their staff members since functional and constructive cooperation contributes significantly to the creation of a positive working environment (Beyer & Trice, 1987; Hampton, Summer, & Webber, 1987). Hence, the leader should be aware that the creation of a positive culture—through which human relations are promoted and the cohesion of staff is sustained—cannot be left to luck. The leader should him-/herself be an example for imitation since their behavior has a great value for the transferal of attitudes and values to the other organizational members (Schein, 2010). Based on the above, the leader should be aware of:

- *The needs of the staff members.* Leaders' opinion of, and behavior toward, the work of the organizational members is of great importance as it can motivate them to take initiatives. At the same time, the leader should not ignore a complaint of a colleague, no matter the significance of it, since in many cases little complaints, left unheeded for a period of time, can grow and develop into unpleasant situations. For this reason, he/she should encourage those employees who have complaints to discuss their issue openly because it is by discussing the problem that solutions can be found.
- *The personality, the tendency, and the special abilities of staff members* when delegating responsibilities and the need to behave objectively toward all staff members. In other words, a fair working environment avoids any discrimination and adopts a transparency in the delegation of work.
- *The basic psychological needs of staff members.* The need for recognition from society, the need to be creative, etc. constitute some of the basic psychological needs of each employee and especially each person in the field of health care. If we accept that the efficiency of each employee depends, to a great extent, on the degree to which their needs are satisfied, then the leader/manager should try very hard to sustain an appropriate psychological climate in their health-care unit.
- *The induction of newcomers* in the health-care unit. The leader/manager should be in the "front line" in helping (new) colleagues to be better in the execution of

their work and by inspiring them to confront new challenges. In other words, the leader should be in the position to encourage staff members to try new ideas and to acquire abilities and skills.

- *The democratic thinking* which the leader should make substantial use of during the decision-making process by applying the method of participatory leadership. In any case, in a democratic society decision-making is closely linked to the participation and cooperation of leaders/managers with staff members, so a leader should not be inflexible. On the contrary, they should be distinguished by their flexibility and be conciliatory in the way they implement their policy without diverging from the purpose of the health-care unit or the legislative framework.
- *Collegiality*, which refers to the social atmosphere within an organization, the friendly environment, the sense of community being shaped among employees. Collegiality may be expressed through established teams that cooperate and celebrate their successes together and within which they can be themselves (Iordanoglu, 2008).

Therefore, the shaping of a positive culture in a health-care unit is not simply a matter of stating some values or principles in the form of interventions and wishes. On the contrary, it demands a series of planned activities and especially requires committed leaders with appropriate leadership behavior so that leaders can be an example for all staff members and thus help create a climate of mutual trust.

2.4.4 Resources of a Health-Care Unit (Hospital)

A hospital's resources include all the available elements used to achieve its aims. The available resources—human, material, and information resources—are categorized as follows:

Human resources: this is the most important element in the analysis of the internal environment of a hospital and contributes substantially to the hospital's aims being achieved and strategies implemented. The human resources apply the other available material resources as required for the hospital to function. In fact, these human resources (medical, nursing, and administrative staff) constitute the only animate and dynamic element of a hospital that possesses desires, emotions, values, and habits. All these make up the control factors of human resource behavior.

Material resources: these are the resources which a hospital imports from the external environment. This type of resources may be split into three main categories:

- Substructure (buildings, furniture, machines) which are used for the provision of health-care services and characterized by long-term use
- Financial resources which refer to the funding available not only to cover functional needs but also creative activities
- Material resources (such as medical supplies, etc.) which are characterized by a continuous flow of supply and demand and constitute an essential element in the smooth functioning of the unit and the provision of health-care services

Information: In the case of a hospital, this is information that describes the behavior of all those factors relevant to its internal and the external environment. The gathering of such information helps the management to take rational and correct decisions and/or to better adapt to new standards. In particular, the decision-making and the implementation of those decisions demand the effective management of information in terms of searching, processing, saving, and transfer. Every manager/leader needs to engage with the management of information. First, they receive the information from the upper management levels and/or from agents of the external environment, which they then process and analyze. If necessary, they may transfer part or all of that information to other staff members of the hospital. In many cases this information is not readily available so the manager needs to search for it.

2.5 Special Environment of Health-Care Units

2.5.1 Cooperation of the Health-Care Unit (Hospital) with Other Units and with Agents of Local Government

A basic duty of the management of a hospital is to create and maintain bonds with other hospitals located in the same district or region. Moreover, all hospitals should demonstrate to the various societal groups of the district/region that they are part of a wider whole (Zacharis, 1985). The close cooperation of different hospitals is considered a crucial factor for the exchange of views, knowledge, and experiences regarding medical issues but also regarding health-care issues in general. Cooperation between the hospitals of a district/region concerns their users—the various societal groups of that district/region—and so is not accomplished simply by establishing links between hospitals but also by presenting them to society as a single and integral part of society's infrastructure. The transfer of information is very important, especially in the field of health care, since this sector is very sensitive and is closely linked with human well-being. However, it should be noted that it is difficult to establish and maintain cooperation among hospitals since there are many different ways of cooperating. To overcome these difficulties, there needs to be close cooperation between hospital managers.

A hospital is a central part of the local community, especially if the unit is located in a rural part of the country. The local community and the environment are both information sources (perhaps the most important sources of information), and for this reason, any possibility for collaboration with these entities should be explored.

Hence, in order for the hospital to be appreciated by the local community, the management should develop a close cooperation with local agents, such as the following.

Local Government This cooperation can be expressed in different types and forms, and its primary purpose is to solve different problems encountered by the health-care units, e.g., noise pollution, improvement/expansion of the building's structure, etc. The latter examples illustrate the positive results that cooperating with local government can bring to a hospital and subsequently to citizens in the area.

Production Units These units could be units in medical technology, pharmaceutical companies, or medical consumables. The cooperation between hospitals and these production units requires caution and should take place within a clearly defined and targeted framework, set up primarily to satisfy the aims and the needs of the hospital.

Patients' Association The main purpose of this association is to liaise between the doctor and the patient to ensure that patients' rights are respected but also to help improve the patient experience. For example, due to the asymmetric flow of information, patients may not have all the necessary information they need to adequately understand the diagnosis of their disease and their subsequent therapy since it is the medical staff who determine "what" therapy is offered as well as "how," "when," and "where" (Chletsos, 2011, p. 61; Ifantopoulos, 2006, p. 248 and p. 318).

Volunteers of Social Work First, we should note that volunteers could be members of the same community or can be members of different communities or societies. Although there are no standard criteria for determining who could be a social volunteer, the reasons that push him/her or a group of people to care for others or for the common good are many and varied, such as moral satisfaction, a feeling of social collegiality, creative use of their free time, the opportunity to develop abilities and special knowledge, etc. Hence, volunteerism is a free action, according to which the offering of help is within the framework of equality from citizen to citizen, with no expected return. Therefore, it is about a spontaneous participation in a social or privileged project with no material reward and stems from one's personal interest for an improved common well-being.

To conclude, a hospital should be open to society in general so as to develop and cultivate between them a cooperation with mutual respect and a common target of providing civilians with high-quality health-care services. For this to happen, the role of the manager should not be restricted only to the internal environment but should be expanded to encompass the social environment. Besides, we should not forget that a hospital is an inextricable part of society which develops, evolves, and exists to serve society and its members.

2.6 External Environment of a Health-Care Unit (Hospital)

It has been mentioned above that a hospital is an open system since it consists of a number of elements such as medical, nursing, and administrative staff, buildings, etc., which function through a number of coordinated actions in order to achieve certain goals while at the same time a hospital is continuously interacting with other (sometimes larger) systems, other sectors, and options of social life. This all means that the members of the hospital take responsibilities and roles within the hospital so as to achieve certain goals. In this process the duty of the manager/leader is to proactively shape the expectations that local citizens have of the hospital, to seek cooperation and support for the hospital's activities, and to establish its public image. Of course, the ultimate goal is to secure the hospital's effectiveness.

Traditionally, according to classical management, an organization is considered to be effective when the organization's goals are achieved with the least possible waste of resources. Today, "the quality of the real role of an organization can be measured only through the democratic application of a free action…" (Beck, 1992, p. 4635). In practice, this means that a hospital should not restrict its activities to its internal environment but should expand its active participation in society.

2.6.1 Environmental Powers of a Health-Care Unit (Hospital)

The external environment of a hospital refers to the wider social, political, technological, economic, cultural, and environmental forces that have a direct influence on it. The main factors that exercise influence on a hospital are the following.

Social Factors The wider social environment impacts upon a hospital in different ways. Each society has its own moral values, habits, and perceptions, and this is evidenced by the different health-care systems worldwide and the historical changes that have occurred in the health-care sector. The rules, habits, and the perceptions of a society will naturally influence the functionality of a hospital and the services it provides. Thus, the culture of a society influences a hospital's function and reflects the lifeblood of that society.

Political/Legislative Factors It is generally accepted that the health-care system of a country functions within a specific national political system and a health-care policy that is usually planned by the central administration of the system. Political factors usually influence hospitals through the legislative framework that is set up for health-care services which all health-care organizations are required to implement. Indeed, the legislative framework has a significant impact on how the organs of hospitals function. For example, among other things, it determines the methods used for recruiting and selecting medical and nursing staff, the medical treatments provided to patients, as well as the hospital's policy for training and developing staff.

Economic Factors Hospitals, like all other social organizations, are heavily influenced by the general economic conditions of each country since their survival and their smooth functioning depend to a large extent on the financial resources made available by the central administration of the health-care system, which in turn determine the quality of the health-care services provided. Moreover, if we consider that the health-care sector contributes significantly to the social and economic development of a country, we may support the view that the state of a health-care system provides a valuable indicator as to the state of economic development of that country.

Cultural Factors The cultural setting of a country is a basic and crucial factor in the development of its health-care system as it adds the "human touch" to its physical infrastructure. For example, the culture of a society influences the type of medical staff, their behavior toward each other, and even their behavior toward their patients. Naturally, the behavior of the medical staff will influence the perceptions and behavior of the patients.

Technological Factors The introduction of modern technology is the most significant environmental factor to radically influence the structure and the provision of the health-care services. For example, advances in biomedicines and biotechnologies in the sector mean that medical conditions can be identified sooner and medical procedures have become less invasive. Subsequently, patients' hospital visits are made shorter, and thus the hospital is able to serve more patients in a given timeframe. Of course, technology requires investment which a manager of a hospital needs to consider along with other essential needs—material and the human resources. A hospital needs to adjust to new technologies, and this adjustment calls for an improved management and programming of the hospital's activities. Here, we take the term "technology" to mean the systematic application of scientific or organized knowledge, the development, and the spread of the new technology (knowledge) so as to increase the importance of innovating to remain competitive (Dubrin, 2009, p. 483).

Ecological Factors These factors concern the physical capital and the ecological characteristics and issues that affect it, where "physical capital" is understood to mean elements such as the air, light, noise, etc. If the spirit of cooperation among hospital community members is considered an important element in a hospital's smooth functioning, then the creation of an appropriate physical environment for staff would be a positive factor in facilitating their efficient performance. Besides, according to relevant research (Terry, 1970), the physical environment directly influences the qualitative and quantitative performance of an organization's human resources.

Thus, the multiple environmental forces that stem from different factors impact upon and influence the shape and the functioning of hospitals.

References

Abdelhak, M., & Hanken, M. A. (2016). *Health information: Management of a strategic resource* (5th ed.). St. Louis, MO: Elsevier.
Abel-Smith, B. (1976). *Value for money in health services*. London: Heinemann.

Anthopoulou, S. S. (1999). Human resource management. In *Management of educational units* (Vol. B, pp. 17–91). Published by Open University in Greece (in Greek).
Arah, O. A., Klazinga, N. S., Delnoij, D. M. J., Ten Asbroek, A. H. A., & Custers, T. (2003). Conceptual frameworks for health systems performance a quest for effectiveness quality and improvement. *International Journal for Quality in Health Care, 15*(5), 377–398.
Argyris, C. (1957). *Personality and organization.* New York: Horperand Row.
Beck, J. (1992). School and society. *Pedagogical psychological encyclopedia dictionary* (pp. 4634–4635) Athens, Greece: Ellinika Grammata (in Greek).
Becker, E. R., & Sloan, F. A. (1985). Hospital ownership and performance. *Economic Inquiry, XXIII*, 21–36.
Beyer, J. M., & Trice, H. M. (1987). How an organization's rites reveal its culture. *Organizational Dynamics, 15*(4), 5–24.
Blair, J. D., Nix, T. W., Payne, T., Rotarious, T. M., & Whitehead, C. J. (2004). Stakeholder management—strategies and styles. In L. Wolper (Ed.), *Health care administration* (4th ed., pp. 157–190). Burlington, MA: Jones and Bartlett Publishers.
Bolman, L. G., & Deal, T. E. (1984). *Modern approaches to understanding and managing organisations.* San Francisco, CA: Jossey-Bass.
Borenstein, J., Badamgarav, G., Henning, J. M., Gano Jr., A. D., & Weingarten, S. R. (2004). The association between quality improvement activities performed by managed care organizations and quality of care. *The American Journal of Medicine, 117*(5), 297–304.
Bouradas, D. (2001). *Management.* Athens, Greece: Benou Publications. (in Greek).
Bouradas, D. (2005). *Leadership.* Athens, Greece: Kritiki Publishing. (in Greek).
Bouzakis, S. (1994). *Educational reforms in Greece* (Vol. A). Athens, Greece: Gutenberg. (in Greek).
Boyne, G. A. (2003). What is public service improvement. *Public Administration, 81*(2), 211–227.
Campbell, J. (1977). On the nature of organizational effectiveness. In P. S. Goodman & J. M. Pennings (Eds.), *New perspectives on organizational effectiveness* (pp. 13–55). San Francisco, CA: Jossey-Bass.
Cardador, M. T., & Rupp, D. E. (2011). Organizational culture, multiple needs and the meaningfulness of work. In Ashkanasy, N.M., Wilderom, C.P.M. & Peterson, M.F. (Eds.) *The handbook of organizational culture and climate*, 2nd edition, (pp. 158–179), U.S.A.: Sage Publications.
Carter, E. E. (1971). The behavioral theory of the firm and top level corporate decisions. *Administrative Science Quarterly, 16*(4), 413–428.
Child, J. (1972). Organizational structure, environment and performance: The role of strategic choice. *Sociology, 6*(1), 1–22.
Chletsos, M. (2011). *Health economics.* Athens: Pataki Publications. (in Greek).
Chrispeels, J. (1992). *Purposeful restructuring: Creating a culture to learning and achievement in elementary schools.* Bristol: Falmer Press.
Counte, M. A., & Meurer, S. (2001). Issues in the assessment of continuous quality improvement implementation in health care organizations. *International Journal for Quality in Health Care, 13*(3), 197–207.
Cuellar, A. G., & Gertler, P. J. (2006). Strategic integration of hospitals and physicians. *Journal of Health Economics, 25*, 1–28.
Daskalakis, D. (2009). *Introduction to modern sociology.* Athens, Greece: Papazisis Publishing. (in Greek).
Deal, T. E., & Kennedy, A. A. (1982). *Corporate cultures: The rites and rituals of corporate life.* Reading, MA: Addison-Wesley Publishing.
Denison, D. R. (1990). *Corporate culture and organizational effectiveness.* Oxford: John Wiley & Sons.
Douglas, C. J., & Ryman, J. A. (2003). Understanding competitive advantage in the general hospital industry: Evaluating strategic competencies. *Strategic Management Journal, 24*, 333–347.
Dubrin, A. J. (2009). *Essentials of management* (8th ed.). Mason, OH: South Western, Cengage Learning.

Fan, Y. (2000). A classification of Chinese culture. *Cross-Cultural Management, 7*(2), 1–10.
Feldstein, M. (1977). Quality change and the demand for hospital care. *Econometrica, 45*(7), 1681–1702.
Georgopoulos, N. (2006). *Strategic management*. Athens, Greece: Benou Publishing. (in Greek).
Gilley, A., Dixon, P., & Gilley, J. W. (2008). Characteristics of leadership effectiveness: Implementing change and driving innovation in organizations. *Human Resource Development Quarterly, 19*(2), 153–169.
Grint, K. (2005). *The sociology of work: An introduction* (3rd ed.). Cambridge: Polity Press.
Guzzo, R. A., & Dickson, M. W. (1996). Teams in organizations: Recent research on performance and effectiveness. *Annual Review of Psychology, 47*(1), 307–338.
Halpin, A. (1966). *Theory and research in administration*. Oxford: MacMillan.
Hampton, D., Summer, C., & Webber, R. (1987). *Organizational behavior and the practice of management*. Glenview, IL: Scott Foresman & Co..
Handy, C. (1981). *Understanding organizations*. London: Penguin Publishing.
Hanlon, N. T. (2001). Sense of place organizational context and the strategic management of publicly funded hospitals. *Health Policy, 58*, 151–173.
Hickson, D., Hinings, C., McMillan, C., & Schwitter, J. (1974). The culture free context of organization structures: A tri-national comparison. *Sociology, 8*(1), 59–80.
Hit, M. A., & Middlemist, R. D. (1979). A methodology to develop the criteria and criteria weightings for assessing subunit effectiveness in organizations. *Academy of Management Journal, 22*(2), 356–374.
Hofstede, G. (1980). *Culture's consequences: International differences in work-related values*. Michigan: Sage Publications.
Hosking, J. E. (2004). Planning healthcare facilities and managing the development process. In L. Wolper (Ed.), *Health care administration* (4th ed., pp. 373–396). Burlington, MA: Jones and Bartlett Publishers.
Hoy, W., & Miskel, C. (1996). *Educational administration: Theory, research and practice*. New York: McGraw Hill.
Ifantopoulos, Y. (2006). *Health economics*. Athens, Greece: Tipothito Publishing. (in Greek).
Iordanoglu, D. (2008). *Human resource management in modern organizations*. Athens, Greece: Kritiki Publishing. (in Greek).
Kantas, A. (1995). *Organizational–industrial psychology. (Part 1 and 3)*. Athens, Greece: Ellinika Grammata Publishing. (in Greek).
Koen, C. (2005). *Comparative international management*. Berkshire: McGraw-Hill.
Kontakos, A. (2009). Shaping a culture of educational change. In A. Kontakos & F. Kalavasis (Eds.), *Issues of educational design: Change and governance of educational systems* (pp. 77–86). Athens, Greece: Atrapos Publishing. (in Greek).
Kontis, T. (1994). *Administrative psychology*. Athens, Greece: Singhroni Ekdotiki Publishing. (in Greek).
Koulougliotis, N. (1992). *Sociology: Introduction to the science of sociology, issues of sociology in education*. Athens, Greece: Singhroni Ekdotiki Publishing. (in Greek).
Levine, S., & White, D. E. (1961). Exchange as a conceptual framework for the study of interorganizational relationships. *Administrative Science Quarterly, 5*(4), 583–601.
Lezotte, L. (1992). *Effective schools practices that work*. Okemos, MI: Effective School Products Ltd..
Li, L. X., Benton, W. C., & Leong, G. K. (2002). The impact of strategic operations management decisions on community hospital performance. *Journal of Operations Management, 20*, 389–408.
Likert, R. (1961). *New patterns of management*. New York: McGraw-Hill.
Mamouz, B., Rousseau, A., & Hudon, P. A. (2016). Strategic management in public administration: A result based approach to strategic public management. *International Review of Administrative Sciences, 82*(3), 411–417.
Marchinko, D. E., & Hetico, H. R. (2013). Overview of operations in health care organizations today: Understanding trends and management objectives. In D. E. Marchinko & H. R. Hetico

(Eds.), *Hospitals and health care organizations. Management strategies operational techniques, tools, templates and case studies* (pp. 3–28). Boca Raton, FL: CRC Press/Taylor & Francis Group.
Martin, J., & Siehl, C. (1983). Organizational culture and counterculture: An uneasy symbiosis. *Organizational Dynamics, 12*(2), 52–64.
Matsagouras, E. (2000). *The classroom*. Athens, Greece: Matsagouras Publishing. (in Greek).
McConnell, K. J., Chang, A. M., Maddox, T. M., Wholey, D. R., & Lindrooth, R. C. (2014). An exploration of management practices in hospitals. *Healthcare, 2*, 121–129.
McKee, M., & Healy, J. (2002). The significance of hospitals: An introduction. In M. McKee & J. Healy (Eds.), *Hospitals in a changing Europe* (European Observatory on Health Care Systems series Edited by Figueras, J., McKee, M., Mossialos, E. & Saltman, R.B.) (pp. 3–13). Buckingham: Open University Press.
Michopoulos, A. (1998). *Educational administration* (Vol. I and II). Athens, Greece: Michopoulos Publishing.
Mintzberg, H. (1979). *The structuring of organizations: A synthesis of the research*. Englewood Cliffs, NJ: Prentice Hall.
Mintzberg, H. (1983). *Power in and around organizations* (The theory of management policy series). Englewood Cliffs, NJ: Prentice Hall.
Mintzberg, H., Lampel, J., Quinn, J. B., & Ghoshal, S. (2003). *The strategy process: Concepts, contexts cases*. Essex: Pearson Education Limited.
Mortimore, P., & Whitty, G. (2001). Can school improvement overcome the effects of disadvantage. In T. Cox (Ed.), *Combating educational disadvantage* (pp. 156–176). New York: Falmer Press.
Mullins, L. J. (2010). *Management and organisational behavior* (9th ed.). London: Prentice Hall.
Noether, M. (1988). Competition among hospitals. *Journal of Health Economics, 7*, 259–284.
Osborn, R. N., & Baughn, C. C. (1994). *An assessment of the state of the field of organizational design*. Alexandria, VA: U.S. Army Research Institute.
Ouinn, J. B. (1980). *Strategies for change: Logical incrementalism*. Homewood, IL: Irwin.
Ouston, J. (2003). School effectiveness and school improvement. In M. Preedy, R. Glatter, & C. Wise (Eds.), *Strategic leadership and educational improvement* (pp. 252–264). Buckingham: Open University Press.
Paisey, A. (1992). *Organization and management in schools* (2nd ed.). London: Longman.
Panagiotopoulou, R. (1997). *Communication in organizations*. Athens, Greece: Kritiki Publishing. (in Greek).
Papanaum, Z. (1995). *School leadership*. Thessaloniki, Greece: Kyriakidis Publishing. (in Greek).
Papoulias, D. (2002). *Business strategic management & change management*. Athens, Greece: Kastanioti Publishing. (in Greek).
Payne, R. (1991). Taking stock of corporate culture. *Personnel Management, 127*, 25–29.
Perry, D., Staudenmayer, N. A., & Votta, L. G. (1994). People, organizations and process improvement. *IEEE Software, 11*(4), 36–45.
Peters, T. J., & Waterman, R. H. (1982). *Search of excellence*. Manhattan, NY: Harper & Row.
Pheysey, D. C. (1993). *Organizational cultures*. London: Routledge.
Robey, D. (1982). *Designing organizations: A macro perspective*. Homewood, iL, Richard D. Irwin.
Sackman, S. A. (2011). Culture and performance. In N. M. Ashkanasy, C. P. M. Wilderom, & M. F. Peterson (Eds.), *The handbook of organizational culture and climate* (pp. 188–224). Thousand Oaks, CA: Sage Publications.
Saiti, A. (2013). Reforms in Greek education 1991–2011: Reforms or something else?. *eJournal of Education Policy*, Spring. Retrieved from http://nau.edu/COE/eJournal/_Forms/spring2013/Saiti. (Online 10 p, pp. 1–10).
Sammons, P., Hilliman, J., & Mortimore, P. (1995). *Key characteristics of effective school: A review of school effectiveness research*. London: Office for Standards in Education.

Schein, E. H. (2010). *Organizational culture and leadership* (4th ed.). San Francisco, CA: Jossey Bass.
Schermerhorn Jr., J. R., Hunt, J. G., & Osborn, R. N. (2002). *Organizational behaviour* (7th ed.). New York: Wiley.
Schneeweiss, C. (1998). Hierarchical planning in organisations: Elements of a general theory. *International Journal of Production Economics, 56–57*, 547–556.
Schwartz, H., & Davis, S. (1981). Matching corporate culture and business strategy. *Organizational Dynamic, 10*(1), 30–48.
Scott, W. (1981). *Organisations: Rational, national and open systems*. Englewood Cliffs, NJ: Prentice-Hall.
Scott, W. R., & Davis, G. F. (2016). *Organizations and organizing rational natural and open system perspectives*. New York, NY: Routledge.
Snook Jr., D. I. (2004). Hospital organization and management. In L. Wolper (Ed.), *Health care administration* (4th ed., pp. 651–662). Burlington, MA: Jones and Bartlett Publishers.
Stoll, L. (2003). School culture and improvement. In M. Preedy, R. Glatter, & C. Wise (Eds.), *Strategic leadership and educational improvement* (pp. 93–108). Buckingham: Open University Press.
Stoll, L., & Myers, K. (1998). No quick fixes: An introduction. In L. Stoll & K. Myers (Eds.), *No quick fixes: Perspectives on schools in difficulty* (pp. 1–14). London: Falmer Press.
Swayne, L. G., Duncan, W. J., & Ginter, P. M. (2006). *Strategic management of health care organizations* (5th ed.). Oxford: Blackwell Publishing.
Taylor, F. (1911). *The principles of scientific management*. New York, NY: Harper and Row.
Terry, G. (1970). *Office management and control*. London: Rizwin Publishing.
Thomas, R. (1974). Environment analysis for corporate planning. *Business Horizons, 17*(5), 27–38.
Tomasik, J. (2013). Collaborating to enhance performance in a changing health care landscape: Opportunities for widespread policy and outcomes improvement. In D. E. Marchinko & H. R. Hetico (Eds.), *Hospitals and health care organizations. Management strategies operational techniques, tools, templates and case studies* (pp. 195–206). Boca Raton, FL: CRC Press/ Taylor & Francis Group.
Trompenaars, F., & Hampden-Turner, C. (1999). *Riding the waves of culture* (2nd ed.). London: Nicholas Brealey Publishing.
Williams, K., & Johnson, B. (2004). *Introducing management: A development guide*. Great Britain: Planta Tree.
Yasin, M., Alavi, J., Kunt, M., & Zimmerer, T. W. (2004). TQM practices in service organizations: An exploratory study into the implementation outcome and effectiveness. *Managing Service Quality: An International Journal, 14*(5), 377–389.
Zacharis, E. (1985). *History, organization and management technique and professional education*. Athens, Greece: OEDB Publishing. (in Greek).

Chapter 3
Process of Strategic Management

Key Concepts All management functions should be interconnected and interrelated on a continuous basis in order to implement an effective strategy.

- It is extremely important for a hospital to analyze the environment (all types of environments) in which it operates so that it can know the extent of its situation and its capabilities before determining its strategic goals.
- An important tool for analyzing a hospital's internal environment is the SWOT Analysis.
- The effective evaluation of a hospital's strategy requires a systematic environmental assessment and feedback on the hospital's performance (both in terms of quality and quantity).
- Since hospitals are complex organizations with individual characteristics, they need to measure their performance and outcomes on a systematic basis so as to maximize patient value and remain focused on a more 'patient-centered' approach.

3.1 Introduction

It was mentioned earlier in this book that the management of an organization, whether public or private, can design a strategy only once it has previously gained a sufficient perception of the environmental conditions within which it functions. In particular, the stating, analysis, and assessment of the current strengths and weaknesses reveal the real picture of an organization's internal environment. The results of this investigation, together with the outcomes of a study of the external environment (e.g., analysis of the political and economic factors), allow the (upper) management of a particular organization to devise a strategic plan for the future development and survival of the organization.

At this point it should be emphasized that it is not possible to separate development from survival. On the contrary, they are interrelated and work in parallel. For

M. Chletsos, A. Saiti, *Strategic Management and Economics in Health Care*,
https://doi.org/10.1007/978-3-030-35370-4_3

example, the central administration of a health-care system cannot move toward improvements in the provision of the health-care services if there is no parallel change in the conditions of the functioning of health-care units (hospitals). Such changes may require adjustments in the system's level of financing.

In view of the above, the design of a strategy should allow for a number of elements, such as the environment within which an organization functions, the available resources (human and material), etc., and should define a specific approach through which management can proceed to actions that support the achievement of specific targets. For the materialization of those targets, the organization should balance the strengths and weaknesses of the internal environment with the emerging opportunities and threats of its external environment. Thus, the process of strategic management results in a carefully devised strategy, followed by its implementation (Georgopoulos, 2006; Mintzberg, 1987, 2012; Porter, 1986; Steiner, 1979; Sun, Wang, & Luo, 2018).

By focusing our interest on the process of strategic management, according to the relevant literature such as Hillestad and Berkowitz (2004); Hitt, Ireland, and Hoskisson (2005); Koontz, O' Donnell, and Weihrich (1982); Liedtka (2000); Mintzberg (1987, 2012); Papadakis (2007); Porter (1986); Steiner (1979); Sun et al. (2018); Swayne, Duncan, and Ginter (2006); and Team FME (2013), this process mainly involves the following steps:

- An analysis of the organization's environment
- The formulation of a strategy
- The implementation of that strategy
- An assessment and review of the outcomes

It should be mentioned that the particular process belongs to the rational model of strategic management (see Table 3.1)—a basic tool for analyzing the strengths, weaknesses, opportunities, and threats, known as SWOT.

3.2 Analysis of an Organization's Environment

3.2.1 Investigation of the External Environment

We have already mentioned in the previous chapter that the external environment has two key features: firstly, the social, economic, and other such factors that are beyond the control of the organization yet influence its function and, secondly, the fact that it tends to change continually and become more complex.

Table 3.1 SWOT analysis of the organizational position

	Internal environment current situation	External environment future situation
What is it?		
Good	Strengths	Opportunities
Bad	Weaknesses	Threats

Given that a strategy should take into consideration an organization's position in its environment, the research and the analysis of its external environment should focus mainly on determining and analyzing the political, economic, and technological trends that are outside the organization's sphere of control and are able to influence, in any way, the effectiveness of its activities.

The analysis of those external factors would help identify key parameters and boundaries within which an organization could devise an effective strategy. Before such a strategy can be formulated, we need answers to the following questions:

When do the external factors influence the organization?

To what extent do these factors influence the organization?

How do these factors influence the organization's development?

Focusing our attention on the field of health care, the basic sectors of research for studying and analyzing the external environment of health-care units are standard (see Chapter 2). However, they also depend on any specific social circumstances that may exist within the society that uses the health-care system. For example, the state of a national economy can be considered as a substantial pre-consideration when working out how to shape and implement a health-care reform.

Moreover, the political, cultural, and social development of a country has an international dimension—due to the high speed of information flow—so subsequently it can be expected that national health (and indeed other) strategies will receive scrutiny from the international community. Due to such phenomena, the philosophy and orientation of health-care units' activities needs careful consideration. Ideally, a central administration should carefully consider the significance of all the factors in an objective way and then formulate their strategy accordingly.

3.2.2 Investigation of the Internal Environment

The elements of an organization's internal environment, with a special emphasis on the environment of a hospital, have been presented in Chapter 2. As has already been mentioned, understanding the factors of an organization's internal environment that influence the organization's functioning is a fundamental issue for strategic analysis.

Thus, the relevant managers of an organization responsible for determining strategies need to make a careful analysis of the organization's environment. Through this analysis, an assessment of the environmental and organizational factors takes place whereby a diagnosis and estimation of the strengths and the weaknesses of the organization is made. This analysis can be achieved through the SWOT analysis (strengths, weaknesses, opportunities, threats).

3.2.3 SWOT: An Assessment of a Health-Care Unit

All the relevant data and information gathered by the managers is organized into a rational structure by using the SWOT analysis.

Then the managers can estimate the internal strengths and weaknesses of the organization as well as the opportunities and the threats that appear in the organization's external environment and so identify the main issues that the organization is faced with and then go on to formulate an appropriate strategy by considering the significant issues highlighted by the above analysis (Burgelman et al., 2018; Georgopoulos, 2006; Lueg & Julner, 2014; Mintzberg, 1987, 2012; Porter, 1986; Reeves, Duncan, & Ginter, 2000; Steiner, 1979; Sun et al., 2018). Information on the required elements can be gathered by the managers through interviews (Ganivelli, 2016; Koontz & Weihrich, 2010; Nilsson, Baathe, Andersson, & Sandoff, 2017; Zavlanos, 1998). From the perspective of a health-care unit, the points below give an example of the sort of feedback that hospital managers might expect when conducting a SWOT analysis:

A. Strengths

The hospital has modern infrastructure.

The hospital has specialized, fully equipped laboratories.

The hospital has a full complement of human resources (medical and nursing staff).

The medical and nursing staff are given incentives.

The hospital's main operating theaters have the latest technological equipment.

B. Weaknesses

Despite incentives, the hospital still experiences a relatively high turnover of medical and nursing staff.

The hospital has no quick way of recovering its functional expenses.

Medical and nursing staff do not receive systematic training.

The hospital is not using its new technologies in an effective way.

Bureaucratic procedures are preventing the hospital from operating smoothly.

C. Opportunities

Harmonious relations with the patient associations contribute to the hospital's effective performance.

The merging of clinics and/or the creation of an executive board for dealing with difficult situations would improve the quality of health-care services that the hospital provides.

Globalization is helping, through the expansion of Internet services, to allow medical knowledge and expert opinions to be exchanged rapidly with other hospitals across the world.

New technologies (e.g., computers and precision instruments in the surgeries) give medical (and nursing) staff the opportunity to perform surgeries less invasively and in a more timely manner, thus reducing patient discomfort and recovery time.

D. Threats

An increase in the number of uninsured patients may be a problem for the sustainable functioning of the hospital.

The national debt may impose cuts in the hospital's finances.

Major catastrophes in quick succession, such as an earthquake, a high-rise fire, etc., may jeopardize the hospital's effective operation.

The increasing cost of new technologies is putting a strain on the hospital's finances.

3.2.4 *Understanding the Current Circumstances of a Health-Care Unit*

Assessment of the Internal Environment of a Hospital

In assessing a hospital's current environment, managers determine the characteristics of their hospital's strengths and areas of weakness that require improvement. At this point it should be emphasized that in order to ensure managers gain a full and sufficient overview of their hospital, they should follow certain rules for an effective SWOT analysis. Basically, a diagnosis of the strengths and weaknesses of a hospital should cover the following areas:

- Medical and nursing staff, which includes the knowledge and the abilities of the hospital staff, the general sense of job satisfaction, any incentives they have, the existing culture, etc.
- The process of health-care service provision, which includes the methods of treatments, the quality of medical technological equipment and labs, the use of new biotechnology, etc.
- The financing of a hospital, which includes the amount and the timing of income received for the functional expenditures of the hospital, the sources of income, etc.
- The administrative function, which includes the knowledge and abilities of the manager/leader, the spirit of cooperation between managers and staff, the hospital's bureaucratic procedures, etc.

Assessment of the External Environment of a Hospital

For the assessment of the external environment of a hospital, managers determine the factors that can be opportunities or threats for their hospital. In the second chapter of the book, we mentioned that the factors related to the external environment of a hospital are:

- Social environment, which includes moral values, beliefs, habits, and other social characteristics such as the expectations of the members of society, population movements, etc.

- Technological environment, which includes the availability and use of new technology in the field of health care
- Economic environment, which includes those external influences that could impact upon the hospital's finances
- Political and legislative environment, which includes the formulation of health-care policy and more generally the legislative framework for health care

A prompt recognition and awareness of the trends and signals of the external environment provide the health-care manager with an integrated view of the information needed for the strategic management of their unit and so help to identify the most appropriate use for all the available resources so as to confront the possible threats that undermine the sustainability of the hospital. In sum, an examination of the internal and the external environment of an organization allows its manager to understand its circumstances. Through this examination, a hospital manager can easily answer the question: "What really is the current status of the hospital?"

3.3 Process of Strategy Development

It is a common perception that each organization, no matter its size or the extent of its activities, adopts some objectives and formulates a strategy. It determines a plan of activities that aims at a variety of achievements. During the process of strategy implementation, the actions and the decisions of the management are of great importance since the survival and the development of the organization depend on the formulation of an appropriate strategy.

A review of the relevant literature (Burgelman et al., 2018; Campbell, Balabanova, & Howard, 2016; David, 2011; Georgopoulos, 2006; Lueg & Julner, 2014; Mintzberg, 1987, 2012; Nilsson et al., 2017; Papadakis, 2007; Porter, 1986; Reeves et al., 2000; Sarsentis, 1996; Steiner, 1979; Sun et al., 2018; Zavlanos, 1998) shows that the process of strategy implementation can be broken down into the following steps.

Step One Determine the organization's mission—as we have already mentioned in Chapter 1, the "mission" answers basic questions regarding the existence of the organization such as:

- Who we are.
- What we are.
- What we want to achieve.

Step Two Determine specific targets—again, as has been previously mentioned, after the mission has been determined, it is absolutely necessary to establish the organization's targets. And this is because a member of the organization needs to know that their role has a context. Hence, the organization's targets should be:

- Within the framework of organization's mission

- Clear and sufficient and express the dynamic of the organization
- Countable and real

Step Three Develop the strategy. After the specific targets have been determined and the necessary elements gathered (strengths and weaknesses), managers are called to create alternative strategies and subsequently choose the best possible one. It is worth mentioning that the development of a strategy is a process that involves quantitative assessment but also follows a type of conditional behavior and the estimations of a conditioned rationality and feeling (Douglas & Ryman, 2003; Mintzberg, 2012; Nickols, 2016; Reeves et al., 2000; Sarsentis, 1996; Steiner, 1979; Team FME, 2013). To make this clearer, there follows a description of targets in two fundamental activities of a hospital with a parallel description of the expected advantages and possible problems.

3.3.1 Provision of Health-Care Services

Targets

(a) *Improvement in the provision of health-care services*

Expected Advantages
Stability of medical and nursing staff
Systematic training of the medical and nursing staff
Possible Problems
Increase in hospital expenditures
Possible reactions of the medical and nursing staff

(b) *Introduction of new biotechnology to the hospital's health-care system*

Expected Advantages
Easier and more effective patient treatments
More robust medical research
Increased high-value health care
Possible Problems
Possible damages
Possible problems in the training of staff
Increase in expenditures due to the maintenance of the new biotechnology

3.3.2 Administrative Function

Targets

(a) *Improvement in the administrative procedures*

Expected Advantages

Faster flow of paperwork within the hospital and hence delivery of a better health-care outcome at lower cost

Less bureaucracy for the administrative, medical, and nursing staff

More secure data storage (printed and electronic)

Possible Problems

Increased cost of equipment maintenance

Possible conflict with/complications in internal functions

(b) *Decentralization of power*

Expected Advantages

Enhanced sense of responsibility for the lower hierarchical level of the hospital.

Faster solutions to problems.

The upper hierarchical level is freed up from routine issues.

Good comprehension of strategies among different internal units.

Possible Problems

Weakness in the ability of less senior staff to solve issues with specialized knowledge

Danger of heterogeneity in the functioning of the different clinics within the hospital

Discrepancies in the interpretation of the legislative framework

Lack of consistency in the implementation of strategies

From the above we can see that the formulation of a strategy in the field of health care is determined by the health-care unit's targets, its strengths and weaknesses, and by the conditions presented by the external environment. Note that there is an interdependency between the strategic targets and the advantages or weaknesses of the health-care units, whereas the general environment is an independent variable in the health-care system.

Regarding the choice of the best possible strategy, we may support the view that the choice of the best proposal can be according to the rational approach in a comparison with the advantages and disadvantages of all the available solutions. In order for this to happen, managers should consider each proposal in light of the following questions:

- To what extent does the proposal help to achieve the organization's objective?
- Would there be any undesirable consequences (e.g., a negative reaction from employees) from implementing the proposal?
- What would be the cost of implementing the proposal?

Essentially, each alternative strategy needs to be assessed against at least three basic criteria: its appropriateness, its cost in real terms, and the degree to which it is accepted (Theriou, 2005, pp. 278–280).

Clearly, the proposal that yields the more positive answers will be selected by the decision makers as the best possible strategy.

Step Four Develop policies, whereby the upper hierarchical levels of an organization (hospital management in our case) provide general guidelines that facilitate managers in making their own decisions and using their own judgment within specific limitations (the meaning of the term "policy" has been presented in the first chapter).

A key challenge facing hospital managers in developing a strategy is to win the cooperation of their medical staff in implementing it. Indeed, enhancing the creativity and the autonomy of the medical staff is crucially important for the shaping and implementation of a hospital's strategy since it is mainly the medical staff who tend to resist change due to greater (perceived) complications and so, in a sense, they exercise a rather autonomous profession. Therefore, it is necessary to win their strong commitment toward their hospital/health-care unit in order for any given strategy to be effective. This can be achieved through fruitful communication and through shared values and targets (David, 2011; Kirkpatrik, Wofford, & Baum, 2002; Mintzberg, 2012; Porter, 1986; Reeves et al., 2000; Speziale, 2015; Steiner, 1979; Swayne et al., 2006).

Ultimately, a well-formulated strategy answers the question: "Where does the hospital want to go?"

3.4 Strategy Implementation

A crucial point in an organization's strategic management is the strategy's implementation phase. The process of strategic management does not stop by choosing the best possible strategy but continues with its implementation through specific activities and actions. At this stage managers will learn whether or not their strategic decision will be accepted and implemented by the organization's members. While it is presumed that the previous steps in the strategy's formulation of the strategy followed due process, the degree of the strategy's implementation is the crucial factor that characterizes it either as an effective one or merely as a good intention, at best. Therefore, it is not enough for a strategic decision to be rational and show the best possible way of achieving a target. It needs to consider the factors (e.g., expenditures, environmental conditions, internal matters, etc.) that could possibly prevent the desired outcome from being achieved.

Therefore, the implementation of a strategy is a functional process that is typically:

- *Complicated* because it often involves substantial changes in people, roles, activities, organization structure, the control system, etc.
- *Difficult* because a new strategy usually demands that the organization moves in a new direction. This tendency causes fear in organization members with perceived unpleasant consequences for some people and hence they react negatively to the proposed changes. In the relevant literature, we see that "organizations often show commitment and devotion to the status quo even though this causes non satisfactory results" (Georgopoulos, 2006, p. 262). In light of this reaction,

managers should put more effort into convincing organization members to accept the proposed changes.

But which activities should the organization's management put forward in order to implement the strategy in an effective way?

First, we may emphasize that in the relevant literature (Ganivelli, 2016; Kaplan & Norton, 2004; Kaval & Voyten, 2006; Mintzberg, 2012; Nilsson et al., 2017; Sarsentis, 1996; Speziale, 2015; Sun et al., 2018) a few methods of strategy implementation are mentioned. These include:

- *The strict management method*, according to which, the upper management decides on an appropriate strategy and the lower levels of management closely oversee its implementation. In this case, there is a swift implementation of the strategic decisions but a low level of acceptance and of course a reaction that is either abrupt (direct resistance) or silent (indirect resistance).
- *The method of training* whereby the organization's staff receive training on the skills they may be lacking to implement the strategy. The success of this method depends heavily on the degree of the employees' training since the training aims to achieve a greater degree of acceptance and certainly a more effective implementation of the strategy.
- *The method of information and participation* whereby the organization members are informed of the organization's problems and the strategic plan devised to address them. The whole process (from strategy formulation to implementation) is explained, along with the impact expected across the organization's sectors/services. The success of this method is increased when the message is transferred in its entirety, convincingly and with no distorting interventions.

In view of the above, we are urged to consider the types of activity that an organization's management should adopt when implementing a strategy.

First, a careful programming should be made that includes a determination of the human and the material resources needed to implement the strategy. With particular reference to the programming of human resources, we may claim that the most important step for the effective implementation of a proposed strategy is the selection of the appropriate staff in significant job positions. For example, managers who are responsible for strategy implementation should (a) be distinguished by their management and leadership abilities and skills so as to be able to influence, motivate, and show sensitivity to other staff members and (b) be in absolute accordance with the upper management and fully accept the content and targets of, as well as responsibility for, the strategic plan's implementation. The same can be said for the staff who will be responsible for implementing the management's decisions.

Second, it is necessary for an appropriate structure to be in place that will facilitate a good cooperation between the different departments' services and that will certainly coordinate and exercise control effectively. It should clarify in detail who will do what, where, how, and when it will be completed. Regarding staff coordination, we may note that, due to the cooperation of numerous staff in different sectors, the implementation stage demands the coordination of all groups and individuals of the organization so as to avoid misinterpretations, conflicts, and consequently a loss of time, money, and human efforts.

Third, a communication network is absolutely necessary so that those who are responsible for implementing the strategy can be informed continually about the process of execution and its outcomes. Indeed, a two-way communication network not only contributes to the development of good human relations and the responsible updating of staff as a whole (managers and nonmanagerial employees) but also helps to win the trust of the organization's members and so strengthen their commitment to the strategy's implementation phase. Indeed, the so-called administrative gap between the hospital management and the medical staff referred to by Mintzberg (2012, p. 3) can be bridged only through a fruitful collaboration. This collaboration can be achieved through efficient communication channels that subsequently establish a positive hospital climate.

Finally, the successful execution of a decision presupposes a stable leadership that will ensure continuity in the organization's policy planning but also ensure continuity in the organization's functionality. For instance, the central hospital management needs to ensure, on an ongoing basis, that the necessary financial resources are available for staff salaries, equipment purchases, etc. This need is particularly strong during a strategy implementation phase. In the case of a hospital, additional finances beyond normal running costs are usually needed to implement the proposed strategy effectively, either due to the increased functional costs or due to the proposed investments in buildings/materials and/or technological equipment. In parallel, a hospital also needs financial resources in order to advance its medical research and to deliver the greatest benefit and high-value health care to individuals (patients) and so meet the needs of society in an efficient and effective way. Indeed, a sufficient budget and hospital workforce are the key factors that contribute significantly to the equitable delivery of health-care services to the whole of society. In any case, a lack of financial support for a hospital and the non-execution of activities necessary for the optimum success of its strategy may undermine the whole implementation process.

3.5 Strategy Assessment

3.5.1 Significance of Assessment

In the first section of this chapter, we mentioned that the process of strategic management involves an analysis of the organization's environment, the formulation of a strategy, the implementation of that strategy, and an assessment and control of the strategic outcomes. In the final step of assessment, once the first outcomes have materialized after a certain period of time, managers are able to evaluate the strategy's implementation according to predefined criteria. This is necessary because during this period of time it is possible for radical changes to have taken place, either in the organization's internal or external environment (or both), on which the formulation of the chosen strategy was based. In practice, this means that managers use strategic control in order to:

- Ensure that the strategic progress is being adhered to
- Evaluate whether or not the environmental changes pose immediate or future problems for the organization's function
- Make necessary adjustments in order for the organization to achieve the desired outcome (Campbell et al., 2016; David, 2011; Dubrin, 1997; Freisen & Johnson, 1995; Georgopoulos, 2006; Mintzberg, 2012; Nickols, 2016; Porter, 1986; Steiner, 1979; Team FME, 2013)

With particular reference to hospitals/health-care units, their environment is in a near-constant state of change due to the rapid pace of technological advances and growing patient demands, which are a driving force for greater innovation in clinical procedures and an expanding knowledge network, which in turn calls for the advancement of medical research. Indeed it is the environment that mainly causes managers to regularly review and assess the strategy implementation process and adapt it as required. Certainly, managers know all too well that if they focus only on long-term results—the main outcome of strategic management—then the immediate or near-term impact is likely to be negative and extremely difficult to reverse (Dubrin, 1997; Freisen & Johnson, 1995; Georgopoulos, 2006; Kaplan & Norton, 2004; Koontz et al., 1982; Mintzberg, 2012; Porter, 1986; Swayne et al., 2006).

However, hospitals (and health-care units in general) face difficulties in satisfying the continuous growing needs of individuals and to keep abreast with the rapid challenges and changes in their external environment. For this reason, more than any other types of organization, hospitals need to measure their performance and outcomes on a systematic basis so as to maximize the value for patients and move swiftly to a more "patient-centered" approach.

In order for a strategy to be assessed effectively, certain prerequisites should be in place, among which are the following:

- Prompt and sufficient feedback (both in terms of quantity and quality) so that managers can readily identify any changes needed and update the strategy accordingly.
- The organization's environment should be monitored on a continuous basis for any changes that may arise. If one does, any potential conflict it may have with the strategy needs to be investigated and, if a threat exists, for the strategy to be adapted so that such an external threat would have minimal or no impact on the activities of the organization. In order for organization members to accept any proposed changes, the focus should be on the activities and the outcomes that are important for the future survival and prosperity of the organization.

3.5.2 The Process of Assessment

The strategy assessment process has four main steps (Dubrin, 1997; Georgopoulos, 2006; Hambrick, 1981; Mintzberg, 1994; Nickols, 2016; Papadakis, 2007; Steiner, 1979; Team FME, 2013):

Determine the standard level of performance. This is defined by the organization's targets and constitutes the basis (or the unit measure) for calculating the results. It expresses specific desired outcomes such as performance levels, targets, behavioral characteristics, and activities. They are not the same in every organization since different organizations have different aims. Moreover, there are some standard frameworks to consider such as time frame (which states the time duration for completing a project), the budget for executing a given project, and the standards of behavior expected of the organization members. It should be noted that all standards of an organization should be realistic, commensurate with the organization's capacities, and, most importantly, acceptable to employees.

Measure the current level of performance. After determining the standard level of performance, the organization's current performance then needs to be measured. Managers usually use four ways of gathering information in order to measure actual performance: (1) personal observation, which provides "first-hand" information about the current state of the organization, (2) statistical reports, (3) verbal accounts that stem from meetings or conversations with staff, and (4) summary reports drawn from documented written reports of staff members (Freisen & Johnson, 1995; Hambrick, 1981; Hillestad & Berkowitz, 2004; Kanellopoulos, 1995; Koontz et al., 1982; Koontz & Weihrich, 2010; Thomas, Clark, & Gioia, 1993). At first glance, measuring actual performance may seem relatively easy. However, there are cases (such as measuring the performance of medical staff or a research clinic) where measurement is ultimately quite difficult. This is because at this stage of the assessment process, in many cases, subjectivity becomes a factor. Therefore, much effort needs to be made in order to establish assessment criteria that are not only quantitative but also sufficiently qualitative.

Compare the current level of performance with the standard level. At this stage of assessment, the actual performance is compared with the standard performance. This comparison helps the organization managers to identify possible deviations from the expected outcomes.

Correct any deviations. Based on the findings of the previous step, if there are any negative deviations, the management needs to devise a remedial course of action that overcomes those deviations and so gets the organization back in line with its strategy. The corrective actions may demand changes in the behavior of some employees, in the organization's activities, in a revision of standards, in a redistribution of duties among staff, etc. At this point it should be emphasized that any positive deviation should also lead to corrective action since it indicates that perhaps the initial targets set are not in line with actual performance achieved by the available staff and material resources, and so those targets should be revised accordingly.

References

Burgelman, R. A., Floyd, S. W., Laamanen, T., Mantene, S., Vaara, E., & Whittington, R. (2018). Strategy processes and practices: Dialogues and intersections. *Strategic Management Journal, 39*(3), 531–558.

Campbell, F. M., Balabanova, D., & Howard, N. (2016). The role of global public health strategy in on profit organizational change at country level: Lessons from the joining of Save the children and Merlin in Myanmar. *The International Journal of Health Planning and Management, 33*(1), 88–101.

David, F. (2011). *Strategic management: Concepts and cases* (13th ed.). Upper Saddle River, NJ: Prentice-Hall.

Douglas, T. J., & Ryman, J. A. (2003). Understanding competitive advantage in the general hospital industry: Evaluating strategic competencies. *Strategic Management Journal, 24*, 333–347.

Dubrin, A. J. (1997). *Essentials of management* (14th ed.). UK: SouthWestern, College Publishing.

Freisen, M. E., & Johnson, J. A. (1995). *The success paradigm: Creating organizational effectiveness through quality and strategy*. Westport, CT: Quorum Books.

Ganivelli, L. (2016). *Business strategies and competitiveness in times of crisis*. London: Palgrave Macmillan.

Georgopoulos, N. (2006). *Strategic management*. Athens, Greece: Benou Publishing. (in Greek).

Hambrick, D. C. (1981). Environment, strategy and power within top management teams. *Administrative Science Quarterly, 26*(2), 253–275.

Hillestad, S. G., & Berkowitz, E. N. (2004). *Health care marketing strategy: From planning to action*. Boston, MA: Jones & Bartlett Publishers.

Hitt, M. A., Ireland, D. R., & Hoskisson, R. E. (2005). *Management competiveness and globalization*. Thomson South-Western: New York.

Kanellopoulos, C. (1995). *Management – Effective administration*. Athens, Greece: Kanellopoulos Publications. (in Greek).

Kaplan, R. S., & Norton, D. P. (2004). How strategy maps frame an organization's objectives. *Financial Executive, 20*(2), 40–46.

Kaval, V. R., & Voyten, L. J. (2006). Executive decision making. Effective processes for making and implementing decisions. *Health Executive, 21*(6), 16–22.

Kirkpatrik, S. A., Wofford, J. C., & Baum, J. R. (2002). Measuring motive imagery contained in the vision statement. *Leadership Quarterly, 13*(2), 139–150.

Koontz, H., O' Donnell, C., & Weihrich, H. (1982). *Management* (7th ed.). London: McGraw Hill.

Koontz, H., & Weihrich, H. (2010). *Essentials of management: An international perspective*. New Delhi: McGraw Hill.

Liedtka, J. (2000). In defense of strategy as design. *California Management Review, 42*(3), 8–30.

Lueg, R., & Julner, P. (2014). How are strategy maps linked to strategic and organizational change? A review if the empirical literature on the balanced scorecard. *Corporate Ownership & Control, 11*(4), 439–446.

Mintzberg, H. (1987). The strategy concept II: Another look of why Organisations need strategies. *California Management Review, 30*(1), 25–32.

Mintzberg, H. (1994). *The rise and fall of strategic planning*. New York: Free Press.

Mintzberg, H. (2012). Managing the myths of health care. *Health Care Leadership, 48*(3), 4–7.

Nickols, F. (2016). Strategy, strategic management, strategic planning and strategic thinking. https://www.nickols.us/strategy_etc.pdf. (online 10 pages)

Nilsson, K., Baathe, F., Andersson, A. C., & Sandoff, M. (2017). Value based healthcare as a trigger for improvement initiatives. *Leadership in Health Services, 30*(4), 364–377.

Papadakis, V. (2007). *Business strategy. Greek and international experience* (Vol. A). Athens, Greece: Benou Publications. (in Greek).

Porter, M. (1986). *Competitive strategy: Techniques for analyzing industries and competitors*. New York: Free Press.

Reeves, T. C., Duncan, W. J., & Ginter, P. M. (2000). Leading change by managing paradoxes. *Journal of Leadership & Organizational Studies, 7*(1), 13–30.

Sarsentis, V. (1996). *Strategy and business policy*. Piraeus, Greece: Stamoulis Publishing. (in Greek).

Speziale, G. (2015). Strategic management of a health care organization: Engagement, behavioural indicators and clinical performance. *European Heart Journal Supplements, 17*(A1), A3–A7.

Steiner, G. (1979). *Strategic planning: What every manager must know*. New York: Free Press.

Sun, J., Wang, S. L., & Luo, Y. (2018). Strategic entry or strategic exit? International presence by emerging economy enterprises. *International Business Review, 27*(2), 418–430.

Swayne, L. G., Duncan, W. J., & Ginter, P. M. (2006). *Strategic Management of Health care organizations* (5th ed.). Hoboken, NJ: Blackwell Publishing.

Team FME. (2013). *Porter's five forces*. Strategy skills. www.free-management-ebooks.com

Theriou, N. (2005). *Strategic business management*. Athens, Greece: Kritiki Publications. (in Greek).

Thomas, J. B., Clark, S. M., & Gioia, D. A. (1993). Strategic sensemaking and organizational performance: Linkages among scanning interpretation, action and outcomes. *The American Management Journal, 36*(2), 239–270.

Zavlanos, M. (1998). *Management*. Athens, Greece: Ellin Publishing. (in Greek).

Chapter 4
Strategic Planning in the Health-Care Sector

Key Concepts

- Strategic planning and programming is the initial and the mandatory managerial tool for any (health-care) organization. It is a rather complicated and difficult process that helps the organization to set its standards and orientation.
- The importance of planning and programming in health care underlies the fact that through this managerial function, the State pursues the best possible capacity-enhancing investment in human resources with the least possible cost in terms of personnel, time, and money.
- During the fulfillment of activity programs, managers discover new elements or the objectives change. Consequently, programmers proceed with corrective changes and naturally return to previous steps of this managerial function.
- As a managerial system, MBO gives an organization's members the opportunity to have a participatory role in, and increase the sense of freedom and flexibility toward the achievement of, the organization's goals. At the same time, as the system has its disadvantages, how these disadvantages impact upon a given organization depends on the way MBO is implemented.
- For effective strategic planning and programming in the field of health care, it is necessary to consider all the dimensions mentioned in the applied models of strategic planning and programming.

4.1 Approaches to Strategic Planning

4.1.1 The Nature of Strategic Planning and Programming

Planning and programming, as an administrative function, includes all those activities of managers that define the organization's goals and the appropriate means in order for those goals to be achieved. Such administrative actions constitute the

M. Chletsos, A. Saiti, *Strategic Management and Economics in Health Care*,
https://doi.org/10.1007/978-3-030-35370-4_4

functional programs of the organization, which were covered in the previous chapter. Furthermore, the function of planning and programming contains a specific type of planning, namely, strategic planning (Koontz & Weihrich, 2010; Mintzberg, 1987; Petridou, 1998).

According to the relevant literature, "strategic planning and programming" has been defined in a variety of ways:

- "A plan that completes the main aims of an organization, the policy and actions in a consequent total" (Quinn, 1980, p. 7)
- "The function of the development of strategic programs on a long-term timeline, which contain the definition of the business's mission, its strategic aims and strategies that will contribute to the achievement of these goals, since its position will be valued in the external environment (Petridou, 1998, p. 99)
- "The procedure through which the organization forms its mission, its vision, its long-term goals and its strategies" (Bouradas, 2001, p. 51)
- "The establishment of basic programs forming the organization's destiny" (Dubrin, 2009, p. 114)

Based on the above definitions, it is clear that strategic planning and programming includes actions that:

- Guide the functional activities of the entire organization
- Provide the organization with the ability to redefine its strategic position and circumstance in its environment

By focusing our attention on the significance of strategic planning and programming, it is clear that its basic aim is achieved "with the prediction and influence, to a degree possible, of the evolvement of the external environment, resulting in the reduction of uncertainty and the minimization of dangers, taking advantage of future opportunities more easily, if it confronts well the reaction to each change" (Petridou, 1998, p. 199). Of course, it is too difficult, if not impossible, for one to predict the future accurately. However, "one can look forward and think what could possibly happen, in order to be better prepared to confront it" (Stylianidis, 2008). No doubt, this concern with the future of the organization, that is, its strategic planning, demands "the collection of much information and the creation and investigation of a wide range of alternative actions, by putting emphasis on the future consequences of short-term decisions. As McCuskey (2003, p. 6) wisely points out, since the strategic planning is the procedure through which organizations use the available information so as to develop plans in order to succeed in their mission, prediction constitutes an excellent tool in the organization managers' hands in order to enrich this procedure.

Consequently, while planning tends to focus on the achievement of predefined goals, prediction helps the organization's managers to envision multiple aims (Bordeaux, 2001; Friebel, 1999; Stilwell, 1999). At the same time it is clear that the procedure of prediction comes first before the procedure of planning, giving the organization's managers the chance to check many scenarios and choose the most appropriate one for their organization."

In conclusion, we may claim that in the case of strategic planning and programming, managers focus on the changeable external environment of the organization by recognizing changes in the organization's direction, by developing all organizational members' skills, and of course by creating competing advantages. And that is why, as has already been mentioned, planning and programming is bound to be more difficult in the future because of the radical social, economic, and technological changes in organizations' external environment. Given that "a new era of changes has been characterized by the extended application of science in each aspect of the human being" (Kanellopoulos, 1995, p. 98), it is rational for the management of modern organizations to be motivated to work more on the procedure of strategic planning and programming. This implies a more dynamic rather than a static approach to planning and programming.

The strategic planning and programming process results in the development of strategic programs, which define long-term goals and certify an organization's position in its environment. These future programs are determined by the upper levels of the managerial hierarchy. Strategic programs have an advantage over other types of programs because, as Kefis (1998) has claimed, a strategic program:

- Is a scientific approach to confronting an organization's problems
- Offers basic quality information about issues of strategic importance, helping to reach rational decisions
- Contributes to the achievement of the organization's targets
- Reduces uncertainty about the future direction and evolution of the organization
- Constitutes an element of democratic management established by the senior managers of the organization
- Provides the appropriate tool for preparing the organization for the environmental challenges of the time

To sum up, the above benefits are positive elements for the sustainability and the welfare of the organization, given that the entire process of strategic planning and programming—which we are going to analyze below—is systematic, methodical, consistent, and collective, allowing an organization to optimize the productivity of its members.

4.1.2 The Process of Strategic Programming

Strategic planning and programming essentially consists of activities that lead to the establishment of an organization's aims and the selection of appropriate strategies that bring about the realization of those aims. It sets in place basic programs that shape the organization's direction.

Nevertheless, for the purposes of this current chapter, we may support the view that the rational clarification of strategic programming is based on a five-stage process (Dubrin, 1997, 2009; Hill, Jones, & Schilling, 2015; Kanellopoulos, 1995; Kotler & Rath, 1984; Saitis & Saiti, 2018). These stages are the following.

Investigate the External Environment The external environment of an organization supplies the resources it needs in order to function, regardless of whether the organization is public (e.g., university institution/State hospital) or private (business/enterprise). The management of the organization should follow the developments (social, economic, ecological) taking place in its environment.

Clarify the Mission The mission's definition must be a long-term vision, based on what the specific organization aspires to become (Dubrin, 2009; Kanellopoulos, 1995; Mintzberg, 1994). Besides, as we have already mentioned in the first chapter, when an organization's management decides to reformulate its mission, it should be answering fundamental questions such as "Who are we?", "What are we?", and "What do we want to accomplish?".

Determine the Organization's Objectives The answer to the question "What do we want to accomplish?" constitutes the organization's objectives and derives from an investigation of the external environment and the organizational capacity. Organization's goals and objectives must be feasible, realistic, countable, and clearly formed (Dubrin, 2009; Petridou, 1998; Saitis & Saiti, 2018).

Determine the Organization's Strategies The answer to the question "where the organization wants to go" determines the organization's strategies.

Create the Strategic Programs At this stage the management continues with the establishment of strategic programs. The question that arises is: What must a manager know in order to correctly program the activities of their (health) organization? Beyond their experience, they must be trained in management issues and be well versed in different techniques (e.g., in decision-making, communication, etc.) so as to:

- Comprehend the methods of planning and programming and determine their key objectives and goals
- Be able to manage their available time effectively to address the problems of the hospital and to choose the best possible solution
- Develop the appropriate level of collaboration with their colleagues that is necessary for establishing a good atmosphere and climate in the health organization

Based on the above, we may support the view that planning and programming in the health-care sector is crucially important, because through this managerial function, the State (of whichever country) can distribute the available resources based on a plan and thus health care can become a key factor for the social, financial, and cultural development of the country. Furthermore, it gives the State the ability to adapt health-care policy according to different environmental conditions.

Historically, the non-systematic or informal type of planning and programming is as old as mankind itself, whereby each conscious decision was typically made prior to the decision about the actions that are followed. However, planning and programming started to become a conscious and systematic duty in each organized human effort as the notion of the "army as a team" emerged toward the end of the eighteenth century (Bell, 1998; Georgopoulos, 2006; Kefis, 2005; Kourtis, 1977).

Scientifically speaking, Taylor (1911) was the first to emphasize the need for the systematic use of planning and programming in each team effort, claiming that "each activity of the worker must be done after a programmed activity of the organization's management" (Taylor, 1947, p. 26 cited by Kourtis, 1977, p. 81). Despite the fact that Taylor's theory became acknowledged by many sectors of social activity, the application of planning and programming was initially limited, at least during the first decades of the twentieth century. Its application and implementation in either the public or private sector appears to have been stunted for two main reasons: firstly, this administrative function had some disadvantages (e.g., the limitations of an individual worker's initiative, an inability to anticipate future situations) as highlighted by several writers (such as Hayek (1945) and Von Mises (1944)) and, secondly, this function was used systematically by the governments of conservative regimes during 1920–1940 (Kourtis, 1977).

A key development that took place in the economic, technological, political, and social sectors in the mid-twentieth century was the recognition by organizations that planning and programming is a fundamental tool in managing all team efforts. Or, as Gide and Rist (1930–1931, p. 113, cited by Kourtis, 1977, p. 82) characteristically put it, "in order for a formal organization to achieve its objective aims, it must be guided by a 'visible hand', namely, the institution of planning and programming".

The inclusion of planning as an actively pursued managerial function in a typical organization such as a hospital is a relatively recent phenomenon. More specifically, in the postwar era the acknowledgment and recognition of the significance of planning resulted in its application to all public organizations and services. Nowadays we are in an economic, technological, and social era where the function of planning and programming is a necessary tool in all organized efforts of social life. And that is because it is socially acceptable for the external environment of organizations to undergo radical transformations, a fact that forces them to adjust to each environmental change (Beer, 1980; Drucker, 1967; Mintzberg, 1994; Pearce & Robinson, 2011; Williams & Johnson, 2004). In other words, in order for organizations to survive the threats posed by increased competitiveness in a globalized world, they need to have continuous and systematic planning and programming.

As has already been mentioned in the previous chapter, planning and programming necessarily occurs prior to other managerial functions because all partial activities (organizing, directing/leading, controlling) aim to achieve the organization's targets, as defined during the planning and programming process.

Today people will share knowledge through meetings/schedules/diaries/action plans in a way that undoubtedly entails planning and programming. But what is "planning and programming"?

First, we have to emphasize that planning and programming do not have identical meanings. According to the relevant literature (Bantaloukas, 1964; Hill & Jones, 2012; Hill et al., 2015; Mintzberg, 1987; Pearce & Robinson, 2011; Perloff, 1961; Zevgaridis, 1983), planning—in the broader sense of the term—refers to the general concept of the goals of a future effort. It is about a pursuit of those things we want to accomplish in the future, in relation to the means we have decided to commit to that purpose. Of course, this pursuit is framed by the commitment of the organization, so that both human and material resources may be utilized in a rational and effective way, leading to the achievement of the organization's goals. So, in the action plan we have the scope of the organization's activities and their overall aim, without a precise specification of details. In general, we may say that planning assists an organization's managers to think in broader terms and to prepare for developments instead of following them.

On the other hand, programming—in the wider sense of the term—refers to the scope of a particular activity (or group of actions) and the means of implementing and/or adapting them to alternative programs of an organization. Through programming, managers predetermine in detail the targets, aims, methods, and means of action, even the place and time of each task's implementation.

From the above, it is evident that the term "planning" may be attributed to a wider set of concepts than the term "programming" since in programming the aims and means of their achievement are described in detail while in the case of planning the setting of goals is general and unspecified.

With this clarification, let us turn to our central question. Concerning the approach about the meaning of the term "planning and programming," researchers such as Dubrin (1997) define this managerial function as a "process of setting goals and objective purposes and proof of how they respond to them" (p. 128). An organization's managers systematically manage the future, rather than being guided by intuition and chance.

Koontz, O' Donnell, and Weihrich (1982) have a similar viewpoint, since they perceive "planning and programming" as "a spiritual, demanding process. It requires conscious determination of action paths, it even requires the decisions to be based on purpose, knowledge and estimated appreciation" (p. 156). By this definition, we may claim that planning and programming requires managers to think thoroughly about what they want to do and how in a predefined timeframe. Thus, any wastage of human and material resources is reduced and a measure of control is exercised on the actual result.

Certainly, a precise optimal (best guess) forecast[1] of the future is rarely achieved, since uncontrolled factors can interfere even in short-term plans and programs. As

[1] We define a forecast/prediction as the estimation of a future activity or action, based on past and present data. It is a fundamental prerequisite of planning and programming since, in the first phase of this function, data are being gathered and calculated and estimations are taking place which lead to assumptions about where the current situation will go. This assumption is evaluated in light of the objectives and then proposed by the senior management of the organization. In the framework of scientific prediction, certain methods are used as mathematical-statistical methods, algebraic methods, etc.

Mintzberg (1987) claims, "for someone to make a path in uncharted waters, it is the perfect way to crash on an iceberg" (p. 26). However, despite the uncertainty inherent in scientifically predicting an organization's future, Fayol (1949) considers forecasting as the beginning of each managerial activity since it provides the basis on which planning and programming is formulated and then implemented. Otherwise, an action of an organization that has not been programmed simply constitutes a random activity that produces nothing other than "chaos" (Goetz, 1949, p. 63). In other words, the lack of planning and programming prevents an organization from effectively mapping out a path that is appropriate for its purposes. Thus, between these contradictory views, the integration of flexible planning and programming may be used as an antidote to the drawback of planning and programming's functionality.

Based on the above, the importance of administrative planning and programming appears to lie in the interrelations of tools and goals, in specifying the expected outcomes, in the analysis of in-between actions and the relevant means (tools) and/or cost. In addition, planning and programming is a premise for the remaining managerial functions—making decisions, organizing, directing (leading), and monitoring. Planning and monitoring in particular are two directly interdependent functions of management, since a programmed action that is not monitored ends up with random results. Conversely, it does not make any sense to put effort into monitoring a situation without plans in place and programs to implement them. In the end, the use of planning and programming assists managers to make decisions about the future within the framework of a wider perspective.

To sum up, we may claim that planning and programming:

- Constitutes the main and fundamental function of management.
- Is a complicated intellectual process that sets the direction that an organization should follow and facilitates control.
- Initially involves deciding between alternative solutions about a future direction of action.
- Generally aims to help the members of an organization to collaborate in a harmonious way without overlapping actions and time-wasting and subsequently reach the best possible result. Relevant studies have mentioned that the quality of programming in an organization, its procedures, and the appropriate application of plans and programs are more likely to contribute to a higher performance than organizations that act without specific plans (Erskine, 1991, p. 61; Robbins, 1991, p. 193).

In conclusion, the function of planning and programming, even recently, has become a mandatory and necessary tool for an organization's members as many positive elements emerge: the formulation of goals, the coordination of efforts, the reduction of overlaps, the eradication of actions without purpose, and a minimized possibility of failure.

4.2 Elements of Strategic Planning and Programming

In order to better understand the function of planning and programming, it is useful to mention the basic elements of a function such as procedures, types, prerequisites, the limitations of the development completed, and adequate plans and programs.

4.2.1 Process of Strategic Planning and Programming

The process of planning and programming contains certain steps that are repetitive and interdependent (Daft, 2007; Dubrin, 2009; Hill et al., 2015; Kanellopoulos, 1995; Koontz et al., 1982; Tzortzakis & Tzortzaki, 1999; Zavlanos, 1998) and are as follows.

Determine the Objectives of the Organization The first step of the planning and programming process is to determine the organization's goals. With the term "goals," we mean "desires or the mission to be achieved by the organization in order to survive" (Kanellopoulos, 1995, p. 78). They constitute the starting point for all the other managerial activities, since—as we previously mentioned—by determining an organization's goals (objectives) we identify the point that an organization desires to reach. Generally speaking, the importance of determining an organization's objectives cannot be underestimated since, without objectives, it is not possible to have motives (desirable situations) and we cannot take advantage of any opportunities or take decisions that would lead to a desirable outcome.

Identify the Organization's Current Situation In this step of planning and programming, managers evaluate the organization's current situation. They examine not only the organization's internal strengths and potential but also the influence coming from its external environment. At the same time, they assess how well the organization—based on specific prerequisites—would be able to attain the defined objectives and goals in the future. This point of planning and programming is a powerful tool for management, because the development of prerequisites for the organization's future environment is based mainly on the forecasting of facts and circumstances (conditions) that may affect the achievement of its goals.

Record Alternative Solutions or Suggestions The third step of the planning and programming process involves the study of the available data and the recording of alternative suggestions for the fulfillment of the organization's objectives. By "alternative solutions or suggestions," we mean the possible directions leading to the final solution of a problem. Each alternative solution or suggestion has different consequences, costs, and prerequisites. So the recording of several (i.e., 3–5) alternative solutions is considered to be a vital condition, since, through these alternative suggestions, we may conduct a deeper analysis of the problem.

Choose the Best Alternative Solution or Suggestion In this step, the evaluation of the alternative solutions takes place, that is, the advantages and disadvantages of each solution are evaluated and then the best solution for the organization is chosen, according to the managers' judgment and assessment.

Implement the Program of Action Managers should apply the chosen program of action. Given that, despite the effectiveness of plans and programs, they alone cannot ensure the success of the organization, managers should coordinate the partial actions, obtain the necessary resources, and generally motivate the organization members.

Evaluate the Results In this final stage, managers first evaluate the results of the action programs in order to verify if the intended goals were achieved. They then analyze new data for plans and programs that would be best for the future of the organization.

Lastly, we note that the steps of planning and programming are not always followed in the order presented above because, during the fulfillment of activity programs, managers discover new elements or the objectives change. Consequently, programmers proceed with corrective changes and naturally return to previous steps of this managerial function.

4.2.2 Basic Types of Program

Programs can be grouped into three main categories:

- *Strategic programs*: They are determined by the upper level of the managerial hierarchy and define the organization's place in its environment and long-term goals.
- *Functional programs*: They are formulated by managers of the middle and lower levels of administration, focus on the internal function of the organization, and define short-term and specific goals.

Hence, a health-care manager/leader, for example, can program the weekly activities in 30 min if they implement the following (Saitis & Saiti, 2018, p. 36).

Objectives (O) What results do you want to obtain by the end of the week? Write them down and rank them according to their significance.

Actions (A) What must you do to achieve your goals and objectives? Write down the necessary activities and put them in order.

Time (T) How much time do you need for each activity? In order to have a realistic program, give yourself more time than you initially estimate. That will give you the additional time you need to confront unforeseeable problems.

Program (P) Check your calendar carefully before you decide when you can carry out each activity. Most people underestimate the contribution a program makes, but you will not achieve much if you do not program (schedule) your time to carry out your work (Dubrin, 2009).

At this point it must be emphasized that functional programs may have the following characteristics (Daft, 2007; Hill et al., 2015; Dubrin, 2009; Mintzberg, 1994; Petridou, 1998; Saitis & Saiti, 2018):

- Understandable, clear, sufficient and simple: firstly, because people perform better when they know what is expected from them and what their area of responsibility is and, secondly, because in this way actual results can exceed the initially prescribed goals at the end of a given time period. Thus, the clarification of targets facilitates the managerial function of control.
- Determined through the participation of all the managers/executives at all management levels: plans and programs are conducted based on an information network in which all the levels of the organization's management are included. Clearly, the general policy of the organization necessarily has to be determined by its senior management. However, this does not mean that managers and staff at the lower hierarchical level cannot contribute to the shaping of the organization's policy. On the contrary, their contribution is significant: first because they can, with their experience and special knowledge, give useful information to the senior executives (of the upper hierarchical level) and second, by participating, will contribute to the best possible implementation of programs. Besides, experience shows that the plans and programs of an organization are more likely to be successful when the people called to implement them have an active participation in their formulation. To conclude, planning and programming should start from the top of the hierarchical pyramid of the organization, but then should be completed by managers/executives of lower managerial hierarchical levels.
- Flexible (elastic): their implementation presupposes certain resources (both human and material), clarity and sufficiency in terms of content, time duration and controlling agent, and their capacity to adjust to unpredictable and changing circumstances. That said, flexibility certainly should not come at the expense of the stability needed to orientate an organized activity.
- Coordinated in the long term according to the strategic program: the complex nature of the many interrelated actions and productive plans and programs must not lose sight of the future aim.
- Specify and accurately determine the time and order for the implementation and execution of the prescribed actions.

Based on the criteria of time duration, programs are distinguished into:

- *Short-term programs*: usually 1–3 years' duration. The time duration of short-term programs is determined by the organization's long-term perspectives.
- *Long-term programs*: usually from 3 to 10 years and are set up to confront major unpredictable issues. The purpose of long-term planning is to facilitate the organization's aims and the distribution of resources in order to fulfill its goals.

Managers may turn to forecasting tools to increase forecasting accuracy, such as sensitivity analysis, regression models, and even computer-based regression models. In this way, they may make some (though limited) improvements.

Despite some weakness, long-term planning improves the effectiveness of strategic decisions. It assists managers in confronting the long-term down effects of decisions and causes them to think about their organization's potential to influence or exploit emerging trends, before the results become evident in the profit/loss account. The issues raised by long-term planning often lead to correct and rational decisions, empowering the long-term competitiveness of the organization (Saitis & Saiti, 2018).

The long-term planning and programming may have a more positive outcome in certain circumstances, such as a high rate of market development, easily predictable tendencies, etc. If these circumstances are absent, then a given plan may be less effective.

As regards the criteria of flexibility, the programs are distinguished into:

- *Rigid or inelastic programs*: these are sufficiently well-defined programs that do not give room for misunderstandings, which would otherwise require readjustments. However, in practice it is doubtful whether a long-term program can nowadays remain fixed, since the element of uncertainty is strong.
- *Flexible or elastic programs*, which determine general guiding directions and allow for adjustments to be made based on the current circumstances of the organization and its environment. No doubt, having the option to change a program without incurring extra costs or substantial modifications is of great value. In practice, though, "flexibility is only feasible within margins" (Koontz et al., 1982, p. 184).

Based on the above, we may conclude that (Saitis & Saiti, 2018, p. 38):

- Programs of all categories are linked to the targets of the organization and to either general or specific purposes
- Managers of all hierarchical levels should be responsible for determining and implementing the programs
- Due to environment uncertainty, long-term programs must have some degree of flexibility so as to allow the organization room for maneuver in confronting unforeseeable and potentially adverse situations

4.3 Strategic Planning and Programming in the Field of Health Care

In the field of health care (mainly in public health care), the planning and programming process can be distinguished into the following.

The Determination of Health-Care Policy As part of general governmental policy, health-care policy aims to (a) satisfy the needs of individuals for their own benefit and (b) satisfy the societal needs and consequently the social, financial, and cultural development of the country.

The Determination of Health-Care Targets These programs determine (a) the specific targets that each health-care organization will try to accomplish, (b) the available resources, and (c) the ways in which these programs will be implemented.

The Determination of Work that Should Be Executed to Achieve the Organization's Targets Depending on the type of health-care plan and program, certain programs of action are determined which, according to their time duration, can be distinguished into:

- Short term (micro planning): programs to implement changes that are due to take place in a short timeframe (usually up to a year)
- Long term (macro planning): programs for long-term changes of the health-care system that mainly aim to define and describe the intended health-care changes

These plans and programs follow the same fundamental principles and procedures as those mentioned in the previous unit of the current chapter. The tendency is for programming at the lower levels of the managerial hierarchy to be limited to functional programs that determine the details and the manner of implementing the organization's aims and targets and are referred to in the health-care unit's strategic program.

4.3.1 Development and Significance of Health-Care Planning

Historically, the roots of planning and programming are old enough. However, the developed aspects of a method appeared for first time in the former Soviet Union in the 1920s (Khoi, 1985; Psacharopoulos, 1999). Thereafter, many countries attempted to connect health-care development with their economic development.

In the Western countries, the idea of planning and programming in health care spread after the Second World War (Cohn & Geske, 1990). Indeed, by the 1970s development strategies about health care had extended to many parts of the world. The essential value of health care became more widely acknowledged and accepted as it was recognized that only when the population of a country is healthy and has an acceptable level of well-being can the productivity of that country increase. This is because healthier workers produce better outputs, both in terms of quantity and quality. According to one view (Khoi, 1985), the main reasons that prompted the State to extend planning and programming to the health sector were the following.

The Population Explosion The population increase was accompanied by a similar increase in State expenditure, a factor that led to the creation of health-care services. At this point it should be mentioned that, in parallel to public expenditure on the health-care sector, public expenditures on education are of equal importance. Capital is indeed crucially important for economic development, but human capital remains the key ingredient for a country's successful and sustainable economic development. A country cannot attain high rates of development without the successful utilization of its available resources and the establishment of fundamental values. Only a healthy and educated population can increase both the quality and quantity of the workforce's outputs and succeed in putting the country on a path to sustainable productivity.

The Consideration of Health Care as an "Investment" The theory of human capital considers health care as an investment since its specialized personnel serve to keep citizens healthy who, in turn, are better able to participate in the national economy and thus contribute to the social and economic development of the country. Indeed, the theory of human capital is based on the principle that if an individual invests in him-/herself (e.g., in their health), then this investment will yield returns in the future, e.g., through prolonged good health, increased productivity/creativity at work, and (potentially) increased financial rewards. This explains why nowadays developed countries strive to maintain modern, efficient, and effective health-care systems. According to Meier (1970), Schultz (1961a, 1961b, 1972), and Tyler (1977), this type of capital is the most important because such investment is the most fruitful and efficient for the economic development of a country.

With particular reference to the implementation of planning and programming in the health-care sector in lesser developed countries of Latin America and Africa, international organizations such as the UN, UNESCO, and the World Bank (among others) have played a significant role. Therefore, we may claim that health-care planning and programming in these countries became a very important managerial component in the field of health care, through which the aims of health care are inaugurated, translated into programs, and implemented. Effective planning is necessary in lesser developed countries where health care constitutes a primary factor for the development of their productivity and the distribution of funds, coming from very limited national resources. Uncoordinated planning is often accompanied by inefficiency, a scarcity of resources where they are most needed, and poor results. Most importantly it can culminate in life-threatening scenarios locally and negative (albeit less severe) consequences at a global level.

Sound decision-making, a keystone for correct planning, is not an easy task to approach due to the difficulty in predicting incidental consequences stemming from different choices. Hence, correct planning in health care is feasible only if the necessary elements are available to the planners, such as a reliable population census and forecasting systems. Unfortunately, these elements are rare in most of the lesser developed countries.

Closing the current unit, we emphasize that the importance of planning and programming in health care underlies the fact that through this managerial function, the State pursues the best possible capacity-enhancing investment in human resources with the least possible cost in terms of personnel, time, and money.

4.3.2 Applied Models of Strategic Planning in Health Care

The direct acknowledgment of planning and programming in the health-care sector across the world has resulted in the development of long-term programs. Initially, there was no specific method and technique for determining such plans and programs in health care. However, by the late 1960s, planning and programming in the field of health care was following a similar pattern to that used by governments in planning the national economy. The relevant literature (Lambropoulos & Stavlioti, 2006; Lourie, 1996; Karageorgou, 1983; Psacharopoulos, 1999) reveals two models that may be applied to the field of health care.

The Manpower Approach This approach recognizes the needs of an economy and of a population regarding health-care standards. It assumes that an economy needs specialized human resources and presupposes that the population should be healthy, while the education level of the population should have particular specializations and not left at a general level. This may be considered to be a rational approach that facilitates the State's correct utilization of both human and material resources for the sake of economic development. However, the main drawback of this approach is that "it is totally mechanistic …" (Psacharopoulos, 1999, p. 127).

The Cost/Benefit Approach Here, specific production goals are determined which require certain levels (standards) of health care.[2] In this model the State must invest resources in the health-care field so as to gain the greatest benefit and returns for the least possible cost. This method seems to have more advantages because it offers important information about the connection between health care and the labor market and consequently contributes to the setting of priorities in investments in proportion to their performance.

However, this method has the following drawbacks: (a) income is not only determined by the level of health but also by other factors (education, social class, individual skills), and (b) the benefits of health care are not only economical but also social/cultural.

[2] Indeed, the health-care sector is one of the two most significant factors (the other being the education sector) in improving the rate of economic development. These two sectors are interrelated, and they are both determinants of increased economic efficiency, mainly through capital accumulation, higher living standards, and increased labor productivity.

In view of the above, evidently planning and programming in health care is difficult—even more difficult than in other sectors of an economy. Therefore, in order to reach an appropriate level of planning and programming in health care, it is necessary to consider all the factors mentioned in the above models.

4.4 Management by Objectives (MBO) and Health-Care Sector

4.4.1 Meaning and Significance of MBO

As has already been mentioned, the target of an organization such as a hospital is indissolubly related to its aims. A hospital's target should be stable, for example, "to provide high-quality health-care services to individuals." On the contrary, aims should consist of specific yet different expressions of the target, taking into consideration the underlying context (economic/social/technological changes) in the hospital's environment.

Based on the above, we may claim that expressing the specific objectives of an organization is a complicated managerial task. This problem caused many management experts (such as Drucker, Barnard) to put the emphasis on managing by objectives, known as MBO (management by objectives). MBO is an organized effort (or "philosophy" or "system") according to which leading managers/executives, in collaboration with their staff members, determine the organization's objectives and targets that should be achieved (Erskine, 1991; Kanellopoulos, 1995; Morrisey, 1976; Odiorne, 1979). It is a way of determining targets at all organizational levels, with the flow beginning bottom-up but also running top-down. It is a participatory approach to the setting of objectives and targets which not only facilitates the establishment of more difficult objectives and targets but also ensures the positive cooperation of all individuals who have drawn up the program or have determined the objectives and targets. And this is perhaps the most crucial and significant part of this management system because, by allowing employees to determine the objectives and targets, either among themselves or together with their managers, it not only reinforces an important advantage, namely, staff motivation, but also allows the organization itself to benefit from their experience and knowledge (Mullins, 2010; Petridou, 1998; Silbiger, 1993).

Historically, Peter Drucker is considered as the "father" of MBO. In particular, in his work *The Practice of Management* (1954), he mentioned, among other things, that each organization needs management based on objectives that will guide managers/executives, contribute to the promotion of teamwork, and encourage self-control. During the same time period, researchers such as Douglas McGregor (1960) endorsed "the personal value of staff members" (p. 113) without predetermined targets and aims. Edward Schleh (1961) mentioned the need to determine organizational objectives as well as the targets of all managers of the organization. Certainly, we must add the so-called classical writers of managerial thinking that have contributed to MBO because a long time before 1954 Fayol (1949), Urwick (1943), and Barnard (1938) had already discerned the meaning of objectives and targets.

To sum up, the above process provides staff members with an active role, increases the sense that they exercise (at least some) control over their environment, and decreases their dependence on their managers.

4.4.2 The Process of MBO

The process of having the objectives defined, understood, and accepted by all organizational members follows a standard procedure which is usually broken down into the following stages (Humble, 1972; Koontz et al., 1982; Kanellopoulos, 1995; Mullins, 2010; Petridou, 1998; Silbiger, 1993; Tzortzakis & Tzortzaki, 1999):

- *Stage 1*: *Preliminary actions of the higher management for the adoption of MBO*. At this initial stage, the higher management of the organization *communicates* with the lower hierarchical levels and *clarifies* a sufficient and effective program of MBO; *explains* thoroughly why they are adopting the program, why it is necessary for staff, and what it is expected to achieve; *clarifies* the relations between the departments participating in the program; and *identifies* and determines specific areas of responsibility relative to the MBO activities at each managerial level.
- *Stage 2*: *Discussion over the requirements of the execution of the project*. At this stage, the manager meets their staff members to discuss the requirements of the work to be executed. Initially, the manager informs their staff about the organizational goals and the departmental goals and then asks their staff to make suggestions about the goals concerning staff duties.
- *Stage 3*: *Development of the staff member's special aims*. Here, the staff member develops their own goals for executing the task assigned to them by the more general objectives of MBO.
- *Stage 4*: *Discussion of the staff member's special goals*. The manager meets the staff member and discusses the special goals which the latter has proposed to execute the project.
- *Stage 5*: *Determination of standards and control points*. The manager and staff member then discuss and agree upon the standards and control points necessary for the completion of the project.
- *Stage 6*: *Evaluation of the results*. After the completion of the project, the manager and the staff member jointly evaluate the task assigned to the employee. The evaluation must be impartial and the discussion should be low-key. If the results are positive, the staff member must gain recognition for their work.

4.4.3 Advantages and Disadvantages of MBO

As with every management system, MBO has certain advantages but also some weaknesses and deficiencies (Dubrin, 2009; Humble, 1972; Petridou, 1998; Zavlanos, 1998). In particular, the advantages of MBO are:

- It helps to clarify the organization's roles and structure and consequently improves the communication level between managers and staff members
- It helps to develop effective techniques of control and coordination
- It contributes to the development of employees in an organization's hierarchical structure
- It facilitates the setting of objectives and the function of programming
- It contributes significantly to efficiency in leadership, since a strong system of staff motivation is created
- It clarifies exactly what is expected of each employee and ensures that they will be involved in determining the results to be accomplished
- Employees are rewarded according to the part(s) of these expectations that is (are) fulfilled
- There is regular communication and support

However, the system is weak/less effective when:

- The objectives are difficult to determine
- The necessary and continuous support from the organization is not in place
- The thought processes are heavily bureaucratic
- Leading managers/executives cannot adapt the objectives to new/emerging data
- The assessment of staff members' work is not impartial
- Importance is given only to the quantitative objectives and measurable performance standards, which reduces staff outputs and human relationships to a mechanical process
- Greater emphasis is put on short-term goals at the expense of long-term ones

If we take a closer look at the abovementioned disadvantages of MBO, we may notice that they arise due to the ways in which this specific system of management is applied and not because of its philosophy.

4.4.4 Factors for the Effective Implementation of MBO

An MBO program will be implemented successfully (Kanellopoulos, 1995, pp. 405–411) when:

- There is substantial organizational support. Given that an MBO program "is an everyday management activity and not just an academic exercise for [the] formulation of goals once a year" (Kanellopoulos, 1995, p. 405), the leading managers of an organization should:

(a) Periodically discuss with each staff member the objectives that were set in the original program
(b) Assess the progress made toward those objectives being achieved
(c) Help and support each staff member so as to overcome any difficulties in the performance of their work

- The organizational members are trained appropriately, mainly in terms of the managerial skills (e.g., skill of formulating objectives) necessary for the successful implementation of MBO. We note that such a training program should be carefully designed so as to give the trainees full knowledge about the motivation behind MBO and the specific skills necessary for the implementation of MBO, such as the drafting and shaping of goals as well as the appropriate managerial attitudes, perceptions, and behavior in exercising authority that are consistent with the philosophy of managing by objectives.
- The managers encourage and motivate staff members through multiple incentives (these can be material or immaterial).
- Each employee gives their consent to adopt MBO, since such a consensus demonstrates that the employee acknowledges their willingness to participate in MBO. Certainly, it is important for employees not to have the impression that the MBO system is merely a technique used by their superiors (managers) to control/monitor their performance.

References

Bantaloukas, K. B. (1964). *Business organization, administration and management*. Piraeus, Greece: School G.O.E.A.B. Publications. (in Greek).
Barnard, C. (1938). *The functions of the executive*. Cambridge, MA: Harvard University Press.
Beer, M. (1980). *Organization change and development: A system view*. Glenview, IL: Scott Foresman.
Bell, L. (1998). From Symphony to Jazz: the concept of strategy in education. *School Leadership Management, 18*(4), 449–460.
Bordeaux, A. V. (2001). *Science education reform for the 21st century: Analyzing policy imperatives for effective teaching through recruitment, renewal, and retention*. Doctoral dissertation, George Mason University in Fairfax, Virginia.
Bouradas, D. (2001). *Management*. Athens, Greece: Benou Publications. (in Greek).
Cohn, E., & Geske, T. G. (1990). *The economics of education*. Oxford, UK: Pergamon Press.
Daft, R. L. (2007). *Organization theory and design* (9th ed.). Mason, OH: South Western, Thomson.
Drucker, P. F. (1967). *The Effective Executive*. New York: Harper & Row.
Dubrin, A. J. (1997). *Essentials of management* (4th ed.). London: SouthWestern College Publishing.
Dubrin, A. J. (2009). *Essentials of management* (8th ed.). London: SouthWestern College Publishing.
Erskine, R. (1991). *Business management*. London: Prentice Hall.
Fayol, H. (1949). *General and industrial management*. London: Pitman Publishing.
Friebel, C. H. (1999). *An application of the Delphi method of forecasting to the future of public education in West Virginia*. Doctoral dissertation, West Virginia University, Morgantown.
Georgopoulos, N. (2006). *Strategic management*. Athens, Greece: Benou Publishing. (in Greek).

Gide, C., & Rist, Ch. (1930–1931). *The history of economic theories*. (Translation into Greek by N. Patseli). Athens, Greece.

Goetz, B. E. (1949). *Management, planning and control*. New York: McGraw-Hill.

Hayek, F. A. (1945). *The road to serfdom*. Chicago, IL: University of Chicago Press.

Hill, W. L., & Jones, G. R. (2012). *Essentials of strategic management* (3rd ed.). Mason, OH: South-Western Cengage Learning.

Hill, W. L., Jones, G. R., & Schilling, M. A. (2015). *Strategic management theory* (11th ed.). Mason, OH: Cengage Learning.

Humble, J. W. (1972). *Management by objectives*. London: Management Publications Limited.

Kanellopoulos, C. (1995). *Management – Effective administration*. Athens, Greece: Kanellopoulos publications. (in Greek).

Karageorgou, D. A. (1983). Methods for educational planning. *Sighroni Ekpaidevsi, 12*, 32–34. (in Greek).

Kefis, V. (1998). The meaning of strategic management and its significance to the diagnosis of changes and the determination of business goals: An indication of strategic planning. *Dioikitiki Enimerosi, 10*, 64–69. (in Greek).

Kefis, V. (2005). *Integrated Management*. Athens, Greece: Kritiki Publishing (in Greek).

Khoi, L. T. (1985). *Programming of education, pedagogical sciences* (Vol. 6). Athens, Greece: Diptycho Publishing. (in Greek).

Koontz, H., O' Donnell, C., & Weihrich, H. (1982). *Management* (7th ed.). London: McGraw Hill.

Koontz, H., & Weihrich, H. (2010). *Essentials of management: An international perspective*. New Delhi, India: McGraw Hill.

Kotler, P., & Rath, A. G. (1984). Design: A powerful but neglected strategic tool. *The Journal of Business Strategy, 5*(2), 16–21.

Kourtis, K. E. (1977). *The theory and the practice of modern administration*. Athens, Greece: Kourtis Publications. (in Greek).

Lambropoulos, H., & Stavlioti, E. (2006). *Assessment, effectiveness & quality in education*. Athens, Greece: Gutenberg Publishing. (in Greek).

Lourie, S. (1996). Educational planning. In G. Mialaret (Ed.), *Introduction to pedagogy* (pp. 76–85). Athens, Greece: Typothito Dardanos. Translation to Greek language G. Zakopoulou (in Greek).

McCuskey, B. M. (2003). *The future of the university housing profession and implications for practitioners: A Delphi study*. Doctoral Dissertation, West Virginia University, Morgantown.

McGregor, D. (1960). *The human side of enterprise*. New York: McGraw–Hill.

Meier, G. (1970). *Leading issues in economic development*. New York: Oxford University Press.

Mintzberg, H. (1987). The strategy concept II: Another look of why organisations need strategies. *California Management Review, 30*(1), 25–32.

Mintzberg, H. (1994). *The rise and fall of strategic planning*. New York: Free Press.

Morrisey, G. L. (1976). *Management by objectives in the public sector*. Reading, MA: Addison-Wesley.

Mullins, L. J. (2010). *Management and organisational behavior* (9th ed.). London: Prentice Hall.

Odiorne, G. (1979). *MBO II: A system of managerial leadership for '80s*. Belmont, CA: Fearon-Pitman Publishers.

Pearce, J., & Robinson, R. (2011). *Strategic management: Formulation, implementation and control* (12th ed.). New York: McGraw Hill.

Perloff, H. S. (1961). *Planning and the Urban Community*. Pittsburg, CA: University of Pittsburg Press.

Petridou, E. (1998). *Administration – Management*. Thessaloniki, Greece: Zygos Publishing. (in Greek).

Psacharopoulos, G. (1999). *Economics of education*. Athens, Greece: Papazisi Publishing. (in Greek).

Quinn, J. B. (1980). *Strategies for change: Logical incrementalism*. Homewood, IL: Irwin.

Robbins, S. P. (1991). *Management* (3rd ed.). London: Prentice Hall.

Saitis, C., & Saiti, A. (2018). *Initiation of educators into educational management secrets*. Basel, Switzerland: Springer.

Schleh, E. (1961). *Management by results*. New York: McGraw-Hill.
Schultz, T. (1972). *Investment in education*. Chicago, IL: University of Chicago Press.
Schultz, T. W. (1961a). Investment in human capital. *American Economic Review, 51*, 1–17. (In Blaug, M. (1968). *The economics of education: selected reading 1*. Penguin books).
Schultz, T. W. (1961b). The concept of human capital: reply. *American Economic Review, 52*(4), 1035–1039. (also in Blaug above).
Silbiger, S. (1993). *The ten day MBA: A step by step guide to mastering the skills taught in America's top business schools*. London, UK: Piatkus.
Stilwell, C. A. (1999). *A delphi study on critical issues facing higher educational for the first decade of the 21st century*. First search, dissertation abstracts online, Accession no. AA 19949353, The George Washington University.
Stylianidis, M. (2008). A model of strategic forecasting and planning for a future school. *Dioikitiki Enimerosi, 45*, 81–94. (in Greek).
Taylor, F. (1911). *The principles of scientific management*. New York: Harper and Row.
Taylor, F. W. (1947). *Scientific Management*. New York: Harper.
Tyler, W. (1977). *The sociology of educational inequality*. London: Methuen.
Tzortzakis, K., & Tzortzaki, A. (1999). *Organization and management*. Athens, Greece: Rosili Publishing. (in Greek).
Urwick, L. (1943). *The elements of administration*. New York: Sir Isaac Pitman & Sons.
von Mises, L. (1944). *Bureaucracy*. New Haven, CT: Yale University Press.
Williams, K., & Johnson, B. (2004). *Introducing management: A development guide*. Doncaster, UK: Plant a Tree.
Zavlanos, M. (1998). *Management*. Athens, Greece: Ellin Publishing. (in Greek).
Zevgaridis, S. (1983). *Management and administration* (Vol. D). Thessaloniki, Greece: Kyriakidis Publishing. (in Greek).

Chapter 5
Strategic Changes in the Health-Care Sector

Key Concepts

- The need for change is imposed by a pool of strong environmental forces linked to the advancement of technology and international economic integration, leading to a globalized economy that has an impact on every organization—whether public or private, large or small—creating new threats and/or opportunities.
- Organizational change is a dynamic process that includes a transitional phase from an existing organizational state to another desired one that allows the organization to operate more sustainably and effectively.
- The terms "change" and "innovation" are not identical. The different types of changes are interdependent, that is, a change in one type often also means a change in another type.
- Resistance to change can be eliminated only when trust, commitment, and collective responsibility are evident within an organization.
- The key elements that can contribute to the success of change in the health-care sector are the following: high-quality leadership, a strong leadership team specifically to manage change, and continual administrative and financial support.

5.1 Introduction

We live in an era of rapid changes brought about by the pace of technological advancement and the dynamics of modern social and economic developments that are shaping the way people relate to each other and to organizations. An issue that derives from the constantly changing environment is that organizations need to move quickly to follow the changes occurring around them, to find ways of operating flexibly in their field of activity, regardless of whether they are looking for new production technologies or new information technologies. In simple words, organizations should be prepared for innovation and change, based on their survival within a world of increased competition (Kotter, 2012). The need for change is imposed by

M. Chletsos, A. Saiti, *Strategic Management and Economics in Health Care*,
https://doi.org/10.1007/978-3-030-35370-4_5

a pool of strong environmental forces linked to the advancement of technology and international economic integration, leading to a globalized economy that has an impact on every organization—whether public or private, large or small—creating new threats and/or opportunities.

Subsequently, in order to manage threats in the best way possible and to take advantage of the opportunities that emerge from an organization's environment, modern organizations are subjecting themselves to dramatic changes in the organizational, functional, and personnel-related fields of their activities (Daft, 2007).

Some organizations have responded to global forces by adopting simple structures that promote communication and collaboration (Daft, 2007). Others have trained their staff to operate electronic equipment, and yet others have adopted changes concerning areas such as the working environment, procedures, the structure of operations, and the organizational culture. However, in many cases the efforts for change have had negative consequences, resulting in "a huge waste of resources and fearful, desperate and devastated professional people" (Kotter, 2001, p. 19).

The health-care sector is no exception to the rule. In such a dynamic society, the improvement of its organizations is imperative because, as open systems, they are affected and influenced by their external environment, that is, the society in which they operate. For instance, a change in the manner of providing health-care services results in a change in the composition of health-care personnel. This change not only affects the health-care unit's managers and other personnel but also its patients. The relations between individuals at various levels of power and their manner of communicating affect the interpersonal relationships of health-care unit members. This inevitably brings with it a change in the culture of the health-care unit. If an imported change in a health-care unit proves to be sustainable, it indicates that any altered expectations among its members are a reflection of a positive culture that exists in these units. In other words, organizational changes in the health-care sector are reflected in a change in behavior of the hospital unit's members (and those of health-care units in general).

To summarize, the rapid changes that occur in the organization's environment (whether social, economical, or technological) lead it to adopt specific adaptation strategies that will ensure its sustainability and effective functioning. Changes in an organization—which may involve the adoption of new types of organizational structures, processes, policies, technologies, and/or culture—are not easy to apply because the organization members often need time, information, and experience of the implications at first hand before they become willing to accept the new set of circumstances, even if it is for their own good.

While health workers' sense of rejection has been addressed earlier in the book, in this section we will be looking at ways of dealing with their reaction to changes in their organization. In practice, introducing dramatic changes in an organization in a way that generates the least possible resistance is a key managerial (leadership) responsibility of the organization.

The next section of this chapter looks at various strategies for change and at how they allow these processes to be addressed in a more effective way.

5.2 What Is Change

5.2.1 *Definition of the Term "Change"*

Based on the fact that organizations are living organs and function within an environment that is dynamic and therefore changeable, organizations should continuously monitor the changes occurring in their environment in order to respond efficiently and effectively.

With particular reference to the definition of the term "change," there are different approaches to describe what we mean when an organization claims to experience change. Based on the relevant literature, there are some elements in the different definitions of "change" that are common, such as the notion of transition—when an organization changes from one state to another.

According to Giannouzas and Carzo (1968), the term "change" is defined as the "transition from a stable pattern or behavior to another stable pattern or situation" (p. 609). In accordance with the abovementioned writers, in order to facilitate the implementation of change, there must be a variable that is significant or powerful enough to overcome steady-state forces. Another definition is given by Papalexandri and Bouradas (2003) who define organizational change as a "conversion from an existing state to a new one" (p. 442). Based on this perception, the change refers to both the transformation of an organization's elements (e.g., structure, procedures, culture, etc.) and to the process of transition from the existing situation to the new one.

According to another perspective (Hytiris, 2006), change is seen as a "transition from one state of reality to another or, put another way, the transition from a given set of conditions to a different one" (p. 336). Moreover, Daft (2007) suggested that, in fact, organizational change comes about with the adoption of something new.

From the above, we may say that organizational change is a dynamic process that includes a transitional phase from an existing organizational state to another desired one that allows the organization to operate more sustainably and effectively.

5.2.2 *Types of Change*

Different types of organizational changes are identified in the relevant literature, which help to understand and handle them better. These organizational changes can be grouped according to the following criteria (Daft, 2007; Kouris, Souliotis, & Philalithis, 2006; Nadler & Tushman, 1998; Papalexandri & Bouradas, 2003): (1) their importance, (2) the change they induce, and (3) their implementation time.

1. Changes of importance are categorized as:
    - Limited, i.e., organizational changes that have low political and social importance (these usually involve changes in the auxiliary body of the organization's services).

- Strategic or structural changes that have a high political and social importance and directly affect the core of an organization's activities by significantly affecting both the services it provides and the image of the entire organization. Papadakis (2009) defines a "strategic change" as an organization's adoption of new methodologies, technologies, and/or strategic options for the organization, with the aim of restructuring/adjusting it to its ever-changing environment in order to exploit new opportunities and create or preserve a competitive benefit (p. 154).

  Strategic change is effectively a plan to change the present state of an organization to an improved one through a set of procedures that involve the participation of all members of the organization. This specific type of change is characterized by a systematic and long-term commitment to change in the organization. Such strategic changes require continuous effort as well as significant resources (human and material) to materialize (McGee, Thomas, & Wilson, 2005). Indeed, if a strategic change is treated as an isolated event that is disconnected from the ongoing development of an organization, it may "provoke such a separation that can demolish each organism" in it (Abrahamson, 2000, pp. 75–79; Papadakis, 2009, p. 154).

2. Any changes induced in the organization can be categorized as:

   - Reactive—such changes are brought about in response to an external stimulus, fact, or force and aim to help the organization adapt to its evolving environment. For instance, demographic changes in the population and economic pressures are elements that prompt reactive changes in a health-care system.
   - Proactive—these changes are the result of predictions made about an organization's environment and about how the organization is expected to be affected by them. Such changes are distinguished by their systematic (rational) character and usually bring better results compared to reactive changes.

3. With regard to implementation time, an organizational change can be gradual or radical. *Gradual* change, which is part of a medium-to-long-term plan, represents a series of continuous improvements that maintain the overall balance of the organization and often affect only one part of it. Gradual change is only feasible through the existing structure and the same management processes. It may include, for example, improvements in technology or service provision. On the other hand, *radical* change pursues rapid changes that will directly transform the entire organization. That practically means the creation of a new structure and new management processes.

The above changes affect vital individual and/or collective activities of an organization and determine their effectiveness. These sectors (Daft, 2007; Hytiris, 2006; McCann, 1991) are:

- The organizational sector, which refers to the managerial part of an organization and includes the structural changes, strategic management, policies, working relationships, information systems, etc.

- The technological sector, which relates to changes occurring in the productive process of the organization, e.g., changes in mechanical equipment or facilities
- The productive sector, which usually relates to changes in the products manufactured (new products) or in the services provided, which in turn contribute to an expansion of the organization's circle of operations
- The human resources sector, which refers mainly to the attitude, culture, aspirations, skills, and behavior of the employees

From the above, it is clear that the different types of changes are interdependent, that is, a change in one type often also means a change in another type. This interdependence does not come as surprise since—as previously mentioned—social organizations are open systems and changing one part often has repercussions for other parts of the organization.

5.2.3 Is "Change" Different from "Innovation"?

By studying the relevant literature, it is clear that attempts to quantify "change" have led researchers, on the one hand, to correlate it with terms such as "innovation," "development," and "reform" and, on the other hand, to produce negative results such as delays, inconvenience, and regression (Iordanides, 2006).

Concentrating our interest on analyses of the terms "change" and "innovation," we may note the following:

As we have seen in the previous section, "change" is defined as the transition from a given state of things to a different state. Organizational change is regarded as the adoption of a new idea or behavior from a typical organization (Pierce & Delbecg, 1977).

On the other hand, the term 'innovation' is regarded as a constant need to change (Daft, 2007) "such as the adoption of an idea or behavior new to the industry, market or to the general environment in which the organism belongs" (Daft, 2004, p. 444).

Furthermore, researchers such as Russell and Russell (1992) claim that "innovation is a procedure of change of one or more elements of the organization, which is completed at the initiative of its members and aims to confront problematic situations, connected directly to the particularities of the specific organization and the environment in which it operates. Therefore, any changes imposed on the organization by external factors (e.g. the adoption of regulations by the State) are not part of its innovative action, since they have not been developed through the organization members' initiative and do not take into consideration the organization's specialties…" (cited by Giannakaki, 2005, p. 245).

Though the term "innovation"[1] implies change, it does however differ from that of "change" since the former refers to any new or varied activity in an organization conducted on the initiative of its members.

Based on the above, we may say that "change" and "innovation" are not identical terms.

5.3 Reasons for Change

If an organization such as a health-care unit desires to achieve a sustainable performance, then monitoring its external environment and adjusting to its requirements is the only way toward efficiency and development. However, an organization's external environment is not the only one that is dynamic. An organization's internal environment is also dynamic and may provide the driver for change.

External factors causing change usually come from:

- The political/legislative sector. Changes in legislation that govern the way health-care services are provided may be a reason for change.
- The economic sector. For instance, if there is a cut in the budget of the health-care sector due to a budget deficit in the national economy, it becomes necessary to initiate a series of changes in the way the country's health-care units are run, so as to compensate (e.g., reduce, or even cancel, orders for new equipment).
- The technological sector. Advances in technology allow organizations to improve their support infrastructure so as to increase their capacity to serve their clients/customers/patients.

Internal factors that cause change are the following (Papadakis, 2009; Zavlanos, 1998):

- The structure of an organization's systems. The existence of subsystems creates a complexity in a health-care unit which does not allow the organization to function with a stable balance. Indeed, the way an organization is structured plays a big part in how it will achieve its targets and establish a balance in its internal relations and interactions.
- The human factor. A change in the upper managerial levels of an organization may bring a change in its culture and orientation and so may bring about changes in personnel and/or procedures.

---

[1] Relevant to the term "innovation" is the term "strategic innovation" and to one view (Papadakis, 2009) is considered as "the discovery of a new way of conducting business activities which not only differs significantly from tradition but also is in conflict with it" (p. 224). It should be noted that strategic innovation does not refer necessarily to an important innovation but rather to an innovation within the framework of an organization's strategy. Strategic innovation falls into two categories: the routine unattractive elements of labor—usually with a low profit margin—and the new developments of labor (Christensen, Raynor, & Anthony, 2003).

According to the systemic approach, an organization (a health-care unit in our case) is an open system, i.e., it consists of a number of interrelated elements that are interactive and cooperate so as to achieve the organization's targets. Within this framework the organization is in direct contact with its environment and has a mechanism of control that continuously monitors the nature and the quantity of inputs and outputs.

5.3.1 Resistance to Change

Although change is indeed part and parcel of an organization, most of the time its members resist it. No matter the type of change, whether gradual or radical, specific or strategic, it causes certain reactions. Among these, according to the relevant literature (Papadakis, 2009; Papalexandri & Bouradas, 2003; Williams & Johnson, 2004; Zavlanos, 1998), the most significant and common reasons for resisting change are the following:

At an individual level: At this level, the reasons for resisting change have their origin in basic human characteristics, the most important of which are the following (Bouradas, 2001; Nadler, 1983; Williams & Johnson, 2004; Zavlanos, 1998):

- The fear of the unknown. Given that each change leads to a new set of circumstances, it is reasonable for people to have difficulty in comprehending what the consequences resulting from that change might be. Change gives people a feeling of insecurity which in turn provokes a feeling of fear that makes people resist change. It should be noted here that certain changes, such as a raise in salaries or a reduction in working hours, may not trigger any resistance among organizational members if they consider those changes to be beneficial for them.
- The fear of losing established rights. Any established rights that could be put at risk with the introduction of a change will draw resistance from the organization's members. Indeed, any changes in the established rights of people require a certain amount of time for staff to be convinced that those changes are beneficial and then accept them. After all, their existing rights would have been accumulatively earned by staff and so they would not be willing to surrender them easily.
- Habit. Human beings are creatures of habit and have a tendency to resist change simply because they have been used to conducting their work in a certain way and any change could potentially disrupt the status quo. For instance, changing the working schedule of medical/nursing staff, even for a valid reason, may invoke a defiant, uncooperative response.
- The loss of control. Individuals may react badly to change because they fear that this change may restrict their freedom to carry out their work as they would like.
- The fear of an increased workload. Individuals most often react to change when they fear that this change will bring extra work.

At a group level: Factors that may provoke resistance to change are the following (Katz & Kahn, 1978; Papadakis, 2009; Saitis & Saiti, 2018, p. 49):

- The organization's structure
- Adjustment in functionality such as a change in the evaluation system
- The inaction of the team
- The organization's culture
- A threat to employees' degree of autonomy
- The reallocation of resources

From the above, it is clear that the organizational climate and the bonds among the organization members are crucially important and significantly influence strategic issues. Despite any initial resistance, people will ultimately accept the changes if they feel reassured by, and trust for, their managers. Leaders should have a deep understanding of the feelings, needs, and visions of the organization members. In order for this to happen, members should be allowed to express their feelings and be provided with the appropriate channels to do so. Hence, the right balance is essential. Only when trust, commitment, and collective responsibility are evident within an organization will it be able to move forward toward a sustainable future.

5.3.2 Confrontation of Change

As has already been mentioned, people react positively to changes that, up to a point, seem reasonable. When the reaction of an organization's members is negative, i.e., when change is resisted, there are some managerial methods that can be used in order to neutralize such a reaction (Dubrin, 2009; Hytiris, 2006; Kanellopoulos, 1995; Papalexandri & Bouradas, 2003; Zavlanos, 1998). The basic approaches for tackling resistance to change are given here:

- *Communicate scheduled changes that are essential/advantageous*. One way to reduce any resistance is to communicate to staff members why a planned change is essential and/or advantageous. Certainly, introducing even minor changes without justifying them only causes anxiety and confusion among employees and gives them reason to resist.
- *Gradually implement the change*. Given that any change imposed suddenly induces a fear of the unknown, implementing it gradually can allay this fear, as the organization's management has the opportunity to prepare employees, through effective communication channels and training, to develop new skills and behaviors so as to accept the proposed change.
- *Provide effective and comprehensive information*. This method consists of the managing directors of the organization systematically informing (e.g., through conferences, speeches, etc.) all relevant stakeholders about the content of the strategic plan. In this way, organization members can get familiar with the purpose it serves and what the organization stands to gain from it. In order for the

information approach to be positive, organizations should have the right to express their objections. This helps to create a good organizational environment in which employees feel they have a say in matters concerning their work.
- *Allow employees to participate in the change's design.* Employee involvement in drawing up the plan for change facilitates their commitment to actively supporting it, simply because they know that this plan is the result of their views. We note that this method requires the participation of employee representatives in committees at all managerial levels. However, the degree of participation in the planning of change for each group of employees depends on the activities of each project.
- *Train employees appropriately.* By providing employees with the knowledge and skills that a given change requires, they are more likely to accept that change, as they would better understand its content and benefits and, most importantly, develop the attitudes and behaviors that the new state of affairs requires.
- *Negotiate with the actors of change.* When a change has negative consequences for the employees, a negotiation technique is imperative (Papalexandri & Bouradas, 2003, p. 427). This is because two-way communication helps to better understand the potential difficulties that come with change and thus reduce some of the frequent concerns that employees have.
- *Exercise authority.* In this approach, the organization's management uses a heavy-handed approach to deal with negative reactions: they reduce the likelihood of employees' resistance with threats (e.g., loss of position/promotion, etc.). This approach can sway employees' initial reactions, but their resentment remains and tends to manifest itself as a type of latent resistance that can cause serious operational problems for the organization in the long term. For this reason, this coercive method should only be used in moments of serious crisis (e.g., an immediate remedial action needed to counter sudden developments that threaten the organization's very existence).

In summary, if we accept that any change (however insignificant) proposed by an organization is to be met with a certain degree of resistance, then the management of that organization should aim to reduce it after a careful analysis of the resisting elements/forces. Ideally, the first five approaches to coping with change should be used, while the latter two should be used only in particularly difficult situations.

5.4 Process of Change

By studying the relevant literature (Dubrin, 2009; Mitchell, Dowling, Kabanoff, & Larson, 1992; Papadakis, 2009; Papalexandri & Bouradas, 2003), evidently there is no commonly accepted model for the process of change in organizations. This lack of agreement is likely to lie in the fact that the nature of change is different from organization to organization but also from situation to situation (Papadakis, 2009). Clearly, this differentiation means that the process of change is not easy for an organization's management to deal with.

Despite the obvious difficulties, certain steps are needed for an organization to introduce any form of change. Mitchell et al. (1992, pp. 524–528) have identified them to be the following:

- *Recognize the problem*: The process of change begins by recognizing the problem. Here, "problem" refers to the difference between the desired situation and the actual one. Based on this notion, an organization's management should recognize and accurately record the critical factors that make up the organization's problematic situation. In a situation where a health-care unit is (for example) observing the frequent absences of health-care personnel or conflicts between patients and health-care employees, the manager should accurately capture the operational status of that unit. In our example, we note that, *firstly*, something is wrong in the health-care unit that prevents it from meeting the requirements of patients and generally from fulfilling its role and, *secondly*, that there is a problem which needs to be solved in a timely manner.
- *Find the causes*: At this stage, the relevant executives try to identify the causes that make the organization's functioning problematic. In many instances this verification is done through the responsible manager's personal observation but also through informal communication with the members of the organization. We note that, for complex problems, the causes are identified through systematic research using various methodological tools to collect information, such as a questionnaire (Likert, 1961; Hackmam & Oldham, 1980; Payne, 1993, 1995; Pearce & Robinson, 2011).
- *Apply the change*: After identifying the causes of a problem, the organization then goes on to establish the type of change and its means of implementation. At this stage the organization discerns whether or not a change is acceptable and can be implemented by its members. In order to effectively implement organizational change, researchers (Nadler, 1983; Payne, 1993, 1995; Pearce & Robinson, 2011) have identified that the following elements should be in place:

  (a) Ensure there is a stimulating climate among the members of the organization who are called upon to implement each program of change. In the case of health-care units, administrators in a hospital should ensure that not only is the necessary legislative regulation in place to complete a change's implementation but also that the members of the hospital community are committed, since the attitude of these members will determine the success or failure of the change undertaken. In addition, regarding the role of human resources in the implementation of change, Papadakis (2009) notes that "employees go through four consecutive stages for change to materialize:

  Refusal: employees refuse to believe that change is necessary and that it is going to be implemented.
  Resistance: this is the individual or even collective efforts of employees to delay the change and persuade those who took the decision of applying the change that it is improper.
  Exploration: employees experiment with behaviors to see the effectiveness of the promising effects of change.

Commitment: the change is accepted and 'embraced' by employees" (p. 185).

(b) Ensure that the direction of the transition state is controlled both during and after the change. More analytically, during the transition from a state A to a state B, an organization goes through varying degrees of disorder, depending on the type of change being undertaken. In practice, this implies that a number of problems can arise that prevent the organization's proper functioning and make it difficult to integrate the change. These problems can be overcome, as long as the change is carefully planned from the beginning and the necessary assets (such as time and resources) are allocated by the management of the organization to facilitate the transition from the existing state to the desired one.

(c) Guide the political dynamics of the organization so as to facilitate the program for change, since in many cases the process is hindered in various ways by the members of the organization.

- *Evaluate the final outcome of the change*: The final stage in the process of change is to evaluate the results of the activities that have been implemented to bring about the change. At this stage, the relevant managing directors examine, on the basis of (qualitative) criteria, whether the desired state has actually been reached, i.e., whether the process has provided a satisfactory solution to the organization's initial problem.

5.5 Introduction to Models for Change

From the above, it becomes clear that, *first*, in all modern organizations the planning and programming of change is the responsibility of the supreme administration and, *second*, any form of change follows a certain process. According to the relevant literature (Dubrin, 1997, 2009; Carnall, 2007; Kotter, 2012; Lewin, 1951; Mitchell et al., 1992; Papadakis, 2009; Papalexandri & Bouradas, 2003; Zavlanos, 1998), there are different models for planning the process of change. This means that a given strategic change is not subject to a particular model of administration (Papadakis, 2009). Instead, each organization applies the model that, at the discretion of management, fits the organization. Nevertheless, we will mention briefly two well-known models relating to the introduction of change, namely, the model of K. Lewin and the eight steps model of J. Kotter.

5.5.1 The Model of K. Lewin

Psychologist Lewin (1951) claimed that a change goes through three stages: *defrosting*, *change*, and *re-defrosting*.

The *first* step provides the stimulus for the organization members to feel the need for change. This is a crucial stage since the introduction of a change usually requires the members to let go of old habits and be willing to try out new ones. However, a change in habit cannot be imposed. In order to overcome this, management should motivate and properly inform employees about the benefits they will derive from the changes, answer their questions, and enable them to participate in those changes. This stage demonstrates that it is very difficult to achieve a change without the readiness and involvement of the organization members.

In the *second* step, the change takes place by applying a method. The new set of circumstances will require new values/attitudes/procedures/etc. to be adopted and this calls for a meaningful two-way communication between all organization members. Furthermore, Lewin claimed that "instead of a one-way flow of orders or advice, the person applying the change should make proposals. Changes should encourage contribution and participation" (cited by Dubrin, 2009, p. 283).

Finally, in the *third* stage change involves standardization whereby the stability of the new set of circumstances is ensured (through new knowledge, skills, behaviors, etc.). Since a change takes a certain amount of time to consolidate, the organization's management needs to highlight the goals that have been achieved, publicly reward all those who have contributed to making it happen, and also positively address any difficulties.

5.5.2 The Eight Steps Model of J. Kotter

In order for an organization to successfully change, Professor Kotter (2001) argues that it should follow a process of eight steps which are the following.

Create a Sense of Necessity First of all, the management should create a sense that a change in the organization is needed, simply because the lack of this sense makes it difficult for the group to "have enough power and credibility to direct the effort or to persuade key people to devote the time needed to create and convey a vision of change" (Kotter, 2001, p. 51). Besides, we should not forget that, without a substantial number of organization members "who will feel the necessity for this venture, the momentum for the change will probably be blown away well before the finish line. People will find thousands of intelligent ways not to cooperate in a process that they consider is not necessary or follows a wrong course" (Kotter, 2001, p. 52).

Create a Guidance Group As mentioned above, major changes are complex managerial challenges and are implemented with great difficulty. Within this framework, Kotter (2001) emphasizes that "because major changes are very difficult to achieve, a powerful force is needed to support the process. No one, even a powerful CEO, will ever be able to develop the right vision, transmit it to many people, eliminate all the major obstacles, create short-term improvements, direct and manage dozens of change programs, and integrate new methods in the philosophy of the organization. There is always a strong leadership coalition, a coalition [heading] in the right direction, with the right degree of trust and a common goal. The formation of such a group is always a key part of the first phases of any effort to restructure, design or re-design a series of strategies" (p. 67).

Create a Clear Vision and Strategy This stage involves the formation of a clear vision and strategy, because in a process of change, a good vision *helps* to clarify the general direction of change, *motivates* the organization members to take actions that lead in the right direction, and *helps* to coordinate the actions of different people. Moreover, as Kotter (2001) argues, "the creation of a vision and strategy is a major investment in creating a better future" (p. 99).

Disseminate the Vision of Change Once the vision has been established, the group should, through bilateral communication, spread the vision and strategy to all members of the organization, so as to convince them of the necessity for, and the benefits of, change. As stated by Kotter (2001), "the true power of a vision is only released when most of those involved in an organization understand its goals and the direction it leads" (p. 100).

Expand the Level of Participation in the Change By this stage the change team should have overcome obstacles (e.g., inflexible structures, lack of skills) and resistances and should then encourage a significant number of organization members to participate in the changes. All these actions aim at empowering employees and help to create a positive climate in the organization.

Achieve Short-Term Results After opening up the level of participation in change, the change team should focus on any short-term results in order to consolidate the cooperation of the members in order to continue their efforts toward the vision. In other words, short-term results help stimulate the personnel and reinforce the benefits of the change (Papadakis, 2009).

Consolidate Successes and Promote Further Changes Achieving short-term results should not be a reason for disrupting the transformation process. Instead, the change group using these results as arguments should push forward new changes. Certainly, we should not forget that change is not only a plan of action but a philosophy of continuous organizational improvement.

Incorporate New Approaches into the Organization's Culture In the last stage, the change team should incorporate the changes as part of the culture of the organization so as to ensure that it will not return to its previous state.

5.6 Why Changes Fail in Organizations

We have mentioned above that adjusting to the external environmental developments is imperative. Despite the importance of change, it is very difficult to get organizations to do so and many attempts to implement change result in failure. In view of these thoughts, the following question arises: Why do organizations' attempts to change often fail? According to Kotter (2001), such failures are due to the following mistakes:

1. *Self-indulgence.* Indeed, when the top management of an organization (e.g., a hospital manager) tries to impress subordinates by changing important aspects within the organization, without adequately preparing the managers and staff members, it is a huge mistake. For Kotter (2001), "this error is fatal, because transformations cannot achieve their goals when there is great self-indulgence" (p. 20).
2. *The inability to create an adequately strong ruling coalition.* As has already been mentioned, significant changes take place when supported by the majority of the organization members. Based on this, we may support the view that in organizations that introduce significant changes without creating a strong leadership coalition, it is very difficult (if not impossible) to acquire the "power needed to overcome often too great sources of inertia" (Kotter, 2001, p. 23).
3. *Underestimating the power of the vision.* While an overwhelming character and strong leadership are necessary conditions, they alone are not capable of bringing about a major change. There still needs to be a comprehensible vision. As Kotter (2001) argues, if there is no vision to guide decision-making, any choice faced by organization members may "evolve into an endless debate. The most important decisions can create intense controversy that drains energy and destroys morale. Minor tactical choices can dominate discussions and valuable time be spent on them" (p. 25).
4. *Transmitting the vision in the wrong way.* In the relevant literature such as Kotter (2001), it is argued that "people do not sacrifice, even when they are dissatisfied with the current situation, unless they believe that the potential benefits of change are attractive and only if they really believe that it is possible to achieve some transformation. If you do not convey the vision convincingly and the extent to which you need it, you will never feel the heart and the spirit of the members of an organization" (p. 25).
5. *The inappropriate handling of obstacles.* As mentioned above, the implementation of a major change requires action by the majority of the members of the organization on the basis of the vision. However, the willful action of these members is often undermined by huge obstacles in the process of change. For example, strictly defined work tasks are likely to undermine their efforts to implement the change.
6. *The nonrecognition of short-term results.* Although the implementation of a change demands sufficient time, however, an organization's management makes a critical mistake when it does not recognize short-term achievements. In this

way many organization members abandon their efforts or ally themselves with those initially reacting negatively toward the transformation.

7. *Celebrating success prematurely*. According to Kotter (2001), it is not bad for an organization's management to celebrate a success, but it is a terrible mistake to suggest that most of the transformation has taken place. This is because it prematurely stops "every momentum, and then overwhelms powerful forces that have to do with tradition (maintenance)" (p. 29).
8. *Failing to correctly incorporate changes into the philosophy*[2] *of the organization*. In order for the organizational transformation to be successful, individual changes should be integrated into the culture and functionality of the organization. Otherwise, if there is no such integration, "there is always the risk of a devaluation of change as soon as the pressures associated with the effort for change are stopped" (Kotter, 2001, p. 30).

From the above, it becomes clear that organizational changes are a complex and difficult process and therefore there is a risk that some mistakes will be made. However, a capable management can significantly reduce the number of mistakes because, as we will see in the next subsection, it has the ability to point out in a timely manner the causes of any resistance to the necessary changes and to follow strategies that can overcome any catastrophic inactivity. It should be noted that the responsibility for timely changes and for constantly improving all elements (e.g., structures, technology, procedures, etc.) is the responsibility of all managers at all hierarchical levels.

5.7 Basic Elements for the Successful Implementation of Change in the Health-Care Sector

It is well known that Greece "has recently been going through the greatest possible fiscal crisis in its history. A crisis that [would have afflicted] Greece sooner or later, regardless of the global crisis, due to the essential lack of financial rules and procedures" (Papadimitriou & Hatzigiannakis, 2010, p. 11). It is also reported in the literature that "effective changes are linked to a multi-phased process that creates a dynamic and activation to an extent that can overcome all sources of inertia" and "this process is effective only if it is implemented by high-quality leadership..." (Kotter, 2001, pp. 54–57). It is therefore useful to point out in this subsection the basic prerequisites for effective change in the field of education. Indeed, we must

[2]The term "philosophy" refers to the behavioral and common values of a group of individuals. The term "behavioral rules" refers to common or usual modes of action that one meets in a group and are imposed because the members of the group behave in a way that teaches these practices to the new members, rewarding those who belong and imposing sanctions on those who do not. Common values are the important interests and goals shared by most members of a group that tend to shape the behavior of the group and often prevail with the passage of time, even when the composition of the group changes (Kotter, 2001, pp. 160–161).

not forget that "education has not only a social and cultural purpose but also an economic value, since its contribution to increasing labor productivity and production is important" (Saiti, 2013).

In order for a change in an educational system to take place, a senior manager will decide upon a strategic change (e.g., upon the evaluation of an educational project), others will develop implementation programs, and yet others in the organization will actually implement those programs. Similarly, the planning, programming, and implementing of a change in the health-care sector is the result of a system of roles and responsibilities assumed by members of the hospital community who are the carriers of the intended change. The success of this change depends on how teams or change actors carry out their roles. In particular, the key elements that can contribute to the success of a change in the health-care sector are the following.

Existence of High-Quality Leadership An extremely significant element in introducing a change is the quality of the leadership that, according to Kotter (2001), *determines* what the organization's future should be, *guides* the members toward this vision, and *inspires* them to make it happen. In practice, the organization leader has to understand the problems thoroughly, *have ideas*, and propose changes with a clearer understanding of the ideological context within which these changes will take place.

An *idea* is a new way to improve something in the organization. It can be something general (such as a vision or a new image for a hospital/health-care unit) or something specific, such as a particular improvement in the health-care services provided. Ideas generally have no hope if there is no sense of urgency regarding change. Despite clear difficulties, a leader of change can overcome any negative reactions by creating a sense of urgency while ensuring that the members of the organization understand the need for the change. Thus, a leader is a person who *develops* the vision as well as the strategies for creating any changes required to achieve this vision, *orientates* people toward the vision, transmits in words and actions the direction to be followed by all organizational members whose cooperation may be needed, and *enables* the channels by which any obstacles (bureaucratic, organizational, etc.) may be overcome, though the satisfaction of basic human needs are often not met in this process (Kotter, 2001).

On the other hand, when the head of a large organization, e.g., a hospital manager, along with his colleagues, decides on a number of changes and then demands a proxy for the entire hospital community to accept them, then such an effort will lead to failure for at least two reasons: *first*, because there was no substantial participation of the hospital staff in the decision-making process and, *second*, because changes in a hospital tend to be implemented by a number of administrative and health-care staff and those who are in favor of such changes tend to be fewer than those who are opposed. Hence, it is important for the hospital leadership to realize that this way of formulating hospital policy is completely inadequate for the current climate of dependence and interdependence. If the attitude and philosophy of this policy does not change, the consequences will undoubtedly be detrimental to the social and economic development of the hospital. Additionally, each manager should accept the fact that any changes cannot be implemented overnight. There must be a firm shift in strategy toward a more practical and sustainable philosophy whereby *all* the components and subsystems of the system are continually improved. In other words, it is very difficult to impose changes even if nowadays these alterations are mandatory for improving the health-care services provided.

From the above, it becomes evident that the effective implementation of a change in the health-care sector requires the pursuit of quality leadership, and such a form of leadership can, through an appropriate strategy and lines of action, overcome the many sources of potential inertia and resistance within the hospital community.

Establish a Strong Leadership Team for Change A health-care system is very large and complex and cannot be transformed by just one leader, however good they are at their job. They need to be supported by many in order to perform their managerial duties effectively. In reality, many managers in health care rely on the establishment of a strong leadership group to manage change, consisting of "distinguished" scientists of various disciplines and health-care professionals. This is because (a) health care is a sensitive area of social life and (b) the political landscape (at least in democratic countries) must be able to adapt to changes in the way the country is governed. The composition of this group should go beyond traditional political party boundaries and its members must have the authority to be able to make critical decisions following an extensive research study and be able to transform an idea for change into action plans. Any recommendations from the above group tend to be more easily adopted by the community in the health-care sector because the whole effort is carried out on a scientific and interparty basis and, most importantly, minimizes the "political cost" for government and possible exploitation by the opposition.

As part of its activities, this leadership group for change should:

- *Act thoroughly and effectively* in conducting research on all health-care issues in order to identify the real weaknesses and shortcomings of the training units. Decision makers of changes in health care have to consider the fact that reforming health-care policy is not an isolated organizational and administrative process. On the contrary, it is part of wider structural changes taking place at the social level, and therefore a change in the health-care sector must be based on a systemic approach in the sense that the success of this change requires the alignment, harmony, and synchronization of the various health-care system elements (Papalexandri & Bouradas, 2003).
- *Create a communication network for at least three purposes*: *First*, to widely disseminate the content of the change in an accurate and clear way to the health-care community in order to create a meaningful dialogue between the members of the team and the medical and nursing staff and patients, developing arguments for the benefits of change, responding to reactions, and dealing with practical issues to help facilitate the change. *Second*, in order to effectively organize the process of applying change during the implementation phase, that is, to define in the lower hierarchical levels of management what exactly needs to be done, how

it is to be done, when it should be done, and who should do it. In summary, the members of the above leadership group should use every possible means to communicate more effectively the vision and strategies that it will support. The goal is to convince the majority of the community in the health-care sector about the necessity and benefits of a given change. *Third*, to have the team members' continuous feedback on the progress made and on the outcomes of implementing the prescribed action programs so that they could then take any corrective measures necessary.

- *Make the best possible effort to change employees' attitudes regarding the issue of change*. This is because the existence of a positive organizational culture is a key component in achieving common decisions or shared values that are also shared or accepted by the central health-care administration and the majority of health-care practitioners. Furthermore, it is argued (Papoulias, 2002) that the culture of a (health-care) organization is directly linked to possible changes which:
  - *Have* emotional and psychological consequences because they intend to alter situations and human relationships that have existed for many years
  - *Are difficult* because they require new efforts to change cognitive objects, a new sense of participation, and new commitments
  - *Have a* personal *effect* on individuals as they may change working conditions, the salaries of staff, etc.

Therefore, the members of the leadership team need to acknowledge the importance of the organization's culture in shaping and implementing changes in the health-care sector. They should create a climate of dialogue, free expression, creative criticism, and disagreement and, most importantly, reward the original and creative ideas of the members of the health-care community. Also, they should not forget that in the area of health care there are no magic recipes, nor does the health-care sector suddenly change with laws and regulatory decisions, but with a change of consciousness and attitude. There is no significant change with a long-term health-care perspective if there is no change in attitudes, if the staff of health-care units are not convinced of their benefits.

Constant Administrative and Financial Support We need to move step by step on the basis of a long-term well-designed strategy. The effectiveness or implementation of changes in health care primarily involves a steady effort and ongoing managerial support from the upper managerial levels.

In addition to managerial support, the effective implementation of a change also requires the provision of the necessary funds, because without financial support, the change remains nothing more than a gesture.

Summarizing the above, we may say that a significant change in the area of health care should not be treated periodically but as a long-term strategy, the success of which depends on organizational support, the design of an appropriate model, the mood/attitude of the members of the health-care community, financial support, and, of course, the abilities and experiences of the decision makers involved in any given change in the health-care sector.

References

Abrahamson, E. (2000, July–August). *Change without pain* (pp. 75–79). Brighton, MA: Harvard Business Review.

Bouradas, D. (2001). *Management*. Athens, Greece: Benou Publications. (in Greek).

Carnall, C. (2007). *Managing change in organizations*. London: Financial Times Press.

Christensen, C. M., Raynor, M. E., & Anthony, S. D. (2003). Six keys to creating new growth business. *Harvard Management Update, 8*(1), 3–6. https://hbswk.hbs.edu/item/six-keys-to-building-new-markets-by-unleashing-disruptive-innovation

Daft, R. (2004). Organization theory and design (Greek translation by Andreas Sokodimou) Athens, Greece: Klidarithmos Publishing (in Greek).

Daft, R. L. (2007). *Organization theory and design* (9th ed.). Mason, OH: South Western, Thomson.

Dubrin, A. J. (1997). *Essentials of management* (4th ed.). London: SouthWestern College Publishing.

Dubrin, A. J. (2009). *Essentials of management* (8th ed.). London: SouthWestern College Publishing.

Giannakaki, M. S. (2005). The implementation of innovations in school units. In M. Kapsaki (Ed.), *Organization and management of school units* (pp. 243–276). Thessaloniki, Greece: University of Macedonia Publications. (in Greek).

Giannouzas, I. N., & Carzo, R. (1968). *The typical organization: Research of the system*. Athens, Greece: Papazisi Publishing. (in Greek).

Hackmam, J., & Oldham, G. (1980). *Work Redesign*. Reading, MA: Addison. H. Wesley.

Hytiris, L. (2006). *Management: Business administration principles*. Athens, Greece: Interbooks Publications. (in Greek).

Iordanides, G. (2006). School management and change management. In G. Bagakis (Ed.), *Educational changes, educators' and school intervention* (pp. 90–97). Athens, Greece: Metaihmio Publishing. (in Greek).

Kanellopoulos, C. (1995). *Management – Effective administration*. Athens, Greece: Kanellopoulos Publications. (in Greek).

Katz, D., & Kahn, R. L. (1978). *The social psychology of organizations* (2nd ed.). New York: Wiley.

Kotter, J. (2001). *Leading change* (Translation into Greek language by A. Sokodimou). Athens, Greece: Kritiki Publishing. (in Greek).

Kotter, J. P. (2012). *Leading change* (2nd ed.). Boston, MA: Harvard Business Review Press.

Kouris, G., Souliotis, K., & Philalithis, A. (2006). The healthcare reforms in Greece: Failure factors and rules of rational reform plan. *Dioikitiki Enimerosi, 39*, 82–90.

Lewin, K. (1951, 1967). *Field theory in social science*. New York: Harper & Brothers.

Likert, R. (1961). *New patterns of management*. New York: McGraw-Hill.

McCann, J. E. (1991). Design principles for an innovating company. *Academy of Management Executive, 5*(2), 76–93.

McGee, J., Thomas, H., & Wilson, D. (2005). *Strategy: Analysis and practice*. New York: McGraw-Hill.

Nadler, D. (1983). Concepts for the management of organizational change. In J. Hackman, E. Lawler III, & L. Porter (Eds.), *Perspectives on behavior in organizations* (2nd ed., pp. 551–561). New York: McGraw-Hill.

Nadler D. & Tushman, M. (1998). *Competing by Design*, Oxford University. New York: Oxford University Press.

Papadakis, V. (2009). *Recent issues of business strategies*. Athens, Greece: Benou Publishing. (in Greek).

Papadimitriou, P. & Hatzigiannakis, G. (2010, April 18). Finally we blame for everything? *Greek Newspaper Kathimerini*.

Papalexandri, N., & Bouradas, D. (2003). *Human resource management*. Athens, Greece: Benou Publishing. (in Greek).

Papoulias, D. (2002). *Business strategic management & change management*. Athens, Greece: Kastanioti Publishing. (in Greek).

Payne, J. H. (1993). Introducing formal project management into traditional functionally structured organization. *International Journal of Project Management, 11*(4), 239–243.

Payne, J. H. (1995). Management of multiple simultaneous projects: A state of art review. *International Journal of Project Management, 13*(3), 163–168.

Pearce, J., & Robinson, R. (2011). *Strategic management: Formulation, implementation and control* (12th ed.). New York: McGraw-Hill.

Pierce, J. L., & Delbecg, A. L. (1977). Organization structure, individual attitudes and innovation. *Academy of Management Review, 2*, 27–37.

Russell, R. D., & Russell, C. J. (1992). An examination of the effects of organizational norms, organizational structure, and environmental uncertainty on entrepreneurial strategy. *Journal of Management, 18*(4), 639–656.

Saiti, A. (2013, Spring). Reforms in Greek education 1991-2011: Reforms or something else? *eJournal of Education Policy*, 1–10. http://nau.edu/COE/eJournal/_Forms/spring2013/Saiti

Saitis, C., & Saiti, A. (2018). *Initiation of educators into educational management secrets*. Basel, Switzerland: Springer.

Williams, K., & Johnson, B. (2004). *Introducing management: A development guide*. Doncaster, UK: Plant a Tree.

Zavlanos, M. (1998). *Management*. Athens, Greece: Ellin Publishing. (in Greek).

Mitchell, T., Dowling, P., Kabanoff, B., & Larson, J. (1992). *People in organizations. An introduction to organizational behavior in Australia*. Sydney, Australia: McGraw-Hill.

Chapter 6
Total Quality Management and Health-Care Sector

Key Concepts

1. Customer diversity makes it difficult for hospitals to operate, because the needs and attitudes of different clients do not always coincide.
2. Since one of the main objectives of TQM is client satisfaction, an organization should listen to, and address in a prompt and fair manner, the demands of all parties.
3. Achieving quality in health care is a matter for all the actors in the health-care process (e.g., doctors, patients, etc.) whereby each in turn should ensure that treatment needs are administered effectively and efficiently.
4. The benefits that can be derived by applying the basic principles of TQM to health-care organizations are significant and many.
5. Sustainability and TQM have a common goal, namely, to satisfy patient needs, and so the two are connected. Hence, a health-care unit should be patient-centered.

6.1 Introduction

Historically, the research for quality has been a significant topic since ancient times, but the focus on the quality of products and services is a phenomenon that has begun to take on huge proportions since the 1950s.

In the world of health-care reality, quality implies the right provision of what each patient needs, according to his needs at the appropriate time, in the appropriate way, ensuring the best possible result (Desai, 2011; Kamra, Singh, & Kumar De, 2016; Papavasiliou, 2018; Talib, Rahman, & Azam, 2011; Verma & Khandelwal, 2011). To do so, hospitals should be effective. Of course, the concept of "efficiency" of formal organizations, and thus of hospitals, is not completely disparate and therefore means different things for different people (Handy, 1981; Katz & Kahn, 1978; Zavlanos, 1998). It is a multidimensional concept that is linked to many factors, such as the best possible care for patients with the least cost, the working climate,

M. Chletsos, A. Saiti, *Strategic Management and Economics in Health Care*,
https://doi.org/10.1007/978-3-030-35370-4_6

the professional satisfaction of the workers in the hospitals, etc. Nevertheless, in the relevant literature (Bouradas, 2005; Handy, 1981; Talib et al., 2011; Verma & Khandelwal, 2011; Zavlanos, 1998, 2003; Zink, 2007), it is stated that an efficient organization, and therefore a hospital, is distinguished for:

- Its competent leadership
- Good working environment
- Employee satisfaction
- Appropriate education and training of all employees
- Adequate organizational support
- Clarity of roles and responsibilities of the members of the organization
- Effective use of resources

A managerial approach to the efficient operation of hospitals is the implementation of the total quality management (TQM), which was formulated in the middle of the last century. It is a modern management model that, on the basis of certain principles, contributes to the efficient utilization of productive resources to achieve specific goals of the organization (Bouradas, 2001; Creech, 1994; Deming, 1986; Mullins, 2010). As we will see later, the TQM adapts to continual change and relies on active mobilization of all members to improve the quality and effectiveness of the organization (Lee, Doi, Tan, & Chong, 2010; Tahir, Nawaz, Butt, & Mahmood, 2012; Talib, 2013; Talib & Rahman, 2010).

6.2 Understanding the Concepts of "Customer" and "Quality"

The clarification of the terms "customer" and "quality" was considered necessary because they are the central concepts of total quality management in this chapter.

6.2.1 What Does "Customers" Mean

Today the modern management mind of an organization emphasizes and prioritizes customer needs. But what is a customer?

There are many definitions to determine the meaning of "customer." In one view (Juran, 1988; Mishra, 1995), this term includes all members that are affected by the processes and products (or services) of an organization. In another view (Edosomwan, 1993; Mullins, 2010), a client means every person or group of people who are on a receiving end of the completion of a job or task. These definitions suggest that employees are also customers since they also accept products or services from other departments or other members of an organization. Therefore, we can argue that the customers of an organization (depending on their location) are either in an internal organizational environment (employees) or in an external organizational environment (final recipients). As a result they can be divided into two categories: internal and external customers (Bourada, 2007; Crawford & Shutler, 1999; Sahney, Banwet, & Karunes, 2004; Zavlanos, 2003). In particular, an external client means any person who is the ultimate recipient of an integrated product or service of an organization. There are, therefore, individuals who are not part of an organization but are still affected by its products or services. It is about serving people outside the organization (Crawford & Shutler, 1999; Creech, 1994; Deming, 1986; Desai, 2011; Mullins, 2010; Powell, 1995; Saha & Theingi, 2009; Saiti, 2012; Zavlanos, 2003).

Consequently, every employee of an organization who receives products or services from suppliers within that organization (Ruckert & Walker, 1987, p. 2) is perceived as internal customer. Therefore, each organization consists of a set of interdependent units (or employees), each of which receives inputs from the previous one and supplies the next internal or external customer (Edvardsson, Thomasson, & Ovretveit, 1994, p. 21; Evans & Dean, 1999, p. 31; Logothetis, 1992, p. 16; Mills & Ungson, 2001). This creates the chain customer-suppliers where the external customer becomes the last link in the chain (Crosby, 1991, p. 11; Rampersad, 2001, p. 342; Williams & Johnson, 2004).

Carrying the above considerations into the sphere of hospitals (and any health-care organization), the term "customer" includes end users, users of products, and employees at all levels who participate in "production" and influence the quantity and quality of health-care services offered (Creech, 1994; Deming, 1986; Malamou, 2016). Patients, for example, who are admitted to a hospital for health care are external customers, and individuals (doctors, nurses, administrative staff, etc.) working in the hospital are external customers.

Given that, (a) customer diversity makes it difficult for hospitals to operate, because the needs and attitudes of different clients are not always coincident, and (b) one of the main objectives of the TQM is the satisfaction of a client, so the organization should listen and face promptly and fairly the demands of all parties. To do this, it is necessary to develop an open communication system with all health-care-related social actors (clients). Besides, we should not forget that contradictions in the health-care sector whether it's in the form of strikes or other actions (e.g., occupations) can be detrimental to all of us.

6.2.2 Dimensions of the Term "Quality"

For the term "quality," there isn't an acceptable definition of what that term means since this can be conceived in many ways (Creech, 1994; Danos & Danos, 2009; Deming, 1986; Hytiris & Anninos, 2015; Kefis, 2005). In particular, some researchers consider quality as "activity that results in customer satisfaction" (Sallis, 2002, p. 12) and as "the group of attributes and attributes of a product" (Michos, 1994, p. 40) or link it "perfection" (Besterfield et al, 1995, p. 30) and "with a system of values, principles, standards and methods of action" (Kefis, 2005, p. 227).

Consequently, the concept of quality in the health-care sector is more complex than any other type of organization and has various approaches. Thus, researchers such as Chassin and Galvin (1998) consider the quality of health care as an extent of the health-care services for both individuals and populations, thereby increases the likelihood of desired health-care outcomes which is consistent with current professional knowledge. Similarly, Kronenfeld (2006) considers the quality of health-care services as an extent of the services provided which increases the likelihood of desirable effects on a particular health-care problem and are in line with modern medical knowledge.

On one hand, the conceptual ambiguity of the word "quality" can be attributed to the fact that it is used in its "absolute" and in its "relative" meaning (Danos & Danos, 2009, p. 26) to describe products made with perfection without calculating the cost of production. This means that it is linked with value and important products that gives great satisfaction to the people who have these products (Mishra, 1995). In other words, rarity and precision are two of the key attributes of quality as an absolute meaning. Based on this, we may say that in terms of health care, the term of quality has a purely "elitist" character directed at those hospitals that can economically choose it.

On the other hand (with "relative" meaning), qualitative elements are not necessarily expensive or exclusive and luxurious as those of the "absolute" concept. They may be common and ordinary. In a hospital, for example, a hospital infrastructure and all health-care equipment related to substructure can only be qualitative if they are intended for their needs. These have to meet specifications and requirements of the "clients" (patients, doctors, nurses, etc.).

According to the above, the broadness of the term "quality" actually creates confusion as it implies different things to different people. But how can we understand the true meaning of quality through different and often opposing views?

There are three main approaches in this direction (Creech, 1994; Murgatroyd & Morgan, 1993):

(a) *Quality assurance*. Historically, this approach is the oldest and refers to standards, appropriate methods, and requirements set out by a specific panel and accompanied by a process of monitoring and evaluation. In the case of the health-care services, quality can be achieved through control (inspection) and evaluation. The patient health-care system, for example, can be considered as a "way of ensuring quality." Take, for example, a patient who is admitted into a public health-care institution undergoes the necessary treatment and remains there until the patient has recovered demonstrates to a certain extent the quality of health care provided in a national health-care system. The quality work of a doctor may also be evaluated by his or her immediate supervisor or a committee, according to the clinical results of the patients and always in relation to their disease(s). The same can be said of the administration in health-care institutions, which complies with the institutional framework and determines the time, the way, the resources, and the kind of action needed in the health-care unit. The Care Quality Commission (CQC), who are health-care inspectors, undertake a check to whether or not the above conditions are met during the day-to-day operation of the hospital.

In this quality process, the standards are exclusively set by a central managerial team, are evaluated by objective criteria, and are presented as a set of requirements that the hospital should satisfy. Moreover, the input from direct health-care providers (doctors, patients, nursing staff, and administrators) is very important and valuable toward the improvement of how the national health-care system should function.

(b) *Contract conference quality*. In this method the quality standards are predetermined by agreement and are applied in various ways. What distinguishes the two above quality approaches is that in the second case (quality modulation) the terms and standards are made "internally" by a person or persons who will take over and not by "specialists."

Here the quality of the project is assessed on the basis of whether and how well the tasks have been performed. Key features of this approach are the following:

- Agreements are better negotiable when they are written and clear and when agreement is reached before the evaluation begins.
- Agreements are made "internally," i.e., within the organization and concern only those who will work.
- Evaluation is done on a continuous basis rather than through an audit.

However, the above approach makes the hospital (and any health-care organization) a "closed" system because the specifications of the agreed quality do not take account of any social and scientific developments in the international community.

(c) *Customer-driven quality*. This type of job quality refers to those who are to receive a service and clarify their expectations in advance. In the case of health care, this means that the quality of health care should be determined by the direct factors of the health-care process, i.e., doctors, nurses, patients, etc.

Certainly, many patients' views or requirements may be characterized as "subjective"; however, there are cases where their opinion should be taken into account when designing the national health-care system (Hendriks, Vrielink, Smets, & De Haes, 2001). The decision, for example, of how a narcotic drug recovery program will be developed and implemented should be a result of a real dialogue between the hospital management, doctors, nurses, and the representatives of patients and relatives, so that the content, duration, and manner of presentation of this program are acceptable to all stakeholders (customers).

From what we have mentioned so far, we may say that none of the approaches mentioned above necessarily implies quality while reducing costs. Therefore, the achievement of quality in health care is a matter for all the actors in the health-care process (e.g., doctors, patients, etc.) where everyone in turn should ensure that treatment demands should be completed in the best way. It should be based not only on quality assurance but also on the formulation of an agreement and to meet the needs of all "customers" so that the final "health-care product" has their full approval and meets the quality requirements they have set.

6.3 Approach to Total Quality Management (TQM)

6.3.1 The Meaning and Importance of TQM in Health Services

The rapid development of technology and the increase in competitiveness within the postindustrial society lead to an ever-increasing demand for quality improvement. Quality improvement of products or services is considered necessary because quality is linked to both the satisfaction and the survival of the organization. To make it clearer, when an organization achieves a better quality of its produced products at the least cost, we may claim that this organization is competitive because it is given the opportunity to offer better and cheaper goods to the market.

Quality improvement is not only about private businesses but any kind of organized human activity. Whether the organization is a car manufacturing company, a ministry, or a hospital, everyone can get involved in a re-evaluation of working methods and the changes that will help to improve the product or service produced. Of course, improving the quality and, by extension, the competitiveness of an organization's products or services is not a matter of the "luck" factor. Instead, it requires a program that will be developed and implemented by the organizational management. Among the various approaches on how to improve the quality of a product or service is total quality management (TQM).

Overall quality ideas were made in the USA by the American Quality Researcher Dr. W. Edwards Deming and Professor Joseph Juran in the late twentieth century. Deming's philosophy for TQM is known as Deming's triangle and is based on three fundamental principles (Crawford & Shutler, 1999; Deming, 1986; Logothetis, 1992; Mullins, 2010; Powell, 1995):

- Commitment of management to improvement, since management is responsible for the organizational competitiveness.
- Application of statistical methodology, since statistical theory is the only way to deal with dispersion, uncertainty, and its different causes. Continuous improvement means a lasting solution to this problem.
- Improving internal relationships, since good interpersonal relationships between employees contribute significantly to productivity growth.

On the other hand, J. Juran's theory of quality is based on the homonymous "quality trilogy" which includes three basic processes (Juran, 1988):

- Quality planning
- Quality control
- Quality improvement

All the other researchers on TQM such as Ph. Crosby, A. Feigenbaum, K. Ishikawa, C. Taguchi, etc. were based on the ideas, values, and principles of Deming and Juran so as to develop and propose the theory of total quality management (Creech, 1994; Deming, 1986; Dervitsiotis, 2001). The three main characteristics of the TQM are:

- Commitment. This means the commitment of senior executives to constantly support every effort that contributes to quality assurance.
- Knowledge. This means continuous training of all parties involved in the process of qualitative research.
- Participation. This means the participation of all human resources in finding the problems, plus proposals for targeting and solving the problem (Kefis, 2005).

But What Is Total Quality Management? In analyzing these three words we have:

- *Total* refers to the influence of the overall effort of employees in an organization (such as in a hospital) as well as all the activities (e.g., as health care, administration) undertaken by the specific health-care organization. In other words, the term "total" expresses the universality of the involvement of hospital staff in improving services (Papakostidi & Tsoukalas, 2012).
- *Quality* is the degree of perfection that a product or service (quality) can provide.
- *Management* is an art on how to handle and guide human resources to meet the goals of an organization.

From the foregoing analysis, it becomes clear that if it wants to improve the quality of a product, it will require a strategy that the organization's leadership plans and implements. Only leadership can ensure that everyone in the organization works in a way that implies high-quality work and constant improvement. Proper leadership facilitates the work of others in order to achieve their goals and to meet or sometimes overcome their expectations.

But What Is the Difference Between Traditional Management and Total Quality Management? The basic difference between the two approaches is how to achieve organizational goals. Thus, while in the traditional approach the focus is on the administration and its responsibilities and involvement, on cost and quality, it is on specification and control. In the case of the TQM, we have, respectively, priority in quality, continuous improvement of quality, and emphasis on prevention. We see, therefore, that quality within the TQM is different. It is not just another new idea, another initiative. Moreover, it is a methodology that helps organizations cope with the plethora of external pressures and problems they present.

In conclusion, total quality management can be defined as an integrated management system that seeks to harmonize three basic parameters:

- Continuous improvement of the quality of the various groups of the organization
- Increasing the competitiveness of the organization
- Maximizing customers (internal and external)

This means that it is a holistic approach that changes the culture and structure of the organization in order to achieve a total commitment to the quality of products or services (Kanji, 1996, p. 331).

Regarding the health-care organizations, the concept of TQM is considered as a set of principles that are the basis of continuous improvement and involves the implementation of quality methods by efficiently using human resources for continuous improvement of the provided health-care services. These are strategies that can guarantee quality, reduce costs, and increase general satisfaction. Therefore, the customer (patient) will gain trust through the continual improvements made in the health-care organizations (Malamou, 2016; Talib & Rahman, 2010; Tountas, 2003).

In summary, the importance of TQM in health-care services is that, on one hand, staff (doctors, nurses, administrative staff, etc.) in health-care organizations have a great responsibility for the effective functioning of these organizations and for the satisfaction of their patients and, on the other hand, the health-care area is constantly facing constant pressure to improve quality (Papavasiliou, 2018). As a consequence, the health sector is a particular challenge for the implementation of the principles of TQM.

6.3.2 TQM Principles in Health-Care Services

Regardless of the type of activity of the organization, the effective application of the TQM is based on the acceptance and observance of certain principles and rules. These elements, which determine how an organization should operate, are (Kefis, 2005; Logothetis, 1992; Malamou, 2016; Schermerhorn, 2011):

Vision, mission, and quality policy. In order for an organization to become effective, it should have:

- A vision defining its future goals (or goals)
- A mission expressing organizational existence
- A policy that suggests how to achieve its goals by employees

Commitment and Participation of Leading Executives The adoption of the TQM is a strategic choice from the top executives of the organization. Therefore, the implementation of a total quality program needs the constant support of all the leading executives of the organization. In order for the organizational leaders to play a leading role, these individuals should:

- Apply the technique of "visits," known as management by wandering around (MBWA). According to the above technique, senior managers-executives have a part of their daily routine to get in touch with their partners, customers, and suppliers.
- Be informed through seminars, conferences, and literature on issues of quality improvement.
- Shape the organizational values of their organizational staff.

- Emphasize open communication and listen carefully to their internal and external customers.
- Recognize and appreciate through rewards the individual and team efforts of their associates.

In the health-care sector, for example, if the supreme and senior leadership of the relevant central administration does not take the initiative to continuously improve the quality of the health care and administrative work of the country's health-care services, then any improvements made by individual efforts will be temporary. This is because the commitment and involvement of employees, in health-care services, depends on the behavior of senior leadership, generating visions and aims to upgrade the country's national health system. Therefore, the heads of the public hospitals of a country and their staff should have time to check the quality and care of the patients (customers). Being in constant contact with all the actors in the health-care process (doctors, nurses, administrative staff, etc.) will form a personal view of the problems presented and will guide their staff accordingly (Malamou, 2016; Marley, Collier, & Goldstein, 2004; Mullins, 2010).

Customer Satisfaction The quality of a product or a public service is assessed by customer preference. Therefore, any organization in order to meet customer requirements each time should be in a position to know:

- Who his customers are
- What their needs are
- What their expectations are of choosing the specific product or service

In order to provide a right answer to the above questions, it is necessary for the responsible organizational managers to carry out, regularly, relevant market research.

With particular reference to the health-care sector, we can say that a primary goal of a health-care unit (and any organization) is to meet the needs and expectations of patients (customers). Furthermore, the satisfaction of external and internal customers (patients, doctors, nurses, etc.) goes through the expectations of:

- Patients and their families
- The medical, nursing, and administrative staff, etc., directly related to the health-care process and its individual requirements
- The State, which has enormous material resources for the operation of health-care services
- Public and private organizations, who, as future employers, want healthy human resources

Continuous Improvement of Quality Achieving higher levels of quality and competitiveness of an organization is not a matter of luck. On the contrary, it requires a continuous and well-planned effort. This effort to improve quality includes a variety of managerial actions (such as the introduction of innovations to reduce errors and imperfections in the production process, etc.). It is also influenced by both customer needs and market conditions. This means that quality is not only a continuous process but also an investment because the survival and competitiveness of an organization depends on the way (in quality and cost) it produces its products. By focusing our attention on a health-care service, we may say that the health-care process is a dynamic concept that has to be adapted to the environmental standards. Continuous adaptation dynamics are of particular importance if we take into account that the health care of the population is the most important factor in the economic development of a country. Of course, the transfer from a given to a desired health level or condition should be done in the context of a strategic planning, thus aiming to analyze continuously and solve specific health-care problems so that hospitals deliver the desired outcome with less negative impact on society.

Participation and Commitment of Human Resources In contrast to the classical concept of management, TQM requires the involvement and commitment of all staff (Dayton, 2003; Desai, 2011). That is, total quality is not a matter of a person, manager, or "specialist" but of all staff under the responsibility and guidance of the senior management of the organization. This way of managing brings multiple benefits to the organization because:

- It ensures the valuable experience of employees on the operation and problems of the organization
- It is possible to motivate all human resources
- The resistance to organizational changes introduced by the administration is diminishing

A basic prerequisite for securing and engaging staff is the change of attitude, which requires:

- Proper information and development of good human relations
- Continuous and systematic training of all employees on issues related mainly on improving communication, encouraging team effort, fostering creativity, and fostering initiative
- Recognizing and rewarding the efforts of employees

Focus on Error Prevention Preventing mistakes means taking care of the present to avoid unpleasant consequences in the future. Based on this, the management of an organization should first assess the information and the requirements of its customers and then proceed to design the product. The best method to minimize errors at the design stage is the ongoing research and the ability of the organization's responsible staff to identify and resolve the emerging problems in time. This is because prevention is preferable to treatment. At this point we should note that there are no small or big problems. In many cases, minor problems have been caused by abandonment or disguise or avoidance of risk sources (such as a damaged product or service) in the organization.

To summarize, the benefits that can be derived from the application of the basic principles of TQM on health-care organizations are many and important, among which are the following (Alexiadis & Sigalas, 1999; Malamou, 2016; Maru et al., 2012; Sodani, Kumar, Srivastava, & Sharma, 2010; Talib, 2013; Tountas, 2003):

- Improving the quality of the services provided
- Increasing competitiveness and productivity
- Reducing the cost of work
- Increasing employee satisfaction and team spirit, etc.

6.4 TQM and Customer Satisfaction

Full customer service is provided by an organization when all its mechanisms and staff are oriented to operating in a way that prioritizes the speed, quality, and high added value of the services provided. Therefore, total customer service is one of the expected results of a successful overall quality program. Indeed, these considerations lead us to the TQM's strategy, which is based on the view that customer satisfaction is the basic purpose of every organization and starts from the view that each employee, in an organization, is a client of another internal customer. By calling "organization," we mean a set of individuals who pursue specific purposes through the shaping of human resources' collective effort. There are several such organizations in the social environment, such as hospitals, businesses, schools, etc. which are set up to fulfill certain clear purposes.

In this chapter, we consider as an internal customer every employee of an organization receiving products or services from suppliers within the organization. Therefore, each organization consists of a "chain" of interdependent functional units (or employees), each of which receives input from the previous unit and supplies the next internal or external customer (Edvardsson et al., 1994, p. 21; Evans & Dean, 1999, p. 13; Logothetis, 1992, p. 16). According to these, in a service organization (such as a hospital) the "quality chain" starts with internal suppliers and ends with external customers (see Fig. 6.1).

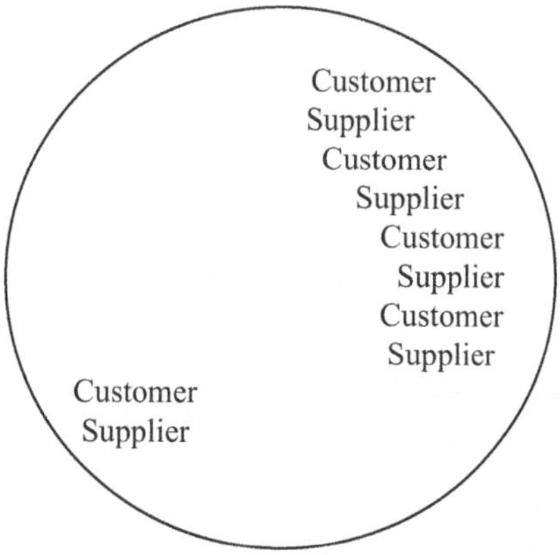

Fig. 6.1 Quality chain, cited by Oakland (1989, p. 8)

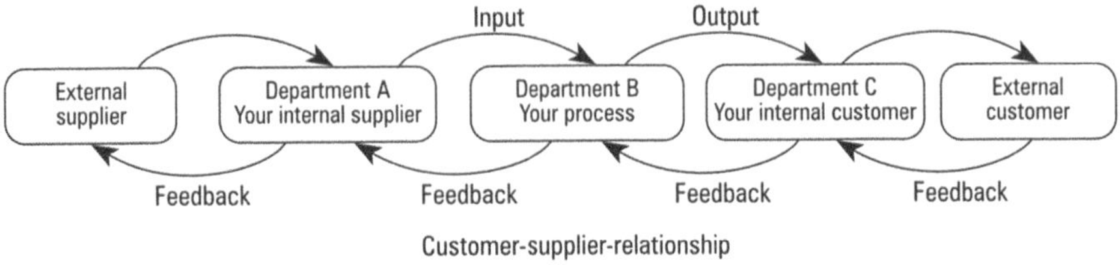

Fig. 6.2 Relations of internal customers and suppliers, cited by Rampersad (2001, p. 342)

Consequently, every employee who is part of this chain is an independent "production unit" that converts inputs from external or internal suppliers to the outflow (Bourada, 2007). Therefore, every employee of the organization contributes with adding added value to a service and delivering it to the next successive department by participating in its own way in the satisfaction of the external customer (Bourada, 2007, p. 71; Crosby, 1991, p. 11). This functional interaction of the organization is shown in Fig. 6.2.

To be clear, we will mention an example of the operation of a health-care institution. In the hospital department of food distribution to patients, employees are considered to be internal customers of the kitchen, while the kitchen is an internal customer of the supply department and an internal supplier, the waiter's employees. All of these may be providers of patients (internal customers of human resources), while patients are external clients of the hospital. If this supply chain works properly, it identifies the needs of customers in each stage, then the hospital will have the ability to adjust to the needs of patients/external customers. According to the philosophy of the TQM, the quality of the products (food) or "services" provided should be "satisfactory" and hence should meet the needs of the hospital's clients (Williams & Johnson, 2004). It should also be noted that in the health-care sector the "satisfaction" of the patient is a multidimensional concept, linked to many factors such as the infrastructure of the health-care institutions, the safety of the care, the bureaucratic process, the professional skills of the staff, etc. For this reason, Kamra et al. (2016) claimed that staff, patients, etc. need to be identified and analyzed, so as to have a plan of the administrative processes and clinical care.

Therefore, TQM's contribution is important because it puts end customers closer to each supply chain, because at all stages managers and employees will have to meet the needs of internal customers who represent the next chain link, which ultimately connects with the external client (in our case with the patient). Besides, as mentioned above, the primary goal of a health-care organization is to cover the patients' needs and expectations.

In terms of identifying the needs of patients and customers, whether they are satisfied with what they receive during health care can be done in a variety of ways such as quality indicators, questionnaires, interviews, etc. (Mylonaki & Markou, 2012).

To summarize, the effective operation of an organization is directly related to the existence of a high level of satisfaction for internal and external customers. Consequently, the importance of quality in a health-care organization is great and fundamental, because it is a factor of growth and survival.

6.5 Implementation of TQM in Health-Care Organizations

It is generally accepted that an economic unit is radically different from a health-care organization in terms of organization, operation, and production. Based on this, the question that arises is: Can the total quality methodology be applied to health-care organizations?

At first sight, one might argue that it is difficult, if not impossible, to implement the TQM in the field of health-care because:

- There is a huge difference between the "product" of a health-care unit and a construction company. A regular product, for example, has to pass a check of raw material control procedures, and the final product (outcome) should meet certain pre-agreed terms. This model cannot fit into health care because quality in the health-care sector is difficult to determine and measure. Distinct features of health care, such as heterogeneity and immateriality, make it difficult to determine and measure quality (Papavasiliou, 2018). Besides, human beings are not "standardized" and brought to health—and not only—a variety of empirical feelings and views that cannot be denied.
- In contrast to the company, the "customers" of the health-care institutions are a diverse set of patients, parents, doctors, employers, etc. Thus, meeting their needs often leads them to different views on what they expect from the health-care system of their country. Undoubtedly, social variations make it difficult for the management to design the health product.
- In contrast to businesses, there is a rigid pay system in public hospitals. This may inhibit (due to lack of incentives) attempts to improve the quality of health care.
- Health-care services are affected or even governed by political criteria, which is not the case in the private sector.

Despite the visible difficulties, a country's public hospitals—key health-care units—which predominantly provide the majority of health-care services have to apply the principles of TQM and include mechanisms to improve quality both before and after providing the necessary health-care services (Tountas, 2003). In the last few decades in many countries of the world, there is an attempt to promote the implementation of the TQM in public health-care systems. This choice is not a transitory social habit of the administration but a substantive solution to address the pathogenesis of administrative systems. Meanwhile, in the sensitive area of health care, it proposed an integrated management system and at the same time an evaluation of the action of administrators, which has been applied both to private health-care organizations and other public sector services. They have contributed decisively to strengthen their competitive capacity and innovative action while addressing adequately the requirements of citizens and patients (Mihailidou & Sakellariou, 2007; Zeithaml, 1988; Zink, 2007). Of course, in order for the above considerations to be realized, certain basic requirements should be fulfilled, such as:

- *The commitment of the health-care system*, at all managerial levels (national, regional, and local), because, as mentioned in the previous section, overall quality concerns all those working in the health-care sector. Regardless of their position, everyone is responsible for the proper performance of their own duties. Given that it is in the long run management in health-care institutions should have a fixed duration in order to be able to follow a specific health-care policy.
- *The existence of voluntary cooperation* between the organizational members is not something that is imposed by laws and ministerial circulars. On the contrary, team effort requires good human relations and a sense of responsibility that starts with managers in the central administration.
- *Changing the way of thinking of all staff*. This takes time to apply because there is a need for a change in methodology and approach, not just the behavior of staff. Also, there is a need for a change in the way health-care authorities operate. Medical staff, for example, need more encouragement and recognition of their efforts and less monitoring. It takes leadership to appreciate their work so as to motivate them to an even greater success. It needs motivation (material and moral) to inspire self-esteem and the quality of the heath-care process.
- *The health-care organization has a good leadership*. Appropriate leadership means that the manager of the health-care unit should (a) have vision and values, such as having the ability to get their message across to doctors, nurses, patients, and the wider community; (b) know that the pursuit of excellence and quality of work is not done behind an office, but by communicating with everyone in the health-care institution; (c) encourage and motivate all members of the health-care community so as to work within their capacities; and (d) be aware of what is more effective for medical and nursing staff (and administrators) to have responsibility and overseeing all projects instead of leaving a manager to deal with the issues in hand. However, the above characteristics of the manager of a health-care institution require meritocratic choice, long-term service, and of course a continuous training program on total quality management. It should be developed in agreement with its members and become a way of thinking. Changing the way of thinking of people in an entire health-care system is a process that takes time and is achieved through continuous training and transmitting all relevant information. It was not always easy to put the customer's wishes first. The message of quality improvement should reach people's thinking, and health care is only going to be a reality if employees are convinced that everyone (patients and employees) will benefit.

To summarize, the introduction and proper implementation of the TQM in the field of health care depends primarily on the political will, the way in which strategies are drawn up, and, of course, the economic resources that the government of a country intends to give. In this case, the TQM's contribution may prove to be crucial to the upgrading of the health-care services provided, as it contributes to the need of a better health-care services in a country and thus to the well-being of its citizens.

6.6 TQM and Sustainability

A sustainable health-care unit (and hence a hospital) continuously seeks to improve the quality of its health-care services for all (with no discrimination) over time, thus contributing to the development and welfare of society. It is a unit where all human and societal dimensions are interactive and draw power from one another. It is sustainable and effective when there is a correspondence between aims and results. In order for this to happen, constructive changes with collective actions and efforts are required. The way to enhance collective activities as well as the foundation for social substructure (i.e., the level of collectivity and teamwork) is through the organization itself since with its policy it can make organizational members be active participants in the policy-making process and therefore in the organizational sustainability.

Organizational sustainability (and leaders who are major proponents of it) needs to be at the heart of every organization (Fullan, 2005). Indeed, sustainable leadership is a key component for organizational sustainability that helps health-care unit to respond in a sustainable and efficient manner to the needs of patients by reinforcing and protecting the values and promoting "civil" health-care organizations (Saiti, 2016). The decision-making process in a sustainable organization stems from a civilized and democratic environment through the appropriate flow of information and sharing of knowledge among the organizational members.

It is true though that all health-care organizations operate in a very complicated environment with multiple internal and external factors. Consequently, it is not easy to determine common organizational aims. Furthermore, a health-care unit is not just an organization developing its social dynamic, "it is also an institution with an evaluative orientation which interacts with the wider social phenomena..." (Papanaum, 1995, p. 40). The most crucial factor for the sustainable functioning of a health-care unit is its leadership. This is because all other elements which are closely linked with sustainability and effective organizational performance—such as the organizational climate (motivation and communication between the staff members and the leader creates a positive organizational climate that positively influences the quality of health-care services), the cooperation between the hospital and patients (effective communication), and the relationship with the local authority—are a matter of organizational leadership. Hence, the sustained effectiveness of a leadership depends on the abilities of the managerial mechanism which programs, organizes, and coordinates all the actions of an organizational system.

Sustainable leadership is not static. It calls for internal communication among people within an organization. Network communications provide information on all the dynamic elements of a health-care unit. Continuous changes create problems in structures, while conflicts between economic, environmental, and societal factors create difficulties regarding issues of sustainable policy, the development of short-term motives, and long-term strategic planning. Therefore, a strong sustainable leadership is critical.

Quality in the health-care context is closely linked with the development of an efficient use of resources and performance appraisal so as to deliver high-quality services on a constant basis with the least possible cost. Therefore, for the organizational sustainability to be achieved, quality needs to be seriously considered. This means that in order for a health-care unit to be sustainable, it should achieve both efficiency and effectiveness. Many researchers such as Creech (1994) and others (Crawford & Shutler, 1999; Deming, 1986; Morgan & Murgatroyd, 1994; Mullins, 2010; Powell, 1995) have converged to the conclusion that total quality is mainly a philosophy rather than tools, techniques, and methods, which means that human resources is the key to the success of efficient and effective performance. Indeed, total quality management helps organizations (and hence health-care unit) to focus on strategy and thus to put the basis for an everlasting performance. The commitment to quality requires an intentional and continuous process. This means cohesion and continuity for the promotion and the enhancement of collaboration, the path toward sustainability. Thus, "all key elements of total quality are closely related to people. Hence, human resources may be considered as an "asset" for an organization rather than a "liability" as it is through a challenging and satisfying working environment, the development of knowledge and skills, the active involvement and participation of people, and the commitment and application of new ideas that human resource management and quality management converge on total quality" (cited by Saiti, 2012, p. 111).

Indeed, cohesion is an absolutely necessary requirement for organizational sustainability because without it, the health-care unit's effectiveness is substantially reduced. Effectiveness refers to the solving of problems and consequently the delivering of qualitative health-care services. Hence, it encompasses (1) *efficiency*, for which available resources (both human and material) need to be gathered together and used effectively in order to respond directly to the challenges and needs, and (2) *effectiveness* which calls for problems to be identified and solutions found. These two elements (efficiency and effectiveness) require balance and certainly need to be maintained if a health-care unit (and hence a hospital) is to perform successfully. Moreover, all aspects of communication should be a leader's top priority to ensure that (1) staff members have the right mentality for achieving the organizational goals and (2) the head is in control of the working environment.

Based on the above, sustainability, in its definition, calls for continuity in the satisfaction of human needs and expectations, and only people can make this happen. Total quality management, even in the context of health care, calls for the satisfaction of patient needs, while the achievement of efficiency and effective performance can be achieved only if the health-care unit is patient-centered. Therefore, the two are connected.

References

Alexiadis, A., & Sigalas, I. (1999). *Health care services/hospital: Characteristics and challenges* (Vol. D). Patra, Greece: Hellenic Open University Publications. (in Greek).

Bourada, A. (2007) *Total Quality Management in Business. and in the provision of services. Investigation of the relation satisfaction of both internal and external customers.* PhD Thesis, University of Piraeus, Piraeus (in Greek).

Bouradas, D. (2001). *Management.* Athens, Greece: Benou Publications. (in Greek).

Bouradas, D. (2005). *Leadership.* Athens, Greece: Kritiki Publishing. (in Greek).

Chassin, M., & Galvin, R. (1998). The urgent need to improve health care quality. *JAMA, 11*(3), 1000–1005.

Crawford, L. E. D., & Shutler, P. (1999). Total quality management in education: Problems issues for the classroom teacher. *The International Journal of Educational Management, 13*(2), 67–72.

Creech, B. (1994). *The 5 pillars of TQM: How to make total quality management work for you.* New York: Plume.

Crosby, L. A. (1991). Expanding the role of CSM in total quality. *International Journal of Industry Management, l2*(2), 5–19.

Danos, A., & Danos, S. (2009). The continuous improvement of quality in the National Health care system. *Dioikitiki Enimerosi, 51*, 65–76. (in Greek).

Dayton, N. (2003). *The demise of total quality management* (TQM). *The TQM Magazine, 15*(6), 391–396.

Deming, W. E. (1986). *Out of crisis: Quality productivity and competitive position.* Cambridge, MA: Cambridge University Press.

Dervitsiotis, K. (2001). *Competitiveness in total quality management.* Athens, Greece: Interbooks Publishing. (in Greek).

Desai, V. V. (2011). Patient satisfaction and service quality dimensions. *Advances in Management, 4*(5), 40–45.

Edosomwan, J. A. (1993). *Customer and market-driven quality management.* Milwaukee: ASOC Quality Press.

Edvardsson, B., Thomasson, B., & Ovretveit, J. (1994). *Quality of service.* New York: McGraw-Hill Inc..

Evans, J., & Dean, J. (1999). *Total quality: Management, organization, and strategy.* Cincinnati, OH: South-Western College Publications.

Fullan, M. (2005). *Leadership & sustainability.* London: Corwin Press.

Handy, C. (1981). *Understanding organizations.* London: Penguin Publishing.

Hendriks, A. A. J., Vrielink, M. R., Smets, E. M. A. v. E. S. Q., & De Haes, J. C. (2001). Improving the assessment of (in) patients' satisfaction with hospital care. *Medical Care, 39*(3), 270–283.

Hytiris, S., & Anninos, N. (2015). *Management and service quality.* Athens, Greece: Sindesmos Ellinikon Akadimaikon Vivliothikon. (in Greek).

Juran, J. (1988). *Planning for quality.* New York: The Free Press.

Kamra, V., Singh, H., & Kumar De, K. (2016). Factors affecting patient satisfaction an exploratory study for quality management in the health-care sector. *Total Quality Management & Business Excellence, 27*(9–10), 1013–1027.

Kanji, G. K. (1996). Implementation and pitfalls of total quality management. *Total Quality Management, 7*(3), 331–343.

Katz, D., & Kahn, R. (1978). *The social psychology of organizations* (2nd ed.). New York: John Willey.

Kefis, V. (2005). *Integrated management.* Athens, Greece: Kritiki Publishing. (in Greek).

Kronenfeld, J. (2006). Access, quality and satisfaction. Three critical concepts in health services and health care delivery. In J. J. Kronenfeld (Ed.), *Access, quality and satisfaction with care: concerns of patients, providers and insurers. research in the sociology of health care* (Vol. 24, pp. 3–14). Bingley, UK: Emerald Group Publishing Limited.

Lee, V. H., Doi, K. B., Tan, B. I., & Chong, A. (2010). A structural analysis of the relationship between TQM practices and product innovation. *Asian Journal of Technology Innovation, 18*(1), 73–96.
Logothetis, N. (1992). *Total quality management: From Deming to Taguchi and the statistical control of processes*. Athens, Greece: Tom Hellas LTD. (in Greek).
Malamou, T. (2016). The implementation methodology of total quality management in health services, as a best practice operation. *Elliniko Periodiko Nosilevtikis Epistimis, 9*(3), 6–15. (in Greek).
Marley, K., Collier, D., & Goldstein, M. (2004). The role of clinical and process quality in achieving patient satisfaction in hospitals. *Decision Sciences, 35*(3), 349–369.
Maru, D. S., Andrews, J., Shwarz, R., Acharva, B., Ramaiya, A., Karelas, G., et al. (2012). Crossing the quality chasm in resource-limited settings. *Global Health, 8*, 41. Retrieved from https://www.ncbi.nlm.nih.gov/pmc/articles/PMC3526495/pdf/1744-8603-8-41.pdf (online 5 pages)
Michos, T. (1994). Systems of Quality insurance. *Dimosios Tomeas, 102*, 40. (in Greek).
Mihailidou, A., & Sakellariou, G. (2007). Quality management in the public health care: The experience of the nephrology department in "Papageorgiou". *Elliniki. Nefrología, 19*(1), 40–50. (in Greek).
Mills, P. K., & Ungson, G. R. (2001). Internal market structures substitutes for hierarchies. *Journal of Service Research, 3*(3), 252–264.
Mishra, D. P. (1995). Total quality management in health services. Historical development, conceptual meaning and comprehensive model. *Journal of Ambulatory Care Marketing, 5*(2), 27–46.
Morgan, C., & Murgatroyd, S. (1994). *Total quality management in the public sector*. Buckingham, VA: Open University Press.
Mullins, L. J. (2010). *Management and organisational behavior* (9th ed.). London: Prentice Hall.
Murgatroyd, S., & Morgan, C. C. (1993). *Total quality management and the school*. London: Open University Press.
Mylonaki, K. & Markou, Z. (2012). *Total Quality Management in the field of health care*. Master Thesis, Upper Technological Educational Institution of Ionian Islands, Lefkada, Greece (in Greek).
Oakland, J. S. (1989). *Total quality management*. Oxford: Heinemann Professional.
Papakostidi, A., & Tsoukalas, N. (2012). The quality of health care services and its assessment. *Arheia Ellinikis Iatrikis, 29*(4), 480–488. (in Greek).
Papanaum, Z. I. (1995). *School leadership*. Thessaloniki, Greece: Kyriakidi Publishing. (in Greek).
Papavasiliou F. (2018). *Total quality management in the health care. The provided health care services in public hospitals of Attika prefecture based on the expectations and attitudes of the staff*. Master Thesis, Hellenic Open University, Patra, Greece (in Greek).
Powell, T. C. (1995). Total quality management as competitive advantage: A review and empirical study. *Strategic Management Journal, 16*(1), 15–37.
Rampersad, H. (2001). 75 painful question about your customer satisfaction. *The TQM Management, 13*(5), 341–347.
Ruckert, W. R., & Walker, O. C. (1987). Marketing's interaction with other functional units: A conceptual frame work and empirical evidence. *Journal of Marketing, 51*(1), 1–19.
Saha, G. C., & Theingi. (2009). Service quality, satisfaction, and behavioral intentions: A study of low-cost airline carriers in Thailand. *Managing Service Quality, 19*(3), 350–372.
Sahney, S., Banwet, D. K., & Karunes, S. (2004). Customer requirement constructs: The premise for TQM in education. *International Journal of Productivity and Performance Management, 53*(6), 499–520.
Saiti, A. (2012). Leadership and quality management: An analysis of three key features of the Greek education system. *Quality Assurance in Education, 20*(2), 110–138.
Saiti, A. (2016). Social capital dimensions: Social justice, morality and the common good. In R. Papa & A. Saiti (Eds.), *Building for a sustainable future in our schools: Brick by brick* (pp. 3–13). Cham, Switzerland: Springer.
Sallis, E. (2002). *Total quality management in education* (3rd ed.). Oxford: Routledge Publishing.

Schermerhorn, J.R. (Jr) (2011). Introduction to management. 11th ed. Hoboken, NJ: John Wiley & Sons.

Sodani, P. R., Kumar, R. K., Srivastava, J., & Sharma, L. (2010). Measuring patient satisfaction: A case study to improve quality of care at public health facilities. *Indian Journal of Community Medicine, 35*(1), 52–56.

Tahir, M., Nawaz, S., Butt, M. Z., & Mahmood, F. A. K. T. (2012). In-patient perceptions, needs, expectations and satisfaction within tertiary care settings. *Journal of Pharmaceutical Sciences and Research, 4*(12), 2025–2031.

Talib, F. (2013). An overview of total quality management understanding the fundamentals in service organization. *International Journal of Advanced Quality Management, 1*(1), 1–20.

Talib, F., & Rahman, Z. (2010). Critical success factors of TQM in service organizations: A proposed model. *Services Marketing Quarterly, 31*(3), 363–380.

Talib, F., Rahman, Z., & Azam, M. (2011). Best practices of total quality management implementation in health care settings. *Health Marketing Quarterly, 28*(3), 232–252.

Tountas, G. (2003). The meaning of quality in medical science and health care services. *Arheia Ellinikis Iatrikis, 20*(5), 532–546.

Verma, D. S., & Khandelwal, U. (2011). Consumers' preferences towards service industry: A factorial study of health care industry. *International Journal of Multidisciplinary Research, 1*(8), 83–89.

Williams, K., & Johnson, B. (2004). *Introducing management: A development guide*. Great Britain, UK: Planta Tree.

Zavlanos, M. (1998). *Management*. Athens, Greece: Ellin Publishing. (in Greek).

Zavlanos, M. (2003). *Total quality in education*. Athens, Greece: Stamouli Publishing. (in Greek).

Zeithaml, V. A. (1988). Consumer perceptions of price, quality and value: A means – End model and synthesis of evidence. *Journal of Marketing, 52*(3), 2–2.

Zink, K. J. (2007). From total quality management to corporate sustainability based on a stakeholder management. *Journal of Management History, 13*(4), 394–401.

Chapter 7
For-Profit Versus Not-For-Profit Hospitals and Public Hospitals

Key Concepts

1. The health-care service is not a commercial service but is a service that promotes social prosperity and society's well-being. No matter the type of hospital ownership, the ultimate goal of a hospital is to function in a most efficient way possible so as to serve society's interests and needs more efficiently.
2. All types of hospital ownership (for-profit, non-profit, and public) are accountable to society. While all types may have a surplus, public and non-profit institutions do not distribute their profits among staff members but reinvest them in improving the quality of the health-care services they provide. On the contrary, private for-profit hospitals distribute their profits to the owners.
3. Private non-profit and public hospitals exhibit many similarities, while any differences may be identified in the mission and the actions developed to achieve that mission.
4. The main difference between private for-profit and the other two types of ownership (namely, public and private non-profit) is that the latter types focus on the better covering of social needs, while their private for-profit counterparts focus on increasing their economic potential.
5. No matter the political system, a government focuses on the quality of the health-care services provided to all social groups (with absolutely no discrimination) and on the promotion of social interest. All types of hospital ownership operate within a legislative framework that has been established by the State and determines the context in which health care is developed, both as a public and as a private asset.

M. Chletsos, A. Saiti, *Strategic Management and Economics in Health Care*,
https://doi.org/10.1007/978-3-030-35370-4_7

7.1 Introduction

The relevant literature indicates that spending on the two most important sectors of the economy, namely, education and health care, contributes significantly to improving the quality of work and consequently to increasing the national product. In addition, the increased productivity of a country's human resources provides a fundamental boost to its social and economic development.

With reference to health care, it is argued that the spending made by the State in this area is considered to be an "investment in human capital and therefore a way for productivity in the economy to grow. Better health increases the quality of the workforce and makes workers more active. Disease control can revitalize areas that people have avoided because of the potential health risks. Ridding a region of diseases may release future wealth from the resources of the region" (Skountzos, 2005, p. 244).

The term "health," in its broadest sense, is perceived as the state of complete physical, mental, spiritual, and social well-being and not only the absence of disease or disability (Kontaratos, 2003; WHO, 1946). Within this framework, health is the most precious asset that a human can possess and, at the same time, is the basis of the prosperity and progress of a country. As public health is so important, its protection must be a top priority for all governments since the social and economic development of any society without a healthy population is not feasible (Sloan, 2000; Vaillancourt Rosenau, 2003). This priority has forced governments to set up rules that define the context in which health care can develop, both as a public and a private asset (Bay, 1979; Chou, 2002; Kekatos, 2010; Newhouse, 2002; Sloan, 2000; Steinberg, 2003; Vaillancourt Rosenau, 2003). In many countries this has taken the form of a national health-care system.

The product of a legislative framework for social policy was the establishment of health-care organizations called hospitals or health-care institutions (Feldstein, 1967; Sloan, 2000; Steinberg, 2003; Theil, 1952; Vaillancourt Rosenau, 2003). In a societal context, a hospital is the cornerstone of the health-care system in every country and is perceived as "a small social system organized specifically for the accomplishment of a specific project: the restoration of health" (Kontaratos, 2003, p. 51). Due to the extremely sensitive nature of the health-care services it provides, the main task of a hospital is to satisfy the social needs of citizens. For this reason, historically speaking, health-care services used to be provided by charitable institutions (Sloan, 2000; Vaillancourt Rosenau, 2003). However, several decades ago this situation changed. Health-care services started to be provided by for-profit organizations, and this entry into the so-called "health-care" market brought several changes in the field of health care. The most important changes to have occurred were the introduction of competition and the emergence of different perspectives on a hospital's priorities, responsibilities, and effectiveness. Indeed, due to the sensitive nature of the health care, these differences in the perception of effectiveness brought to the surface a new challenge, giving rise to a new entity (which, before for-profit organizations entered the field of health care, was taken for granted), namely, the public trust (Hirth, 1999; Rodrigues, Trigg, Schmidt, & Leichsenring, 2014; Sloan, 2000; Vaillancourt Rosenau, 2003).

Depending on the way health-care services are funded, organized, produced, and distributed, hospitals are categorized as either public or private. Private hospitals can be further distinguished into non-profit and for-profit hospitals. However, they all have multiple goals:

- To provide health care to patients that enter them.
- To implement health policy and protect patients (e.g., through vaccinations, etc.).
- To ensure staff are highly trained and up to date with the latest developments in medical science and nursing practices (Ballou & Weisbrod, 2003; Bay, 1979; Goering, 2007; Hunter, 2006; Intzesiloglou, 1992; Pappa, 2016; Sarros, Coopen, & Santoro, 2011; Vaillancourt Rosenau, 2003). This means that hospitals offer not only health-related services but also valuable knowledge to further the evolution of medical science.

In order to achieve its goals and objectives, a hospital should function effectively. For this to happen, certain conditions should be met (Bay, 1979; Machlup, 1967; Moore, 2000; Vaillancourt Rosenau, 2003):

- Capable leadership. Both the head and the members of the hospital's board of directors should have all the requisite qualifications, knowledge, experience, and personality that are consistent with the operation of a hospital.
- The appropriate human resources (medical, nursing, administrative, etc.) necessary for running a hospital.
- Harmonious cooperation between and among all stakeholders (managers, doctors, nurses, other support staff) and across departments.
- The necessary substructure, for example, the availability of the essential material resources (buildings, furnishings, technological equipment, etc.).

Despite the importance of hospitals, health protection is currently in crisis in many countries whose hospitals (and their equivalents) are in a stage of transition. This crisis has a global dimension, although its roots and depth vary from country to country. We might consider that this crisis in the health-care sector may be the result of high health-care costs and disruptions to health-care systems. Any such disruptions can be attributed to factors such as a lack of coordinated control, insufficient financial resources, a lack of rationalization and management of financial resources, and/or a lack of adequate and appropriate health-care staff (Bay, 1979; Bayindir, 2012; Kessler & McClellan, 2002; Kuttner, 1999). Indeed, with questions being raised about prospects for development in the health-care sector, hospital ownership becomes a very important issue as hospitals tackle structural problems and increasing health-care costs that perhaps have been intensified due to the global economic crisis. Ways need to be found that will facilitate a hospital's smoother, more efficient functioning so as to be sustainable and satisfy the needs of citizens more effectively.

In this chapter we will examine the assets of public, for-profit, and non-profit hospitals, what the theory says about each type of hospital, and the role the government could play when different types of hospitals coexist.

7.2 Hospital Ownership

In the previous section, we mentioned that the hospital is the basic unit of a country's health-care system, offering not only health care but also medical specialization and wider health-care education. At the same time, however, the hospital is a social organization that is active within its social environment, i.e., hospitals affect, and are affected by, society.

Within this framework, system theory considers a hospital to be a system that is open and influential and, in turn, emits outflows (health-care services) within a wider system. Therefore, it is considered as a subsystem that operates within the wider system (the social environment). It works in the social field to achieve goals, and its basic mission is to care for people who are in need of its health-care services.

In order for a hospital to harmonize its functions and processes, which is necessary for the achievement of its objectives, it uses a set of principles and tools. From this perspective, the hospital is an organization of a socio-technical nature, since the contribution of various material or intangible resources (e.g., money, information, etc.) is a supplement to the human factor. The term "property" is defined as the sum of the economic goods, the tangible (such as buildings, machinery, etc.) and intangible (such as reputation, knowledge, etc.), and applies to all organizations, both public or private (Baumol & Bowen, 1965; Bayindir, 2012; Georgiadis, 1967; Marwell & McInerney, 2005; Rothenberg, 1951; Sloan, 2000; Vaillancourt Rosenau, 2003).

The inherent attributes of an organization (and hence a hospital, whether public, non-profit, or for-profit) can be distinguished into material and nonmaterial, directly productive and indirectly productive (i.e., those that contribute indirectly to the care process), fixed assets (buildings, etc.), portable (medicines, etc.), and monetary (budgets, deposits, bills, etc.) (Bay, 1979; Bayindir, 2012; Georgiadis, 1967; Vaillancourt Rosenau, 2003).

By focusing on the organization of a hospital, we may observe the following resources in its internal environment:

Human resources: The human factor is the most important element in the analysis of its internal environment and contributes substantially to the achievement of the stated goals and to the implementation of the proposed strategies by the top management of the health-care system. Human resources are those that help all the other tangible elements in a hospital to function.

The human resources (medical, nursing, administrative, etc.) constitute the only living and dynamic element in the health-care unit with desires, feelings, values, and habits that determine a hospital's behavior.

Based on the above, the central administration of the hospital should:

- Acquire the employees that are necessary
- Put the right people in the right place, since know-how is a strategic resource for the sustainability and growth of the organization and is concentrated in the minds of the staff
- Provide incentives for effective human performance, leading to acceptable levels of labor productivity
- Assess the performance of each employee

Material resources (natural resources): The resources of a hospital include facilities and mechanical equipment and are characterized by a lasting use. It should be noted that the main factors determining the type and geographical position of the hospital are the demand for health-care services by the population of the wider region, the supply of health-care services by competition, the availability and the cost of land, and the proximity of the location to major roads (Bay, 1979; Kontaratos, 2003; Leone & Van Horn, 2005; Vaillancourt Rosenau, 2003).

Technological resources are resources that relate to the level of technology applied in a hospital. The management has to choose the appropriate technological equipment for the health-care organization in relation to its objectives and the capacity of the human resources to use the equipment. For example, biomedical equipment is the most effective tool currently available in medical science for the detection, diagnosis, and treatment of diseases as well as for the rehabilitation of patients. However, in order for the equipment to work properly and efficiently, the institution must have the appropriately trained staff to use it.

The financial resources: All public and private organizations need funding for both their existing functions and their future development. In the field of health care:

- Public hospitals are funded out of revenues stemming mainly from the State budget and the budget for public investment. They act as public agencies and, because of globalization, they face financing problems combined with time-consuming bureaucratic procedures that do not allow for the prompt acquisition of biomedical technologies or other modern equipment and consequently are slow to respond to the increasing demand for high-level diagnostic services.
- Non-profit hospitals receive income in the form of donations, social security contributions, and private payments. This is a mixed financing system with no distribution of profits.
- The for-profit hospitals are only funded by one or more owners who are also responsible for the sustainability of the hospital. They operate based on the principles of a private legislative framework and the dynamics of the market while their main purpose is profit. However, if it is acceptable by the owners of the hospital (since the earnings are distributed to the owners), the money earned can be invested in human resource education, research, new equipment, and social contributions.

The flow of information: In the case of hospitals, information refers to the status of all those factors relating to the hospital's internal and external environment. The gathering of information helps the hospital administration to make the right decisions or better adapt to new medical data. This is particularly important if we consider that the efficient and effective performance of the modern hospital is based on the intense, valid, timely, and continuous interdisciplinary exchange of information that only the establishment of an integrated hospital information system can ensure today.

To sum up the above considerations, we may note that all types of hospital operate under the same working environments. However, there are differences in their operating costs and their effectiveness. This differentiation should be investigated in terms of their organization and administration and in terms of the human factor. For example, is the hospital staffed (from the head of the organization to the last employee) according to the principles of human resource management?

To conclude, whether or not a hospital will achieve its goals depends not only on its finances but also on the ability of the administration to effectively manage the available resources of the hospital.

It has been mentioned above that, with the health-care sector in many countries facing problems, attempts are being made to achieve better results through different organizational forms of ownership. For this reason, in recent decades a new type of organizational form has been developed which is a hybrid form of ownership in between that of the public and private sectors. The main reason for this collaboration in the health-care sector is to overcome the disadvantages of each type of organizational form and to enhance the advantages of each form through the efficient utilization of the available resources, so as to result in the provision of better qualitative health-care services.

Indeed, in recent years, more countries have adopted this new hybrid organizational form of hospital ownership. The coexistence of the public and private sectors in one hospital may bring a balance between the disadvantages and the advantages of these sectors and provide more competition in terms of quality health-care services. This collaboration is based on a better distribution of risk between the two sectors (public and private) in such a way that it can be handled according to the capacity of each one (Anagnostopoulos, 2005; Barr, 2007; Brogaard & Petersen, 2018; Languille, 2017; Nikolic & Maikisch, 2006; Pomeroy, 2008). For the hospital, this results in a more efficient economic behavior. The public form of a hospital, due to its public and social character, has quality as an advantage and takes on the risk of offering high-cost health-care services. However, due to low motivation, complicated bureaucratic procedures, and interventions of the State, they cannot easily follow technological progress or acquire new infrastructure in order to properly adjust to the new technological environment (Anagnostopoulos, 2005). The private form of hospital ownership, on the other hand, is more economically efficient in terms of its orientation, it does not take on the high risk of offering complicated and high-cost health-care services, while attempts to increase the monetary benefits may be attributed to the owners (as they are likely to be more concerned with the distribution of profits) (Brogaard & Petersen, 2018; Johnston & Finegood, 2015; Nikolic & Maikisch, 2006; Torchia, Calabrò, & Morner, 2015). Through this collaboration, the expectation is to bring a balance in the hospital's priorities and to secure the sustainability of the institution.

Certainly this coexistence is a complicated process because too many agents are involved in pursuing the desired outcome. From the public sector's perspective, the priority is to reassure the public interest and the common good of society, while for the private sector, it is profit. It is a challenge to have these two concurrently since the quality of the health-care services provided cannot easily be determined or measured, while in such collaborations any reimbursement can happen only when the investment (which in this case is high risk) brings some income (Barr, 2007; Johnston & Finegood, 2015; Nikolic & Maikisch, 2006; Pomeroy, 2008; Sekhri, Feachem, & Ni, 2011). However, despite these difficulties and complications, the private sector tends to take the risk of such an investment as it has a motive—the assurance of economic efficiency—while the public sector proceeds with such collaborations since it can achieve lower production costs and at the same time has control of the project in terms of the monitoring of the hospital's performance and responsiveness regarding social needs and interests.

To conclude, health care is not a commercial service. Furthermore, no matter the form of ownership, the ultimate goal of a hospital is to promote the satisfaction of social needs and social justice and certainly not to increase its economic potential. It is true that changes in the forms of ownership are implemented in the name of "quality improvement" so as to develop a more effective way of serving societal interests. However, we should not forget that no matter the form of hospital ownership, the focus should be on the hospital's social responsibility and its commitment to serve social interests and needs.

7.3 What Makes a For-Profit Hospital: What the Theory Says

Private hospitals are divided into for-profit and non-profit. Regardless of whether a hospital is for-profit or non-profit, it aims to return patients to good health. This means that, beyond any economic objectives, due to the prospect of good health offered by a hospital, the purpose of any type of hospital also includes a social dimension. The performance of private for-profit hospitals is based on the earnings and the maximization of efficiency. The primary concern of private for-profit hospitals is that good health is a private good (Chletsos, 2011; Duggan, 2002; Kaye, Harrington, & LaPlante, 2010; Nett, 1993). Therefore, the function of this type of hospital is based on the dynamics of the health-care market. In addition, the for-profit hospital considers that the health-care user has all the necessary information about the quality of the health-care services and the quantity he/she wants to consume. The primary source of revenue for a private for-profit hospital is the sale of health-care services to users who wish to purchase services (Duggan, 2002; Moore, 2000). Such hospitals focus on the efficiency of their health-care services to make them more cost-effective and user-friendly, since greater efficiency means more profit. Hence, for-profit hospitals are primarily interested in the swift identification and satisfaction of their users' needs.

The strategy for the operation of for-profit hospitals is based on cost-efficient economic behavior, with profits distributed to shareholders (Bay, 1979; Bayindir, 2012; Horwitz & Nichols, 2009). Maximizing hospital welfare is the hospital's primary goal without compromising the well-being of users, staff, and suppliers. In addition, user satisfaction is the key to the sustainability of the hospital. Within this framework, the social goal of for-profit hospitals is to maximize user satisfaction and the benefits derived from this satisfaction.

With reference to earnings, private hospitals have more margins for increased profits, since they operate in a competitive environment and have access to capital markets, which allows for more efficient pricing (Bayindir, 2012; Forsberg, Montagu, & Sundewall, 2011; Goering, 2007; Layton, Ellis, McGuire, & Van Kleef, 2017; Patouillard, Goodman, Hanson, & Mills, 2007; Rosenthal & Newbrander, 1996). A private for-profit hospital has the potential to minimize complex bureaucratic procedures and thus speed up the decision-making process. By drafting and implementing a business plan, it can accelerate the pace with which health-care services are provided and reduce the waiting and retention time of patients.

The competitive environment in which profit-making hospitals operate (particularly their coexistence with non-profit and public hospitals) is forcing them to maximize user satisfaction in order to provide added value. This constitutes the basis for the sustainability of any for-profit hospital. Due to its focus on service efficiency and profit sharing, a profit-making hospital usually provides less specialized health-care services so as to achieve cost savings.

The type of hospital a user chooses is based on their financial capacity, their insurance cover, and/or the type of treatment they need. Usually, users who choose a for-profit hospital are insured and therefore have (at least a substantial part of) their health-care costs covered.

For-profit hospitals attract more profitable patients by the quality of health-care services they provide. However, since the operation of for-profit hospitals is based on patterns of demand, if the demand for their quality health-care services is not as expected, then it is more likely that less emphasis will be put on quality (Baumol & Bowen, 1965; Bay, 1979; Horwitz & Nichols, 2009; Newhouse, 1970, 2002; Zhao, 2016). Certainly, for-profit hospitals offer a mixture of services, and the efficiency of service quality refers to the entire package of this mixture.

Attracting more profitable users of health-care services enables for-profit hospitals to increase their market share, thus securing their sustainability and increasing their profits. Of course, the latter will only occur if the revenue from the provision of services exceeds the cost of the treatments (Duggan, 2002; Horwitz & Nichols, 2009; Layton et al., 2017; Newhouse, 1970, 2002; Sloan, 2000).

Based on the above, a common factor among all types of for-profit hospitals is their sustainability, the efficient continuity of their operation, and the satisfaction of their users' needs. In addition, the sustainable operation of such hospitals depends on their interaction with society, the level of service, the social benefits, and the perceived value. Social prosperity is of interest to all types of hospitals. What is changing is the perception of social prosperity. Private for-profit hospitals perceive social well-being through the efficient allocation and optimal use of their available resources. They recognize social justice but at the same time perceive that the health-care market is functioning in the same way as the markets for other private goods. Thus, consumer demand for health-care services is influenced by users' incomes, while the cost of those services is determined according to their supply and demand.

7.4 What Makes a Non-profit Hospital: What the Theory Says

The type of organization plays an essential role for the mission and purpose of that organization. Indeed, depending on their type, organizations aim to plan and maintain a stability in the functions of their work. The source of finance is what determines the type of ownership of the organization. Based on the theory, organizations are broadly distinguished into public and private (Bjorvatn, 2018; Hunter, 2006; Marwell & McInerney, 2005; Moore, 2000). No matter the type of organization (hospital), all organizations implement a strategy and adapt the organization (in a controlled manner) to environmental changes. Regarding private non-profit hospitals, they exhibit many similarities to public ones, and the differences between them are identified in the mission and the actions developed to achieve this mission (Bjorvatn, 2018; Hunter, 2006; Marwell & McInerney, 2005; Moore, 2000). Private non-profit hospitals are characterized by a homogeneity in their organization, while more strict policies are applied so that they develop customer relationships, particularly with their financial contributors (Cornelius, Todres, Janjuha-Jivraj, Woods, & Wallace, 2008; Haugh, 2012; Kondilis, Antonopoulou, & Benos, 2008; Stevens, Moray, Bruneel, & Clarysse, 2015).

Private non-profit hospitals work for the good of the community and their financial contributors. The latter is because non-profit private hospitals have donors or sponsors as their main source of funding, and hence there is a dependency relationship with them (Brown & Moore, 2001; Lewis, 2002, 2003; Spyridaki, 2008). A common point that could be identified regarding public hospitals and private non-profit hospitals is their interaction with society, particularly in terms of social support and acceptance by the community; in a sense, they are accountable to society. Private non-profit hospitals in particular have profits that cannot be distributed to the owners or key shareholders of the hospital. Hence, there is no profit distribution (Bjorvatn, 2018; Horwitz & Nichols, 2009; Moscelli, Gravelle, Siciliani, & Gutackor, 2018). This is because any profit is used to help achieve the basic purpose of a non-profit hospital, which is social cohesion and the well-being of the community. So a private non-profit hospital has the ultimate goal of solidarity and the provision of health-care services to citizens in order to maximize social values—a process which benefits the community. The purpose of private non-profit (and public) hospitals is therefore purely social.

Moreover, private non-profit hospitals, due to their social character, have a responsibility toward society. As a source of health-care services mainly for citizens with limited income capacity, private non-profit hospitals are seen as promoters of prosperity and social equality. Indeed, the "health" good is a social good and all citizens have a right to access it (Chletsos, 2011; Goering, 2007; Haugh, 2012; Horwitz & Nichols, 2007, 2009; Hunter, 2006; Ifantopoulos, 2006; Leone & Van Horn, 2005; Sloan, 2000; Stevens et al., 2015). Therefore, private non-profit hospitals also have a humanitarian character, which is fulfilled through charitable contributions (Machlup, 1967; Marwell & McInerney, 2005). For this reason, and because of the dependency relationship with their financial contributors, private non-profit hospitals are accountable to society regarding how the financial resources are managed and how they are being used to achieve their goals. Certainly, private non-profit hospitals are also accountable to their financial contributors for the same reason.

Based on the above, private non-profit hospitals are required to have control mechanisms on a systematic basis that will result in better decisions and more transparent procedures and collaborations and so further improve efficiency (Horwitz & Nichols, 2009; Jordan & VanTuijl, 2006; Lee, 2004; Leone & Van Horn, 2005). This in turn facilitates careful management of their financial resources, enhances their self-awareness of the services they offer, nurtures a philosophy of governance that is free of any corruption, and builds a foundation for qualitative performance in their projects, namely, effectiveness. Certainly, the issue of efficiency and effectiveness is not just a function of economic factors. It is linked to the hospitals' impact on society. Because of their special type of funding and their humanitarian nature, private non-profit hospitals should constantly provide society with evidence of their work and maintain a climate of mutual respect and confidence in the assessment of their results.

Private non-profit hospitals are organizations that play an active role in communities, and their action is linked to social benefits. These hospitals have a special relationship and cooperation with local actors, since their activities are part of the social services sector. For this reason, private non-profit hospitals are open to voluntary contributions in order to help meet the demand from society for effective health-care services (Brown & Moore, 2001; Kaye et al., 2010; Lewis, 2002, 2003; Liarikos, 2008; Rodrigues et al., 2014; Spyridaki, 2008).

Efficiency in the provision of health-care services is not easily achieved, as the effects of their action are not immediately apparent. Nevertheless, it remains a challenge for hospitals of this type. Due to the social and humanitarian nature of such hospitals and the sensitivity of the sector in which they operate (health), ongoing efforts are needed to win and maintain trust. The key to building trust and social equity lies in the consistency of their services, a close cooperation with the community, and a constant effort to improve the quality of their services.

Another issue that arises in relation to a hospital's organization type is resource efficiency and the pricing of its health-care services. Private non-profit hospitals (like public hospitals) are not competitive and have no business plan (Horwitz & Nichols, 2009; Hughes & Luksetich, 2010; Kessler & McClellan, 2001; Pauly, 1987). The funding they receive is mainly used to sustain the provision of the health-care services they offer, while the primary users of these services, who are usually not able to pay for their health care, come from a larger pool of potential users (Ballou & Weisbrod, 2003; Horwitz & Nichols, 2009; Hughes & Luksetich, 2010; Hunter, 2006; Moscelli et al., 2018; Preston, 1988).

However, it is well known that, in order for a hospital (or indeed any organization) to be effective, it needs to achieve its goals with a minimum of cost and effort. In order for a private non-profit (or public) hospital to offer its services to the community and at the same time ensure its sustainability as an organization, the production cost of providing health-care services must be kept low so that the selling price can also be low. However, in the particular case of private non-profit hospitals, the relationship between price and cost tends to be negative because the cost of meeting social needs often exceeds the price of health-care services due to the limited ability of users to pay for these services (Horwitz & Nichols, 2009; Leone & Van Horn, 2005). They often cover this shortfall by channeling the funds received by donors or hospital sponsors into the production costs so that they do not operate at a loss. Furthermore, they often need to subsidize the health-care services provided in order to survive in the market (Horwitz & Nichols, 2009; Leone & Van Horn, 2005; Moore, 2000). Certainly, private hospitals (for-profit and non-profit) generally provide fewer services than public hospitals, while the health-care services offered are specialized and low cost. The sustainability of private non-profit hospitals as organizations is their main priority, but at the same time their ultimate goal is to consolidate social values. The efficient financial management of these hospitals is a goal but not a top priority in their mission. Indeed, it is of interest for these types of hospitals to have a good financial return with transparency in the way they manage their financial resources, but what matters most is to ensure they are able to meet social needs. Ultimately, however, they can achieve their goal only by securing their economic sustainability.

According to theory, the economic behavior of private non-profit hospitals depends on the nature of the market and on the policy and strategy of a country's health-care system. With reference to the nature of the market, what is important is whether private non-profit hospitals operate in an environment where competition is dominated by for-profit hospitals, that is, whether or not the market is more profitable. There are three basic theories that could be mentioned regarding the economic behavior of non-profit hospitals (Horwitz & Nichols, 2007, 2009; Leone & Van Horn, 2005). The first theory aims to maximize the output of non-profit hospitals. According to this theory (and taking into account that there is no distribution of profits to financial contributors), a non-profit hospital will maximize its provision of health-care services as long as its profits amount to zero (Baumol & Bowen, 1965; Horwitz & Nichols, 2009; Newhouse, 1970; Pauly, 1987; Rothenberg, 1951; Theil, 1952). That said, as mentioned above, users of this type of hospital come from a larger "pool." If there is competition in the market, then other non-profit and for-profit hospitals will try to attract more affluent patients, and this will increase the diversity in the pool of users which, in turn, will force a non-profit hospital to limit its net cash flow in order to offer more competitive prices for its services. If there are no competitors in the market, then the non-profit hospital will not need to change its economic behavior. Therefore, the economic behavior of the non-profit hospital depends on the nature of the market (whether it is more for-profit or non-profit).

The second theory maximizes market output, according to which non-profit hospitals exhibit an economic behavior aimed at maximizing the market outcome for the benefit of society (Goering, 2007; Horwitz & Nichols, 2007; Hughes & Luksetich, 2010; Pauly, 1987; Preston, 1988). This is either because public hospitals are failing to meet social needs or because the market output approach is being demanded by their financial contributors (Francois, 2001, 2003; Frank & Salkever, 1991; Kessler & McClellan, 2002; Nett, 1993; Steinberg, 2003). It is true that the nature of the market and the competition between hospitals play a role in this theory. However, this theory also concludes that the economic behavior of non-profit hospitals depends on the existence of for-profit hospitals in the market.

The differentiation is that non-profit hospitals will behave similarly to for-profit ones regardless of the differentiation in goals. However, on the other hand, due to the social and humanitarian nature of non-profit hospitals, the apparent convergence of economic behavior with for-profit hospitals will ultimately result in a higher satisfaction of social needs and possibly lead to for-profit competitors offering unprofitable health-care services (Gravelle & Sivey, 2010; Horwitz & Nichols, 2009; Kaye et al., 2010; Nett, 1993; Rose-Acerman, 1996; Steinberg, 2003; Steinberg & Bradford, 1993).

The third theory is a mixture of theories, known as the "for-profit in disguise theories" (Feldstein, 1967; Hirth, 1999; Horwitz & Nichols, 2009, p. 926; Zhao, 2016). Based on this theory, the economic behavior of non-profit hospitals is not expected to differentiate according to whether the market is more profitable or not. There are profits for both types of private hospitals while there is a difference in the distribution of profits. Private for-profit hospitals distribute profits to owners, while non-profit hospitals, due to internal accountability and the incentives offered to their human resources, distribute profits among their staff.

The basic element of all theories is whether a non-profit hospital will behave economically as a profitable organization or not. The key issue for a non-profit hospital is the relationship between the efficiency of its actions (provision of health-care services) and social equality. Certainly, the nature and orientation of a country's health-care system affects the economic behavior of non-profit hospitals (Gravelle & Sivey, 2010). This is because the orientation of the health-care system and the nature of the health-care market are based on the ideology and culture of nations. The asymmetry of information to users and the diversity and heterogeneity of user preferences apply to any health-care system.

7.5 Public Hospitals: What the Theory Says

As has already been mentioned, the hospital is the basic unit of a health-care system where the process of providing health-care services is carried out. At the same time, it is a social organization that operates in a certain geographical area, consists of people, pursues specific objectives, and is based on a set of principles and rules aimed at the structuring, coordination, and coherence of its activities, which are necessary for the realization of its goals. In order for a hospital to achieve its objectives, a number of essential elements need to be in place (such as sound leadership, staff stability, a positive climate, etc.), but it is also crucially important for the necessary organizational support to be in place, such as the provision of the necessary material resources so that they may be used appropriately to achieve the best possible results.

In terms of organizational support, public hospitals are funded by the State. The source of funding for public hospitals is the State's tax revenue. The primary objective of a public hospital is to fulfill citizens' expectations. This objective is particularly important because public hospitals are funded with public money and are accountable to society. In addition, they operate within a certain legislative framework set by the State itself. The rules of operation determine the degree of freedom of public hospitals, and the investment of public money in a hospital requires collective action (Moore, 2000; Steinberg, 1990a, 1990b).

Sometimes public hospitals operate under strict operating conditions imposed by the State. These strict frameworks are likely to be an obstacle to the dynamics of public hospitals, but at the same time, they might provide the leverage necessary for a better adjustment to their external environment. Indeed, due to their "public" nature, sometimes their mission may seem inelastic (especially with regard to the perception of quality), even if the environment in which hospitals operate imposes change. It is what Moore (2000, p. 192) called "mission stickiness." This is because the provision and investment of public money must be productive in nature and aimed at the social good. A public hospital has a public value and the good "health" is perceived as a social good.

In the case of public hospitals, the State is the main mechanism for establishing both resources and operating rules for public hospitals. Public funding directly affects the efficient functioning of public hospitals, while the State must ensure that the way public hospitals are financed is in line with the objectives it has set (Buchanan & Tollison, 1972; Feldstein, 1967; Newhouse, 1970; Shleifer & Vishny, 1994; Steinberg & Bradford, 1993; Tiemann, Schreyogg, & Busse, 2012). Public hospitals have no expectation of increasing their income through the sale of health-care services. The attraction of greater funding to public hospitals is through the realization that they have achieved their goal of meeting social needs and have the potential to achieve higher goals (McClellan & Staiger, 2000; Moore, 2000; Oster, 1995).

Like private non-profit hospitals, public hospitals perceive the value of their services only in terms of their mission and not in terms of their economic behavior. While users of a hospital's health-care services may do so for their own individual benefit, by using these services, they help increase the demand for them and thus secure the benefits that hospitals offer for the wider community (Moore, 2000). The key characteristics of public hospitals are the overall maximization of satisfaction and equal access of users to health-care services (Chletsos, 2011; Hirth, 1999; Horwitz & Nichols, 2009; Newhouse, 1970; Steinberg & Bradford, 1993; Theil, 1952).

Public hospitals do not aim to be efficient or competitive but aim solely to deliver quality health-care services. To enable them to reduce costs that cannot be passed on to users or donors (as in the case of non-profit hospitals), they subsidize the health-care services they provide. Health-care services of public hospitals are nonprofitable. Due to the public nature of hospitals, they deal with often complicated incidents and provide advanced emergency services at considerable cost to the State. In addition, because of their public character, they serve citizens who have no access to health insurance, nor do they have the economic resources to pay for the use of these health-care services.

Although most studies support the view that the preferences and choices of health-carc users depend on the type of illness and success rate or failure of treatments developed in a hospital, public hospitals are chosen by users with a particular preference for quality. Indeed, owing to the public character of hospitals, citizens tend to trust public hospitals in the quality of the health-care services they provide.

7.6 The Role of Government Toward Different Hospital Types

One of the key features that determines the level of civilization of a modern society is the way in which its government confronts the quality of the health-care services provided to its citizens, regardless of the political system, i.e., regardless of whether or not the statutory functions established by the State determine the context in which health care is developed, either as a public or as a private asset.

Given that (a) hospitals are now operating in a particularly demanding environment characterized by the scarcity of resources and the increased needs of society to prevent or address problems in health care, (b) it is necessary for hospitals to have the appropriate organizational framework, specialized staff, and capable leadership, (c) in modern societies, health-care services are provided both by public and private hospitals, but they differ from one another (Angelopoulou, Kangis, & Babis, 1998; Horwitz & Nichols, 2007; Jabnoun & Chaker, 2003; Sussex, 2009), and (d) the trend in recent years is for a growing collaboration between the public and the private sectors (Weil, 2003), then a question arises: What should be the health-care policy of a government toward the different hospital types?

First of all, it should be noted that for-profit and non-profit hospitals are distinct categories of organizations (Frank & Salkever, 1991; Harris, 1977; Jamali, Hallal, & Abdallah, 2010; Newhouse, 1970).

In order to justify this distinction, one could argue that:

(a) The public health-care system is hierarchically structured and public hospitals, like all public sector organizations, operate within a complex and bureaucratic system-based social justice, the protection of public health, and social prosperity. On the other hand, private hospitals mainly aim to generate a profit.

(b) Management decisions in public hospitals, as opposed to those of their private counterparts, are governed by political planning and political feasibility (e.g., the pricing policy of medicines, the establishment or merger of hospital units and health-care centers).
(c) The work offered by public hospitals cannot be quantified, which makes it difficult to assess their productivity.
(d) Public organizations, including public hospitals, are subject to an enhanced monitoring and accountability (e.g., in terms of how they operate, their objectives, and results) from either top-level organizations or specific governmental bodies. For example, a public hospital's medical, nursing, and administrative staff are under the supervision of central or regional government bodies responsible for public health.
(e) There are significant differences between public and private hospitals concerning how human resources are managed. Typical examples are the permanence of employment and the promotion system based on seniority in a public hospital, as opposed to the flexibility of dismissal in the private hospitals and their promotion system based on performance criteria.

However, the above differences between public and private hospitals could be described as "differences on the surface." This is because (a) they are not always or equally applicable to all hospitals and to all national health-care systems, and (b) both public and private hospitals are characterized by similar requirements: to protect public health, to address the health-care problems of their citizens in an effective and timely manner, and to make rational use of their available resources. Within this framework, we may support that:

- Both types of hospitals have multiple purposes (Dranove, 1988; Hoerger, 1991; Leone & Van Horn, 2005). For example, a public health-care institution does not aim only for public good and to serve the public interest, neither does a private hospital solely aim to make a profit. In particular, at the top hierarchical level of administration in both hospital types where important strategic decisions are made for the future, both the responsible/rational management of resources (human, material) and their impact on society are taken into account. In practice, this means that the central administration (e.g., of a health-care ministry) will not only provide for the allocation of resources but also for the provision of quality public health-care services to society at the least possible cost. Similarly, the management of a private hospital will plan the future, taking into account both the profit and the appeal of their services to the community. It should be noted that the latter is particularly important for the survival, prestige, and further development of private hospitals.
- Both large private and public hospitals are characterized by uniformity and consistency in the way they operate and manage their staff. Moreover, as has been mentioned, the larger the organization (public or private), the more bureaucratic it is in terms of its structure and processes (Keeling, 1972). It is a common objective for both types of hospitals to be interested in the social and political consequences of their choices. Although public hospitals are considered to be

more receptive to society's views and to criticism or control from other public authorities (at central, local, or regional level) regarding their performance and purpose, it does not mean that private hospitals are indifferent to the social impact of their actions. Putting it simply, both private and public hospitals are equally accountable to society. Public hospitals are primarily controlled by government bodies as well as by the rules and limitations they place in the exercise of public authority. But the single-member or collective body of a private hospital is accountable to the owner (or owners) of that particular institution. Moreover, the junior executives of both types of hospitals are under heavily control and are obliged to justify their actions. They act more as recipients of data and information transmitters in their administrative and professional hierarchy rather than sources of data (Gamm, 1996; Sutton & Stensland, 2004; US Government Accountability Office, 2008).

- The two types of hospitals are subject to quantitative assessment, despite the fact that the measurement of public hospital performance can only be measured in terms of quality, like any other public organization (Van Thiel & Leeuw, 2002). No doubt, the greatest difficulty is to evaluate the work/service offered by a public hospital. This is a common difficulty for all public institutions, such as those in health and education, because any benefit of these actions cannot be quantified directly and precisely.
- Despite the impression that, as private organizations, large private hospitals are flexible in their human resource management (e.g., incentive schemes, promotions, dismissals, etc.), it is equally true that they operate in a similar manner to public hospitals: they usually work with bureaucratic standards and manage their staff in a uniform manner. In the case of public hospitals, it is worth mentioning that in the last few years (a) it is a dominant perception that permanence and promotion are awarded on the basis of seniority; (b) staff mobility, resignations, and dismissals (e.g., due to professional misconduct) have increased; and (c) hierarchical promotion on a wage-based scale has been established based on performance. This may all be due to the fact that hospitals today, due to social challenges, want to have competent and appropriately motivated staff (El-Jardali, Tchaghchagian, & Jamal, 2009).

To sum up the above considerations, we may support the view that the way in which a private health-care unit is managed cannot be substantially different from one in the public sector because (a) the concept of "social/common interest" does not make the management of resources totally unbiased, (b) the decision-making process takes into consideration the social cost and benefit, (c) in both types of hospitals there is a balance of income and expenditures, (d) the decisions are discussed and left open to public scrutiny and criticism, (e) the way in which they function should not raise any social objections or challenge society in a negative way, and (f) their staff have access to equal career opportunities and professional development.

References

Anagnostopoulos, K. P. (2005). The economics of cooperation between public and private sector. Theoretical framework and crucial issues. In P. Ipsilantis & K. Syrakoulis (Eds.), *Project management the Greek experience* (pp. 67–89). Athens, Greece: Propobos Publishing. (in Greek).

Angelopoulou, P., Kangis, P., & Babis, G. (1998). Private and public medicine: A comparison of quality perceptions. *International Journal of Health Care Quality Assurance, 11*(1), 14–20.

Ballou, J. P., & Weisbrod, B. A. (2003). Managerial rewards and the behavior of for-profit, governmental, and nonprofit organizations: Evidence from the hospital industry. *Journal of Public Economics, 87*(9–10), 1895–1920.

Barr, S. A. (2007). A research protocol to evaluate the effectiveness of public–private partnerships as a means to improve health and welfare systems worldwide. *American Journal of Public Health, 97*(1), 19–25.

Baumol, W. J., & Bowen, W. G. (1965). On the performing acts. *The American Economic Review, 55*(2), 495–502.

Bay, C. W. (1979). Cost comparisons of for profit and non-profit hospital. *Social Science & Medicine. Part C: Medical Economics, 13*(4), 219–225.

Bayindir, E. C. (2012). Hospital ownership type and treatment choices. *Journal of Health Economics, 31*(2), 359–370.

Bjorvatn, A. (2018). Private or public hospital ownership. Does it really matter? *Social Science & Medicine, 196*, 166–174.

Brogaard, L., & Petersen, O. H. (2018). Public-private partnerships (PPPs) in development policy: Exploring the concept and practice. *Development Policy Review, 97*(s2), O729–O747.

Brown, D., & Moore, M. (2001). Symposium: New roles and challenges for NGOs. *Nonprofit and Voluntary Sector Quarterly, 30*(3), 569–587.

Buchanan, J. M., & Tollison, R. D. (1972). *Theory of public choice*. Ann Arbor, MI: University of Michigan Press.

Chletsos, M. (2011). *Health economics*. Athens, Greece: Pataki Publications. (in Greek).

Chou, S. Y. (2002). Asymmetric information, ownership and quality of care: An empirical analysis of nursing homes. *Journal of Health Economics, 21*(2), 293–311.

Cornelius, N., Todres, M., Janjuha-Jivraj, S., Woods, A., & Wallace, J. (2008). Corporate social responsibility and the social enterprise. *Journal of Business Ethics, 81*(2), 355–370.

Dranove, D. (1988). Pricing by non-profit institutions: The case of hospital cost-shifting. *Journal of Health Economics, 7*(1), 47–57.

Duggan, M. (2002). Hospital market structure and the behavior of not-for-profit hospitals: Evidence from responses to California's disproportionate share program. *The Rand Journal of Economics, 33*(3), 433–446.

El-Jardali, F., Tchaghchagian, V., & Jamal, D. (2009). Assessment of human resources management practices in Lebanese hospitals. *Human Resources for Health, 7*(84), 1–9. Retrieved from https://human-resources-health.biomedcentral.com/articles/10.1186/1478-4491-7-84

Feldstein, M. S. (1967). *Economic analysis for health service efficiency*. Amsterdam: North Holland Publishing.

Forsberg, B. C., Montagu, D., & Sundewall, J. (2011). Moving towards in depth knowledge on the private health sector in low and middle income countries. *Health Policy and Planning, 26*(Suppl.. 1), i1–i3.

Francois, P. (2001). Employee care and the role of nonprofit organizations. *Journal of Institutional and Theoretical Economics, 157*(3), 443–464.

Francois, P. (2003). Not for profit provision of public services. *The Economic Journal, 113*(486), C53–C61.

Frank, R., & Salkever, D. (1991). The supply of charity services by nonprofit hospitals: Motives and market structure. *RAND Journal of Economics, 22*(3), 43–45.

Gamm, E. D. (1996). Dimensions of accountability for not-for-profit hospitals and health systems. *Health Care Management Review, 21*(2), 74–86.

Georgiadis, M. E. (1967). *Business economics*. Athens, Greece: Papazisis Publishing. (in Greek).

Goering, G. E. (2007). The strategic use of managerial incentives in a non-profit firm mixed duopoly. *Managerial and Decision Economics, 28*(2), 83–91.

Gravelle, H., & Sivey, P. (2010). Imperfect information in a quality-competitive hospital market. *Journal of Health Economics, 29*(4), 524–535.

Harris, J. E. (1977). The internal organization of hospitals: Some economic implications. *The Bell Journal of Economics, 8*(2), 467–482.

Haugh, H. (2012). The importance of theory in social enterprise research. *Social Enterprise Journal, 8*(1), 7–15.

Hirth, R. A. (1999). Consumer information and competition between nonprofit and for-profit nursing homes. *Journal of Health Economics, 18*(2), 219–240.

Hoerger, T. J. (1991). Profit variability in for-profit and not-for-profit hospitals. *Journal of Health Economics, 10*(3), 259–289.

Horwitz, J. R., & Nichols, A. (2007). *What do nonprofits maximize? Hospital service provision and market ownership mix* (NBER Working Paper 13246). University of Michigan Law School. Retrieved from https://repository.law.umich.edu/cgi/viewcontent.cgi?referer=https://scholar.google.gr/&httpsredir=1&article=1073&context=law_econ_archive

Horwitz, J. R., & Nichols, A. (2009). Hospital ownership and medical services: Market mix, spillover effects, and nonprofit objectives. *Journal of Health Economics, 28*(5), 924–937.

Hughes, P., & Luksetich, W. (2010). Modeling nonprofit behavior. In B. A. Seaman & D. R. Young (Eds.), *Handbook of research on nonprofit economics and management* (2nd ed., pp. 120–141). Northampton, MA: Edward Elgar Publishing.

Hunter, D. E. K. (2006). Using a theory of change approach to build organizational strength, capacity and sustainability with not-for-profit organizations in the human services sector. *Evaluation and Program Planning, 29*(2), 193–200.

Ifantopoulos, Y. (2006). *Health economics*. Athens, Greece: Tipothito Publishing. (in Greek).

Intzesiloglou, N. (1992). *Society and new technology*. Thessaloniki, Greece: Sakkoulas Publishing. (in Greek).

Jabnoun, N., & Chaker, M. (2003). Comparing the quality of private and public hospitals. *Managing Service Quality: An International Journal, 13*(4), 290–299.

Jamali, D., Hallal, M., & Abdallah, H. (2010). Corporate governance and corporate social responsibility: Evidence from the healthcare sector. *Corporate Governance. The International Journal of Business in Society, 10*(5), 590–602.

Johnston, L. M., & Finegood, D. T. (2015). Cross-sector partnerships and public health: Challenges and opportunities for addressing obesity and noncommunicable diseases through engagement with the private sector. *Annual Review of Public Health, 36*(1), 255–271.

Jordan, L., & VanTuijl, P. (2006). Rights and responsibilities in the political landscape of NGO accountability: Introduction and overview. In L. Jordan & P. Van Tuijl (Eds.), *NGO accountability: Politics, principles & innovation* (pp. 3–20). London: Earthscan.

Kaye, H. S., Harrington, C., & LaPlante, M. P. (2010). Long-term care: Who gets it, who provides it, who pays, and how much? *Health Affairs, 29*(1), 11–21.

Keeling, D. (1972). *Management in government*. London: George Allen & Unwin.

Kekatos, E. B. (2010). *Human hospital*. Athens, Greece: Parisianou Publishing. (in Greek).

Kessler, D. & McClellan, M. (2001). *The effects of hospital ownership on medical productivity* (Working Paper 8537). Retrieved from http://www.nber.org/papers/w8537

Kessler, D., & McClellan, M. (2002). The effects of hospital ownership on medical productivity. *RAND Journal of Economics, 33*(3), 488–506.

Kondilis, E., Antonopoulou, L., & Benos, A. (2008). Cooperations between public–private sector in hospitals. *Archives of Hellenic Medicine, 25*(4), 496–508. (in Greek).

Kontaratos, A. (2003). *The art of hospital management*. Athens, Greece: Parisianou Publishing. (in Greek).

Kuttner, R. (1999). The American health care system: Wall street and health care. *New England Journal of Medicine, 340*(8), 664–668.

Langulle, S. (2017). Public private partnerships in education and health in the global south: A literature review. *Journal of International and Comparative Social Policy, 33*(2), 142–165.
Layton, T., Ellis, R. P., McGuire, T. G., & Van Kleef, R. (2017). Measuring efficiency of health plan payment systems in managed competition health insurance markets. *Journal of Health Economics, 56*(December), 237–255.
Lee, J. (2004). *NGO accountability: Rights and responsibilities, programme on NGO and civil society*. Geneva, Switzerland: CASIN.
Leone, A. J., & van Horn, L. R. (2005). How do nonprofit hospitals manage earnings? *Journal of Health Economics, 24*(4), 815–837.
Lewis, D. (2002). Organization and management in the third sector: Towards a cross cultural research agenda. *Non Profit Management & Leadership, 13*(1), 67–83.
Lewis, D. (2003). Theorizing the organization and management of non-governmental development organizations: Towards a composite approach. *Public Management Review, 5*(3), 325–344.
Liarikos, K. (2008). Accountability in project management from environmental NPO: Theoretical approach and tools. In K. Syrakkoulis & A. Afouxenidis (Eds.), *The dynamic and the limit of citizens' society* (pp. 29–56). Athens, Greece: Propobos Publications. (in Greek).
Machlup, F. (1967). Theories of the firm. Marginalist behavioral, managerial. *The American Economic Review, 57*(1), 1–33.
Marwell, N. P., & McInerney, P. B. (2005). The nonprofit/for-profit continuum: Theorizing the dynamics of mixed-form markets. *Nonprofit and Voluntary Sector Quarterly, 34*(1), 7–28.
McClellan, M. M., & Staiger, D. O. (2000). Comparing hospital quality at for-profit and not-for-profit hospitals. In D. M. Cutler (Ed.), *The changing hospital industry: Comparing not-for-profit and for-profit institutions* (pp. 93–112). Chicago: University of Chicago Press.
Moore, M. H. (2000). Managing for value: Organizational strategy in for profit, nonprofit and governmental organizations. *Nonprofit and Voluntary Sector Quarterly, 29*(1), 183–204.
Moscelli, G., Gravelle, H., Siciliani, L., & Gutackor, N. (2018). The effect of hospital ownership on quality of care: Evidence from England. *Journal of Economic Behavior and Organization, 153*, 322–344.
Nett, L. (1993). Mixed oligopoly with homogenous goods. *Annals of Public and Cooperative Economics, 64*(3), 367–393.
Newhouse, J. P. (1970). Toward a theory of nonprofit institutions: An economic model of a hospital. *The American Economic Review, 60*(1), 64–74.
Newhouse, J. P. (2002). Why is there a quality chasm? The barriers to good performance are more fundamental than simply the lack of organized systems. *Health Affairs, 21*(4), 13–25.
Nikolic, I. A., & Maikisch, H. (2006). *Public-private partnerships and collaboration in the health sector*. Washington, DC: The International Bank for Reconstruction and Development/The World Bank. Discussion Paper.
Oster, S. M. (1995). *Strategic management for nonprofit organizations: Theory and cases*. New York: Oxford University Press.
Pappa, C. H. (2016). *Health care management and job satisfaction*. Master Thesis, Medical School, University of Patra, Greece. (in Greek)
Patouillard, G., Goodman, C. A., Hanson, K. G., & Mills, A. J. (2007). Can working with the private for profit sector improve utilization of quality health services by the poor? A systematic review of literature. *International Journal for Equity in Health, 6*(17), 1–11. Retrieved from https://equityhealthj.biomedcentral.com/articles/10.1186/1475-9276-6-17 (Online 11 pages)
Pauly, M. V. (1987). Nonprofit firms in medical markets. *The American Economic Review, 77*(2), 257–262.
Pomeroy, B. (2008). The limits to public – Private partnership. *The RUSI Journal, 143*(4), 27–29.
Preston, A. E. (1988). The nonprofit firm: A potential solution to inherent market failures. *Economic Inquiry, XXVI*(July), 193–506.
Rodrigues, R., Trigg, L., Schmidt, A. E., & Leichsenring, K. (2014). The public gets what the public wants: Experiences of public reporting in long-term care in Europe. *Health Policy, 116*(1), 84–94.

Rose-Acerman, S. (1996). Altruism, nonprofits and economic theory. *Journal of Economic Literature, XXXIV*(June), 701–728.
Rosenthal, G., & Newbrander, W. (1996). Public policy and private sector provision of health services. *International Journal Health Planning Management, 11*(3), 203–216.
Rothenberg, J. (1951). Welfare implications of alternative methods of financing medical care. *Journal of the American Association of University Teachers of Insurance, 18*(1), 96–106.
Sarros, J. C., Coopen, B. K., & Santoro, J. C. (2011). Leadership vision, organizational culture, and support for innovation in not-for-profit and for-profit organizations. *Leadership & Organization Development Journal, 32*(3), 291–309.
Sekhri, N., Feachem, R., & Ni, A. (2011). Public-private integrated partnerships demonstrate the potential to improve health care access, quality, and efficiency. *Health Affairs, 30*(8), 1498–1507.
Shleifer, A., & Vishny, R. W. (1994). Politicians and firms. *The Quarterly Journal of Economics, 109*(4), 995–1025.
Skountzos, T. (2005). *Economic development* (Vol. A). Athens, Greece: Stamoulis Publishing. (in Greek).
Sloan, F. (2000). Not-for-profit Ownership and Hospital Behavior. In A. J. Culyer & J. P. Newhouse (Eds.), *Handbook of Health Economics* (Vol. 1, pp. 1141–1174). Amsterdam: Elsevier.
Spyridaki, H. (2008). Non-governmental organisations or developing enterprises: Modern challenges for the role of North developing nongovernmental organizations. In K. Syrakkoulis & A. Afouxenidis (Eds.), *The dynamic and the limit of citizens' society* (pp. 57–80). Athens, Greece: Propobos Publications. (in Greek).
Steinberg, R. (1990a). Taxes and giving: New findings. *Voluntas: International Journal of Voluntary and Nonprofit Organizations, 1*(2), 61–79.
Steinberg, R. (1990b). Labor economics and the nonprofit sector: A literature review. *Nonprofit and Voluntary Sector Quarterly, 19*(2), 151–169.
Steinberg, R. (2003). Economic theories of nonprofit organizations. In H. K. Anheier & A. Ben-Ner (Eds.), *The Study of Nonprofit enterprise. Nonprofit and civil society studies* (pp. 277–309). Boston, MA: Springer Publications.
Steinberg, R., & Bradford, G. (1993). The role of nonprofit enterprise in 1993: Hansmann revisited. *Nonprofit and Voluntary Sector Quarterly, 22*(4), 297–316.
Stevens, R., Moray, N., Bruneel, J., & Clarysse, B. (2015). Attention allocation to multiple goals: The case of for profit social enterprises. *Strategic Management Journal, 36*(7), 1006–1016.
Sussex, J. M. (2009). *How fair? Competition between independent and NHS providers to supply non-emergency hospital care to NHS patients in England (September 1, 2009)*. (Office of Health Economics Briefing, No 50). Retrieved from SSRN: https://ssrn.com/abstract=2640148 or https://doi.org/10.2139/ssrn.2640148 (Online 32 pages)
Sutton, J. P., & Stensland, J. (2004). Promoting accountability: Hospital charity care in California, Washington and Texas. *Journal of Health Care for the Poor and Underserved, 15*(2), 237–250.
Theil, H. (1952). Qualities prices and budget inquiries. *The Review of Economic Studies, 19*(3), 129–147.
Tiemann, O., Schreyogg, J., & Busse, R. (2012). Hospital ownership and efficiency: A review of studies with particular focus on Germany. *Health Policy, 104*(2), 163–171.
Torchia, M., Calabrò, A., & Morner, M. (2015). Public–private partnerships in the health care sector: A systematic review of the literature. *Public Management Review, 17*(2), 236–261.
U.S. Government Accountability Office. (2008). *Non-profit hospitals: Variation in standards and guidance limits comparison of how hospitals meet community benefit requirements*. (Report to the Ranking Member, Committee on Finance, U.S. Senate, GAO-08-880). Washington, D.C.: General Accounting Office.
Vaillancourt Rosenau, P. (2003). Performance evaluations of for profit and nonprofit U.S. hospitals since 1980. *Nonprofit Management and Leadership, 13*(4), 401–423.
Van Thiel, S., & Leeuw, F. L. (2002). The performance paradox in the public sector. *Public Performance & Management Review, 25*(3), 267–281.

Weil, T. P. (2003). Governance in a period of strategic change in US healthcare. *International Journal of Health Planning and Management, 18*(3), 247–265.

World Health Organization. (1946). *Constitution of the World Health Organization*. Washington, D.C.: U.S. Department of State.

Zhao, X. (2016). Competition, information, and quality: Evidence from nursing homes. *Journal of Health Economics, 49*(September), 136–152.

Chapter 8
The Economics of Hospitals

Key Points
- The most important element for a cost-effective hospital behavior is cost control.
- Hospitals need to use debt in constructive investments such as capital structure in order to upgrade and develop services and at the same time have a rational economic behavior.
- The health-care system plays a significant role in the hospital financing since it influences, to a great extent, the insurance coverage of citizens for the use of the hospital services which is one of the basic sources of hospital revenues.
- None of the determinants can influence the behavior of the hospital alone. The most important determinant of hospital behavior is the human capital and the decisions of how the productive resources will be used and how the changes, costs, and benefits will be managed.
- Nonprofitable hospitals have other goals besides the maximization of profits, such as the maximization of revenues, maximization of quantity, and the improvement in the quality of hospital services.

8.1 Introduction

In the second and third chapters of the book, we have analyzed in detail both the factors that influence hospital strategy and what we mean by the term hospital. Starting with the definition of hospital, we should consider that in all civilized societies, a well-organized system of health is used for well-defined purposes in which it takes into account and exploits the contribution of society, the state, and the environment as a whole. Within this framework, one could argue that the hospital is a living organization and as a form of the social system has become a product of political and social evolution.

M. Chletsos, A. Saiti, *Strategic Management and Economics in Health Care*,
https://doi.org/10.1007/978-3-030-35370-4_8

The hospital is, therefore, the basic unit of the health-care system where the health-care service is performed. At this point, we should emphasize that a hospital, depending on its type (e.g., cooperation with a University), may justify investing in services that are different from purely health care such as teaching. As a unit and social organization, it is a system which is broadly adapted to all expressions of life. As a system, as we have already mentioned in earlier chapters of the book, it has subsystems and inputs that are transformed and produce outputs. At the same time, of course, it also has a feedback mechanism, which is a mechanism for checking whether or not the hospital has achieved its goals. This control mechanism, as we shall see further down in this chapter, is the most important element for the economic efficiency and effectiveness of the hospital. In addition, what is important for the hospital's economic viability is the legislative framework and rules of the health-care system.

No matter the type of hospital ownership, its main objective is sustainability and profit maximization, while the rules and legal framework of the health-care system have a significant influence on the control and especially on the costs shifting. Indeed, the hospital is an organization that operates within an uncertain environment with frequent turbulence since patient insurance coverage, which is one of the main sources of hospital funding, is at risk. Therefore, the hospital industry does not operate under the same conditions with an organization at the service sector. This is because for a business organization in a service sector such as hotel industry, fully occupation would mean profit, for a hospital we cannot say that with certainty, since it works mainly with fixed costs and whether or not it will achieve profits depends heavily on the insurance coverage of patients.

Moreover, another factor that affects hospitals' economic efficiency is the fact that a hospital has more labor and capital intensity than any other social organization. The size of the hospital affects the economies of scale that largely determine the success or failure of the hospital (Bai & Anderson, 2016; Gruca & Nath, 1994). According to the relevant literature (Cowing, Holtmann, & Powers, 1982, cited by Gruca & Nath, 1994; Shortell, 1988; Wheeler, Burkhardt, Alexander, & Magnus, 1999), a multihospital system is more likely to disperse costs and, thus, display economies of scales. Of course, hospitals in the system chain need to be geographically close since otherwise the achievement of economies of scale will be difficult. However, the question that usually arises is whether or not large hospital units are able to achieve economies of scale themselves. The answer from the literature is that this depends on the number of beds that is its capacity (Bai & Anderson, 2016; Cowing et al., 1982, cited by Gruca & Nath, 1994; Ginn & Young, 1992; Handel et al., 2010; Spaulding, Edwardson, & Zhao, 2018). And this is because if a hospital has multiple beds, it means it can accommodate more patients and thus be able to spread the cost of services. Of course, there is also a limit, which does not mean that economies of scale are increasing as the number of beds increases. A relevant research by Cowing et al. (1982, cited by Gruca & Nath, 1994, p. 350) showed that economies of scale are up to 500 beds. Moreover, economies of scale depend on the service mix of the hospital (economies of scope). In any case, investment and diversification of the services affect economic efficiency. The hospital market is different and presents fluctuations and differentiations. As a result, the special character of the services offered and the financial sources of a hospital, profit maximization, and economic efficiency mainly depend on the number of available services, the case and patient mix, system membership, and type of patients' admission in the hospital (whether it is an emergency or nonemergency admission).

Based on the above, we may say that a hospital consists of a multiple number of elements (people, services, regulations, teaching, etc.), each of which performs its own work, all working together, collaborating and working together to achieve the hospital's goals and sustainability.

8.2 Which Are the Purposes of Hospitals

As it has already mentioned, the hospital is the basic unit of the health-care system and of a social organization. It operates in a specific geographical area, is composed of people, is pursuing specific goals, and is based on a set of principles and regulations aimed at structuring, coordinating, and cohering of necessary activities for the achievement of its goals. To accomplish its goals, a hospital requires, among other things (e.g., strong leadership, staff stability, and positive climate) (Bai & Anderson, 2016; Duran, Kutzin, Martin Moreno, & Travis, 2012; Sloan & Becker, 1981; Stall & Mortimore, 1997), the necessary organizational support, that is, the provision of the necessary material resources to use them appropriately in order to achieve the best possible result at the least possible cost. Indeed, the economic viability of a hospital requires good management and control over the cost of its services. Controlling and managing the costs of a hospital's services is not an easy task. It needs continuous monitoring by the managerial leadership, flexibility to respond to market demand, provision of quality services, and re-assure of funding resources so as to be able to operate in a cost-effective manner. These are the main purposes of a hospital. However, these purposes may vary in intensity, and this depends mainly on organizational factors such as the type of hospital and its type of ownership but also its external environment such as the hospital system and membership. Indeed, given that, hospitals have as their primary goal the maximization of profit and utility at the lowest possible cost. For example, a nonprofitable hospital which operates with low-profit margins will respond to having a better economic behavior, when it is more likely to have a cost shift on patients with private payment and less likely to shift the cost on patients with social insurance (Champagne, Leduc, Denis, & Pineault, 1993; Deneffe & Masson, 2002; Gruca & Nath, 1994; Handel et al., 2010; Hoerger, 1991). Moreover, it is more likely, for purely reasons of economic sustainability, a hospital to merge with another hospital unit. However, the conditions that a merger can take place depend on the system's regulations and the relevant legislative framework. The decisions of hospital upper hierarchical management as to which hospitals should merge depend largely on the type of hospital ownership. Hence, it is more likely that a nonprofitable hospital will merge with a not-for-profit hospital than with profitable counterpart (Deneffe & Masson, 2002; Spaulding et al., 2018). Therefore, the type of ownership affects the economic behavior of hospitals.

Indeed, decisions about hospital goals, as an economic entity, are related to the choices for investment in services and by system membership, that is, whether the hospital belongs to a multihospital system or not. Decisions on investment in services (e.g., investment in subacute or acute medical care or electronic medical records) always take into account hospital goals and follow the same rationale as a regular economic unit. Although the hospital like any other economic unit has assets, costs, and financial resources, their main purpose is to capture the opportunities and not expose the economic unit at risk.

Moreover, decisions regarding hospitals' aims also depend on financing resources and financing restrictions. With reference to the organizational support, we should mention that funding of hospitals is heavily based on the nature and culture of the health-care system. The culture of a country's health-care system influences the system membership as well as the emphasis on the type of hospital ownership (e.g., nonprofitable, for profit or investor owned, and public). The structure of the health-care system determines, to a great extent, the market conditions of the hospital industry, which consequently influences the hospital objectives.

We will discuss the main sources of funding for hospitals that affect hospital goals, later on this chapter; however, we would like to point out that in the case of financing hospitals, every health-care system is governed by certain regulations and legislative framework. The degree of relaxation and flexibility of these regulations also determines the degree of freedom in the operation of both the hospital units as a whole, their various departments, and their overall staff. Moreover, the economic conditions of the hospital's external environment have a positive or negative impact on the financial sources of hospitals' revenues. To conclude, there is a need for a drastic funding policy for hospitals in terms of how the budgets and funding resources are implemented in order to constantly improve the quality of health-care services and reach the goals of the hospital.

8.3 Determinants of Hospital Behavior

As we have already mentioned, hospitals are dynamic economic and social organizations that operate within an uncertain environment and therefore undergo a process of change which entails a number of fundamental changes. In addition to the key factors of production (labor and capital), we will discuss other determinants such as organizational factors, managerial and market factors, and the regulations and legislative framework, which, to a more or less extent, influence a hospital's behavior.

At this point, we may say that the hospital as an open system for through its subsystems it exchanges information and activities with its external environment (Al-Amin, Schiaffino, Park, & Harman, 2018; Fennell & Alexander, 1987; Kast & Rozenzweig, 1972; Sloan & Becker, 1981; Spaulding et al., 2018). This means that the system receives energy and influence from its external environment and the hospital itself is influenced by its actions to the environment. Therefore, there is an interactive relationship between the factors that determine a hospitals' behavior. The following are among the factors that may influence hospitals' behavior and hence its structure and function (Abernethy & Lillis, 2001; Al-Amin et al., 2018; Bai & Anderson, 2016; Champagne et al., 1993; Fennell & Alexander, 1987; Ginn & Young, 1992; Gruca & Nath, 1994; Handel et al., 2010; Kallapur & Eldenburg, 2005; Miles, Snow, Meyer, & Coleman Jr., 1978; Spaulding et al., 2018; Wheeler et al., 1999).

Market Factors These factors are often referred to as environmental factors in the literature because they are related to the conditions of the hospital environment (hospital industry). The shape of these conditions is influenced by the general economic conditions and the particular characteristics of the community in which the hospital operates. It is well known that hospitals operate not only in urban centers but also at regional and local levels. The communities and regions of a country, even the urban centers of a country, differ in social and economic characteristics, while in some countries, for example, USA, the difference between regions or urban centers among different states can be even on the level of legislative framework and regulations. This means that there are differences between communities (local, regions, and urban centers) in terms of wage rate, supply and density of physicians, patient income, hospitals' concentration, and competition. Indeed, all these factors influence the behavior of hospitals in their operation as they determine the degree of uncertainty and possible market environment shocks. Hospitals are under pressure from the market, and in order to survive and develop improved cost-effective behavior, they need to respond in an efficient manner to environmental conditions. The extent and intensity of market pressures are largely determined by the mentioned characteristics of the area where hospitals operate. At this point, we should emphasize that the influence of market characteristics, regarding the degree and intensity, depends on the ownership type of the hospital. This means that public hospitals, which are autonomous units that mainly serve a wider range of services to a larger socioeconomic part of the population and are not related to each other, are a different group of hospitals that exhibit heterogeneity (Champagne et al., 1993; Sloan & Becker, 1981). Within this framework, the degree of market complexity for public hospitals depends primarily on the number of public hospitals in an area. The number of hospitals plays a role in making decisions about investing in services. When many hospitals function in one area and offer specific services (usually offering and investing more in acute care), this makes it more difficult to decide whether to diversify services (e.g., in subacute care) or invest in a more innovative service. When a hospital operates in an area where income is high enough, and there are increased sources of funding, the hospital will operate differently from another, operating in a low-income area with limited financial resources (Al-Amin et al., 2018; Bai & Anderson, 2016; Kimberly & Evanisko, 1981; Wheeler et al., 1999). This is because higher income area means more demand for health-care services since the population can either cover their income expenditure or have private insurance coverage

(Wheeler et al., 1999). Regarding the income of the districts or regions, a wealthy area of public money will be able to cover and subsidize hospitals with more public money. Public funding (or financing by local or regional government) of hospitals depends primarily on the culture and ideology of the health-care system and the general economic conditions of a country. However, a wealthy area means more money where combined with good management they generate more chances for better service and flexibility that consequently lead to further socioeconomic development of the area.

Hospitals which function in urban centers also cooperate with universities, while hospital staff in many cases come from universities and have university affiliations (Champagne et al., 1993). Indeed, according to Swanson Kazley and Ozcan (2007), hospitals that have more financial sources of income can adopt innovative services such as electronic medical records. This means that in such a case, the hospital is more likely to invest in research and adopt innovative ideas.

Organizational Factors Organizational factors include ownership type, system membership, size, patient and case mix, outpatient activity, subacute and acute care, people, and teaching status. These factors affect the functioning (and behavior) of hospitals either positively or negatively. Indeed, the type of ownership and system membership (more for private profitable hospitals) affect the behavior of hospitals. Private hospitals have the potential to develop different types of hospital groups and chains. This, within the organization framework, enables them to operate with greater flexibility. In contrast, public hospitals, which are independent and unique units, do not have the flexibility to diversify their services. However, public hospitals are more likely to work with a university, and hence to develop research and specialized services. Indeed, Kimberly and Evanisko (1981) indicated that an efficient organizational response to the problem of hospital acute care services heterogeneity is investing in technology. This will boost the effectiveness of the hospital, as it will attract both medical staff and patients. The only thing that is necessary in such cases is the continuous cost control and careful analysis of the population's insurance coverage. However, both types of hospitals exhibit labor and capital intensity when comparing the hospital industry with another industry service (Al-Amin et al., 2018; Bai & Anderson, 2016; Gentry & Penrod, 2000; Handel et al., 2010; Kimberly & Evanisko, 1981; Wheeler et al., 1999). Regarding the organizational factors, the relevant literature (Champagne et al., 1993; Handel et al., 2010; Kallapur & Eldenburg, 2005; Kimberly & Evanisko, 1981; Sloan & Becker, 1981; Wheeler et al., 1999) converged to the conclusion that the size of the hospital and whether it has invested in acute or subacute care are crucial important elements. The size of the hospital, as we have already mentioned, affects the quantity and type of services provided. Large public hospitals, for example, are more likely to provide outpatient care in relation to their private counterparts. This is because outpatient activity is a cost-raising service, and therefore, an investor-owned hospital cannot easily afford it since the prime goal is profit. It is true though that most hospitals are more likely to invest in acute care and less in subacute care. The emphasis on the type of services differentiates their behavior. For example, shifting services to subacute care should be combined with good management of available beds and analysis of patient insurance coverage. Considering the type of hospital and the emphasis on services, nonprofitable hospitals are more likely to invest in subacute care, whereas the supply of health-care staff may determine the investment in subacute care in any type of hospital ownership. According to relevant literature (Abernethy & Lillis, 2001; Al-Amin et al., 2018; Bohigas et al., 1996; Champagne et al., 1993; Hage & Dewar, 1973; Kallapur & Eldenburg, 2005; Kimberly & Evanisko, 1981; Miles et al., 1978; Sloan & Becker, 1981; Wheeler et al., 1999), high importance is given to hospital staff mainly for hospital upper management. Indeed, hospital staff and management are critical to its financial performance. No investment or diversification of services will achieve high growth rates if there is a maladministration or exploitation of the available resources due to a lack of fundamental ideas. Capital alone cannot replace organizational and management ideas. Therefore, skilled and qualified human resources are crucial and essential for the efficient combination of available resources and the delivering of quality services at the lowest possible cost. Finally, in terms of patient and case mix, patients' needs depend, to a great extent, on the area within which the hospital functions and, in particular, the age structure of the population and per capita income of the area.

Regulations and Legislative Framework The regulations and the legislative framework have a positive or negative impact on the financial performance of the hospital. In particular, the legislative framework has a close link to reforms (changes) taking place in the health-care sector and in the hospital industry. Changes sometimes reduce and sometimes increase problems in the hospital field. Regulation (as well as the legislative framework) concerns about the control mechanisms necessary to better regulate the functioning of the hospitals. According to Gruca & Nath (1994, p. 346), the main categories of control mechanisms are focused on investment, utilization, and reimbursement control. With reference to *investment controls,* the regulations refer to the bureaucratic procedures that a hospital needs to follow and the investment limitations so that a hospital can move on, if it wants to expand its investment activity in terms of services offered. The orientation of a hospital's investment opportunities and limitations (e.g., a merger) is important and necessary because this will better regulate the market (competition in the hospital industry) and it will also have a better control of the conditions in the area where a hospital operates. *Utilization control* relates to the services offered and is about the regulation of the hospital's internal operation. This type of control ensures, through legislative regulations, that patients are offered a specific and necessary level of health care in terms of quality. At the same time, a kind of cost control is achieved since regulations can regulate issues such as unnecessary hospitalization and length of hospital stay. Certainly, with particular reference to the latter, the will of the hospital management is essential. This means that regulation alone cannot have good cost management and control. Human intervention (of managers) is absolutely necessary. We may also note at this point that utilization control affects public hospitals more in the sense that they operate more with public money. Finally, *reimbursement control* regulates issues of hospital charges and hospital reimbursement. Of course, the hospital (especially the private ones) charges their services based on their cost, and this does not depend on the method of payment. Although hospitals (and the private sector) often agree on service charges, the nature of these regulations tends to regulate the costs of hospitals and the provision of better quality services. In this way, hospital management can better manage their budget and overall hospital operations. At this point, it is necessary to mention that the impact of these regulations has an influence on public hospitals.

Managerial Factors These factors are related to the decisions of hospital upper management regarding the labor intensity, debt utilization, and service mix. They are also related to the hospital infrastructure (technology equipment), which is the main prerequisite for the modernization of the hospital. These are very important factors that greatly influence the hospitals' behavior. Although they may not be purely economic factors, they include the most important crucial determinant factor of economic behavior that is the human factor. Work intensity affects employment relationships, and ultimately, if the hospital's financial and investment decisions are not based on a consensus basis, then they cannot thrive and promote proper functioning. With reference to debt utilization, the rational use of a hospital's debt leads to cost-effectiveness. Here too, the rational use of debt requires rational decision-making by hospital management. The same applies for the service mix. The mix of services offered requires careful planning and strategy so that the hospital can achieve the lowest cost and best possible performance.

From the above, it is evident that hospitals are in a bidirectional relationship with their environment (internal and external). This means that the hospital has to adjust to the environmental data and conditions. A rational policy and strategy is absolutely necessary so as any change to be acceptable by all involved including stakeholders and, most importantly, from an organizational perspective to be economically sound. The production factors such as capital, labor, and technology alone are not enough to improve the financial situation of hospitals. The most important factor that determines and will increasingly determine the sustainable development of a hospital will be human capital, as a culture and attitude of life.

Based on the above, none of the factors mentioned above can alone determine the behavior of a hospital. The fact that:

a. The picture of hospitals' financial effectiveness is relatively unclear and complex due to the special and sensitive character of the hospital industry and the services that are offered.
b. There are discrepancies between the hypothetical world of economic theory and the real world of economic life.

In reality, the environment of a hospital creates situations that do not meet the optimal solutions that deliver financial well-being. The essence is, therefore, in how the productive resources are used and how the changes, costs, and benefits are managed by hospitals.

8.4 Which Are the Sources of Revenues and the Expenditures of Hospitals

8.4.1 *Hospital Revenues*

One of the main methods used to allocate state resources is the process of budget programs (or budgets). It is a short-term program of economic action through which the economic and social policy of the government is implemented (Lee, Johnson, & Joyce, 2013). The budget seeks to rationalize the allocation of 1-year resources available to meet public needs and implement the government's economic and social policy.

The state budget is financed from two main sources: the state operating expenditure budget and the public investment budget. The main source of funding for hospitals, regardless of the type of health-care system, is the state. In cases where the philosophy of the health-care system (e.g., national health-care system) allows, hospitals funding, mainly public hospitals, from the state, is high. The final decision, therefore, on the question of how much money will be spent mainly on public hospitals is a matter of the state.

Expenditure on hospital funding has a large portion of public spending and derives money from various sources. Based on the relevant literature (Chletsos, 2011), two ways of calculating the amount of public expenditure can be identified. The first method calculates the amount of public health-care expenditure based on the needs of the system and then identifies the revenue (e.g., the money raised) to cover the expenditure. The second way of calculating starts with the planning of public expenditure, this means the state revenue comes first and then the covering of the needs. The main source of revenue for a state is taxation (direct and indirect). Apart from the state, however, in some countries, public funding of hospitals is a subcategory and comes, to a lesser extent, from regional or local authorities. One of the key features of health-care policy is the relationship between the return on investment in health care and equality of opportunity. Since taxes are the main source of revenue for the state and are paid compulsorily by citizens depending on their income, citizens should have the same opportunity to have equal treatment in public hospitals in a country. This means that the way a country's state budget operates should enable it to solve serious operating problems faced by hospitals and contribute to the developmental character of the hospital.

The relevant literature (Bai & Anderson, 2016; Chletsos, 2011; Gruca & Nath, 1994; Harris, 1977; Lee et al., 2013; Miles et al., 1978; Xenos, Nektarios, Polyzos, & Ifantopoulos, 2014) shows that public financing of hospitals should be effective and not bureaucratic. The state has to be an effective producer by providing motives. Taking into consideration that the state finances and other sectors of the economy, effectiveness is a necessary condition for an effective financing of hospitals. The distribution of health-care costs in hospitals needs to be efficiently organized so that the participation of the state in the allocation of health-care expenditures results in a high profitability with the lowest possible cost (Burnell, 1991).

However, besides taxation, hospitals receive funding from social insurance and private payments. Social insurance refers to the hospital covering of the needs of the population by the state, while the health-care systems which exercise this type of social insurance are the social insurance system and the national health-care system. With reference to the former, the financing of the system is largely wage related since it comes from sharing contributions between employers and employees. Regarding the national health-care system, the financing of the system comes from taxation (both direct and indirect). For the particular case whereas a country has a national health-care system, which provides full coverage of the population, then the payment for the use of services in a public hospital is made through social insurance. The use of services in a private hospital based on the national health-care system is only partially covered by social insurance, and the remaining will be paid for by private payment. Private payments refer to citizens' private hospital coverage (private insurance) and patients' direct payments, for example, payment coming from patients' income when they do not have any (social or private) hospital care insurance. With reference to private payments, the liberal or free market health-care system is more likely to be related, and this is because in a free market health-care system, citizens have private insurance paid by their employers only when they are employed. If the citizens are not working, then they have to pay for their own income for the use of hospital services. In any case, we should mention that the population of any country is, in theory, obliged to have health-care insurance. The main difference between the two sources of hospital revenue is the time the hospital payment is made. In the case of social insurance, there may be a delay in hospital repayment due to bureaucratic procedures.

8.4.2 Hospital Expenditures

With particular reference to hospital expenditures, we may divide into fixed and variable expenditures. Fixed costs include operating costs for hospital functions such as building maintenance, while variable costs depend on the level of hospital occupation and the number of medical and administrative staff. In particular, the main categories of hospital expenditures can be divided into the following categories (Al-Amin et al., 2018; Bai & Anderson, 2016; Bohigas et al., 1996; Champagne et al., 1993; Handel et al., 2010; Karasoulos, 2014; Spaulding et al., 2018; Suhrecke, Sauto Arce, McKee, & Rocco, 2012; Swanson Kazley & Ozcan, 2007; Xenos et al., 2014).

Pharmaceutical and Clinical Costs This type of expense varies and depends, to a great extent, on the type of inpatient care and length of hospital stay. At this point, it is worth to mention that the cost of health-care services is interdependent and thus may be a constraint on service mix changes (Gruca & Nath, 1994, p. 359; Handel et al., 2010). Another limitation is the regulations and the legislative framework which may limit the chances of diversification of services in order to reduce the cost of clinical and pharmaceutical costs.

Providers' Payment Hospital suppliers are another major category of costs. According to the relevant literature, the hospital suppliers market is related to the structure of the hospital industry as well as to the philosophy of a country's health-care system. When we have a competitive market with a large number of hospitals, then hospitals have a choice so they can have better management costs for suppliers in terms of both cost and quality. In addition, as has already mentioned above, hospital costs are related to economies of scale and scope (Al-Amin et al., 2018; Gruca & Nath, 1994; Handel et al., 2010; Sloan & Becker, 1981; Xenos et al., 2014). This means that in relation to the cost of suppliers, the hospital occupancy rate plays an important role. The functioning of competition between health-care providers and purchasers can be ensured through control mechanisms.

Wages of Medical and Administrative Staff This expenditure consists of the largest proportion of total hospital expenditure. This is because the hospital, like any organization, in order to function properly, has the necessary human resources. Hospitals (private and public) are usually large organizations and have three human resources specialties: administrative, medical, and nursing staff. Hence, the cost of wages is high, as is the case with any economic entity.

To conclude, the hospital financing policy needs constant consideration and drastic action to ensure a quality upgrade of the system. Based on the above and considering that the financing of hospitals from the state influences directly the effective performance of hospitals, the state should be certain that the way of financing hospitals fits the hospitals' aims.

8.5 How Do the Hospitals Achieve Their Goals: A Theoretical Explanation?

The behavior of the hospital is determined by the economic model in which hospitals belong. According to Jacobs (1974), hospitals can be placed in two different categories of economic models. In the first category, hospitals are considered as an "organism" which has its own goals. These goals could be maximization of profits or quantity or the quality of the product. In the second category, hospitals are organizations where there functions help different groups (physicians, administrative board, etc.) to maximize their utility function under economic constraints such as the capacity of patients to pay for health services. Concerning the hospitals which belong to the second category, the owners are not the managers. According to the managerial theories, owners are employed managers who are responsible to achieve the objectives of the hospitals (McGuire, Henderson, & Moone, 1988). These goals could be the maximization of profit or the maximization of revenues, etc (Baumol, 1959). The managers take decisions about the functions of the hospital having in mind their managerial utility function. Their utility depends on the level of the salary they get, their bonus, security, power, and status (McPake & Normard, 2008).

A number of theories emphasize the role of clinicians upon the decision-making process. Brown (1970) plays emphasis on the role of the hospital management in the determination of hospital functions. Under this concept, the clinicians are not hired and paid by the hospitals; the role of clinicians is to serve as agent for the consumers. Additionally, Feldstein (1968) adds that the role of the hospital management is to maximize output for a given quality level. The same is the thesis developed by Rice (1966). The different point of the theory of Rice (1966) is the distinction of the goods and services produced by the hospital to those categorized as medically necessary treatments and amenities. This categorization of goods provided by the hospital implies that the hospital operates in two different markets. There is an intermediate market for the health care supplied by the hospital (McGuire et al., 1988) and a final market for the amenities. McGuire (1985) notes that in Rice's theory complete inelasticity of demand for health care does not exist in the intermediate market. Therefore, hospitals compete with each other and with other inputs in the production function of the clinician—hospitals.

Another group of theories which try to explain the behavior of the hospital are the behavioral theories. These theories support that hospitals are not a single decision-making unit, but there are different objective functions because they are made up of diverse sets of actors (McPake & Normard, 2008). The hospital behavioral theory is based on the work by Simon (1957).

The necessity to develop an economic model which explains the behavior of the hospitals arises from the different structure of hospitals. As Joshi and Krishnan (2017) mention the fact that there is simultaneous presence of different types of hospitals (for-profit, nonprofit, and government/public hospitals), this implies that they have different missions and different objective functions. Chang & Jacobson (2012) categorize the different objectives of nonprofit hospitals in four streams. These categories are as follows: (a) "for-profits in disguise," (b) "output maximizers," (c) "perquisite maximizers," and (d) "social welfare maximizers." Hospitals which belong in the first category could operate as a profit-maximizing entity. This is because of the lack of enforcement or the ambiguity of law to allow nonprofits to act as profit maximizers. Nonprofit hospitals of the second category have an aim to maximize quantity and quality as Newhouse (1970) states in his theory. The third group of models posits that nonprofit hospitals maximize perquisites and more specifically the perquisites of the physicians as these enter into the welfare function of the physicians. According to the last category ("social welfare maximizers"), the hospitals are nonprofit because their managers have altruistic motives, and they care more about the output than wealth.

In the case of a for-profit hospital, the profit motive leads the production of health services (Rice & Unruh, 2009). According to traditional economic theory, the for-profit hospital is considered as a firm which maximizes its profit. The maximization of profit is achieved by producing the level of output (health services) to the point where marginal revenue equals marginal cost. In the case of a perfect competitive market, the hospital is a price taker (the price is fixed in the market and it is constant for each hospital) and the demand curve is identified by the marginal revenue curve. In the case of a monopolistic or monopolistic competitive market, the hospital is a price maker and the demand curve is different from the marginal revenue curve. At the equilibrium condition, the hospital determines the quantity of health-care services provided where the profit is maximum, and therefore, the price is determined by the demand curve which is different from the marginal revenue curve. The managers of a hospital should choose the level of output where goals have been achieved. So the level of output should vary between the levels of output at which profit is maximized (the equilibrium condition is Marginal Revenue (MR) equals to Marginal Cost (MC)) and the levels of output at which profit is zero (Average Revenue equals to Average Cost). Although there are economic and behavioral theories which attempt to explain the hospital's behavior, there are serious doubts about the effectiveness of these theories. The fact that there is a great diversity in the structure of hospitals and the output produced by a hospital is not the same; this is an obstacle to treat a hospital as a cohesive unit. The heterogeneity of the hospitals is shown by Sloan (1979). He found that there are significant organizational differences between different types of hospitals. As McGuire (1985) mentions, the problem raised by the work of Sloan is the effort of the theories to aggregate different types of hospitals while there is no a single category of model to be general enough to analyze hospitals.

8.5.1 The Role of Physicians in Maximizing Hospitals' Profits: The Model of Pauly and Redisch

Pauly and Redisch (1973) proposed a model of the US hospitals which is similar to the traditional economic model of firm based on the profit-maximization rule. They refer to the US hospitals because the structure of US hospitals is different than the structure of European hospitals. In Europe, physicians are employees of the hospital, and they are paid by the hospital in order to provide treatment to the patients. In contrast with USA physicians are not employees of these hospitals. They attract patients and provide them with a treatment within the hospital, and their remuneration depends on the number of patients and the kind of treatment. This is a profit-maximizing model. The clinicians dominate among other groups of hospitals. They have control over the resource allocation, and they attempt to maximize their income. There are two main groups in this nonprofit hospital. The first group consists of the physicians and second group of the equity holders (so-called trustees). There are residual profits which go to the physicians. As the physicians attempt to maximize these residual profits, they perform the role of the manager. As we said, this model of the nonprofit hospital could contrast the orthodox model of the profit-maximizing firm. As Pauly & Redisch (1973, p. 90) indicate, "the only difference between this model and the physician-profit-maximization model of the hospital is that in the latter it is the physician input, rather than the nondebt capital input, which obtains economic profits, residual income." Thus, the physicians are the decision makers (McPake & Normard, 2008), and the objective functions of the hospitals consist of the income of the physicians. Hospitals function in a way to maximize the net income of physicians at any point in time. The output produced by the hospital is "hospitalization services" (Q), and it is produced by physical capital (K), nonphysician labor (L), and physician or medical staff labor (M). The production function is:

$$Q = F\left(K,L,M\right) \tag{8.1}$$

The "hospitalization services" (Q) is sold to patients at a price (P_T) for which the hospital has no gain or loss. The gross total revenue ($P_T{\cdot}Q$) equals to the revenue goes to pay nonphysician labor and capital ($P_h{\cdot}Q$), and the residual revenue goes to the physician. The P_h is the price that the hospital charges for the use of nonphysician labor and capital. The wage rate for the nonphysician labor is w, and user cost of capital is w. On the basis of the above:

The revenue goes to the nonphysician labor and capital is:

$$P_h{\cdot}Q = w{\cdot}L + c{\cdot}K$$

The residual revenue goes to the physician is:

$$P_T{\cdot}Q - P_h{\cdot}Q = P_T{\cdot}Q - \left(w{\cdot}L + c{\cdot}K\right) \tag{8.2}$$

The demand curve is given by:

$$Q = Q\left(P_T\right) \tag{8.3}$$

The number of physicians (M) is constant in short-run period:

$$M = M_c \tag{8.4}$$

In short-run period, the hospital has to maximize the equation (8.2) subject to Eqs. (8.1), (8.3), and (8.4). The equilibrium in short-run period is to hire units of L and K until their prices equal to their marginal contribution to the value of output (Jacobs, 1974).

In the long-run period, the number of physicians is not fixed and it is variable over time. The question raised is to fix the optimal level of hospital's staff, and the optimal level depends on the assumption made about the hospital's staff. There are three possible cases: (a) closed staff model, (b) discriminatory sharing or hiring, and (c) open staff model. In the first model (closed staff model), the physicians are able to regulate their members in order to maximize average net revenue. Physicians will accept to add new members as long as it causes each member's net income rise. McPake & Normard (2008, p. 157) indicate that in the: (a) "closed staff" model, the physicians regulate the number of their numbers in order to maximize their revenues and each member takes an equal share, (b) "discriminatory hiring" model, some of the physicians are partners and share equally the net revenues and other

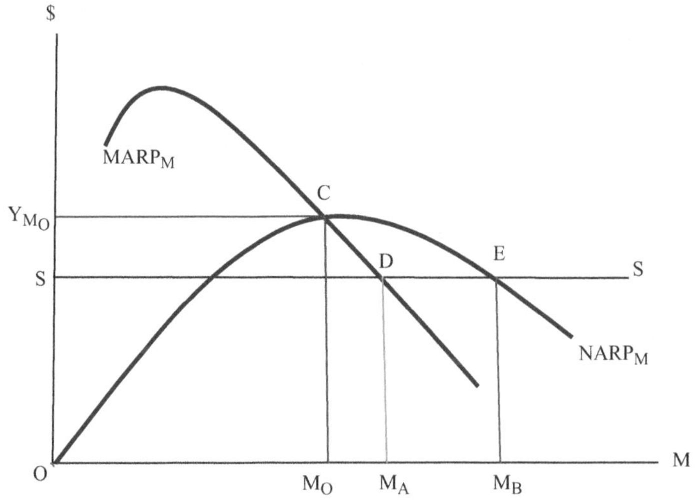

Fig. 8.1 Equilibrium in Pauly–Redisch model, where *SS* is physician supply curve which is infinite inelastic and it is at a low level relative to income possibilities in this particular hospital, *M* is number of physicians, $NARP_M$ represents the maximum attainable income per physician for each specific value of M, and MRP_M represents the value of the marginal product of physicians

physicians are payed their marginal product, and (c) "open-staff" model, any physicians who want to join the hospital can do so and share equally the net revenue.

Figure 8.1 shows the physician equilibrium in the Pauly–Redisch model.[1] More specifically, the optimal size of physicians is determined in three models.

On the horizontal axes of Fig. 8.1, the number of physicians is measured, and on the vertical axes, the price of remuneration of physicians is presented. The three different models explain the determination of the size of the physicians based on the assumptions made about the possibilities of new entries of physicians into this particular hospital. In the first model ("closed staff" model) where physicians control the number of their members, they share equally the total revenue. As the number of physicians increases, the total revenues increase. The rate of the increase of revenues is decreasing. The increase of the revenues is shown by the upward sloping of the curve O $NARP_M$. The decreasing rate of the change of total revenues is presented by the downward part of the MRP_M curve. Taking into consideration that the purpose of the physicians is to maximize their total revenues, the equilibrium point is the point *C* and size of the physicians at this point is M_O.

In the second model ("Discriminatory sharing or hiring" model), the number of physicians employed in this hospital will be increased until the marginal revenue product (MRP_M) equals to the price of the physicians (OS). As MRP_M is greater than OS, more physicians are added in the hospital. The equilibrium point will be the point *D* and the size of physicians is M_A.

[1] This figure is presented by Pauly and Redisch (1973, p. 92). This physician equilibrium in the Pauly–Redisch is presented and analyzed by Jacobs (1974, p. 93).

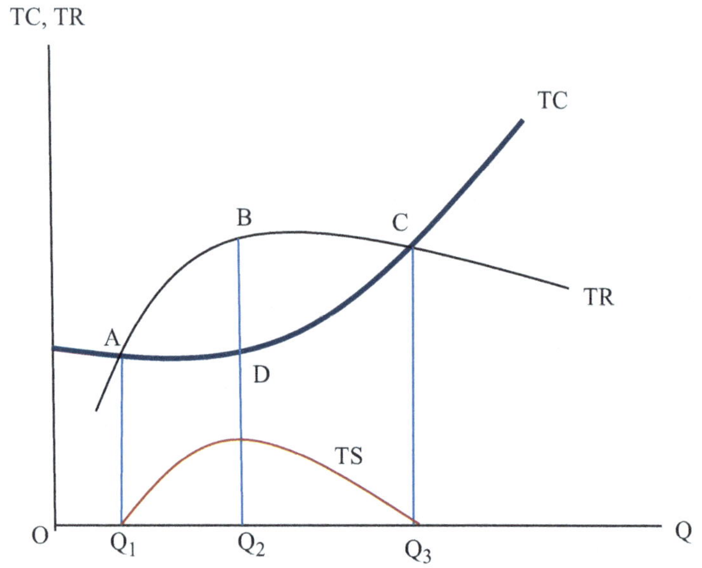

Fig. 8.2 The quantity-maximizing model (this figure is presented by Jacobs (1974, p. 88) and by Liu & Mills (2008, p. 279)). *TR* total revenue, *TC* total cost, *TS* total surplus (profit or loss), and *Q* health services provided

In the last model ("Open Staff" model), there is free entry of physicians and each new member becomes a "full partner" of this hospital. Each of these physicians receives as income the part of average income per person which equals to the marginal price of physicians. The equilibrium point is the point E, and the number of physicians is M_B.

8.5.2 *Quantity/Revenues Maximizing Model of Hospitals*

Profit is not the main goal for most hospitals (Liu & Mills, 2008). Other objectives are quantity maximizing and revenue maximizing. According to Rice (1966) and Brown (1970), hospitals are quantity maximizers. The quantity is the number of patients. The revenue function of the hospitals depends on the number of patients under the hypothesis that the price paid by patients does not change. As the number of patients increases, the total revenues also increase with a decreasing rate. In contrast, the total cost has an upward sloping, and this indicates that as the number of patients increases, the hospital has to use more input in order to provide sufficient health-care services. Figure 8.2 presents the model of quantity maximizing.

In the case of a profit-maximizing hospital, the output produced will be Q_2 at which the profit (it is the difference between total revenues and total cost) BD is the highest. In the case of a nonprofit output-maximizing hospital, the output is Q_3. At this level of output, the profit is zero. More specifically, according to the theory of Rice (1966), the hospital will produce until it achieves a minimum profit. If profit does not exist, then this level of output, as we mentioned above, is Q_3. The government can push the nonprofit hospital to produce more health services if the government decides to subsidies total revenues or cost. In both cases, the new output is to the right of Q_3.

If the government subsidizes total revenues, the total revenues curve shifts upward and the new output produced is Q_4 (Figs. 8.3 and 8.4), or if the government subsidizes the total cost, the total cost curve shifts downward and the output produced is Q_5.

Finkler (1983) extends the Baumol sales-maximization theory[2] to the nonprofitable hospitals and develops the revenue-maximizing model. He considers that the hospital is a revenue-maximizing entity. The basic hypotheses of Finkler's theory are as follows: (a) owners of not-for-profit hospitals are rewarded on the basis of revenues and not on the basis of profits and (b) hospitals are not perfect competitive units and the demand curve for each hospital is finite for each of its products. It is also assumed that physicians are related to the hospital and are affiliated with the hospital, as a result the hospital is in greater demand. The revenue-maximizing hospital implies that hospitals offer those products that return the largest amount of revenue per unit of cost and the hospital can still break even. There are cases in

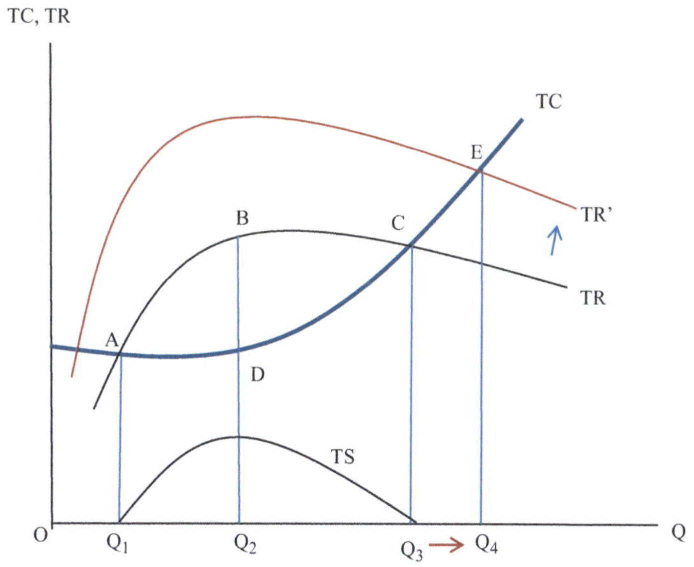

Fig. 8.3 The quantity-maximizing model in the case of subsidizing revenues

[2] Baumol developed the sales-maximization theory in his work in 1959.

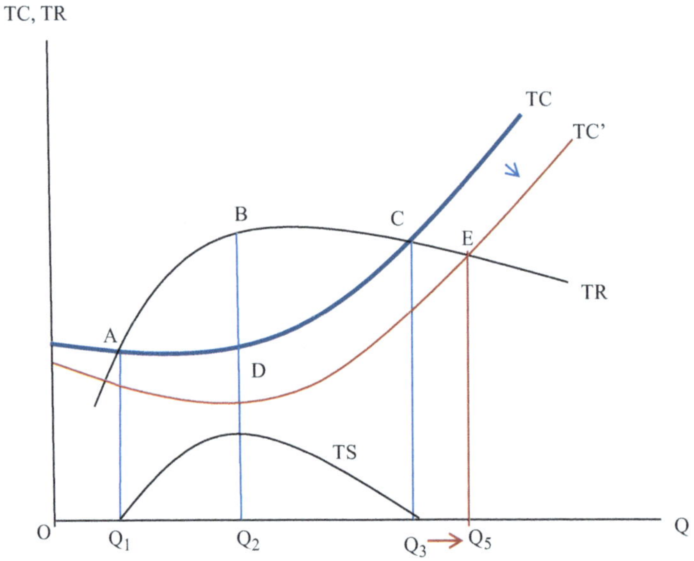

Fig. 8.4 The quantity-maximizing model in the case of subsidizing total cost

which some products will be offered at a loss if their effect on the demand of other products supplied by the hospital makes a profit at least equal to the loss.

8.5.3 Quality-Maximizing Model of Hospitals

In the previous model, the maximization rule was upon the quantity or the revenues of hospitals. Lee (1971) focuses on the quality of health services. He assumes that there is interdependency between ownership and administration of the hospitals. The administrator is seen to be the main actor who is interested in maximizing a utility function, which is the objective function of the hospital operation. This utility function includes variables such as salary, prestige, security, power, and job satisfaction. Utility maximization is linked to status (prestige) rather than income. The administrator perception about the status is related to the prestige of other hospitals (Jacobs, 1974). Lee emphasizes on the quality of inputs which enter into the hospital's objective function and not on the quality of inputs and outputs. The basic assumption of his production theory is that the hospital attempts to minimize the gap between its desired status and its prevailing status. The hospitals compete not for the profit but for the status. Hospitals compete in terms of the methods of treatment and the use of equipment and the personnel (Lee, 1971). On the basis of these assumptions, Lee argues that a kinked demand curve exists in the factors market and the hospitals will respond to an increase of input usage of any hospital but not to the decrease. The rise of the status is related to the increase of revenues, and the latter is determined by the prices of services and insurance schemes. The price elasticity of demand is closed zero, and this will raise revenues without affecting the output levels. The model proposed by Lee (1971) has been criticized because of its assumptions and because of the lack of explanation of the behavior of model to external changes (Jacobs, 1974).

8.5.4 Quantity- and Quality-Maximizing Models of Hospitals

Newhouse (1970) proposes another economic model to explain the behavior of nonprofitable hospital. As in the previous presented models, Newhouse focuses upon the administrator as the decision maker of maximizing a utility function. The first difference with the other models is that the "decision maker" in the Newhouse's model is a mixed group which consisted of trustees, doctors, and hospital administrator (Jacobs, 1974). This amalgam of different persons seeks to maximize a weighted function of quality and quantity subject to a budget constraint. Each of the group of the amalgam has different objectives. It is not clear how different objectives are combined in order to determine the objectives of the common utility function. In the model developed by Newhouse, it is not clear if "quality" refers to inputs or outputs. Furthermore, there is a lack of clarity in what each group of the management considers as "quality." According to McGuire (1985), the Newhouse's model is based on specific assumptions:

a. The hospital is considered as a single product firm whose physical product is measurable and the decision-making process is maximizing the quantity/quality trade-off.
b. There are entry restrictions.
c. The hospital can implement market decisions subject to budget constraint without taking into account any other competitors.

Another assumption made by Newhouse is that patients pay the full cost of hospital care and therefore the hospitals' revenues are calculated according to an individual demand curve. Given the quality, income, the price of health care, and other factors, there is a specific demand at each price which determines the demand curve. If there is a change in the quality, then the price of health care increases (patients have the willingness to pay more for a higher quality health services), and a new demand curve is fixed. As far as the average total cost is concerned, Newhouse assumes that this is U-shaped. This also shifts upward with an increase in the quality. For each level of quality, there is at least one equilibrium point where average revenue (AR) equals to average total cost. This equilibrium is shown in Figures 8.5 and 8.6.

Figures 8.5 and 8.6 show that the hospital determines its output at different level of quality. As the quality increases, the total cost and demand curve shift upward, and the new output could be greater (Fig. 8.5) or smaller (Fig. 8.6) than the previous.

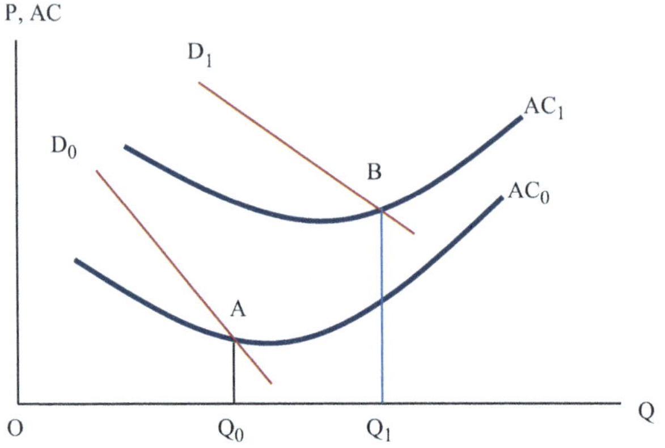

Fig. 8.5 Output maximizing at different quality levels

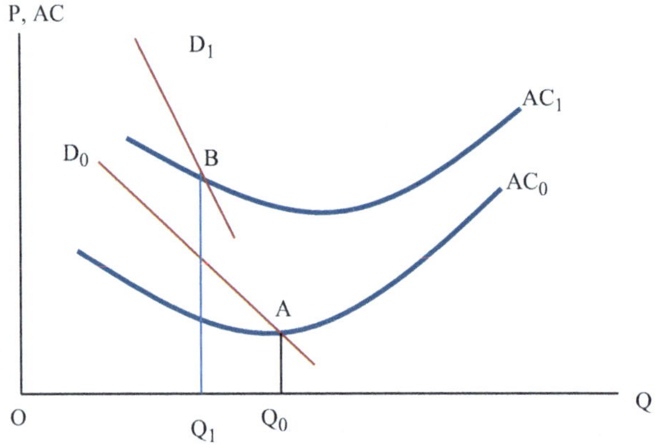

Fig. 8.6 Output maximizing at different quality levels

Combining all different equilibrium points at which output is maximizing for different given levels of quantity, the trade-off curve between quantity and quality is drawn. This curve is downward sloping[3] showing that as the quantity of the health care increases, the quality of this health care decreases. As we said above, the administrator should maximize his utility function. According to Newhouse, the decision maker must choose the point of the trade-off curve which maximizes his utility, given by the utility curve (Fig. 8.7).

The equilibrium point at which the decision maker maximizes his utility is the point at which the trade-off curve is tangent at the utility curve.

[3] The trade-off curve may have an upward slope over some ranges, although it usually has a downward slope (Jacobs, 1974).

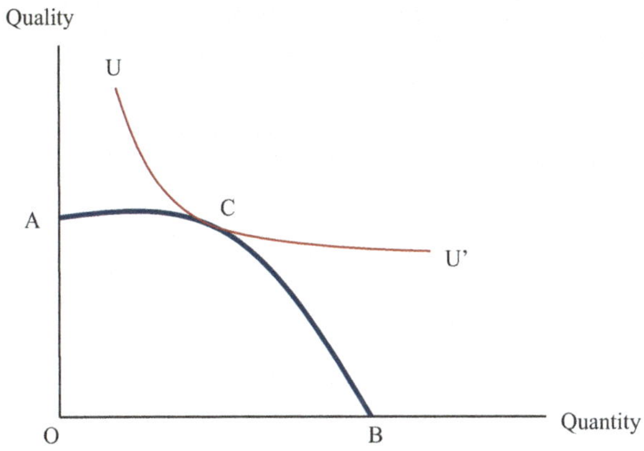

Fig. 8.7 Equilibrium in Newhouse's quantity–quality maximizing model (this figure is presented by Newhouse (1970, p. 68) and Jacobs (1974, p. 88)). *UU'* utility function, *AB* trade-off curve between quantity and quality

One of the implications of the Newhouse's model is least-cost production. This indicates that the hospital could produce health services at a lower unit cost. Newhouse states two reasons for which the hospital does not achieve an optimal outcome. First, there is a bias in favor of higher quality products. Second, there are barriers for entrance resulting from nonprofit status of the hospitals.

The presentation of the Newhouse's model was based on the assumption that hospital produces only one quality which is unclear. However, the hospital produces several services of a different quality. Jacobs (1974) considers that the major problem with Newhouse's model is that hospital is placed in a theoretical context as a "firm" with a single decision maker ("administrator") and with a single utility function which is not realistic. Moreover, the least-cost production and the average cost pricing is questionable.

Harris (1977) considered the hospital as two separate firms. One of the firms is made up of medical staff that comprises a demand division, and the second firm is for the administration which is the supply division. These two firms have different structures. Each of these two firms has its own managers, objectives, pricing policies, and constraints. Each firm attempts to maximize its utility, but the objectives set up by its managers are sometimes contradictory. Medical staff is considered to be the more powerful group. Within this organization, the staff (medical staff and administration) operate in a noncooperative oligopoly type model. The maximization of the quantity and the quality is the main objective of the hospital. The main differences between Harris' model and the Newhouse's model are the different organizational structure of the hospital and the existence of conflicts between the medical staff and administration which influence the operation of the hospitals.

Feldstein (1971) developed an economic model in order to explain the hospital cost inflation. This model consists of several equations which describe both demand

and supply. Using the market mechanism demand and supply is equilibrated by price. Given that in short-run period the supply of health-care services—based on the use of beds—remains constant, an increase of demand will lead to an increase of price. In this model, any change to the health-care services provided had no effect on the demand for health-care services. In the next work of Feldstein (1977), he incorporates the variable "quality" in his model, and he shows that more expensive "quality" increases the demand for health-care services. Since the patient may only be given limited information, Feldstein (1977) proceeded to explain the role of physician in the determination for the demand of health-care services. The physician is well aware of the financial and economic position and the insurance coverage of the patient, as well the patient's medical problem, and he may determine the demand for health care. As far as the hospital utilization is concerned, Feldstein (1971, 1977) states that this is affected by admissions (ADM) and average duration of stay (MS). Admissions and average duration of stay depend on the price per patient, the quality of care, the extent of a patient's insurance, and a variety of other variables including income, demographic composition of population, availability of hospital facilities, and alternative sources of care. The total demand bed days is defined as follows:

$$\mathrm{BDD} = \mathrm{ADM}\cdot\mathrm{MS}$$

Bed supply (BEDS) is determined exogenous in short-run period. If R is a constant number of bed occupied, then BDS = 365·R·BEDS, where BDS = desired bed days supplied. As we have mentioned, Feldstein (1971) indicated that quality is not a determinant and demand curve does not shift with quality, while in his second work in 1977, he considered quality as a determinant which affects the demand curve. Equalizing demand for beds (BDD) to the fixed bed supply (BDS), we find the equilibrium price. This price is consistent with the demand curve. According to Feldstein (1971), hospitals will respond to an increase in the equilibrating price by adjusting their actual price upward. If the price is less than the equilibrium price, then there is an excess in demand. Until now, Feldstein (1971) explained the determination of the price of hospital care based on the demand and supply for beds. He explained the rising of hospital prices keeping constant the number of hospital beds without any reference to input prices and quantities. The next step in his analysis is to explain the relation between hospitals price and the components of hospital cost. The budget constraint is:

$$P = C - D,$$

where P is the price charged per bed day, C is the average cost per patient, and D is the deficit per patient day.

If there is no deficit ($D = 0$), then the price charged per bed day equals to the average cost per patient ($P = C$).

The average cost per unit can be defined in terms of the cost of employees and cost of materials.

$$C = w\cdot N + \pi\cdot J + K$$

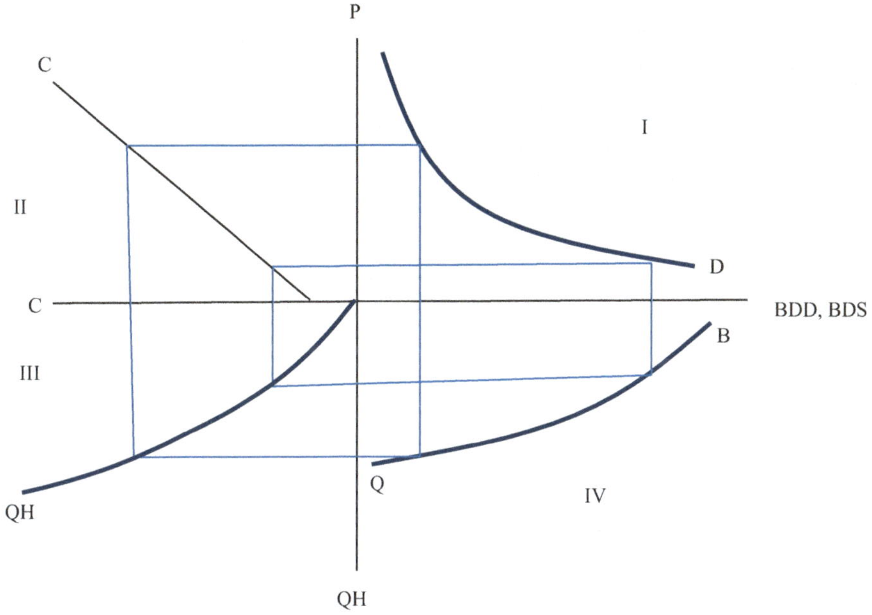

Fig. 8.8 Presentation of Feldstein's model

where N is the number of employees per patient day, W is the average wage, π is the price of materials, J is the quantity of materials, and K is the interest and other fixed costs associated with previously acquired capital stock.

Given that in this model the quality (QH) is constant, constant returns to scale will be constant. Maximizing quality of health care (QH) implies choosing N and J such as C is on the budget frontier. This means that higher the P the higher the C and maybe the QH. Figure 8.8 presents the basic relations of the Feldstein's model.[4]

The first quadrant shows the relation between the hospital's price (P) and the number of bed days demanded (BDD). The labeling of the horizontal axis implies the equality of demand of beds to supply of beds. The line in quadrant II shows the linear relation between the price and the cost per patient day. Each point on the line shows that $P = C$. The quadrant III shows the relation between the cost per patient and the maximum attainable level of quality. In other words, the quality is related positively to the cost. The curve QB in the quadrant IV shows the relation between the number of patient bed days (BDS) and the quality of care. Given the demand for beds (D), the cost-price relation (C), and the production function of the quality (QH), the trade-off curve (QB) is derived.

[4]The graphical presentation of the Feldstein's model is based on Feldstein (1971, p. 857–858) and Jacobs (1974, p. 90).

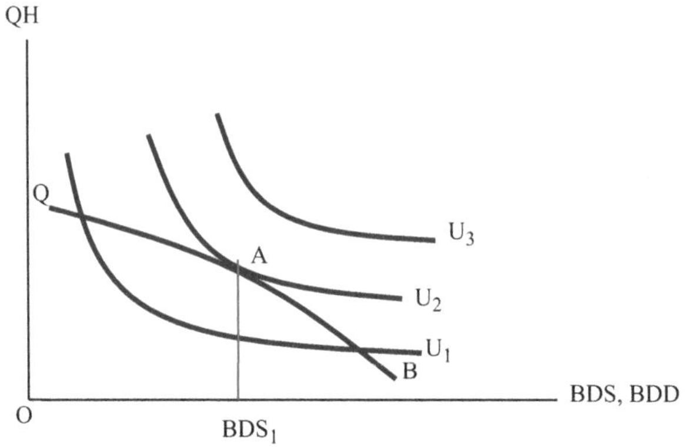

Fig. 8.9 Equilibrium in Feldstein's model

Hospital's preferences are presented by a utility function whose components are the number of patient bed-days and the quality of hospital care:

$$U = U(\text{BDS},\text{QH})$$

The hospital attempts to define the number of beds that maximizes the utility function, subject to the constraints of the price of health care, of the average cost, and of the quality of health. The equilibrium is shown in Figure 8.9.

The Feldstein's model tries to explain the hospital cost inflation. He supports that the reasons of the increase of the hospital cost inflation are the rising demand induced by an increase in insurance coverage, personal incomes, and the availability of hospital services. Any increase of the components of cost is the result and not the cause of higher prices.

The presentation of the economic models of the hospitals' operation shows that hospitals are economic units and they follow the principles of the economic theory. The structure of the hospital and the nature of the hospital care services make a difference between hospitals and firms. In order to understand and explain the behavior of hospitals, the differences between hospitals and firms imply to use other economic practices rather than the traditional economic models seen in firms. The role of physicians in the decision-making process is major one, and the quality of the health-care services is an important constraint for those who determine the objectives of the hospital's operations.

References

Abernethy, M. A., & Lillis, A. (2001). Interdependencies in organization design: A test in hospitals. *Journal Accounting Management Research, 13*(1), 107–129.

Al-Amin, M., Schiaffino, M., Park, S., & Harman, J. (2018). Sustained hospital performance of health care providers and systems survey measures. *Journal of Healthcare Management, 63*(1), 15–28.

Bai, G., & Anderson, G. F. (2016). US hospitals are still using charge master, makeups to maximize revenues. *Health Affairs, 35*(9), 1658–1664.

Baumol, W. (1959). *Business behavior, value and growth*. New York: Macmillan Co..

Bohigas, L., Smith, D., Brooks, T., Donahue, T., Heidemann, E., Donaldson, B., et al. (1996). Accreditation programs for hospitals: Funding and operation. *International Journal for Quality in Health Care, 8*(6), 583–589.

Brown, M. (1970). An economic analysis of hospital operations. *Hospital Administration, 15*, 60–74.

Burnell, B. (1991). The effect of school district structure on education spending. *Public Choice, 69*(3), 253–264.

Champagne, F., Leduc, N., Denis, J. L., & Pineault, R. (1993). Organizational and environmental determinants of the performance of public health units. *Social Science & Medicine, 37*(1), 85–95.

Chang, T., & Jacobson, M. (2012). What do nonprofit hospitals maximize? Evidence from California's Seismic Retrofit Mandate, Rand and NBER, August 2012.

Chletsos, M. (2011). *Health economics*. Athens: Pataki Publications.

Cowing, T. G., Holtmann, A. G., & Powers, S. (1982). Hospital cost analysis: A survey and evaluation of recent studies'. In R. M. Scheffler & L. F. Rossiter (Eds.), *Advances in health economics and health services research* (Vol. 4, pp. 257–303). Greenwich, CT: JAI Press.

Deneffe, D., & Masson, R. T. (2002). What do not-for-profit hospitals maximize? *International Journal of Industrial Organization, 20*(4), 461–492.

Duran, A., Kutzin, J., Martin Moreno, J. N., & Travis, P. (2012). Understanding health systems: Scope, functions and objectives. In J. Figueras & M. McKee (Eds.), *Health systems, health, wealthy and societal well being. Assessing the care for investing in health systems* (pp. 19–36). Maidenhead, UK: McGraw Hill Open University Press.

Feldstein, M. S. (1971). Hospital cost inflation: A study of nonprofit price dynamics. *The American Economic Review, 61*(5), 853–872.

Feldstein, M. S. (1977). Quality change and the demand for hospital care. *Econometrica, 45*(7), 1681–1702.

Feldstein, P. J. (1968). Applying economic concepts to hospital care. *Hospital Administration, 13*(1), 68–89.

Fennell, M. L., & Alexander, J. A. (1987). Organizational boundary spanning in institutionalized environments. *Academy of Management Journal, 30*(3), 456–476.

Finkler, S. (1983). The hospital as a sales-maximizing entity. *Health Services Research, 18*(2), 117–133.

Gentry, W. M., & Penrod, J. P. (2000). The tax benefits of not-for-profit hospitals. In D. M. Cutler (Ed.), *The changing hospital industry: Comparing for-profit and not-for-profit institutions* (pp. 285–324). Chicago: University of Chicago Press.

Ginn, G. O., & Young, G. J. (1992). Organizational and environmental determinants of hospital strategy. *Hospital & Health Services Administration, 37*(2), 291–302.

Gruca, T. S., & Nath, D. (1994). Regulatory change, constraints on adaptation and organizational failure: An empirical analysis of acute care hospitals. *Strategic Management Journal, 15*(5), 345–363.

Hage, J., & Dewar, R. (1973). Elite values versus organizational structure in predicting innovation. *Administrative Science Quarterly, 18*(3), 279–290.

Handel, D. A., Hilton, J. A., Ward, M. J., Rabin, E., Zwemer, F. L., & Pines, J. M. (2010). Emergency department throughput, crowding, and financial outcomes for hospitals. *The Society for Academic Emergency Medicine, 17*(8), 840–847.

Harris, J. E. (1977). The internal organization of hospitals: Some economic implications. *The Bell Journal of Economics, 8*(2), 467–482.

Hoerger, T. J. (1991). Profit variability in for-profit and not-for-profit hospitals. *Journal of Health Economics, 10*(3), 259–289.

Jacobs, P. (1974). A survey of economic models of hospitals. *Inquiry, 11*(2), 83–97.

Joshi, S., & Krishnan, R. (2017). *Economic models of hospital behavior, international encyclopedia of public health* (2nd ed.pp. 410–416). Oxford: Academic Press.

Kallapur, S., & Eldenburg, L. (2005). Uncertainty, real options, and cost behavior: Evidence from Washington State Hospitals. *Journal of Accounting Research, 43*(5), 735–752.

Karasoulos, C. (2014). Modern approach to the operation of a hospital. *To Vima tou Asklipiou Journal, 12*(1), 7–19.

Kast, E. E., & Rozenzweig, J. E. (1972). General systems theory: Application for organisation and management. *Academy of Management Journal, 15*(4), 447–465.

Kimberly, J. R., & Evanisko, M. J. (1981). Organizational innovation: The influence of individual, organizational, and contextual factors on hospital adoption of technological and administrative innovations. *Academy of Management Journal, 24*(4), 689–713.

Lee, L. M. (1971). A conspicuous production theory of hospital behavior. *Southern Economic Journal, 38*(1), 48–58.

Lee, R. D., Johnson, R. W., & Joyce, P. G. (2013). *Public budgeting systems* (9th ed.). Burlington, MA: Jones & Bartlett Learning.

Liu, X., & Mills, A. (2008). Economic models of hospital behavior. In *International encyclopedia of public health* (pp. 276–282). Amsterdam: Elsevier.

McGuire, A. (1985). The theory of the hospital: A review of the models. *Social Science & Medicine, 20*(11), 1177–1184.

McGuire, A., Henderson, J., & Moone, G. (1988). *The economics of health care*. London: Routledge & Kegan Paul.

McPake, B., & Normard, C. (2008). *Health economics. An international perspective*. London/New York: Routledge Taylor & Francis Group.

Miles, R. E., Snow, C. C., Meyer, A. D., & Coleman Jr., H. J. (1978). Organizational strategy, structure, and process. *The Academy of Management Review, 3*(3), 546–562.

Newhouse, J. P. (1970). Toward a theory of nonprofit institutions: An economic model of hospital. *The American Economic Review, 60*(1), 64–74.

Pauly, M., & Redisch, M. (1973). The not-for profit hospital as a physicians' cooperative. *The American Economic Review, 63*(1), 87–99.

Rice, R. (1966). An analysis of the hospital as an economic organization. *Modern Hospital, 106*, 87–91.

Rice, T., & Unruh, L. (2009). *The economics of health reconsidered* (3rd ed.). Chicago: HAP – AUPHA.

Shortell, S. M. (1988). The evolution of hospital systems: Unfulfilled promises and self-fulfilling prophesies. *Medicare Care Research and Review, 45*(2), 177–214.

Simon, H. (1957). *Models of man, social and rational: Mathematical essays on rational human behavior in a social setting*. London: Wiley.

Sloan, F. (1979). The internal organization of hospitals: A description. *Health Services Resources, 14*, 203–230.

Sloan, F. A., & Becker, G. R. (1981). Internal organization of hospitals and hospitals costs. *Inquiry, 18*(3), 224–239.

Spaulding, A., Edwardson, N., & Zhao, M. (2018). Hospital based purchasing performance. *Journal of Healthcare Management, 63*(1), 31–48.

Stall, L., & Mortimore, P. (1997). School effectiveness and school improvement. In J. White & M. Barber (Eds.), *Perspectives on school effectiveness and school improvement* (pp. 9–24). London, UK: Institute of Education.

Suhrecke, M., Sauto Arce, R., McKee, M., & Rocco, L. (2012). Economic costs of ill health in the European region. In J. Figueras & M. McKee (Eds.), *Health systems, health, wealthy and societal well being. Assessing the care for investing in health systems* (pp. 61–100). Maidenhead, UK: McGraw Hill Open University Press.

Swanson Kazley, A., & Ozcan, Y. A. (2007). Organizational and environmental determinants of hospital EMR adoption: A national study. *Journal of Medical Systems, 31*(5), 375–384.

Wheeler, J. R. C., Burkhardt, J., Alexander, J. A., & Magnus, S. A. (1999). Financial and organizational determinants of hospital diversification into subacute care. *Health Services Research, 34*(1), 61–81.

Xenos, P., Nektarios, M., Polyzos, N., & Ifantopoulos, I. (2014). Modern methods of hospital funding, competition and financial incentives. *Archives of Hellenic Medicine, 31*(2), 172–185.

Chapter 9
Hospitals as Suppliers of Healthcare Services

Key Points

- In the short term, technology is constant and the quantity of healthcare services depends on the variable factor, namely, the medical and nonmedical personnel
- A hospital can achieve economies of scale in the earliest stages of production where capital is fixed and not used efficiently
- Independently of the nature of the market, a hospital decides on the level of its output based on the profit maximization rule
- Hospitals generate profits mainly in the short term because the competition between them reduces the margins for making high profits
- A perfectly competitive market is considered as the ideal market for the consumer/patient since it improves the quality of healthcare services provided and the price at which they are sold is kept to a minimum due to the competition between hospitals.

9.1 Introduction

Hospitals all over the world strive to deliver healthcare services to their patients. They date back to ancient Greek and Egyptian times, when illnesses were attributed to religious shortfalls such as a lack of faith. Nowadays, hospital healthcare services are understood to serve a societal need and are delivered by hospitals in two forms: public and private. Many studies have investigated the differences in the healthcare services provided by public and private hospitals and a general conclusion is that patients prefer private hospitals because they are better technologically equipped, have shorter waiting lists, and provide more personalized care (Shabbir, Malik, & Malik, 2016). Research in this field identified many barriers, including inadequate health insurance systems and limited purchasing power, which should be taken into consideration when delivering quality health care (Kasturi Rangan, Quelch, Herrero, & Barton, 2007). Due to the limitations of the health care offered by the public

M. Chletsos, A. Saiti, *Strategic Management and Economics in Health Care*,
https://doi.org/10.1007/978-3-030-35370-4_9

sector, private healthcare provision has grown but it has also received criticism, mainly for being inaccessible to people on low incomes and occasionally for providing profit-generating services that are unnecessary (Bennett, McPake, & Mills, 1997).

The World Health Organization (2010) acknowledges that even developed countries are expected to face challenges in the way that healthcare services are provided because of an aging population, an increased life expectancy, and population growth. In debates regarding healthcare problems, hospitals have a key role to play: based on an OECD report (OECD, 2018), the healthcare expenditures were increased up to 2017 in all countries examined.

An extremely important component in the economics of providing healthcare services is innovation (Lansisalmi, Kivimaki, Aalto, & Ruoranen, 2006). In the healthcare industry, innovations enhance life expectancy, the quality of life, diagnostic and treatment options, and indeed the cost-effectiveness of the whole healthcare system (Varkey, Horne, & Bennet, 2008). For example, innovations are applied in the delivery of health care (Varkey & Athyal, 2005), in surgical interventions, and in medications (Varkey et al., 2008).

Another important component of healthcare services linked to economics is their quality. The quality of services provided by hospitals is associated with customer satisfaction (Johns, Avci, & Karatepe, 2004; Kara, Lonial, Tarim, & Zaim, 2005), customer retention (Reichheld & Sasser, 1990), costs (Wilson, Zeithaml, Bitner, & Gremler, 2008), and the financial performance of the hospital (Buttle, 1996). However, unlike ordinary products, this kind of quality is not so easily defined or measured (Lee, Delene, Bunda, & Kim, 2000). Nevertheless, researchers maintain that the quality of healthcare services is the most important element of those services (Lee & Yom, 2007). Padma, Rajendran, and Sai Lokachari (2010) go further, saying that hospitals are obliged to provide superior healthcare services.

Healthcare organizations should aim to maximize their efficiency by reducing their costs while offering quality services at the same time (Kounetas & Papathanassopoulos, 2003). The range of healthcare services offered is mainly determined by their relevant cost, the decision-making approach(es), and the price level set for those services. An accurate estimation of healthcare service costs is the key to preventing undesirable consequences that would affect the quality of those services (Waters & Hussey, 2004).

All over the world, hospitals constitute the most important healthcare expenditure in their local economy. As such, hospitals (both public and private) can be considered as economic units with specific goals. Hospitals have to provide health services which are the result of a production process. In economic terms, the production function explains the relationship between inputs and outputs in the short term and in the long term. According to the production theory, hospitals are obliged to choose the optimal combination of inputs in order to produce the optimal level of output(s). Thus, the hospitals first have to decide about the optimal level of outputs (or services) they would like to offer, given the amount of inputs they have, and secondly, to set the optimal price at which they can sell their outputs in order to achieve their goals. Public and private hospitals have a different approach for setting the price of their healthcare services, depending on whether or not the aim is to maximize profit.

This chapter deals with economic issues of hospitals as production units and looks more in depth at the operation of hospitals under different market structures.

9.2 Short-Term and Long-Term Production Theory

Economists have developed many theories in order to explain the main aspects of the economy. A typical example is the microeconomic theory of production which is a well-known, highly standardized theory that can be applied to a variety of sectors and explains how firms operate. Just as other scientific theories that aim to explain and predict, the production theory can be applied to hospitals in order to explain their operation by considering their main financial aspects.

Health can be attained through the healthcare services provided by hospitals and related organizations. Those healthcare services constitute the productive outputs of a hospital and require financial expenditure. All business units aim to produce goods or services in order to have an income. Hospitals produce healthcare services in order to make a profit or to produce a specific output/benefit. A healthcare service (a hospital's production function) aims to maximize the level of health in a patient by a specific set of inputs in a defined time frame (Santerre & Neun, 2010). A hospital's output consists not only of its performance in improving and maintaining patients' health but also in its capacity to satisfy demand (Zweifel & Breyer, 1997). However, it is difficult to measure the hospital outputs and establish a production theory for hospitals due to the considerable amount of heterogeneity that exists in hospitals with regard to the different treatments offered (Sloan, 1979). The output could be expressed in terms of the number of days of a patient's stay (patient days), the number of patients, or types of treatment. Zweifel and Breyer (1997) differentiate the types of treatment along various dimensions such as the type of illness, the severity of the illness, and complications arising during the treatment, the stage of the disease, concomitant diseases, and patient characteristics.

Gaynor and Vogt (2000) stated that it is difficult to analyze hospital productivity, even if there is a large amount of data available regarding the hospital's costs. The diversity of treatment types and patient characteristics calls for the development of a patient classification system that can facilitate an estimation of the treatment cost. Zweifel and Breyer (1997) mention three different patient classification systems: (a) the international classification of diseases (ICD), (b) diagnosis-related groups (DRGs), and (c) patient management categories (PMCs).

The production process of any economic unit can be described by the production function, which shows the highest level of output the economic unit can produce from a given combination of inputs (Katz & Rosen, 1998).

Generally speaking, economists describe the production of an output as a function of labor and capital, where:

$$Q = f(L,K)$$

In the healthcare sector, Q refers to the hospital services which are measured as patient days or treatment types, L refers to the medical and nonmedical staff, and K constitutes the medical equipment and the building infrastructure. In the traditional neoclassical model proposed by Pauly and Redisch (1973), there is a distinction of labor between nonphysician and physician/medical staff.

The financial outcome of hospital activity, from an economic perspective, is based on certain indicators (Breyer, 1987):

- Factors of production: hours worked by the staff, dressings, drugs, electricity, fuel, etc.
- Individual medical and nursing services: examinations, medications, injections, meals, etc.
- Number of patient days, which indicates the intensity of care
- Number of patients

The hospital can be considered as a production unit, where the fundamental elements of the production theory can be applied. Production theory involves short-term and long-term time frames. In the short term, at least one factor of production remains constant while in the long term all factors are variable. In the case of a hospital, the quantity of the productive coefficients remains stable. For example, there are no changes in the fundamental elements of a hospital such as the building infrastructure and medical equipment. A fixed cost (FC) is an amount spent for the productive coefficients to remain stable over the short term. On the other hand, a variable cost (VC) includes factors that can change in the short term, such as the number of patients. The total cost (TC) is the result of summing the fixed and variable costs.

In the short-term production of a hospital, "K" (medical equipment and building infrastructure) remains stable while "L" (medical personnel) is variable. Short-term production is based on the equation:

$$Q = f\left(L, \overline{\overline{K}}\right)$$

where: $\overline{\overline{K}}$ indicates that K is constant and independent of the output produced. Thus, the hospital output depends on variations in labor (L).

In the short term, the total cost changes only because of the changes in labor cost ($w \cdot L$) since the capital cost ($r \cdot K$) is constant and does not vary along with the variations in the output

where: w = wage rate for medical personnel and r = rental price of capital.

The short-term cost function is given by the equation:

$$\text{SRTC} = w \cdot L + r \cdot \overline{\overline{K}}$$

while the long-term cost function is given by the equation:

$$\text{LRTC} = w \cdot L + r \cdot K$$

Santerre and Neun (2010) defined generalized short-term health production as follows:

$$\text{Health} = f\left(\text{medical care, technology, profile, lifestyle, environment, socioeconomic status}\right)$$

where: Health represents the level of health at a specific point in time; medical care is the quantity of medical care consumed; technology is the medical technology used; profile refers to the individual's mental and physical profile; lifestyle covers the lifestyle variables (diet and exercise); environment refers to environmental variables; socioeconomic status represents social and economic factors such as education and income.

On the other hand, while long-term production is based on the same functional formula $Q = f(L, K)$, the K is no longer stable. In a long-term time frame, all factors of production can change. A typical example of a nonstable K is the development of a new facility that requires a hospital's building structure to be expanded or more beds to be added. In long-term production, there are no fixed inputs and the firm has the flexibility to make its own production decisions. In the long term, a hospital can either expand or reduce its production in order to reduce its costs, according to its economies of scale.

The difference between short-term and long-term production is that factors deemed to be "fixed" cannot be changed in the short term but only in the long term, while the variable factors can be amended in either case. Long-term production can be estimated either by estimating short-term costs, by using the envelope condition to calculate the long-term cost function (Preyra & Pink, 2006), or by estimating short-term costs directly without using the envelope condition (Aletras, 1999).

Long-term production is based on the economies/diseconomies of scale. In an economy of scale, it is assumed that a hospital's average costs will fall when its specialized labor and capital are increased. On the other hand, diseconomies of scale arise when a firm becomes too large (Santerre & Neun, 2010) and all inputs increase. Certainly, it is difficult to apply production theory in situations of radical change (Amendola, Gaffard, & Saraceno, 2005).

The production function (Katz & Rosen, 1998) makes the following assumptions:

1. The hospital services increase, if at least one of its inputs increases and all other inputs remain constant. Thus, an extra amount of output is produced when the hospital uses one more additional unit of input. The marginal product of input[1] (MP) must be ≥ 0.

[1] Marginal product of input is the ratio of the change of output over the change of input ($MP = \Delta Q/\Delta X$).

Fig. 9.1 Production function in the short term

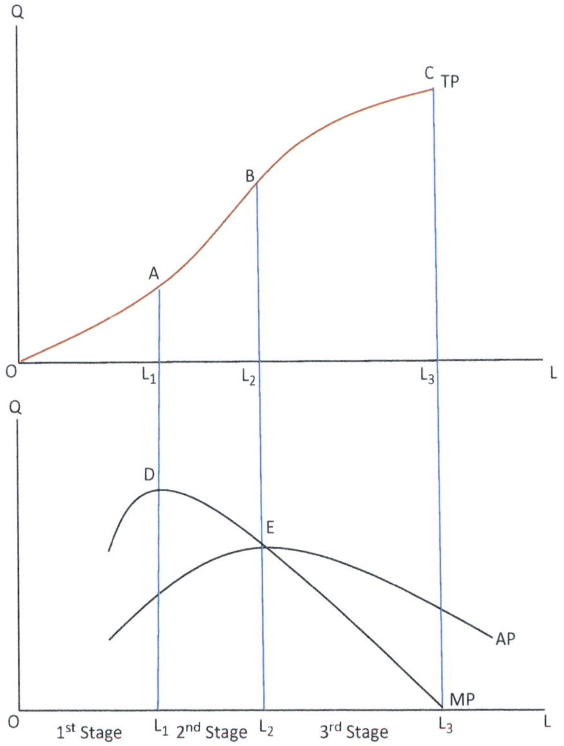

2. The law of diminishing marginal returns applies. This law states that as a given input increases, with the amount of the other inputs remaining constant, then output increases at a decreasing rate.

The next figure shows the production function for the short term, followed by an explanation of how the hospital assesses the optimal level of output produced (Fig. 9.1).

In the short term, the production function consists of three parts, each with a different slope. In the upper diagram, the total output is presented as a function of labor.[2] In the lower diagram, average product (AP) and marginal product (MP) curves are presented. The average product (AP) is the total output divided by the amount of variable input. The marginal product (MP) is the change in total output divided by the change in variable input.

A hospital, just like any other firm, has to determine the optimal level of variable input (labor) that produces the optimal output. In the first stage of production, we remark that the total product (TP in the upper diagram) and the marginal product (lower diagram) show increasing marginal returns for an increase in labor. The

[2]Total output depends on factors of production. Since the amount of capital is assumed to be constant in the short term, changes in outputs are caused only by changes in labor.

medical technology (capital) exhibits increasing marginal returns for an increase in labor: as we increase the quantity of labor, the marginal product of labor rises and so the slope of the marginal product is positive (upward sloping). The slope of the TP curve becomes steeper: the hospital continues to use more and more labor as it gets more and more output. The second stage shows decreasing marginal returns: the marginal product (MP) has a negative (downward) slope, indicating that the use of extra labor increases the total output at a decreasing rate. In this second stage of production, the total output reaches its maximum (upper diagram), as does the average product (AP in the lower diagram). The marginal product intersects the average product at its maximum point (lower diagram). In the third stage, technology continues to exhibit decreasing marginal returns for an increase in labor. However, when the amount of labor exceeds L_3, the total output decreases and the marginal product becomes negative. This indicates that, at this point, an extra use of labor causes a decrease in the total output. Therefore, it is not in the interest of any economic unit, hospitals included, to use a level of labor greater than L_3 in the third stage of production because the marginal productivity becomes negative. The optimal stage at which a hospital must set its level of labor in order to produce optimal outputs is the second, at which the optimal level is reached that maximizes average productivity.

For the long-term time frame, all inputs are variable. The hospital unit has to choose the optimal combination of labor and capital: it can either aim to produce the maximum output for a fixed cost of inputs or produce a given output at minimal input cost. Both actions represent the concept of efficiency. The hospitals are efficient when they use all available resources to produce the maximum output.

Thus, the decision that the hospital has to take can be described as follows:

$$\max Q\left(L,K\right) \text{under the constraint} : \text{TC} = w \bullet L + r \bullet K$$

where: Q = total output, TC = total cost, w = price of labor, L = quantity of labor, r = price of capital, and K = quantity of capital.

The production function is represented by the isoquant curve (Fig. 9.2) that shows all different combinations of labor and capital for which the total output is constant.

In Fig. 9.2, the curve Q_1 is the isoquant curve that shows all different combinations of labor and capital for which the output produced (Q_1) is constant. Thus, as we move along the isoquant curve we produce the same output using different combinations of labor and capital. The isoquant curve is downward sloping, which indicates that as we use increase one input the other input decreases. The main hypothesis is that there is a substitution (or trade-off) between labor and capital. The marginal rate of technical substitution (MRTS) is the rate at which the available technology allows the substitution of one factor for another (Katz & Rosen, 1998). As we move from A to B, we can decrease the labor by increasing the capital. MRTS is the change of capital over the change of labor and it indicates how many units of labor the hospital unit could save when increasing the capital by one unit ($\Delta K/\Delta L$). When labor and capital are perfect substitutes, the isoquant curve is a straight line. In the

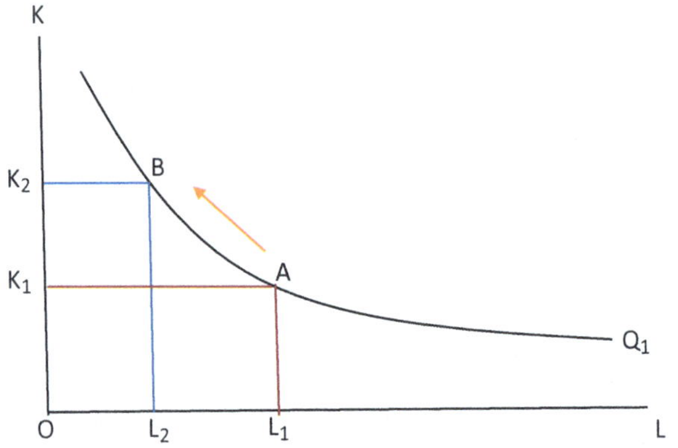

Fig. 9.2 Isoquant curve of a hospital unit

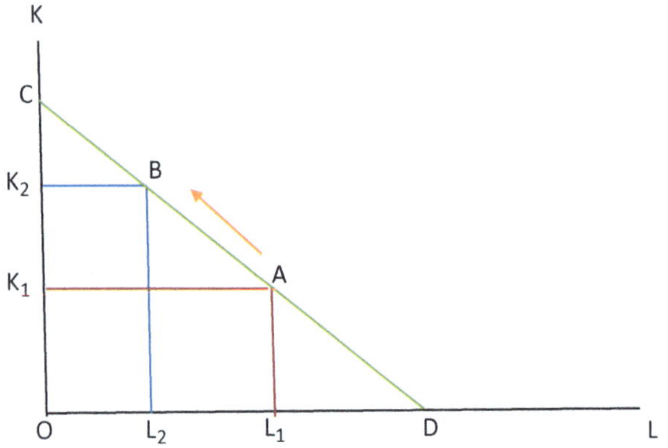

Fig. 9.3 Isocost line of the hospital unit

case that labor and capital are not substitutes, the isoquant curve is a right angle. The slope of the isoquant curve is −1 times MRTS. Each isoquant curve with a trajectory that is upward and to the right represents a greater amount of output produced since more inputs were used.

The cost of inputs is a constraint that a hospital unit has to take into account when it decides which hospital services it will offer. As we mentioned above, the cost function for the long term is given by the equation:

$$\mathrm{TC} = w \cdot L + r \cdot K$$

where: TC = total cost, w = price of labor, L = quantity of labor, r = price of capital, and K = quantity of capital.

The cost function is presented in Fig. 9.3.

The line CD in Fig. 9.3 is the isocost line that shows all different combinations of labor and capital for which the total cost is constant. Any combination to the right

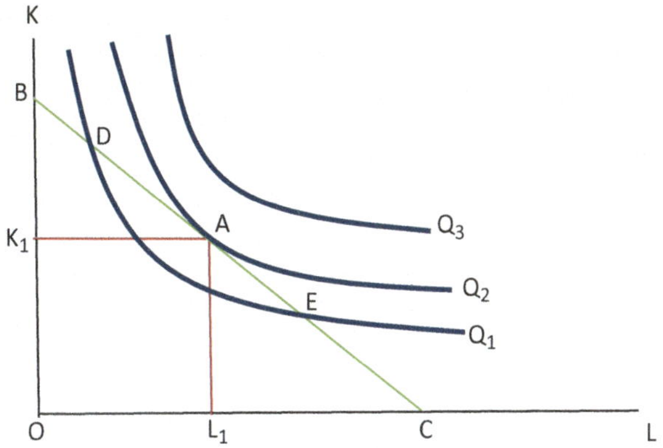

Fig. 9.4 Equilibrium of the hospital unit over the long term

of CD cannot be achieved due to the constraints in the prices of inputs and the total available budget. Any combination to the left of the isocost line is possible but it is not efficient since it means that inputs are not used to their full capacity. The slope of the isocost line is −1 times the ratio of prices ($-w/r$).

Given a hospital's total available budget and the prices of inputs, the challenge is for the hospital to identify the optimal combination of labor and capital for which the maximum output can be produced. At this point, the hospital unit aims for the optimal combination between labor and capital which allows it to maximize hospital services in the long term.

Figure 9.4 presents the equilibrium of the hospital unit in the long term. As already mentioned, the hospital has to choose the optimal combination of labor and capital for which it maximizes its output under the constraint of the total cost. Thus, the hospital unit can choose any combination along the isocost line (e.g., A, D, or E) but not any other combination to the right of the isocost line. The optimal combination is found at the point where the isoquant curve with the highest Q value (output produced) meets the isocost line. This occurs for the isoquant curve Q_2 at point A. At this point, the slope of Q_2 is the same as the slope of the isocost line, which is the condition for equilibrium: MRTS = w/r.

9.3 Short-Term Costs, Long-Term Costs, and Decision-Making in Health Services

9.3.1 Short and Long-Term Costs

Cost can be defined as the value of resources used in order to produce something. A community hospital's expenditures can be broadly categorized into the payroll, professional fees, supplies, capital depreciation, and interest. These costs vary from hospital to hospital as a result of differences in the severity of factors such as the patient's illness, the quality of care, the intensity with which the services are used, the shifting of costs to pay for teaching and research, the billing method, efficiency, the cost of labor, and other inputs (Getzen, 2006). Healthcare organizations also generate costs through the use of outsourcing services.

The concept of cost can be considered in the short term and the long term. Short and long-term costs are frequently found in healthcare administration. However, they are not easily distinguished, something that becomes evident when looking at how assets on the yearly balance sheet are recorded (Finkler, Ward, & Baker, 2007). Generally, a cost is considered as fixed in the short term but variable in the long term. The full cost of a hospital consists of both fixed and variable costs.

The fixed costs (*short-term costs*) remain constant and do not affect outputs in the short term. Typical examples of fixed costs are:

- Purchase of equipment—without taking into consideration the operating and maintenance costs
- The current rent of the hospital building
- Building maintenance
- Salaries—without taking into consideration potential overtime costs or annual increases in salaries.
- Utilities

The short-term costs of a hospital can be estimated by calculating its weekly or monthly costs. In the calculation of short-term costs, a reduction in the number of patients will increase the average cost per patient.

The variable costs (long-term costs) are mainly linked to the activity of a hospital. Typical examples are the drugs, consumables, worker supplies, lab supplies, fuel, and food. The number of patients has no impact in the short term while the patient volume is a factor in the long term. Actually, what is fixed in the short term becomes variable in the long term. For example, the unit supervisor's cost is fixed in the short term but it can be varied in the long term by eliminating a unit or by changing the number of employees (Finkler et al., 2007).

In the long term, directors might have more time to train the management, hire clinical staff, replace existing building infrastructure, and take steps that help to minimize production costs and achieve the desired level of output (Getzen, 2006). The majority of hospital costs derive from equipment, building infrastructure, labor, and overheads (Landon, Normand, Frank, & McNeil, 2005), so reducing these costs can make the medical practices of hospitals more stable and resilient.

The labor cost ($w \cdot L$) is the variable cost or the short-term cost. This cost depends on the price of labor (w) and on the quantity of labor used in the production. As the price of labor is considered to be constant, the short-term cost depends on the change in the quantity of labor. Changes in the total cost due to the changes in the variable cost can be measured by the marginal cost. The marginal cost (MC) is the change in short-term variable cost due to the change to the production of one more unit of output (Katz & Rosen, 1998). As the hospital wants to produce more, it increases

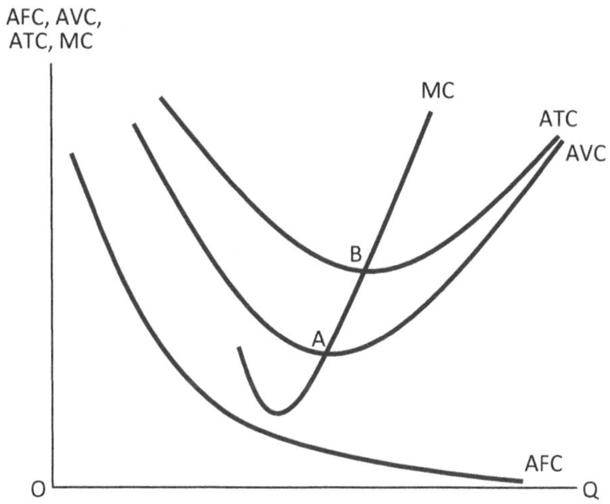

Fig. 9.5 Average fixed cost, average variable cost, average total cost, and marginal cost

the quantity of labor used and thus increases the variable cost and therefore the total cost.

The properties of a short-term cost are as follows[3]:

1. The variable cost curve is upward sloping. This shows that, as more labor is used, the total cost of labor (variable cost) increases
2. The variable cost also depends on the fixed cost which is the capital cost. The amount of capital is constant in the short term. If the capital is not used to its full capacity in the short term, then it is necessary to increase labor, and therefore its cost, in order to use the remaining capital and become more efficient.

It is worth noting that a firm (or hospital in our case) is more interested in the average cost rather than the total cost. The average variable cost (AVC) is the variable cost per unit of output (AVC = VC/Q). The average fixed cost (AFC) is the fixed cost per unit of output. The marginal cost is the change in variable cost due to the change of variable input.

In Fig. 9.5, the average and the marginal cost curves are presented.

The average fixed cost, average variable cost, average total cost (ATC), and marginal cost are given by the following equations:

$$\mathrm{AFC} = \mathrm{FC} / Q = (r \bullet K) / Q$$

$$\mathrm{AVC} = \mathrm{VC} / Q = (w \bullet L) / Q$$

$$\mathrm{ATC} = \mathrm{TC} / Q = (w \bullet L + r \bullet K) / Q$$

[3] See Katz and Rosen (1998)

$$\mathrm{MC} = \Delta TC / \Delta Q = \Delta VC / \Delta Q$$

In the short term, the change in the total cost is due to the change in the variable cost since fixed costs remain constant.

The AFC is highly inelastic at the beginning of production and becomes more elastic when more and more output is produced. At the beginning of production, only a part of the capital is used in the production process and therefore the capital cost per unit is high. As the hospital unit produces more and more, it uses more and more capital and the average fixed cost decreases. This happens because the numerator of the AFC remains constant while the denominator increases. The other curves (AVC, ATC, MC) are U-shaped. Along the downward part of AVC and ATC, the production is characterized by economies of scale. As a hospital produces more output by using factors of production more efficiently, the increase in output is greater than the increase in the total cost and hence the ATC (and ACV) decreases. Diseconomies of scale occur along the upward part of AVC and ATC. In this case, the rate of increase of output is smaller than the rate of the increase of total cost and therefore AVC and ATC increase. The hospital achieves the lowest AVC and ATC at points A and B. As far as the marginal cost (MC) is concerned, it decreases and then increases. It intersects AVC and ATC at their lowest level (points A and B).

9.3.2 Decision-Making

The decision-making process of healthcare and hospital services is based on economic evaluations (Hoffmann & Graf von der Schulenburg, 2000). Initially, such evaluations were used by decision makers in situations of resource constraints and uncertainty (Weinstein, 2006). However, research suggests that there is a discrepancy between theory and practice regarding the role of economic evaluation (Lessard, Contandriopoulos, & Beaulieu, 2010). Based on previous research, there are different approaches that can be used in a hospital's decision-making process. To begin with, decision makers sometimes fail to consider economic evaluations in decision-making and pay more attention to therapeutic value and acquisition costs (Walkom, Robertson, Newby, & Pillay, 2006; Williams, McIver, Moore, & Bryan, 2008). Furthermore, sometimes the decision-making is vulnerable to context-related factors such as the power of shareholders and political powers (Teerawattananon & Russell, 2008). Nevertheless, the economic perception of decision-making is the most dominant perception.

Regarding the economic perception of decision-making in hospitals, the time frame of a decision is defined by the type of cost (fixed or variable). As concerns outputs, the management has to deal with foreseeable but also unknown costs. A key factor that drives management's decision-making is the budget (Berman & Weeks, 1990). A budget that does not change in relation to volume is called a fixed budget and includes all the short-term costs while a flexible budget changes with volume.

Both fixed and flexible budgets create the hospital's operating budget (Getzen, 2006). Therefore, the decision-making is based on the hospital's budget that takes into account both short and long-term costs. A tool that helps decision makers set budgets is called budget impact analysis, which estimates the financial consequences of a new intervention's implementation in a specific healthcare context (Mauskopf et al., 2007) and measures the amount of resources needed to implement an investment (Donaldson, Currie, & Mitton, 2002).

Another factor influencing a hospital's decision-making is known as cost-effectiveness analysis (CEA). The CEA takes into account resource constraints, options for using the available budget, and ethical or political constraints (Baltussen et al., 2003). Moreover, this analysis can provide information regarding the relevant costs (short and long term) and health benefits for different strategies. The CEA is a formal economic decision-making method used in the health sector that analyzes the allocative efficiency of a hospital and is frequently used in countries such as Australia, Canada, Sweden, and the United Kingdom. There is a growing awareness of using CEA as a decision-making tool, mainly in the reimbursement of pharmaceuticals (Pritchard, 2002). A similar approach for decision-making in hospitals is cost-consequence analysis (CCA) which evaluates predictive effects such as the impact on quality of life, utility impact, humanistic outcomes, and resources such as direct medical costs, hospital costs, and direct nonmedical costs (Williams et al., 2008). Through this process, the decision-making is based on the relevant costs and the consequences they may have for the hospital.

Another approach to decision-making as regards costs is through marginal analysis. This approach has been developed as part of a model that aims to set priorities for the allocation of resources (Mitton & Donaldson, 2004; Ruta, Mitton, Bate, & Donaldson, 2005). Based on this approach, the stakeholders set questions about the economic notions of margin and opportunity cost (Mitton & Donaldson, 2004). This makes the reallocation of resources feasible.

The decision-making process can derive from a combination of the above approaches—a practical process that evaluates all possible parameters in the hospital. The economic evaluation is an essential tool for decision makers and provides substantial help in a situation where there are conflicting objectives and/or uncertainty (Weinstein, 2006). Different types of information and methodologies should be combined during the decision-making processes in order to achieve effective decisions that can be applied to a hospital.

9.4 How Hospitals Determine Optimal Price Levels for Their Health Services Under Different Market Structures

The determination of an optimal price level for health services is based on a hospital's costs and decision-making processes and therefore can vary among different market structures. The resource allocation and the price determination for healthcare services are affected by several factors such as the availability of information and the characteristics of purchasers and providers. Nowadays, hospital costs have risen (OECD, 2018) due to a wide variety of factors.

Waters and Hussey (2004) state that the determination of hospital prices relies on two main factors: the type of payment (specifically, whether a payment is retrospective or prospective) and the payment system (whether it is variable or fixed). In variable systems, the prices are fixed, while in fixed systems the price per service varies according to the volume of services.

High-income countries have different strategies for the determination of prices for hospital services. Research suggests that hospital payments are either case-based, DRG-based (i.e., based on a patient's diagnostic related grouping) or based on a budget allocation model. Austria is an example of a country where the budget allocation model is used to determine optimal price levels. There, costs are derived from a subset of hospitals that provide data for average costs and the financial calculation is performed centrally (Kobel & Pfeiffer, 2011). Other European countries follow different approaches for setting prices. For example, Denmark receives information on each single patient. In Estonia, the costing system sometimes relies on negotiations between professional associations and hospitals and on data that are retrieved from the annual cost of resources, the total use of resources and on the different types of services provided (Kahur, Allik, Aaviksoo, Laarmann, & Paat, 2011). In France, cost-based pricing was also applied during the 2000s. The costs are calculated according to the level of severity of patient conditions and the length of stay. In England, activity-based funding was introduced in 2003. All public hospitals provide their data and prices are determined from cost data accumulated over the previous two years (Epstein & Mason, 2006). In 2009, a voluntary patient-level information and costing system was also applied in order to determine the cost of each medical case according to actual records (NHS, 2012–2013).

A DRG-based model was introduced into the public health sector of the United States in 1984. At the beginning, prices were determined based on the data related to costs of specific DRGs. The system was subsequently updated whereby the prices were based on data from hospitals' cost centers and on data of the total charges of individual cost centers (CMS, 2010). The US approach to determining prices for hospital services relies on the assumption that cost-based weights and charge-based weights are similar (Cotterill, Bobula, & Connerton, 1986). However, there is a body of research that questions this assumption (Price, 1989). Consequently, the price of the final product depends on the present charge.

In Australia, case-based payments were applied to all hospitals in 2012 (Department of Health and Ageing, 2011). The cost of each case is based on the treatment given and on the allocation of services to individuals. There, the public sector purchasers apply diagnostic-based per-case payment methods (Imai, Jacobzone, & Lenain, 2000).

Africa has yet another market structure, for which the principal constraint in low- and middle-income countries is the restricted information on volumes, costs, and patient characteristics (Maceira, 1998). Subsequently, while access to drugs is increasing (Knippenberg et al., 1997), there is reduced service utilization (James et al., 2006) and access to health care is restricted (Gilson, Doherty, Loewenson, & Francis, 2007). In African hospitals, sometimes funding agencies influence the closure of certain health services (Witter & Adjei, 2007). On the other hand, Ridde and Morestin (2010) stated that the user fees have been abolished in many countries of Africa. For example, in Uganda, all services are generally free for low-income patients but the hospitals do charge those who can afford their services (Nabyonga-Orem et al., 2008). In South Africa, basic services are free and in Kenya the services are free, apart from laboratory tests. Overall, the closure of certain services in African hospitals makes it hard to determine the optimal pricing level for a health service. Research suggests that in low- and middle-income countries, the determination of price and services is linked to line-items and global budgets (Bitran & Winnie, 1998). Elsewhere in the world, countries such as Argentina, Brazil, Nicaragua, and Thailand use capitation in order to control and determine healthcare costs but the available documentation for these countries is limited (Mills, Bennett, Siriwanarangsun, & Tangcharoensathien, 2000).

Clearly, the approaches used around the world to determine the optimal price level for hospital services are quite diverse, as are the regulations applied to determine the structure of cost categories, the designation of supporting cost centers, and the form of the intermediate and final products. Nevertheless, regulations have been criticized for failing to control the overall cost of health care (Getzen, 2006).

Market micro-costing methodologies for tracing and determining costs can be classified into top-down and bottom-up methodologies. Top-down costing is the approach where each cost is calculated based on comprehensive sources about relevant costs (Chapko et al., 2009). On the other hand, bottom-up costing is where each cost component of a patient's hospitalization is calculated individually (Wordsworth, Ludbrook, Caskey, & Macleod, 2005). The bottom-up approach has been characterized as a more accurate method because the cost allocation is based on resources actually used (Berlin & Smith, 2004), while some researchers suggest that the optimal approach comes from combining top-down and bottom-up micro-costing (Baker, 1995; Kaplan, 1988).

Other factors that have been identified as determinants of price are the operating costs of hospitals and the integrating costs of new technologies, which can lead to price adjustments (Tompkins, Altman, & Eilat, 2006). The optimal price of hospital services also relies on the characteristics of the healthcare providers and the relationship they have with their purchasers. Waters and Hussey (2004) indicated that provider autonomy can determine contractual relationships with purchasers. Hence, providers with greater autonomy have more flexibility in determining the price of the services. Provider negotiating power can also be an important determinant in optimal price setting. For example, in Germany the healthcare system allows for negotiation regarding prices.

Another key determinant in price setting for health services is the competition that exists among hospitals: areas with higher competition tend to have relatively low costs in comparison with areas that have fewer providers of healthcare services (Keeler, Melnick, & Zwanziger, 1999). Competition is a complex issue because hospitals compete not only for patients but also for physicians and contracts. While the literature tends to assume that hospitals are local monopolists (Barros & Olivella, 2005; Olivella, 2002), competition remains a significant factor that can force hospitals to provide services which are better and more efficient.

Consequently, the optimal price of a hospital's services is the result of the interaction of different, sometimes conflicting, factors. The unique accounting system that each hospital has for cost allocation can also help determine the optimal price. Furthermore, hospitals do not have a standardized management information system (Tompkins et al., 2006) and this further allows for price differentials in the costing of their services.

Considering the hospital to be a typical economic unit, we can explain how the price and outputs are determined. The purpose of a firm is to maximize its profit. Marginal analysis is a decision-making tool that can help a firm achieve such a goal. Marginal analysis focuses on the cost or benefit of the *next* unit produced by a firm. If the extra benefit that the firm gets from the production of the last unit is greater than the extra cost of this unit, then the firm proceeds to produce this unit. Otherwise, the firm does not produce this unit. The equilibrium condition is that marginal revenue is equal to marginal cost. Marginal revenue and marginal cost are given by the following equations:

$$\text{Marginal Revenue}(\text{MR}) = \Delta TR / \Delta Q = \Delta(P \cdot Q) / \Delta Q$$

where: P = price and Q = quantity of the product.

$$\text{Marginal cost}(\text{MC}) = \Delta TC / \Delta Q = \Delta VC / \Delta Q$$

The equation for marginal revenue shows that the marginal revenue is the price. In a perfectly competitive model, the price is exogenous and constant. Each firm is price-taking which means that each firm sells the product at the price which is fixed in the market by aggregate demand and aggregate supply. In this case, marginal revenue is constant and independent of the quantity produced. In a noncompetitive market, the price is not constant since the price is set by the firm. Marginal revenue is not constant and the marginal revenue curve is downward sloping.

The marginal cost depends on the price of the factor of production. If the price of input is constant, then the marginal cost is constant. Otherwise, the marginal cost is upward sloping. The next figure presents the decision-making tool of a hospital unit, based on the marginal analysis.

Figure 9.6 shows that the marginal revenue (BQ_2) of producing Q_2 is greater than its marginal cost (CQ_2). Thus, the hospital unit decides to produce this last unit. The opposite is true when the hospital investigates the implications of producing output quantity Q_3 since the marginal revenue (EQ_3) of this output is smaller than its marginal cost (DQ_3). The optimal output is Q_1 for which its marginal revenue equals its marginal cost.

As mentioned above, the hospital unit must determine the price and the output for which the hospital unit can maximize its profit. The decision-making tool is

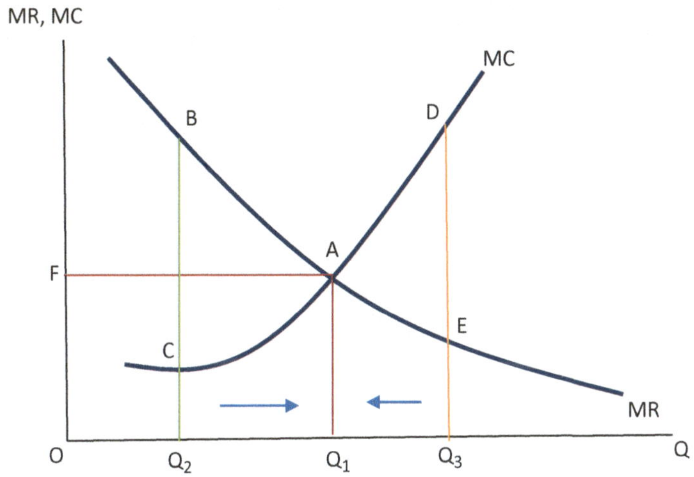

Fig. 9.6 Determination of the optimal output for which the hospital unit maximizes its profit

based on the marginal analysis, as was presented above, but it also depends on the market structure. Katz and Rosen (1998) mention the main characteristics of the market structure to be the following:

a. the size and number of buyers and sellers
b. the degree of substitutability among different sellers' products
c. the extent to which buyers are informed about prices and available alternatives
d. the conditions of entry

On the basis of these characteristics, a perfectly competitive market is determined as one in which:

1. there are a great number of buyers and sellers, neither of which is large relative to the overall market to be able to influence the actions of the others
2. the output produced is homogeneous
3. there is perfect information about the product
4. there are no barriers to entering or exiting the market

When considering a perfectly competitive market, we need to distinguish between short-term and long-term time frames. The main difference between the short term and the long term is that all inputs are variable in the long term and the hospital can achieve economies of scale by producing a greater amount of health services and by making full use of all available capital. Thus, the firm can operate at a lower average total cost in the long term, compared to that of the short term. The slope of the average total cost in the long term is more elastic than in the short term. Due to the competition that exists between different economic units, the price at which the output is sold is lower in the long term than it is in the short term and so the profit margin is also lower. The consumers (patients), who pay for health services in a competitive market, pay a lower price and the buy products of higher quality.

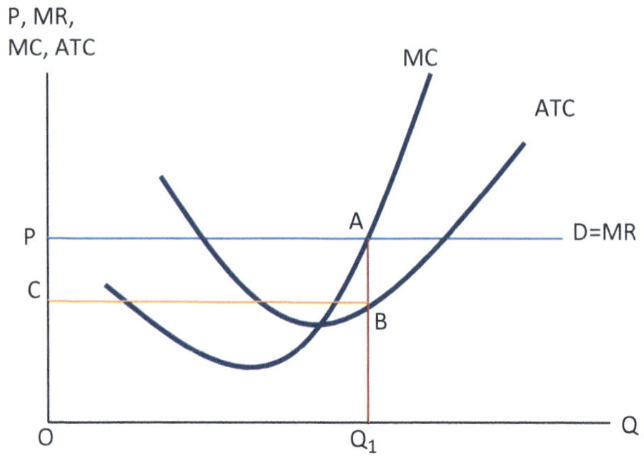

Fig. 9.7 Equilibrium condition of a perfectly competitive hospital in the short term

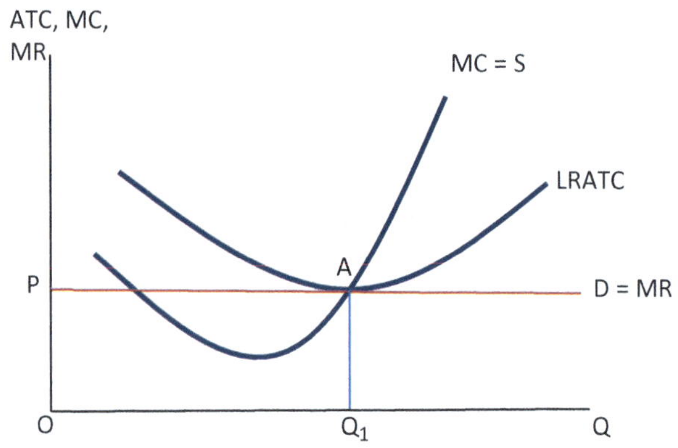

Fig. 9.8 Equilibrium in the long term in a perfectly competitive market

Figures 9.7 and 9.8 present the short-term and long-term equilibrium of a price-taker hospital, respectively.

The equilibrium condition at which a hospital can identify the optimal output for maximum profits is MR = MC. The equilibrium point is A and the quantity produced is Q_1. The profit per unit (Π = P–ATC) is AB (namely, AQ_1–BQ_1) and the total profit is PABC (profit per unit quantity = AB·CB[4]). The profit can be explained by the fact that the price, which is given by the line PD, is above the average total cost, which is the ATC curve). If the price of a hospital's health services were set below the average total cost, then the hospital would operate at a loss. The question is: what would the hospital decide to do if losses were incurred in the short term? If the price is greater than the average variable cost, the hospital continues to produce because all

[4]The quantity produced is OQ_1, which is equal to CB.

the variable costs and a part of fixed costs are covered by the price, which is the revenue from producing and selling one unit. On the contrary, if the price cannot cover all the variable costs, it is because the average variable cost exceeds demand (or marginal revenue). Then, it makes economic sense for the hospital to stop producing since in this situation it has to pay all fixed costs and the part of variable costs which are not covered by the price. If the hospital does not operate, it only has to cover its fixed costs.

In the long term, the hospital has to choose the optimal combination of inputs and produce its services at a lower average total cost than that of the short-term time frame. The price of the product is constant in the short term. The existence of profits or losses in this market causes other hospital units to enter or leave the market and therefore a change in production affects the equilibrium price. The existence of no profit in a perfectly competitive market is only a theoretical concept. In practice, if there is a profit, this tends to be kept low in the long term.

In the above diagram, the equilibrium of the hospital in the long term is presented. The equilibrium condition is MR = MC, as it is in the short term. At the equilibrium point A, the hospital produces an output equal to OQ_1. The price at which the output is sold is OP. The price (or the marginal revenue), which is OP, equals the average total cost (AQ_1). Thus, we remark that the hospital in the long term does not make profit. As we mentioned above, a perfectly competitive market is considered to be the ideal market for the consumer (in our case, the patient) who benefits by receiving hospital services at a higher quality yet at a lower price.

A noncompetitive market can be considered to be a monopolistic market, the main characteristics of which are:

1. There is one seller who is the price maker (they set the price)
2. There are many buyers
3. There are no close substitutes to replace the product
4. There are barriers to entering the market

The price is determined by the monopolistic firm and therefore is not constant. The marginal revenue curve differs from the demand curve and is downward sloping.

Figure 9.9 presents the equilibrium in a monopolistic market. The equilibrium condition is MR = MC. At the equilibrium point B, the output produced is Q_1. The price at which the monopolistic hospital unit sells the quantity of health services Q_1 is OP. This price is found if the quantity in demand is replaced by Q_1. At this quantity, the price (OP) is greater than the average total cost (BQ_1) and the hospital makes a profit. The profit per unit is EB (P–ATC = OP–BQ_1 = EQ_1–BQ_1) and the total profit is PEBC (profit per unit quantity = EB·OQ_1 = EB·BC).

In a monopolistic market, a firm often applies a price discrimination policy whereby the monopolistic firm charges different prices to different consumers for the same good. The classical firm differentiates the price of the good in order to increase the demand of a specific group of consumers or in a specific period of time. The hospital can differentiate the price of health services according to the personal characteristics of the patient (e.g., age, insured/uninsured, etc.).

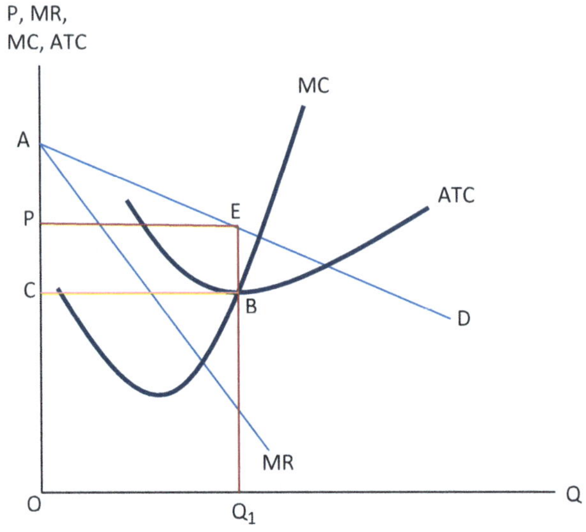

Fig. 9.9 Equilibrium in a monopolistic market

Another important market structure is the monopolistic competitive market, the main characteristics of which are based on those of the perfectly competitive market and of the monopolistic market. It is important to mention that the main characteristic of this market is the differentiation of the product. The competition between hospitals is based on the differentiation of their health services and each hospital determines the price of its health services as in the case of a monopolistic market.

The equilibrium of a monopolistic competitive market in the short term is identical to the equilibrium of the monopolistic market. The difference between these two markets is that in the long term there is no profit for the monopolistic competitive hospital due to the competition between hospitals. The profits that hospitals earn in the short term attract new hospitals into the industry of hospital services. The increase in hospitals, which are suppliers of health services, shifts the demand and the marginal curve lower and therefore the profit decreases. In the next figure, the long-term monopolistically competitive equilibrium is presented (Fig. 9.10).

The equilibrium condition is attained when the marginal revenue equals the marginal cost. At the equilibrium point B, the quantity supplied by the hospital is Q_1. The price at which this quantity is supplied is OP. The price (OP) is equal to the average total cost (CQ_1) and the profit per unit ($OP-CQ_1$) is zero.

Another market structure is the oligopolistic market. The main characteristic of this market is that there is mutual interdependence between the firms (Katz & Rosen, 1998). Each firm is concerned with the actions of the other rival firms and it is also aware that the other firms are watching its decisions about the quantity it produces and at what price. The main characteristics of this market are:

1. There is mutual interdependence between rival firms which behave strategically
2. Each firm is a price maker

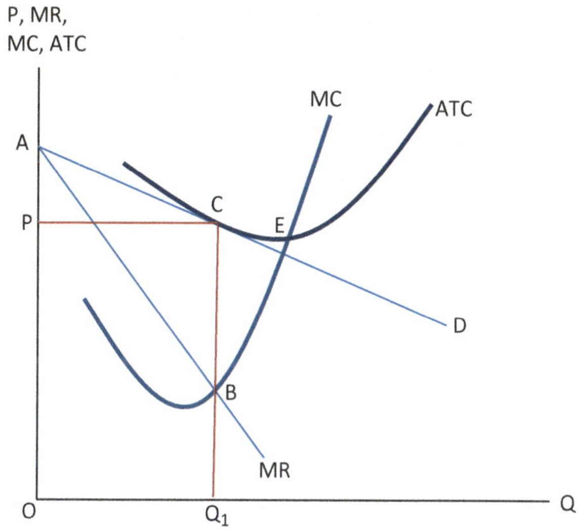

Fig. 9.10 Long-term monopolistically competitive equilibrium

3. Buyers are price takers
4. Entry into the market may or may not be obstacle-free

How do the oligopolistic firms behave as far as the price and the quantity of product are concerned? The market influence that each firm has is an important determining factor regarding their behavior. If a firm has a significantly greater market influence relative to the other firms, then that firm is considered to be a leader firm. The leader firm can determine the output and price in order to maximize its profit and the other firms are obliged to follow the policy applied by the leader firm. In the case that no firm has a significant market power, the firms can arrive at a collaborative agreement in order to reduce their uncertainty and keep their profit. Their agreement mainly concerns a consensus on pricing but may also include the quantity supplied. To agree on the price, the firms should be able to exert some control on the market supply. Such an agreement between the firms would change the structure of the oligopolistic market to a monopolistic market. In many countries, there are antitrust laws which prevent monopolistic conditions from prevailing in the market.

In the case of no agreement between the firms, there are models which try to explain the behavior of firms in an oligopoly. One of these models is the so-called "Kinked Demand Curve,[5]" in which competing oligopoly firms commit to match price cuts but not price increases. The kinked demand curve can be applied to an oligopolistic market and delineates two different demand curves that each firm faces. The first part of the kinked demand curve is inelastic and shows that if one of

[5]This model has been developed by Sweezy (1939).

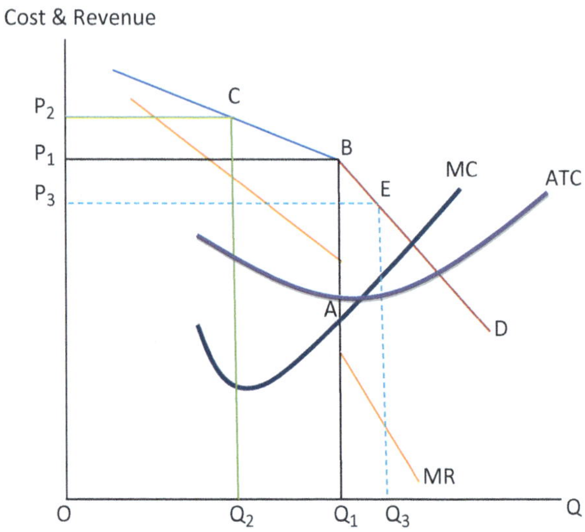

Fig. 9.11 Kinked demand curve in an oligopoly model

the firms decides to increase its price then the other firms do not follow. The opposite happens if the firm decreases the price of the product. In this case, we remark that all the other firms would also decrease their prices. The kinked demand curve shows the interdependence that exists between the oligopolistic firms. The equilibrium price is at the intersection of the two demand curves (Fig. 9.11).

The equilibrium price and quantity are $P1$ and $Q1$, respectively, and correspond to point B. The part of the demand curve above point B is more elastic than the part of the demand curve below it. This change in slope shows the degree of reaction of the rival firms. If the oligopolistic firm decides to increase the price of the product (the part of the curve above point B), the decrease in quantity is greater because the other firms do not follow this price policy and attract consumers from the first firm. The opposite happens if the oligopolistic firm decreases its price. The other firms do the same and subsequently there is a small increase in the quantity of the first firm.

Each of the firms in an oligopolistic industry chooses the strategy that maximizes its profit in view of the strategies of other firms. In such a case, the market is said to have established a Nash equilibrium whereby every firm in a group makes the best decision for itself, based on what it thinks the others will do. A market in which any firm chooses a certain level of output taking into consideration the reactions of other firms is said to have attained a Cournot-Nash equilibrium.[6] Each firm has a reaction curve that tells us the profit-maximizing output choice it would make, given what this firm believes about the output level of other firms. We can illustrate an oligopoly with two firms (a duopoly is a form of oligopoly), with each firm having a reaction curve (Fig. 9.12).

[6] Cournot (1838) introduced a model to analyze the market structure of oligopoly.

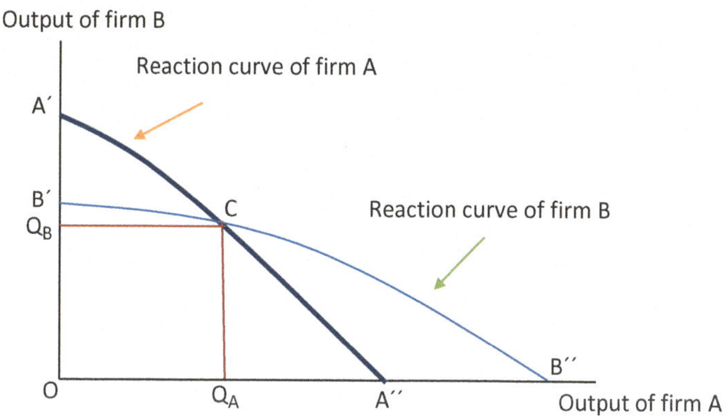

Fig. 9.12 Cournot equilibrium in an oligopoly model

The above figure illustrates the Cournot equilibrium in a duopoly model. As mentioned above, each firm decides its output on the basis of the predictions of the actions of the other firm. These decisions are shown in the reaction curve of the firm. The equilibrium point is the point where the reaction curves meet, at point C. This point indicates the common level of output which is optimal for both firms.

In this section, we examined the basic market structures (perfect competition, monopoly, monopolistic competition, and oligopoly), as they are presented in a microeconomics textbook. We also used the term "firm" instead of "hospital." We do this because the analysis of the market structure could be applied to many different industries. Clearly, instead of the term "firm" we could use the term "hospital" or "healthcare unit." The main issue is to explain the market structure of the healthcare sector. The theoretical background of different basic market structures was given above. It is not so easy to indicate which market structure most characterizes the healthcare industry because of the market conditions and the particularity of the provided good ("healthcare services"). The nature of healthcare services raises questions. If healthcare services are considered as a purely private or public good, then it is easier to define the market structure of the industry. In particular, health care, which is provided by hospitals, is not purely a private or public good. To put it differently, there are arguments which support that health care could be a private or a public good. The most important is that health care generates positive externalities and therefore the government intervenes in order to support the provision of health care to poor people. Healthcare services are not a typical good. Their demand is determined not by consumers but by their suppliers. This is the so-called induced demand. This happens because the consumers/patients suffer from perfect information concerning their healthcare status and the type of health care they need. The development of healthcare insurance affects the price and the quantity of healthcare services supplied. People who are fully covered by their health insurance do not have any incentive to decrease their consumption of healthcare services (moral hazard). If we focus on the structure of the market for hospitals without thinking about the particularities of healthcare services, we may see that the size and the structure of the market in the healthcare industry differ from country to country and from region to region but nevertheless may be characterized as one of monopolistic competition. Hospitals compete against each other by offering a "different" healthcare service. This is true to some extent but this does not apply in all cases. The size of the market and the structure of society influence the behavior of private hospitals and affect pricing policy and the quantity of services produced. The existence of a public healthcare system (public hospitals) is another factor that influences the development of hospitals in the private sector. To conclude, we consider monopolistic competition to be the most viable market structure for the healthcare industry without excluding the case of a perfectly competitive or an oligopolistic model.

References

Aletras, V. H. (1999). A comparison of hospital scale effects in short-run and long-run cost functions. *Health Economics, 8*(6), 521–530.

Amendola, M., Gaffard, J. L., & Saraceno, E. (2005). Technical progress, accumulation and financial constraints: Is the productivity paradox really a paradox? *Structural Change and Economic Dynamics, 16*, 243–261.

Baker, J. J. (1995). Activity-based costing for integrated delivery systems. *Journal of Health Care Finance, 22*(2), 57–61.

Baltussen, R., Adam, T., Edejer, T., Hutubessy, R., Acharya, A., & Evans, D. (2003). Methods for generalized cost-effectiveness analysis. In T. Edejer, R. Baltussen, T. Adam, R. Hutubessy, A. Acharya, & D. Evans (Eds.), *Making choices in health: WHO guide to cost-analysis*. Geneva: World Health Organization.

Barros, P., & Olivella, P. (2005). Waiting lists and patient selection. *Journal of Economics and Management Strategy, 14*, 623–646.

Bennett, S., McPake, B., & Mills, A. (1997). *Private health providers in developing countries: Serving the public interest*. London: Zed Books.

Berlin, M. F., & Smith, T. H. (2004). Evaluation of activity-based costing versus resource-based relative value costing. *The Journal of Medical Practice Management, 19*(4), 219–227.

Berman, H., & Weeks, L. (1990). *The financial management of hospitals* (5th ed.). Ann Arbor, MI: Health administration Press.

Bitran, R., & Winnie, C. Y. (1998). *A review of health care provider payment reform in selected countries in Asia and Latin America. Major applied research 2, working paper 1*. Bethesda: Abt Associates Inc.

Breyer, F. (1987). The specification of a hospital cost function: A comment on the recent literature. *Journal of Health Economics, 6*, 147–158.

Buttle, F. (1996). SERVQUAL: Review, critique, research agenda. *European Journal of Marketing, 30*(1), 8–32.

Chapko, M. K., Liu, C., Perkins, M., Li, Y., Fortney, J. C., & Maciejewski, M. L. (2009). Equivalence of two healthcare costing methods: Bottom-up and top-down. *Health Economics, 18*, 1188–1201.

CMS. (2010). *The provider reimbursement manual*. Retrieved from https://www.cms.gov/Regulations-and-Guidance/Guidance/Transmittals/2018Downloads/R13P240.pdf

Cotterill, P., Bobula, J., & Connerton, R. (1986). Comparison of alternative weights for diagnosis-related groups. *Health Care Financing Review, 7*(3), 37–51.

Cournot, A. (1838). *Researches into the Mathematical Principles of the Theory of Wealth. Trans.* N.T. Bacon, New York: Macmillan.

Department of Health and Ageing. (2011). *Australian hospital patient costing standards*. Retrieved from http://www.ihpa.gov.au/internet/ihpa/publishing.nsf/Content/Australia-Hospital-Patient-Costing-Standards.htm

Donaldson, C., Currie, G., & Mitton, C. (2002). Cost effectiveness analysis in healthcare: Contraindications. *BMJ, 325*, 891–894.

Epstein, D., & Mason, A. (2006). Costs and prices for inpatient care in England: Mirror twins or distant cousins? *Health Care Management Science, 9*(3), 233–242.

Finkler, A., Ward, D. M., & Baker, J. J. (2007). *Essentials of cost accounting for health care organizations* (3rd ed.). Sudbury, MA: Jones and Bartlett Publishers.

Gaynor, M., & Vogt, W. B. (2000). Antitrust and competition in health care markets. In A. J. Culyer & J. P. Newhouse (Eds.), *Handbook of health economics* (Vol. 1B, pp. 1405–1487). New York: North-Holland.

Getzen, T. (2006). *Health economics: Fundamentals and flow of funds* (3rd ed.). New York: John Wiley and Sons.

Gilson, L., Doherty, J., Loewenson, R., & Francis, V. (2007). *Challenging inequity through health systems. Final report of knowledge network on health systems*. Geneva: WHO Commission on the Social Determinants of Health.

Hoffmann, C., & Graf von der Schulenburg, J. M. (2000). The influence of economic evaluation studies on decision making. A European survey. The EUROMET group. *Health Policy, 52*(3), 179–192.

Imai, Y., Jacobzone, S., & Lenain, P. (2000). *The changing health system in France*. Organization for Economic Cooperation and Development (OECD). Economics Department, Working Papers No. 269 (Online 41 pages).

James, C. D., Hanson, K., McPake, B., Balabanova, D., Gwatkin, D., Hopwood, I., et al. (2006). To retain or remove user fees? Reflections on the current debate in low- and middle-income countries. *Applied Health Economics and Health Policy, 5*, 137–153.

Johns, N., Avci, T., & Karatepe, O. M. (2004). Measuring service quality in travel agents: Evidence from Northern Cyprus. *The Service Industries Journal, 24*(3), 82–100.

Kahur, K., Allik, T., Aaviksoo, A., Laarmann, H., & Paat, G. (2011). Estonia: Developing NordDRGs within social health insurance. In R. Busse, A. Geissler, W. Quentin, & M. Wiley (Eds.), *Diagnosis-related groups in Europe: Moving towards transparency, efficiency and quality in hospitals* (pp. 301–320). Maidenhead: McGraw-Hill/Open University Press.

Kaplan, R. S. (1988). One cost system isn't enough. *Harvard Business Review, 66*(1), 61–66.

Kara, A., Lonial, S., Tarim, M., & Zaim, S. (2005). A paradox of service quality in Turkey: The seemingly contradictory relative importance of tangible and intangible determinants of service quality. *European Business Review, 17*(1), 5–20.

Kasturi Rangan, V., Quelch, J., Herrero, G., & Barton, B. (2007). *Business solutions for the global poor creating social and economic value*. San Francisco, CA: Jossey-Bass.

Katz, M., & Rosen, H. (1998). *Microeconomics*. 3rd Edition. Boston: McGraw-Hill Education.

Keeler, E. B., Melnick, G., & Zwanziger, J. (1999). The changing effects of competition on non-profit and for-profit hospital pricing behavior. *Journal of Health Economics, 18*, 69–86.

Knippenberg, R., Soucat, A., Oyegbite, K., Sene, M., Broun, D., Pangu, K., et al. (1997). Sustainability of primary health care including expanded program of immunizations in Bamako Initiative programs in West Africa: An assessment of 5 years' field experience in Benin and Guinea. *International Journal of Health Planning and Management, 12*(1), 9–28.

Kobel, C., & Pfeiffer, K. (2011). Austria: Inpatient care and the LKF framework. In R. Busse, A. Geissler, W. Quentin, & M. Wiley (Eds.), *Diagnosis-related groups in Europe: Moving towards transparency, efficiency and quality in hospitals* (pp. 175–196). Maidenhead: McGraw-Hill/Open University Press.

Kounetas, K., & Papathanassopoulos, F. (2003). How efficient are Greek hospitals? A case study using a double bootstrap DEA approach. *The European Journal of Health Economics, 14*, 979–994.

Landon, B. E., Normand, S.-L. T., Frank, R., & McNeil, B. J. (2005). Characteristics of medical practices in three developed managed care markets. *Health Services Research, 40*(3), 675–696.

Lansisalmi, H., Kivimaki, M., Aalto, P., & Ruoranen, R. (2006). Innovation in healthcare: A systematic review of recent research. *Nursing Science Quarterly, 19*, 66–72.
Lee, H., Delene, L. M., Bunda, M. A., & Kim, C. (2000). Methods of measuring health-care service quality. *Journal of Business Research, 48*, 233–246.
Lee, M. A., & Yom, Y. H. (2007). A comparative study of patients' and nurses' perceptions of the quality of nursing services, satisfaction and intent to revisit the hospital: A questionnaire survey. *International Journal of Nursing Studies, 44*(4), 545–555.
Lessard, C., Contandriopoulos, A. P., & Beaulieu, M. D. (2010). The role (or not) of economic evaluation at the micro level: Can Bourdieu's theory provide a way forward for clinical decision-making? *Social Science & Medicine, 70*(12), 1948–1956.
Maceira, D. (1998). *Provider payment mechanisms in health care: Incentives, outcomes, and organizational impact in developing Countries. Major applied research 2, working paper 2.* Bethesda, MD: Abt Associates Inc.
Mauskopf, J. A., Sullivan, S. D., Annemans, L., Caro, J., Mullins, C. D., Nuijten, M., et al. (2007). Principles of good practice for budget impact analysis: Report of the ISPOR Task Force on good research practices e budget impact analysis. *Value in Health, 10*(5), 336–347.
Mills, A., Bennett, S., Siriwanarangsun, P., & Tangcharoensathien, V. (2000). The response of providers to capitation payment: A case-study from Thailand. *Health Policy, 51*, 163–180.
Mitton, C., & Donaldson, C. (2004). *Priority setting toolkit: Guide to the use of economics in healthcare decision making*. London: BMJ Books.
Nabyonga-Orem, J., Karamagi, H., Atuyambe, L., Bagenda, F., Okuonzi, S. A., & Walker, O. (2008). Maintaining quality of health services after abolition of user fees: A Uganda case study. *BMC Health Services Research, 8*, 102. https://doi.org/10.1186/1472-6963-8-102
NHS. (2012–2013). *Reference costs guidance for 2012–2013*. Retrieved from https://www.gov.uk/government/uploads/system/uploads/attachmentdata/file/213206/Draft-reference-costs-guidance-for-2012-13-not-accessible.pdf
OECD. (2018). *Health statistics 2018*. Retrieved from https://stats.oecd.org/index.aspx?DataSetCode=HEALTH_STAT#_ga=2.58058926.560407070.1560235889-1343015259.1560235889
Olivella, P. (2002). Shifting public-health-sector waiting lists to the private sector. *European Journal of Political Economy, 19*, 103–132.
Padma, P., Rajendran, C., & Sai Lokachari, P. (2010). Service quality and its impact on customer satisfaction in Indian hospitals: Perspectives of patients and their attendants. *Benchmarking: An International Journal, 17*(6), 807–841.
Pauly, M., & Redisch, M. (1973). The Not-For Profit Hospital as a Physicians' Cooperative, *The American Economic Review, 63*(1), 87–99.
Preyra, C., & Pink, G. (2006). Scale and scope efficiencies through hospital consolidations. *Journal of Health Economics, 25*(6), 1049–1068.
Price, K. F. (1989). Pricing medicare's diagnosis-related groups: Charges versus estimated costs. *Health Care Financing Review, 11*(1), 79–90.
Pritchard, C. (2002). Overseas approaches to decision making. In A. Towse, C. Pritchard, & N. Devlin (Eds.), *Cost effectiveness thresholds. Economic and ethical issues* (pp. 56–68). London: King's Fund and Office of Health Economics.
Reichheld, F., & Sasser, W. (1990). Defections: Quality comes to service. *Harvard Business Review, 68*(1), 106–107.
Ridde, V., & Morestin, F. (2010). A scoping review of the literature on the abolition of user fees in health care services in Africa. *Health Policy and Planning, 26*(1), 1–11.
Ruta, D., Mitton, C., Bate, A., & Donaldson, C. (2005). Programme budgeting and marginal analysis: Bridging the divide between doctors and managers. *BMJ, 330*, 1501–1503.
Santerre, R. E., & Neun, S. P. (2010). *Health economics: Theory, insights, and industry studies*. Mason, OH: Cengage Learning.
Shabbir, A., Malik, S. A., & Malik, S. A. (2016). Measuring patients' healthcare service quality perceptions, satisfaction, and loyalty in public and private sector hospitals in Pakistan. *International Journal of Quality & Reliability Management, 33*(5), 538–557.

Sloan, F. (1979). The internal organization of hospitals: a description, *Health Services Resources, 14*, 203–230.

Sweezy, P. (1939). Demand under conditions of oligopoly. *Journal of Political Economy, 47*, 568–573.

Teerawattananon, Y., & Russell, S. (2008). A difficult balancing act: Policy actors' perspectives on using economic evaluation to inform health-care coverage decisions under the Universal Health Insurance Coverage scheme in Thailand. *Value in Health, 11*(1), S52–S60.

Tompkins, C. P., Altman, S. H., & Eilat, E. (2006). The precarious pricing system for hospital services. *Health Affairs, 25*(1), 45–56.

Varkey, P., & Athyal, V. P. (2005). Service delivery innovations at Mayo Clinic. *Minnesota Medical, 88*, 39–42.

Varkey, P., Horne, A., & Bennet, K. E. (2008). Innovation in health care: A primer. *American Journal of Medical Quality, 23*, 382–388.

Walkom, E., Robertson, J., Newby, D., & Pillay, T. (2006). The role of pharmacoeconomics in formulary decision-making. *Formulary, 41*(8), 374–386.

Waters, H. R., & Hussey, P. (2004). Pricing health services for purchasers—a review of methods and experiences. *Health Policy, 70*, 175–184.

Weinstein, M. C. (2006). Recent developments indecision analytic modelling for economic evaluation. *PharmacoEconomics, 24*(11), 1043–1053.

Williams, I., McIver, S., Moore, D., & Bryan, S. (2008). The use of economic evaluations in NHS decision-making: A review and empirical investigation. *Health Technology Assessment, 12*(7), 1–175.

Wilson, A., Zeithaml, V. A., Bitner, M. J., & Gremler, D. D. (2008). *Services marketing: Integrating customer focus across the firm*. New York: McGraw Hill Inc.

Witter, S., & Adjei, S. (2007). Start-stop funding, its causes and consequences: A case study of the delivery exemptions policy in Ghana. *The International Journal of Health Planning and Management, 22*, 133–143.

Wordsworth, S., Ludbrook, A., Caskey, F., & Macleod, A. (2005). Collecting unit cost data in multicentre studies. Creating comparable methods. *The European Journal of Health Economics, 6*(1), 38–44.

World Health Organization. (2010). *The world health report 2010: Health systems financing: The path to universal coverage*. Retrieved from http://apps.who.int/iris/

Zweifel, P., & Breyer, F. (1997). *Health economics*. Oxford: Oxford University Press.

Chapter 10
Financing Hospitals

Key Points

- There is an inverse relationship between economic efficiency and social justice/equality
- Financing health care by income tax enhances equality and equity in health care
- Prospective methods control health expenditures more than the retrospective methods
- DRG payments link the payment to economic activity and therefore money is distributed more equally to health providers according to their activity
- P4P programs are used to enhance the quality of healthcare services but the empirical results are mixed.

10.1 Introduction

Financing an economic activity is the crucial point in the production process of healthcare services. While patients consume healthcare services, they are not the direct purchasers of healthcare services. Public or private insurance agencies collect money from people and transfer this money to health providers (hospitals). Consumers pay a fixed amount of money which does not correspond to the cost of the healthcare services they consume. The purpose of the government is to control spending on health care. Factors that exacerbate spending on health care are an aging population, technological advances, changes in consumer preferences due to higher incomes (Murthy & Okunade, 2016), and the asymmetric nature of information in health care which causes an induced demand beyond what is actually necessary (Evans, 1974; McGuire, 2000). Although the control of health spending is one of the objectives of a nation's health policy, promoting equality and equity is among the first priorities of health policy makers. Equality refers to the distribution of health services among a population. In a market economy, the allocation of resources and the distribution of output are based on the market mechanism. It could be optimal in the sense that it

M. Chletsos, A. Saiti, *Strategic Management and Economics in Health Care*,
https://doi.org/10.1007/978-3-030-35370-4_10

achieves the Pareto optimum, but this does not guarantee that the allocation/distribution is also fair or equal. The latter depends on what society considers as fair or equal and is attained only through the transfer of resources/income from one social group to another. In general, efficiency and justice are considered to be inversely related. Furthermore, equity is not the same as equality. As the World Health Organization (WHO) states[1] "Equity is the absence of avoidable, unfair, or remediable differences among groups of people, whether those groups are defined socially, economically, demographically or geographically or by other means of stratification. 'Health equity' or 'equity in health' implies that ideally everyone should have a fair opportunity to attain their full health potential and that no one should be disadvantaged from achieving this potential." Another aspect of equity in health is the equity in health financing. De Graeve et al. (2017, p. 569) consider that "equity in health financing is about fairness in the distribution of health-care payments across the population." Financing health care influences the economic and social process since it is related to the transfer of money from persons to health providers through public or private agencies. Thus, financing is an extra cost for individuals. It is one matter for the costs to be distributed equally but it is another matter for individuals to have equal access to the healthcare system. Both are among the main priorities of health and public policy. From the one side, taxes imposed on individuals or on firms affect their decisions and therefore the development of the economy. From the other side, the financing of health care stimulates economic activity in the health sector and permits individuals to obtain health care and ameliorate their health status. The main sources of revenues for healthcare activities are taxes on income, payroll taxes/social security contributions, and out-of-pocket money. Tax on income is characterized by progressivity and distributes the cost of financing according to the income of each individual. Equality in financing is therefore achieved and equal access to health care is enhanced. Reimbursement methods indicate the way health providers are paid for the provision of health services. The reimbursement method could affect the amount of spending on health. A retrospective method, such as fee-for-service, would help to increase the spending on health, while a prospective method, such as a global budget, could limit the cost of health services and enhance the efficiency of the health providers. In recent years, one of the more popular methods of health payments has been the DRG method (diagnostic-related groups) which relates the payment to the health services delivered. Empirical studies show that DRGs promote efficiency and equality in the distribution of payments. Although the efficiency of the health sector is crucial, relevant literature also focuses on the effect of payments on the quality of the health services offered. The Pay-for-performance (P4P) method is used simultaneously with a prospective reimbursement method (such as DRGs) in order to give financial incentives to health providers to ameliorate the quality of health services.

The purpose of this chapter is to discuss not only the concepts of efficiency, equality, and equity in the health sector, but also the different financing and reimbursement methods that hospitals use.

[1] This definition is in the web page of the WHO: https://www.who.int/topics/health_equity/en/.

10.2 Equity and Efficiency in Financing Hospitals

One of the major priorities of the welfare state is to reduce inequalities which very much depend on the way in which resources are distributed. A key factor is income distribution, namely, how the nation's gross domestic product (GDP) (or income) is distributed among its population (Atkinson & Bourguignon, 2001). Classical economists, such as Adam Smith, David Ricardo, etc., concern themselves mainly with the various factors of production in total income (functional distribution of income). Today, economists are also interested in the distribution of income among individuals, independently of their social status (personal distribution of income). Of course, income may be distributed equally or unequally. However, defining equality is not only a matter of economic, social, or political science but it is also a central issue of ethical analysis, which aims to identify where there should be equality and why (Sen, 1992). However, this does raise the question: If everyone has the same income and the same amount of resources, could we say that they are all equal?

For the sake of simplicity, let us assume that in society only one good is produced—hospital services—and that they must be distributed between just two persons. Then, those services can be considered to have been distributed equally if each person receives the same amount of hospital services (Fig. 10.1).

All the combinations on the line OC show that there is an equal distribution of health services. For all other combinations, the hospital services are distributed unequally. For example, for any point on any line OD below the line of equality, person A receives more hospital services than person B. The opposite is the case for any line OE found above the line of equality. In this case, person B receives a greater amount of hospital services than person A.

Figure 10.2 presents the distribution of hospital services which, for illustration purposes, we are assuming to be the only good produced in the economy. The percentage of the population is presented on the horizontal axis, while the percentage of hospital services is presented on the vertical axis. The diagonal line OO′ indicates perfect equality in the sense that, at each point on this line, any given percentage of the population consumes the same percentage of the available hospital services. The curve OO′ describes an unequal distribution of hospital services since, other than points O and O', at each point on the curve the percentage of available hospital services being consumed is less than the percentage of the population consuming them. At point B, the proportion of services consumed, OH_1 is less than OP_2, the percentage of the population that has benefited from this quantity of services. As the curve OO′ (which is the Lorenz curve) shifts to the right, the inequality increases.

The allocation of output produced in the economy is based on the Pareto efficiency principle.[2] Assume that two goods are produced in the economy—hospital services and other consumption goods—and that there are two consumers.

[2] See Katz and Rosen (1998, p. 386–388).

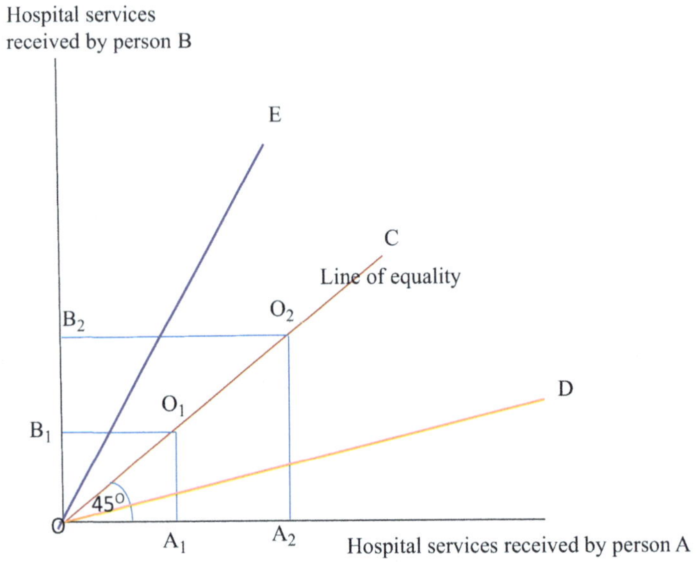

Fig. 10.1 Equality map of hospital services (this figure is drawn from Fig. 4.2 presented by Amiel & Cowell (2003, p. 33))

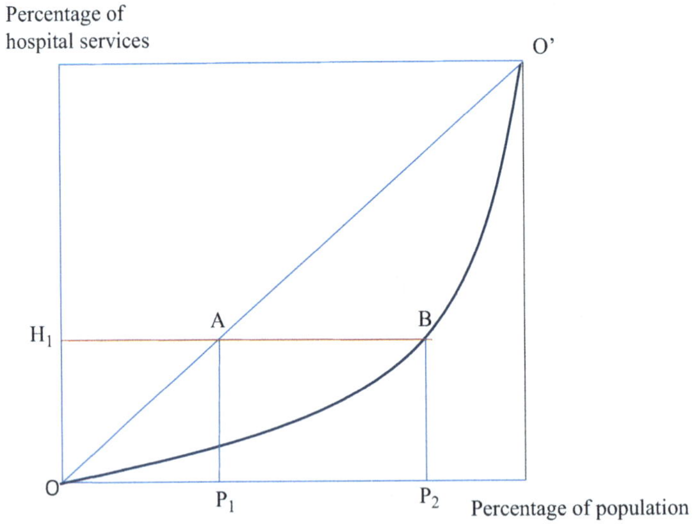

Fig. 10.2 Lorenz curve

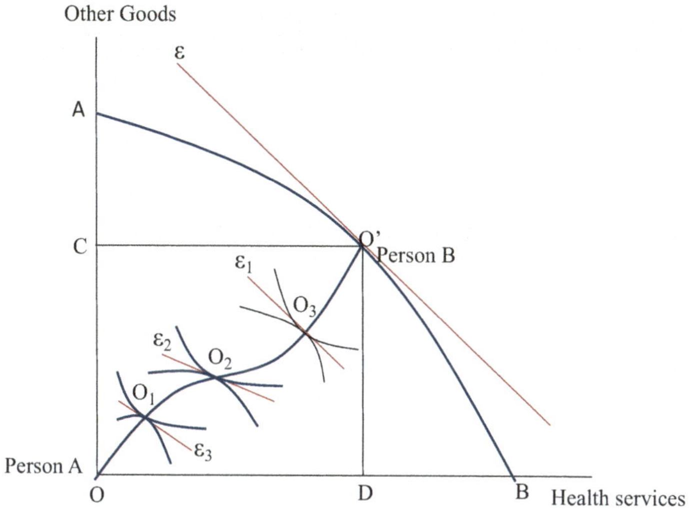

Fig. 10.3 Pareto efficient allocation (this figure is based on the figure presented by Katz & Rosen (1998, p. 388))

The price mechanism determines the allocation efficiency[3] of goods between the two consumers. According to Pareto, efficient allocation requires efficiency not only in allocation but also in production. Pareto efficiency implies that an action of consumers or producers cannot improve the welfare of one person without worsening that of the other person. Pareto efficiency is illustrated in the following figure (Fig. 10.3).

On the above figure, we remark the following:

- AB is the production possibilities frontier, which shows all the optimal combinations between health services and other goods that are produced by using all available resources with maximum efficiency.
- The line ε shows the slope of the production possibilities curve. The point O' is the equilibrium point, at which there is Pareto efficiency in production.
- The curve OO′ is the contract curve which shows that there is Pareto efficiency in consumption. At all the points on the contract curve, the combination of the two goods is Pareto efficient.

[3]The allocation is considered to be efficient if the marginal rate of transformation between two goods is equal to the marginal rate of substitution between two goods (Katz & Rosen, 1998, p. 387). The marginal rate of transformation (or the marginal rate of substitution) is the rate at which the economy can exchange one good with another. More specifically, the marginal rate of substitution refers to the producers of goods and services while the marginal rate of transformation concerns the consumers of goods and services.

The point O_3 is the equilibrium point at which Pareto efficiency is achieved in production and consumption simultaneously. The equilibrium condition is:

Marginal rate of substitution of person A = Marginal rate of substitution of person B = Marginal rate of technical substitution.

The purpose of each consumer is to maximize their utility by consuming goods and services. Thus, the utility function of each person is:

$$U_A = f(X,Y,\ldots Z)$$

The utility of person A depends on the quantity of the goods that they consume. As their consumption increases, their utility increases at a decreasing rate. The latter implies that the person's marginal utility (namely, when the extra utility that the person obtains by consuming a good increases by one unit) decreases (Fig. 10.4).

The total utility function is presented in the upper diagram and the marginal utility function is illustrated in the lower diagram. As a person consumes more health services, they obtain less extra utility and so the marginal utility decreases.

The distribution of the output (health services) to different people may be economically efficient but may not necessarily be equal or fair. If this distribution is not economically efficient, it may become so if the prices of the goods are changed. Thus, the market mechanism can lead to Pareto equilibrium (first theorem of welfare economics). If society considers that this distribution is not fair in the sense that some persons with certain conditions should receive more health services than others, then a new redistribution is necessary. This could succeed only if the government transfers income (or in-kind income) from one person to another person (second theorem of welfare economics). In the case that we transfer health services from one person to another, the utility of one person increases while the utility of the other person decreases. The frontier of utility possibilities is the locus of Pareto-efficient points. This curve illustrates the changes in the utility of person A caused by changes in the utility of person B (Fig. 10.5).

As we transfer health services from person B to person A, the utility of person A increases and the utility of person B decreases.

In order to determine the distribution of income (or in-kind income, e.g., health services), we need to use the social welfare function (Rosen & Gayer, 2007). The purpose of society, which is identical to the purpose of each person, is to maximize the welfare of society, that is, social welfare. Different schools of economic, political, and philosophical theory have their own social welfare function and have a completely different way of maximizing this function. As Stiglitz (2000, p. 98) says, "the social welfare function gives the level of social welfare corresponding to a particular set of levels of utility attained by members of society."

Libertarianism supports that social welfare increases as there is Pareto improvement.[4] According to the utilitarian theory, social welfare is the sum of the utility of

[4] Pareto Improvement occurs if the reallocation of goods makes one person better off without making anyone else worse off.

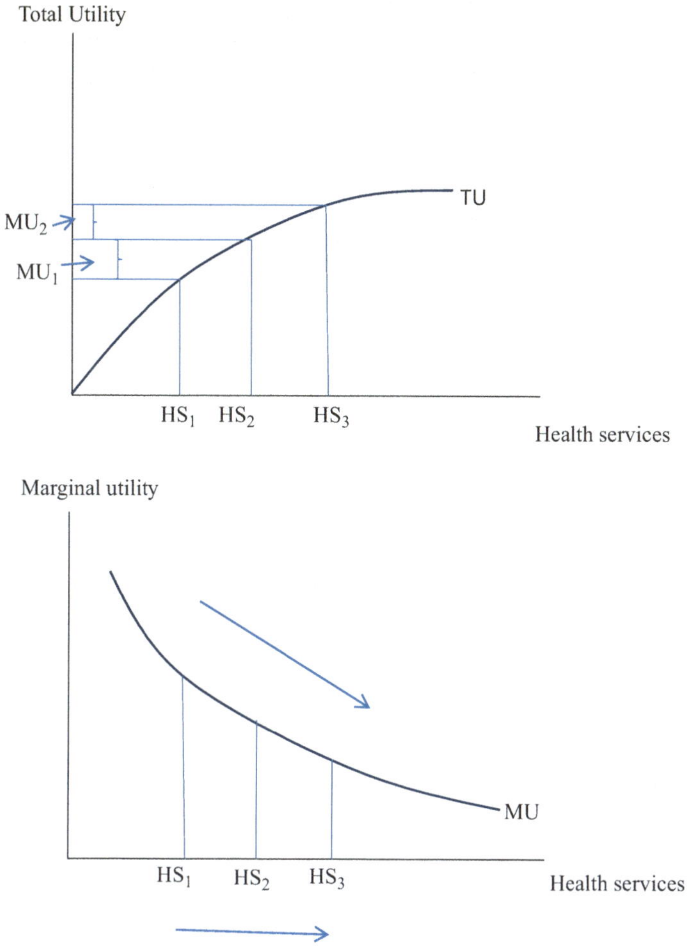

Fig. 10.4 Total and marginal utility of a person who consumes health services (this figure is based on the figure presented by Stiglitz (2000, p. 124))

all members of society and welfare is maximized by maximizing the utility of each member. Rawls' theory supports that social welfare depends on the welfare of those persons who are in the worst economic and social situation. Social welfare is maximized by ameliorating the economic situation of these persons.[5]

Just as an individual can maximize their utility by choosing the combination for which the budget line is tangent to the highest indifference curve, society maximizes social welfare by choosing the combination for which the utility possibilities frontier is tangent to the highest social indifference curve (Fig. 10.6).[6]

[5] See Barr (2004, p. 44–51).

[6] The social indifference curve is the locus of different combinations of utility of person A and person B for which the total utility is constant.

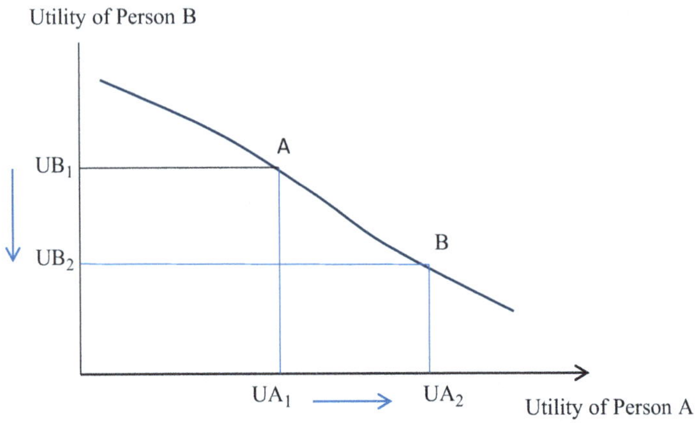

Fig. 10.5 Utility possibilities frontier (this figure is based on the figure presented by Katz and Rosen (1998, p. 389))

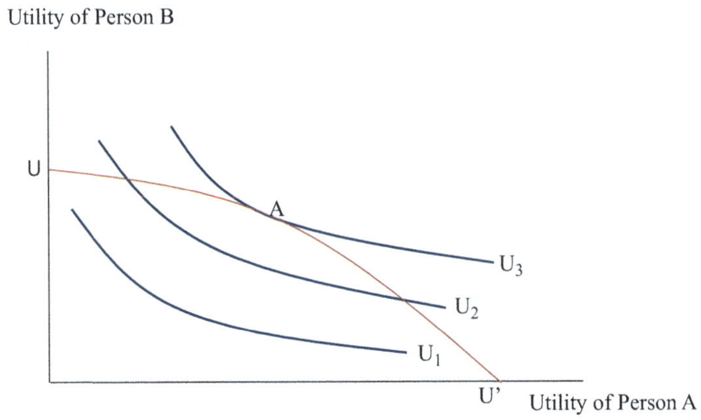

Fig. 10.6 Maximization of the social welfare (the figure is based on the figure presented by Katz & Rosen (1998, p. 401))

The equilibrium point is the point A at which society maximizes its social welfare.

The allocation of resources and goods among individuals is based on the principle of allocative efficiency in production and consumption. As we mentioned above, allocative efficiency does not imply that the allocation of goods is fair or equal. The second theorem of welfare economics states that the market mechanism is unable to improve the level of fairness in the allocation of goods. Only the state could change an unequal distribution of income to a more equal distribution. This is achieved by the transfer of income (in cash or in kind) from one person to another. In this case, resources are transferred from one person to other persons and thus economic

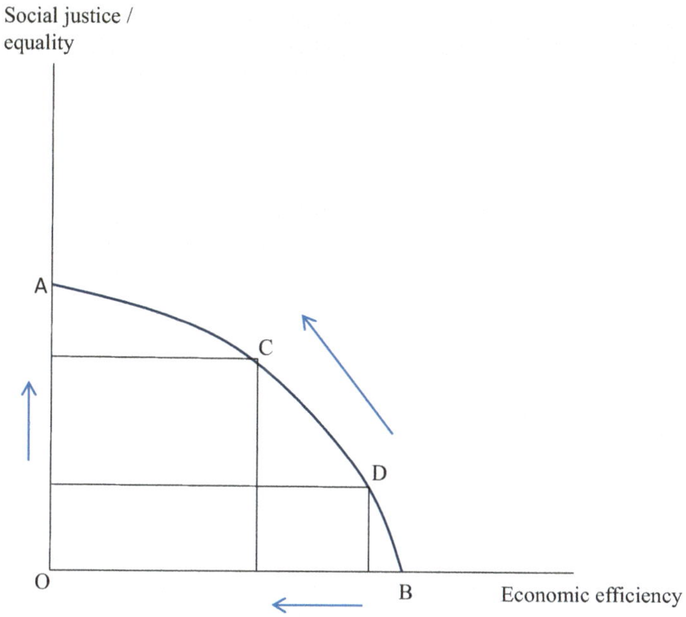

Fig. 10.7 The relation between economic efficiency and social justice/equality

efficiency is altered. The relation between social justice (or equality) and economic efficiency[7] is illustrated in the figure below (Fig. 10.7).

As shown in the above figure, there is a trade-off between economic efficiency and social justice or equality. When a society takes measures to improve social justice, that society loses in terms of economic efficiency.

Equality is the effect of treating each person in the same way. There is income equality if the income that a person gets is the same as everyone else's. So, inequality can be described as the effect of treating an individual (or individuals) differently from others. Health equality/inequality refers to the health status of each person. Health equality exists when the health status of all people is the same, regardless of personal characteristics (such as age, sex, educational background, etc.). Thus, health inequalities refer to differences in health between persons with different socioeconomic characteristics (Braverman, 2014; Braverman et al., 2011; Chittleborough, 2017; Whitehead, 1992). Braverman et al. (2011) use the concept of health disparities, instead of the concept of health inequalities when they refer to the health status of a different racial or ethnic group. Whitehead (1992) emphasizes the unfair and unjust character of health inequalities. Braverman (2006) indicates that health inequalities are not only health differences between persons of different race or ethnicity, but they also refer to persons with different socioeconomic status.

[7] Economic efficiency is achieved when all resources are used efficiently and produce the maximum output at the minimum cost.

The poorest people are expected to have an inferior health status, compared to that of richer persons. Income, education, employment status (Galobardes, Lynch, & Davey Smith, 2007), ethnicity, and gender (Galobardes, 2012) are some of the determinants of health inequalities. According to McCartney, Popham, McMaster, and Cumbers (2019), the use of health inequalities by Americans does not imply that health differences are not necessarily unfair. The unfair character of health inequalities has been emphasized by Whitehead and Dahlgren (2007) in their WHO report. They use the concept "inequities" instead of "inequalities" but they mention that these two concepts are synonymous. They support that all health differences between socioeconomic groups within the country can be considered "unfair" and therefore they can be classified as "health inequities." The definition given by Krieger (2001, p. 698) is similar and more detailed. He uses the concept of social inequalities (or inequities) in health, instead of health inequalities. What is new in his definition is his notion that social inequalities… "systematically burden populations rendered vulnerable by underlying social structures and political, economic and legal institutions." He also considers that social inequalities are not synonymous with health inequalities, which are broader than social inequalities since the former concept does not imply that health differences are necessarily unjust and unfair. Thus, social equity refers to the absence of unjust health disparities (Krieger, 2001, p. 698). The main difference between health inequality and health inequity mentioned by Kawachi, Subramanian, and Almeida-Filho (2002) is that health inequality refers to all differences and disparities in the state of health while health inequity specifically refers to those health inequalities that are unfair. Details on health inequality defined by many authors are presented explicitly by McCartney et al. (2019, p. 27).

The definitions of equity proposed above indicate that equity is related to fairness and equity in health outcomes. Whitehead (1992, p. 431) defines health inequity as "differences in health which are not only unnecessary and avoidable, but in addition are considered unfair and unjust." These definitions consider that equity is an ethical concept. Braverman and Gruskin (2003) consider that health equity is also linked to human rights principles and they propose to define equity based on measurable criteria and on the purpose of operationalization. The right to health is close to the notion of an equal opportunity to remain healthy. Braverman & Gruskin (2003, p. 254) define equity in health as "the absence of systematic disparities in health (or in the major determinants of health) between social groups that have different levels of underlying social advantage/disadvantage—that is, a different position in the social hierarchy." In related work, Braverman et al. (2001, p. 679) stated that "Equity concerns a special subset of health disparities that are particularly unfair because they are associated with underlying social characteristics, such as wealth, that systematically put some groups of people at a disadvantage with respect to opportunities to be healthy."

Theories about social justice also refer to the concept of equity and consider access to health to be its main determinant. Various views on these theories about equity are presented extensively by Wagstaff and Doorslaer (2000), Williams and

Cookson (2000), and Williams (1993). Libertarians[8] reject the necessity of government intervention to assure efficiency and equity in the provision of health services. In contrast, they point toward a privately financed health system where health care is distributed according to an individual's willingness (and ability) to pay. Egalitarianism, as a school of thought, prioritizes equality for all people. As Wagstaff and Doorslaer (2000, p. 1809) mention, egalitarians support that in a publicly financed health system health care should be distributed according to need and financed according to "the ability to pay."

Another important key to defining equity in health care is the role of access to health care.[9] Access could be measured in terms of money or in terms of the time that people spend waiting to receive healthcare services (Le Grand, 1982; Mooney, 1983). Goddard and Smith (2001) focus on equal access to health care for equal need in order to define equity in health. This concept of equity in health is independent of ethical belief. Access could refer to delivering health care (Le Grand, 1982; Mooney, 1994) or to receiving health care. Olson and Rodgers (1991) support that income is among the determinants of access to health. They define access as the maximum attainable quantity of healthcare services, given a household's income and the prices of healthcare services. According to Goddard and Smith (2001), equity of access needs to be considered from the supply side and any variations in access are due to either: (a) the availability of health services, (b) the quality of health services, (c) the cost of health services, or (d) information that the availability of the health services is known to everyone.

Another aspect of equity in health concerns health financing. As de Graeve et al. (2017, p. 569) mention, "equity in health financing is about fairness in the distribution of health-care payments across the population." Universal health coverage is also an important element to ensure that all people have access to needed health services. In a publicly financed health system, the equity in financing could take the form of vertical equity (persons of different income capacities contributing unequally to finance health care) or the form of horizontal equity (that people with the same ability to pay taxes should pay the same amount of taxes) (Wagstaff & Doorslaer, 2000, p. 1819). As Culyer & Wagstaff (1993) commented, the point of view that health care should be distributed according to "need" for the sake of justice is illustrated by both the horizontal and the vertical versions. In their work (2000, p. 433), they further state "the horizontal version implies that persons in equal need should be treated the same, while according to the vertical version persons with greater need should be treated more favorably than those with lesser needs."

In a publicly financed system, people should have access to healthcare services without paying for the delivery of those services. In many healthcare systems, people contribute to the cost of health services at the time they receive those services—a type of payment often referred to as OOPs (out-of-pocket payment). The questions "who pays" and "how much should they pay for health care" are at the core of health

[8] Libertarians are represented by Nozick (1974) and Locke (1967).

[9] See Wagstaff and Doorslaer (2000).

policy analysis. The amount of money that households give to obtain health services constitutes the financial burden. De Graeve et al. (2017) consider that a household's capacity to pay (ctp) is essential in measuring equity in health. "A household's capacity to pay is equal to the total resources that a household can mobilize for purchasing health services, including savings, selling assets and borrowing from financial institutions, relatives and friends" (De Graeve et al., 2017, p. 569). Xu et al. (2003, p. 112) define the household's capacity to pay as "effective income remaining after basic subsistence needs have been met." Thus, ill-health could lead individuals to spending catastrophic amounts for their care, which in turn could push them into poverty. Catastrophic expenditures occur when the amount that a household pays for health care is greater than 40% of their capacity to pay (Yerramilli, Fernandez, & Thomson, 2018). A household is considered poor when its capacity to pay (ctp) becomes negative after subtracting the budget needed to cover their basic needs (Cylus, Thomson, & Evetovits, 2018). Yerramilli et al. (2018) considered that households are further impoverished if consumption budgets are reduced by OOPs to less than the cost of their basic needs.

10.3 Financing Versus Payment of Hospital Services

Hospitals are economic units and as economic units they use resources in order to produce healthcare services and deliver these services to the population. The production and the distribution of healthcare services are illustrated by the circular flow diagram presented in the next figure (Fig. 10.8).

Hospitals use inputs (Personnel, Technology, and Materials) in order to produce health services and supply these services to households. Hospitals need money in order to produce health services and this amount of money constitutes the financing of hospital services. Hospitals pay the health providers in order to buy inputs and organize the production. Note that there is a clear distinction between a payment and financing. The latter answers the question "who pays for the hospital services" and refers to the manner in which hospitals apportion the total cost of their services among the population (Evans, 2002, p. 33). The payments to health providers answer the question "who gets what and how much" (Evans, 2002, p. 41). Therefore, the financing equation could be written as follows (Mossialos & Dixon, 2002, p. 3):

$$\begin{aligned}\text{Total revenues} &= \text{Total health expenditures}\\ &= \text{Total incomes} + \text{profits of those working in hospitals}\end{aligned}$$

Total revenues, which are the funding side, come from the government, from social and private insurance, and from households. Total revenues are: taxation (direct or indirect, national, or local taxes), social health insurance, private insurance, and out-of-pocket money. Social insurance is levied on earnings and is like income tax. Health expenditures amount to the health services produced multiplied by their prices. Total incomes amount to the units of factors of production multiplied by their prices.

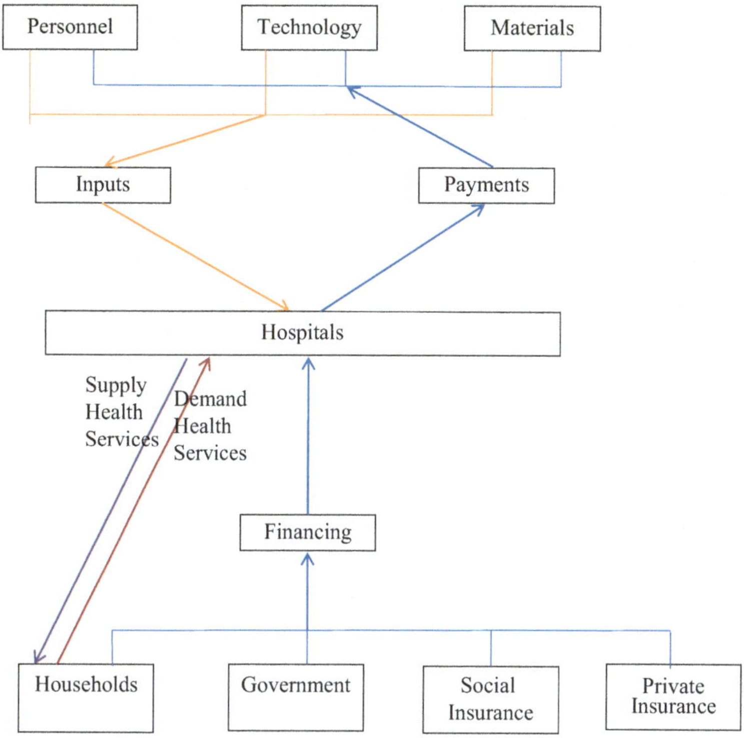

Fig. 10.8 Circular flow diagram

The financing process consists of three parts: (a) the collection of revenues, (b) the pooling of funds, and (c) the purchasing of health services (Mossialos & Dixon, 2002; Murray & Frenk, 2000; Phua & Lee, 2017). The first part, which is the collection of revenues, is implemented through different mechanisms.[10] According to Kutzin (2001, p. 175), these mechanisms are: direct taxes, indirect taxes, payroll taxes, other compulsory contributions, voluntary prepaid contributions, grants, and loans. Mossialos and Dixon (2002, p. 5) add two more mechanisms which are medical savings[11] and out-of-pocket payments.[12] Co-payment is a fixed amount established by an insurance policy and paid by the consumer at the time of using the

[10] See Kutzin (2001), Mossialos and Dixon (2002), and Sheiman, Langenbrunner, Kehler, Cashin, and Kutzin (2010).

[11] In medical savings, individuals contribute a proportion of their income. This amount of money is spent at the time that persons use health services (Mossialos & Dixon, 2002, p. 21). There is a huge amount of literature on the role of medical savings (among others, see Scheffler and Yu, 1998; Hsiao, 1995).

[12] Out-of-pocket money includes costs paid by the consumer at the time of using the health services. They consist of formal and informal payments.

health service. The implementation of co-payment is based on the plan for sharing the cost of certain health services between the insurance company and the insured customer.

OECD (1992) classifies healthcare financing into seven models based on the hypothesis that there are two main types of financing: (a) voluntary and (b) compulsory. The health financing models are: (a) the voluntary out-of-pocket money, (b) the voluntary reimbursement model, (c) the public reimbursement model, (d) the voluntary contract model, (e) the public contract model, (f) the voluntary integrated model, and (g) the public integrated model. As far as hospital financing in Europe is concerned, there are two main models. The first is the public compulsory insurance model and the second is the tax-based model. Private insurance and out-of-pocket money are supplementary sources of financing. In the case of public-owned hospitals, the role of the state in the financing process of these hospitals is crucial. Even in the case of privately owned hospitals, the role of the state is important, especially in the case of the nonprofit private hospitals.

Hospital financing is strongly related to the equity principle. The question that arises is how the financial burden is distributed among the population. It is believed that the most equitable approach is a progressive distribution whereby those with a greater ability to pay, as measured by consumption, income, or wealth, should pay a greater marginal tax rate than those with a lower ability to pay (Auerbach, 2009). Income tax is a progressive tax while the consumption tax [value-added tax (VAT)] is a regressive tax. Payroll tax or social security contributions are less progressive than income tax. Musgrave and Thin (1948) aimed to examine the progressivity of the tax system by comparing income inequality before and after income tax was deducted. A tax system is considered as progressive when income inequality, after income tax is deducted, decreases while in the case of a regressive tax system the income inequality increases. A measure of the progressivity of tax on incomes, proposed by Pigou (1928), is an increasing change in the average tax rate as the change in income increases. If the ratio of change in tax rate to the change in income increases, then the tax system is described as progressive. It is considered to be proportional if this ratio is equal to 1 and regressive if less than 1. In the next figure, the average tax rate across incomes is presented in different tax systems (Fig. 10.9).

Kakwani (1977), inspired by the Gini coefficient, proposed a measurement of tax progressivity. The graphical presentation of Kalwani's index is presented explicitly by Wagstaff and Doorslaer (2000, p. 1823). The Lorenz curve shows the distribution of income for each proportion of the population. As the distance between the equality line and the Lorenz curve increases, the income inequality increases. With regard to the financing of health care, two Lorenz curves are drawn. The first curve is the Lorenz curve for prepayment income $L_{\text{pre(p)}}$ which represents the distribution of income before the financing of health care. The second curve is the payment concentration curve $L_{\text{pay(p)}}$ which is the distribution of tax payments among different proportions of the population. In the case of a proportional tax, the two curves coincide. If the tax is progressive, the $L_{\text{pay(p)}}$ curve is found below the $L_{\text{pre(p)}}$ curve ($L^1_{\text{pay(p)}}$ in the diagram). If the tax is regressive, the $L_{\text{pay(p)}}$ curve is found above the $L_{\text{pre(p)}}$ curve ($L^2_{\text{pay(p)}}$ in the diagram) (Fig. 10.10).

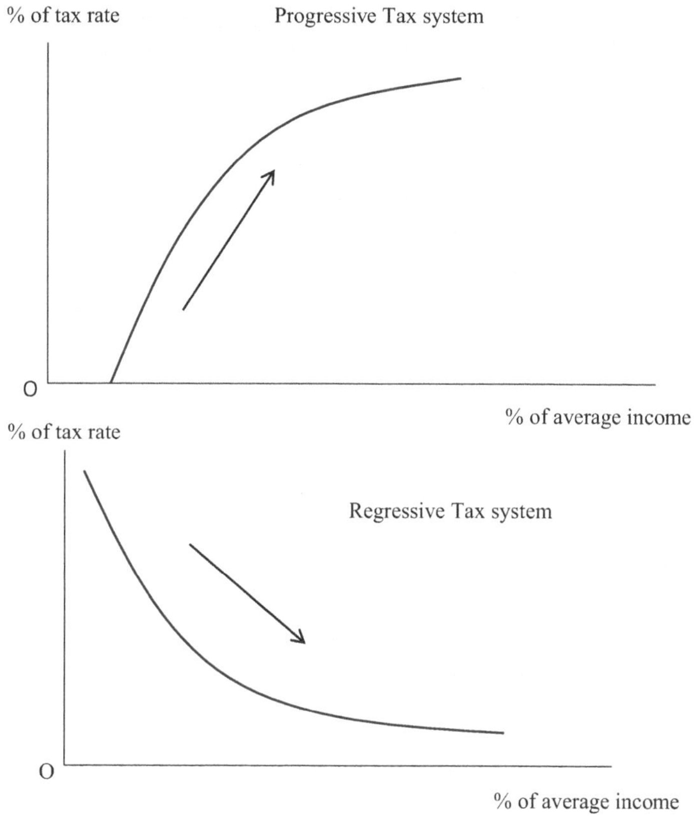

Fig. 10.9 Average tax rate across income

The Kalwani's index is based on the use of the Gini coefficient for the prepayment income G_{pre} and the concentration index for payments (C_{pay}) and is defined as: $\pi\kappa = C_{\text{pay}} - G_{\text{pre}}$ (Wagstaff & Doorslaer, 2000, p. 1823). The index $\pi\kappa$ is positive if the system is progressive and negative if the system is regressive.

The financing of hospital care has its limits, with consequences for individuals and for the economy as a whole. A key means of increasing hospital financing is for the national government to increase its spending on health and this is achieved by increasing income tax, which inevitably affects the decisions of individuals and firms. Disposable income (income minus taxes) decreases which affects private consumption and therefore aggregate demand and consequently aggregate supply. Firms' decisions are also affected by the increase in their taxes. As taxes for firms increase, profits decrease and therefore investments decrease. An increase of payroll tax increases the cost of labor, which has a negative effect on firms' recruitment of staff. Also, firms have a vested interest to substitute labor with capital and this can further reduce employment opportunities for households. Hospital financing also impacts upon the welfare of society, as it affects income inequality and the extent to which the health needs of the population are satisfied.

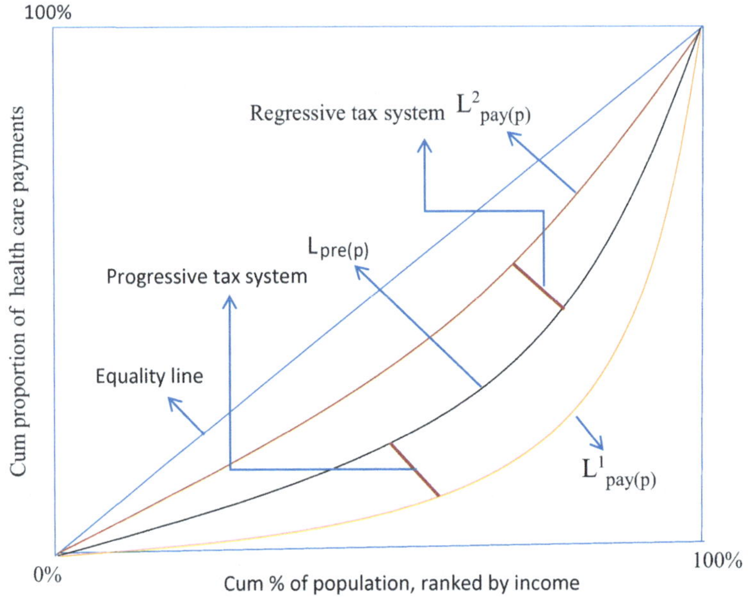

Fig. 10.10 Lorenz curve for prepayment income and healthcare payments (this figure is presented in Wagstaff and Doorslaer (2000, p. 1823))

10.4 Traditional and Modern Hospital Payments (DRGs and P4P)

The way hospitals are financed for the services they provide is a crucial point in any health policy. Hospital costs constitute the main portion of health expenditures (Mathes, Pieper, Mosch, Jaschinski, & Eikermann, 2014). Health providers (hospitals) may or may not have incentives to affect a hospital's costs. In the past, health policy makers used reimbursement methods in order to incite hospitals to control their costs (Abel-Smith & Mossialos, 1994; Dixon, 2004; Draper et al., 1987). Although the relevant literature includes some analysis of the impact of payment methods on hospitals' costs and on the quality of their care, it remains difficult to predict their impacts (Campbell et al., 2007). The relation between a health provider's income and their activity is under research. In systems where the remuneration is variable, a hospital has the capability to influence their earnings, while this is not the case of systems where the remuneration is constant (Jegers, Kesteloot, de Grave, & Gilles, 2002).

As far as payments to hospitals are concerned, these could be classified into two major categories: (a) Retrospective healthcare systems and (b) prospective healthcare systems. In a retrospective payment system, the hospital's costs are reimbursed fully or partially ex post. This payment system does not give an incentive to the hospital to decrease their costs since they are reimbursed for the cost of providing their services (Eastaugh, 1987). The cost of providing hospital services determines the price of hospital services which is the price of reimbursement. It seems that there is a positive relationship between hospital costs and payments to hospitals. In the prospective payment system, payments to hospital are determined ex ante (Jegers et al., 2002) and can take the form of a regular payment or a set budget. In this payment system, the payment is independent of the actual cost of the hospital's services since the reimbursement is fixed ex ante. It seems that this system incites hospitals to stimulate efficiency by decreasing their cost and increasing their profits (or decreasing their losses in the case that hospitals are faced with losses). Prospective payment systems have the potential for applying a cost containment policy.[13] Although such a prospective payment system has the advantage of controlling a hospital's costs, one disadvantage from a patient's perspective is that, in an attempt to reduce costs, hospitals using this system tend to provide care that has less diversity and lower quality.

The provision of an extra unit of health care has a marginal cost and a marginal benefit. An economic unit (hospital) may decide to produce an extra unit if the expected benefit is greater than the extra cost. As long as the prospective payment system is not cost-neutral, hospitals have incentives to increase the provision of health care, even if this is not absolutely necessary. Induced demand, which is when demand for health services is increased to more than the level that society actually needs, is caused because of the asymmetric nature of the information that patients have about their health.

As far as the specific reimbursement schemes are concerned, WHO[14] proposes six main approaches, as follows:

- *Line-item budget*. This is a centrally planned budget that is allocated according to different resource categories (staff, medicines, etc.).
- *Payment per procedure (Fee-for-service)*. This is a payment for each individual procedure. Reimbursement is based on a set of listed charges for various procedures.
- *Payment per day (or bed)*. There is a fixed charge per day, regardless of the treatments given to the patient.
- *Payment per case*. A fixed payment is made for each admission, regardless of the actual cost of the care. Fees are set according to diagnosed medical conditions and standardized treatment costs (OECD, 1995, p. 31).
- *Global budgeting*. A lump sum is given to the hospital to cover all specified services during a given period.

[13] The cost containment policy consists of actions that aim to control operational costs.

[14] See World Health Organization. How are hospitals funded and which payment method is best? Summary of a HEN network member's report. http://www.euro.who.int/en/data-and-evidence/evidence-informed-policy-making/publications/hen-summaries-of-network-members-reports/how-are-hospitals-funded-and-which-payment-method-is-best. These main types of reimbursement schemes are also presented by Mathes et al. (2014, p. 2).

- *Capitation*. A fixed amount for each person is covered for specified services for a given time period.

Pay per procedure (Fee-for-service) is a retrospective mechanism while all the others are prospective mechanisms. As we mentioned above, while a fee-for-service incentivizes hospitals to increase their activity and therefore health expenditure, it does not encourage efficiency. It may create competition between health providers (hospitals) but this competition would be based on the quality of hospital services provided rather than on lower prices (Weisbrod, 1991). Prospective mechanisms enhance the measure of control over hospital costs and incentivize hospitals to be more efficient. However, there has been no evidence of any improvement in the quality of the health care provided (OECD, 2016). Davis and Rhodes (1988, p. 121) support the view that the prospective payment mechanism provides incentives that encourage cost-conscious behavior among hospitals and helps to secure a certain level of inpatient care.

The payment mechanism based on a global budget has two main advantages. The first is that it is relatively simple from an administrative point of view. Secondly, it helps to control the cost of health services.

In recent years, many countries have used the payment per case model to reimburse the cost of hospital services. A well-known payment per case system is the Diagnostic-Related Groups (DRGs) system. The first DRG system was implemented in New Jersey in the beginning of 1980 and it was the basis for reimbursing providers under the US Medicare system (Wiley, 2011, p. 4). Initially, the purpose of the DRG system was to serve as a patient classification system. It also helped to classify diseases according to clinical complexity and the utilization of resources. McGuire (1991, p. 98) noted that DRGs were primarily used as a tool to regulate increases in hospital spending. Indeed, DRGs do serve as a basis for budgeting and cost control in hospital management (Vogl, 2013, p. 290). Another purpose of DRGs as a payment mechanism is to encourage the efficient delivery of healthcare services and to discourage the provision of unnecessary services. The implementation of DRGs as a payment mechanism affects the behavior of health providers (hospitals). From one perspective, hospitals could increase their activity in order to increase their profit if they expect that hospital costs will be less than the reimbursement rate (Miranda & Cortez, 2005; Wiley, 2011). From another perspective, hospitals could decrease admissions in order to avoid exceeding the expected costs (Chalkley & Malcomson, 2000; Cutler & Zeckhauser, 2000). As far as the consequences of the implementation of DRGs are concerned, it has been found that DRGs decrease the average length of stay in hospitals (Husser, Guerin, & Bretones, 2012) and subsequently hospital utilization (Davis & Rhodes, 1988). A literature review on the usefulness of DRGs to pay hospital costs revealed that there are also some negative effects (Street, O' Reilly, Ward, & Mason, 2011). Hospitals can choose their patients and apply the "cream skimming practice" (Martinussen & Hagen, 2009). There is also a risk of hospitals being unfairly financed whereby they choose/attract the patients who are likely to incur the lowest bills (Husser et al., 2012, p. 33). The impact of hospitals using a DRG-based payment system on the quality of health care is ambiguous and depends on the hospital's practices. The impact could be negative if the hospital decides to decrease the cost per admission or it could be ameliorated if it decides to increase the number of admissions. The latter would give the hospital an incentive to use new technology (Quentin, Scheller-Kreisen, & Buss, 2011).

Summarizing, we can say that the implementation of DRGs in many countries has not only many advantages but there are also some weak points. According to Husser et al. (2012, p. 32), DRGs help to:

- Establish a link between healthcare production and financing
- Encourage the providers to be more efficient, otherwise they will be penalized with deficits
- Enhance the development of management tools to control costs
- Encourage harmonization between the public and private sector
- Reduce the length of stays
- Cause cream skimming whereby hospitals apply patient selection in order to avoid the most severe cases (and the highest costs)
- Cause a coding effect (overcoding/upcoding of patient diagnosis)
- Increase the tendency for hospitals to transfer patients to units that do not operate under a DRG system.

A new payment method, which can be used in addition to the existing basic reimbursement methods, is pay-for-performance (P4P). This method is not actually a payment or reimbursement method. The purpose of this method is to provide incentives to health providers to improve efficiency (Eijkenaar, Emmert, Scheppach, & Schoffski, 2013) and the quality of their services (Milstein & Schreyoegg, 2016). The use of the P4P method in health care originated in the private sector in the USA in the late 1990s (Cashin, Chi, Smith, Borowitz, & Thomson, 2014). In many countries where P4P programs have been implemented, healthcare providers have had financial incentives to achieve goals relating to performance measures (Eijkenaar et al., 2013, p. 115), to increase their coverage of preventative services, and to enhance their management of chronic diseases in order to achieve better patient outcomes (Cashin et al., 2014, p. 4).

There is no commonly accepted definition of a P4P program. The OECD (2010) offers definitions given by the following six organizations/institutions: the Agency for Healthcare Research and Quality (AHRQ), the Centers for Medicare and Medicaid Services (CMS), the RAND Corporation (RAND), the World Bank, the United States Agency for International Development (USAID), and the Center for Global Development. The definitions proposed by AHRQ, CMS, and RAND relate to an extra payment being made in order to improve quality. The definition proposed by the RAND Corporation includes the attainment of efficiency as a measure of the performance needed in P4P programs. The definitions given by the World Bank, USAID, and the Center for Global Development include incentives for both the supply side (providers) and for the demand side (patients) (OECD, 2010, p. 110).

In a typical market, decisions about the price and the quantity supplied are based on perfect information concerning the product and the needs of the consumers. The transaction between consumers and producers causes maximum utility of both economic units. However, the health market is characterized by asymmetric information between patients and health providers (Arrow, 1963). Moreover, health providers have a greater knowledge of patients' health status than the patients have. They decide, on behalf of their patients, about the treatment and generally about the quantity of the health services a given patient should receive. As hospitals aim to maximize their interests, this may cause demand to increase more than is necessary. This is known as the phenomenon of induced demand. Patients who are insured and have their health needs fully covered do not have an incentive to reduce their demand for health services. This is a moral hazard. The relationship between provider and patients in the healthcare market could be characterized as a principal–agent relationship (Nguyen, 2011). The framework of the pay-for-performance program can be analyzed based on the principal–agent theory (Christianson, Knutson, & Mazze, 2006; Eisenhardt, 1989; Golden & Sloan, 2008; Robinson, 2001; Town, Wholey, Kralewski, & Dowd, 2004; Trisolini, 2011). Agency describes the relationship between the principal (i.e., the patient or the organization that finances the provision of healthcare services) and the agent (i.e., the physician or medical unit, such as a hospital). The prospective payment method implies that there is a financial risk for the health provider (hospital) in the case that the reimbursement is less than the cost of healthcare services. Hospitals have an interest in reducing the cost of healthcare services in order to increase the number of admissions. The cost of health care may be reduced by decreasing the amount of health care provided to the patient. However, this could be to the detriment of the patient's health. P4P programs give the health provider an incentive to improve performance and therefore to increase quality by linking payment to performance. It is considered that P4P programs have two main goals: to improve the quality of health services and to improve efficiency. The first questions to arise when measuring quality and efficiency are: should health providers be rewarded for good quality/efficiency? Should they have a penalty imposed for

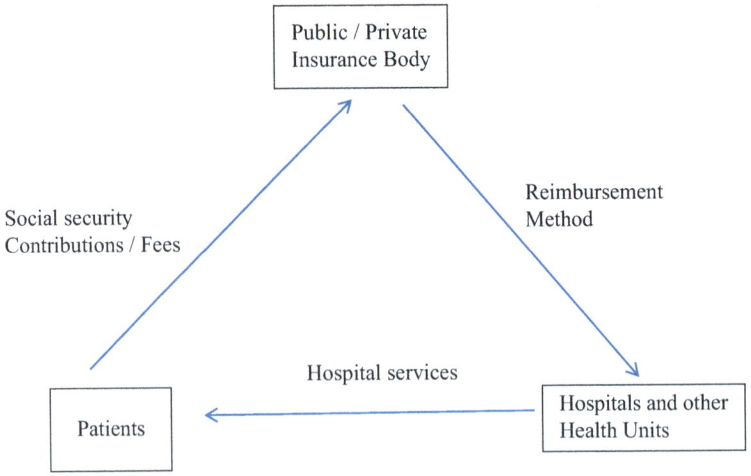

Fig. 10.11 Relationship between patients, public and private insurance institutions, and hospitals

poor quality/efficiency? The next step in the P4P process is to determine the basis for reward/penalty and the third step is to ensure the reward/penalty is administered. In the case of a prospective payment system, reimbursement to the hospital comes from the purchaser of hospital services, which could be a public or private insurance group. The relationship between the patient (principal), the public/private purchaser of health services, and the health units/hospitals (agents) is illustrated in the following figure (Fig. 10.11).

A P4P program is set up by a public/private insurance body and it is linked to the main payment method. The measures used can be split into quality and efficiency measures (Scheffler, 2010). The performance domain refers to: (a) structure, (b) process, and (c) outcomes. Efficiency measures refer to cost savings or productivity improvements. The basis for reward could be the absolute level of measure or ranking system. The type of reward is mainly a financial bonus but could also be a nonfinancial incentive. Scheffler (2008) developed the following framework for a P4P program:

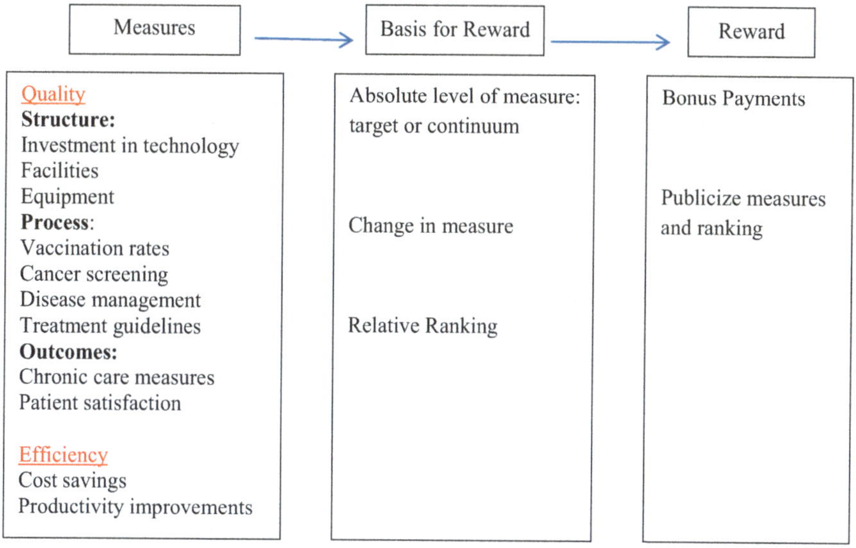

Framework of P4P programs. *Source:* **Adopted from Scheffler RM: Is There a Doctor in the House? Market Signals and Tomorrow's Supply of Doctors, Stanford University Press, 2008**

The effects of P4P programs on the quality of health services remain mixed (Damberg et al., 2009; Gurthrie, Auerback, & Binman, 2010). Frolich, Talavera, Broadhead, and Dudley (2007) studied the impact of P4P programs on service quality and they found that in two programs there was an improvement of quality while in three other programs there was no significant effect. Sutton et al. (2012) found that a P4P program in hospitals in one region of England had clinically significant effects on in-hospital mortality. As regards the impact of using P4P programs on inequalities, a review of many studies carried out by Eijkenaar et al. (2013) showed that P4P seems to have narrowed socioeconomic inequalities. The unclear effect of the use of P4P is also shown by Milstein and Schreyoegg (2016). In their review of 34 P4P programs in 14 OECD countries, they mention two positive effects of the use of P4P programs: a greater awareness of how personal data were being recorded and the development of public records.

Summarizing, we can say that the new methods of paying for healthcare services aim to control health spending, promote efficiency, improve service quality, and decrease inequalities.

References

Abel-Smith, B., & Mossialos, E. (1994). Cost containment and health care reform: A study of the European Union. *Health Policy, 28*(2), 89–132.

Amiel, Y., & Cowell, F. A. (2003). *Thinking about inequality: Personal judgment and income distributions*. Cambridge: Cambridge University Press.

Arrow, K. J. (1963). Uncertainty and the welfare economics of the medical care. *American Economic Review, 53*(5), 941–973.

Atkinson, A. B., & Bourguignon, F. (2001). Income distribution. In *International encyclopedia of the social & behavioral sciences* (Vol. 3, 2nd ed., pp. 7265–7271). Oxford: Elsevier.

Auerbach, A. (2009). Public finance in practice and theory. *CESifo Economic Studies, 56*(1), 1–20.

Barr, N. (2004). *The economics of the welfare state* (4th ed.). London, UK: Oxford University Press.

Braverman, P. (2006). Health disparities and health equity: Concept and measurement. *Annual Review of Public Health, 27*, 167–194.

Braverman, P. (2014). What is health equity: And how does a life-course approach take us further towards it? *Maternal and Child Health Journal, 18*(2), 366–372.

Braverman, P., & Gruskin, S. (2003). Defining equity in health. *Journal of Epidemiology & Community Health, 57*(4), 254–258.

Braverman, P., Kumanyika, S., Fielding, J., LaVeist, T., Borrell, L. N., Manderscheid, R., et al. (2011). Health disparities and health equity: The issue is justice. *American Journal of Public Health, 101*(S1), 149–155.

Braverman, P., Starfield, B., & Geiger, J. H. (2001). World Health Report 2000: How it removes equity from the agenda for public health monitoring and policy. *BMJ, 323*, 678–681. https://doi.org/10.1136/bmj.323.7314.678

Campbell, N. C., Murray, E., Darbyshire, J., Emery, J., Farmer, A., Griffiths, F., et al. (2007). Designing and evaluating complex interventions to improve health care. *The BMJ, 334*, 455–459. https://doi.org/10.1136/bmj.39108.379965.BE

Cashin, C., Chi, Y.-L., Smith, P. C., Borowitz, M., & Thomson, S. (2014). Health producer P4P and strategic health purchasing. In C. Cashin, Y.-L. Chi, P. C. Smith, M. Borowitz, & S. Thomson (Eds.), *Paying for performance in health care. Implications for health system performance and accountability* (pp. 3–21). Berkshire, UK: Open University Press/McGraw-Hill Education.

Chalkley, M., & Malcomson, J. (2000). Government purchasing of health services. In A. J. Culyer & J. P. Newhouse (Eds.), *Handbook of health economics* (Vol. 1, pp. 841–890). Amsterdam, The Netherlands: Elsevier/North Holland.

Chittleborough, C. (2017). Health inequalities. In *International encyclopedia of public health* (Vol. 3, 2nd ed., pp. 406–412). Oxford: Academic Press.

Christianson, J. B., Knutson, D. J., & Mazze, R. S. (2006). Physician pay-for-performance. Implementation and research issues. *Journal of General Internal Medicine, 21*(suppl 2), S9–S13.

Culyer, A. J., & Wagstaff, A. (1993). Equity and equality in health and health care. *Journal of Health Economics, 12*(4), 431–457.

Cutler, D., & Zeckhauser, R. (2000). The anatomy of health insurance. In A. J. Culyer & J. P. Newhouse (Eds.), *Handbook of health economics* (Vol. 1, pp. 543–643). Cham, The Netherlands: Elsevier/North Holland.

Cylus, J., Thomson, S., & Evetovits, T. (2018). Catastrophic health spending in Europe: Equity and policy implications of different calculation methods. *Bulletin of the World Health Organization, 96*(9), 599–609.

Damberg, C. L., Raube, K., Teleki, S. S., & Cruz, E. D. (2009). Taking Stock Of Pay-For-Performance: A Candid Assessment From The Front Lines. *Health Affairs, 28*(2), 517–525.

Davis, C. K., & Rhodes, J. D. (1988). The impact of DRGs on the cost and quality of health care in the United States. *Health Policy, 9*(2), 117–131.

De Graeve, D., Xu, K., & Van Gestel, R. (2017). Equity in health financing. In *International encyclopedia of public health* (Vol. 2, 2nd ed., pp. 569–576). Oxford: Academic Press.

Dixon, J. (2004). Payment by results – new financial flows in the NHS. *The BMJ, 328*, 969–970. https://doi.org/10.1136/bmj.328.7446.969

Draper, D., Rogers, W. H., Kahn, K. L., Keeler, E. B., Reinisch, E. J., Sherwood, M. J., et al. (1987). *Effects of Medicare's prospective payment system on the quality of hospital care*, RAND Corporation, Document Number: RB-4519-1. Retrieved from https://www.rand.org/pubs/research_briefs/RB4519-1.html

Eastaugh, S. R. (1987). *Financing Health care: Economic Efficiency and Equity*. Dover MA: Auburn House Pub. Co.

Eijkenaar, F., Emmert, M., Scheppach, M., & Schoffski, O. (2013). Effects of pay for performance in health care: A systematic review of systematic reviews. *Health Policy, 110*(2-3), 115–130.

Eisenhardt, K. (1989). Agency theory: An assessment and review. *Academy of Management Review, 14*(1), 57–74.

Evans, R. (1974). Supplier-induced demand: Some empirical evidence and implications. In M. Perlman (Ed.), *The economics of health and medical care* (pp. 162–173). London: Macmillan.

Evans, R. G. (2002). Financing health care: Taxation and the alternatives. In E. Mossialos, A. Dixon, J. Figueras, & J. Kutzin (Eds.), *Funding health care: Options for Europe* (European observatory on health care systems series) (pp. 31–58). London, UK: Open University Press.

Frolich, A., Talavera, J. A., Broadhead, P., & Dudley, R. A. (2007). A behavioral model of clinician responses to incentives to improve quality. *Health Policy, 80*(1), 179–193.

Galobardes, B. (2012). Socioeconomic inequalities in health: Individual or area level: Does it matter? *BMC Public Health, 12*, 171. https://doi.org/10.1186/1471-2458-12-171

Galobardes, B., Lynch, J., & Davey Smith, G. (2007). Measuring socioeconomic position in health research. *British Medical Bulletin, 81-82*(1), 21–37.

Goddard, M., & Smith, P. (2001). Equity of access to health care services: Theory and evidence from the UK. *Social Science & Medicine, 53*(9), 1149–1162.

Golden, B., & Sloan, F. (2008). Physician pay for performance: Alternative perspectives. In F. Sloan & H. Kasper (Eds.), *Incentives and choice in health care* (pp. 298–318). Cambridge, MA: MIT Press.

Gurthrie, B., Auerback, G., & Binman, A. (2010). Competition for Medicaid enrolls based on performance does not improve quality of care. *Health Affairs, 29*(8), 1507–1516.

Hsiao, W. C. (1995). Medical savings accounts: Lessons from Singapore. *Health Affairs, 7*(4), 260–266.

Husser, J., Guerin, O., & Bretones, D. (2012). The incentive effects of DRGs' reimbursement rates for health care establishments in France : Toward a new allocation of surgical procedures? *International Business Research, 5*(12), 31–37.

Jegers, M., Kesteloot, K., de Grave, D., & Gilles, W. (2002). A typology for provider payment systems in health care. *Health Policy, 60*(3), 255–273.

Kakwani, N. C. (1977). Measurement of tax progressivity: An international comparison. *The Economic Journal, 87*(345), 71–80.
Katz, M. L., & Rosen, H. S. (1998). *Microeconomics* (3rd ed.). Boston: Irwin/McGraw-Hill.
Kawachi, I., Subramanian, S. V., & Almeida-Filho, N. (2002). A glossary for social epidemiology. *Journal of Epidemiology & Community Health, 56*(9), 647–652. https://doi.org/10.1136/jech.56.9.647
Krieger, N. A. (2001). A glossary for social epidemiology. *Journal of Epidemiology & Community Health, 55*(10), 693–700. https://doi.org/10.1136/jech.55.10.693
Kutzin, J. (2001). A descriptive framework for country – level analysis of health care financing arrangements. *Health Policy, 56*, 171–204.
Le Grand, J. (1982). *The strategy of equality: Redistribution and the social services*. London: Allen & Unwin.
Lockc, J. (1967). *Two treatises of government*. Cambridge: Cambridge University Press.
Martinussen, P. E., & Hagen, T. P. (2009). Reimbursement systems, organizational forms and patient selection: Evidence from day surgery in Norway. *Health Economics, Policy, and Law, 4*(2), 139–158.
Mathes, T., Pieper, D., Mosch, C. G., Jaschinski, T., & Eikermann, M. (2014). Payment methods for hospitals. *Cochrane Database of Systematic Reviews, 6*, CD011156. https://doi.org/10.1002/14651858.CD011156
McCartney, G., Popham, F., McMaster, R., & Cumbers, A. (2019). Defining health and health inequalities. *Public Health, 172*(July), 22–30.
McGuire, T. (2000). Physician agency. In A. J. Culyer & J. P. Newhouse (Eds.), *The handbook of health economics* (Vol. 1, pp. 462–536). Amsterdam, The Netherlands: Elsevier/North Holland.
McGuire, T. E. (1991). DRGs: The state of the art, circa 1990. *Health Policy, 17*(2), 97–119.
Milstein, R., & Schreyoegg, J. (2016). Pay for performance in the inpatient sector: A review of 34 P4P programs in 14 OECD countries. *Health Policy, 120*(10), 1125–1140.
Miranda M., & Cortez L. (2005). *The Diagnosis Related Groups (DRGs) to adjust payment – mechanisms for health system providers*. In Conference paper presented at Conferencia Interamericana de Seguridad Social (Inter-American Conference on Social Security).
Mooney, G. (1983). Equity in health care: Confronting the confusion. *Effective Health Care, 1*(4), 179–185.
Mooney, G. (1994). *Key issues in health economics*. New York: Harvester Wheatsheaf.
Mossialos, E., & Dixon, A. (2002). Funding health care: An introduction. In E. Mossialos, A. Dixon, J. Figueras, & J. Kutzin (Eds.), *Funding health care: Options for Europe* (European observatory on health care systems series) (pp. 1–30). Buckingham, UK: Open University Press.
Murray, C. J., & Frenk, J. (2000). A framework for assessing the performance of health systems. *Bulletin of the World Health Organization, 78*(6), 717–731.
Murthy, V. N., & Okunade, A. A. (2016). Determinants of US health expenditure: Evidence from autoregressive distributed lag (ARDL) approach to cointegration. *Economic Modelling, 59*(December), 67–73.
Musgrave, R. A., & Thin, T. (1948). Income tax progression 1929–1948. *Journal of Political Economy, 56*(6), 498–514.
Nguyen, H. (2011). The principal-agent problems in health care: Evidence from prescribing patterns of private providers in Vietnam. *Health Policy and Planning, 26*(1S), 153–162.
Nozick, R. (1974). *Anarchy, state and utopia*. New York: Basic Books.
OECD. (1992). *The reform of health care. A comparative analysis of seven OECD countries*, Paris, France.
OECD. (1995). Health care reform: Controlling spending and increasing efficiency. *OECD Economic Studies, 24*, 7–55.
OECD. (2010). *Value for money in health spending, OECD health policy studies*. Paris, France: OEDC.
OECD. (2016). *Focus on better ways to pay for health care*, Paris, France

Olson, E. O., & Rodgers, D. L. (1991). The welfare economics of equal access. *Journal of Public Economics, 45*(1), 91–106.

Phua, K. H., & Lee, K. (2017). Governance issues in health financing. In *International encyclopedia of public health* (Vol. 3, 2nd ed., pp. 330–341). Oxford: Academic Press.

Pigou, A. C. (1928). *A study in public finance*. London: Macmillan.

Quentin, W., Scheller-Kreisen, D., & Buss, R. (2011). Technological innovation in DRG-based hospital payment systems across Europe. In R. Busse, A. Geissler, W. Quentin, & M. Wiley (Eds.), *Diagnosis – related groups in Europe. Moving towards transparency, efficiency and quality in hospitals* (European observatory on health systems and policy series) (pp. 131–148). Buckingham, UK: Open University Press.

Robinson, J. C. (2001). Theory and practice in the design of physician payment incentives. *Milbank Quarterly, 79*(2), 149–177.

Rosen, H. S., & Gayer, T. (2007). *Public Finance*. 8th edition, USA.: McGraw Hill Higher Education.

Scheffler, R., & Yu, W. (1998). Medical savings accounts: A worthy experiment. *European Journal of Public Policy, 8*(4), 274–278.

Scheffler, R. M. (2008). *Is there a doctor in the house? Market signals and tomorrow's supply of doctors*. Redwood City: Stanford University Press.

Scheffler, R. M. (2010). *Pay for performance (P4P) programs in health services: What is the evidence? world health report, background paper, 31*. Geneva: World Health Organization.

Sen, A. (1992). *Inequality reexamined*. Oxford: Clarendon Press.

Sheiman, I., Langenbrunner, J., Kehler, J., Cashin, C., & Kutzin, J. (2010). Sources of funds and revenue collection: reforms and challenges. In J. Kutzin, C. Cashin, & M. Jakab (Eds.), *Implementing health financing reform. Lessons from countries in transition* (European observatory on health systems and policies) (pp. 87–118). Copenhagen, Denmark: World Health Organization.

Stiglitz, J. E. (2000). *The economics of public sector* (3rd ed.). New York/London: W.W. Norton & Company.

Street, A., O' Reilly, J., Ward, P., & Mason, A. (2011). DRG-based hospital payment and efficiency: Theory, evidence and challenges. In R. Busse, A. Geissler, W. Quentin, & M. Wiley (Eds.), *Diagnosis – related groups in Europe. Moving towards transparency, efficiency and quality in hospitals* (European observatory on health systems and policy series) (pp. 93–114). Buckingham, UK: Open University Press.

Sutton, M., Nikolova, S., Boaden, R., Lester, H., McDonald, R., & Martin, R. (2012). Reduced mortality with hospital pay for performance in England. *New England Journal of Medicine, 367*, 1821–1828.

Town, R., Wholey, D. R., Kralewski, J., & Dowd, B. (2004). Assessing the influence of incentives on physicians and medical groups. *Medical Care Research and Review, 61*(3 Suppl), 80S–118S.

Trisolini, M. G. (2011). Theoretical perspectives on pay for performance. In J. Cromwell, M. G. Trisolini, G. C. Pope, J. B. Mitchell, & L. M. Greenwarld (Eds.), *Pay for performance in health care: Methods and approaches* (pp. 77–98). Research Triangle Park: RTI Press Publication.

Vogl, M. (2013). Improving patient – level costing in the English and the German "DRG" system. *Health Policy, 109*(3), 290–300.

Wagstaff, A., & Doorslaer, E. (2000). Equity in health care finance and delivery. In A. J. Culyer & J. P. Newhouse (Eds.), *Handbook of health economics* (Vol. 1, pp. 1804–1862). Amsterdam, The Netherlands: Elsevier/North Holland.

Weisbrod, B. A. (1991). Health care quadrilemma: An essay on technological change, insurance, quality of care and cost containment. *Journal of Economic Literature, 29*(2), 523–552.

Whitehead, M. (1992). The concepts and principles of equity and health. *International Journal of Health Services, 22*(3), 429–445.

Whitehead, M., & Dahlgren, G. (2007). *Concepts and principles for tackling social inequities in health: Levelling up Part 1. Studies on Social and Economic Determinants of population Health No 2*. Copenhagen, Denmark: World Health Organization Publications.

Wiley, M. (2011). From the origins of DGRs to their implementation in Europe. In R. Busse, A. Geissler, W. Quentin, & M. Wiley (Eds.), *Diagnosis – related groups in Europe. Moving towards transparency, efficiency and quality in hospitals* (European observatory on health systems and policy series) (pp. 3–8). Buckingham, UK: Open University Press.

Williams, A., & Cookson, R. (2000). Equity in health. In A. J. Culyer & J. P. Newhouse (Eds.), *Handbook of health economics* (Vol. 1, pp. 1864–1910). Amsterdam, The Netherlands: Elsevier/North Holland.

Williams, A. H. (1993). Equity in health care: The role of ideology. In E. van Doorslaer, A. Wagstaff, & F. Rutten (Eds.), *Equity in the finance and delivery of health care* (pp. 287–298). Oxford: Oxford University Press.

Xu, K., Evans, D. B., Kawabata, K., Zeramdini, R., Klavus, J., & Mur, C. J. L. (2003). Household catastrophic health expenditure: a multicountry analysis, *THE LANCET, 362*, 111–117.

Yerramilli, P., Fernandez, O., & Thomson, S. (2018). Financial protection in Europe: A systematic review of the literature and mapping of data availability. *Health Policy, 122*(5), 493–508.

Chapter 11
Hospital Efficiency and Performance

Key Points

- Hospital efficiency involves the cost of, and prices charged for, the provision of health-care services as well as the quality of those services and the cost effectiveness of their production method.
- Attaining both technical and allocative efficiency is the primary economic target of a hospital and requires the realization of an optimal quantity of qualitative medical care services provided at minimal production cost.
- Marginal and average total costs are fundamental economic elements that determine the minimum operating cost for a given number of medical care services.
- Among the factors that influence hospital efficiency, the most influential are the size of the hospital, the range of the medical care services, and changes in technology.
- The relationship between hospital efficiency and financing depends, to a great extent, on the national payment structure (the funding system a country uses) and the appropriate management of hospital fees. At hospital level, a useful tool for managing the efficient use of hospital budget is efficiency variance analysis.

11.1 Introduction

As has already been mentioned, a public or private hospital is an open system designed to provide health-care services to the community as a whole, and is therefore a social organization. This sense of purpose is the primary reason for a hospital's creation. In order to determine whether it is working effectively, the degree to which individual objectives are being achieved needs to be measured. This measurement is necessary firstly because operational costs of modern hospitals are huge (Bevan, Helderman, & Wilsford, 2010; Donaldson & Magnussen, 1992; Farrell, 1957; Hollingsworth, 2008; Hopp & Lovejoy, 2013; Hussey et al., 2009; Linna, Hakkinen, & Magnussen, 2006; Sullivan, 2012; Wagstaff, 1989) and secondly

M. Chletsos, A. Saiti, *Strategic Management and Economics in Health Care*,
https://doi.org/10.1007/978-3-030-35370-4_11

because healthy citizens make healthy workers, which helps to increase the quality of their work and thus a nation's productivity (Chletsos, 2011; Saiti & Mylona, 2015a, 2015b; Skountzos, 2005). Within this framework, the management of a health-care organization has to resolve any operational problems (such as organizational, structural, medical, and financial) in order for the organization to achieve maximum efficiency through the utilization of the available resources (human and material) at the lowest possible cost and without altering the quality.

In theory, measuring an organization's performance may seem relatively easy, but, in practice, determining efficiency is quite difficult. This is because there is no commonly accepted theoretical model that takes into account the production process, the behavior of hospital costs, the complexity of service provision, the different types of hospital organization, different operating environments, etc. (Bates, Mukherjee, & Santerre, 2006; Bevan et al., 2010; Chletsos, 2011; Donaldson & Magnussen, 1992; Dranove, 1988; Feldstein, 1967, 2012; Flatters, Henderson, & Mieszkowski, 1974; Helmig & Lapsley, 2001; Hopp & Lovejoy, 2013; Jacobs, Smith, & Street, 2006; Newhouse, 1970, 1992; Prior, 2006; Wagstaff, 1989; Zagga, 2017; Zuckerman, Hadley, & Iezzoni, 1994). This forces health-care agency administrations to resort to practices and intervention measures to improve efficiency.

In addition, the operation of a hospital institution refers mainly to the supply of services and not to the production of material goods. In contrast to the outputs of industrial processes, "good health" is not so marketable since patients who attain good health through appropriate care are not themselves marketable products. In other words, "good health" is not easily measurable and cannot be separated from the person in possession of it.

According to economic theory, efficiency requires the inputs to be used in a cost-effective way so that the organization can perform efficiently and achieve the desired outcome. Determining cost/prices indexes in the health-care industry has significant and serious problems concerning their measurement (Arrow, 1963; Hollingsworth, 2008; Newhouse, 1992; Prior, 2006), the most significant of which are the following:

The price to be paid for health-care services cannot be measured based on the cost of the treatment, but rather on the number of days a patient stays in hospital. However, this estimation can differ significantly from the actual cost of health-care services, since the provision of medical care is most intense at the beginning of a patient's stay in the hospital, so the cost of the patient's first day in hospital will certainly be higher than the cost of their last day. Hence, the estimated price fails to consider any cost savings that might occur during the patients' stay in the hospital.

The calculation of the price index is based on the standard listed price for health care and not on the actual costs (Newhouse, 1992, p. 10).

The estimation of the price index does not anticipate adjustments for any changes that may occur in terms of quality. This is a very real problem because medical science is moving fast and it is very likely that qualitative changes in the provision of medical care will have a significant impact on the cost/price index.

Health-care systems vary around the world, not least in terms of the proportion of the patient's hospital bill they cover. For this reason, it is extremely difficult to find a given method for estimating a cost/price index for medical care. Moreover, in most countries, the health-care system includes both private and public health insurance coverage. These two types of health insurance have differences in their coverage of hospital bills, medicines, visits to medical staff, etc. in terms of the contribution the patient makes to their medical expenses. In some cases, public medical insurance requires no contribution from the patient to health-care costs. Even among the private health insurance packages, there can be substantial differences in the contribution that the patient makes to their health-care costs.

In view of the above, the study of efficiency among health-care organizations is becoming more and more essential, especially nowadays that organizations around the world face problems that are many and varied, mainly in the fields of economy and labor.

Further in this chapter, we will see how the efficiency of health-care organizations can be conceptually determined and the difficulties in assessing it.

11.2 Defining Efficiency (Technical and Allocative Efficiency)

Efficiency refers to the relationship between attributable results and the inputs spent to achieve the result, usually expressed as a cost-effectiveness ratio/percentage. The goal of efficiency is to produce outputs of good quality with the least possible cost using the most efficient production method available.

One way in which an administration may monitor the performance of their organization is by its productivity. This term counts the quantity and quality of the organization's output in relation to input costs (Assaf & Matawie, 2008; Bates et al., 2006; Bevan et al., 2010; Biorn, Hagen, Iversen, & Magnussen, 2010; Farrell, 1957; Hollingsworth, 2008; Hopp & Lovejoy, 2013; Hussey et al., 2009; Jacobs et al., 2006; Newhouse, 1992; Schermerhorn, 2010; Zuckerman et al., 1994). It examines how well an organization uses the resources available to achieve its goals and produce its services.

Productivity includes two common performance measures:

- The effectiveness of a 'nursing unit,' that monitors the degree to which management's goals are achieved through planning and programming (Zagga, 2017, p. 47), and
- The efficiency that expresses the cost of resources associated with achieving a result (Assaf & Matawie, 2008; Bates et al., 2006; Bevan et al., 2010; Farrell, 1957; Flatters et al., 1974; Gruen & Howarth, 2005; Hollingsworth, 2008; Hopp & Lovejoy, 2013; Hussey et al., 2009; Jacobs et al., 2006; Jensen & Morrisey, 1986; Prior, 2006; Schermerhorn, 2010; Segal & Richardson, 1994; Varabyova & Schreyogg, 2013; Wagstaff, 1989). According to this perception, efficiency is measured by an indicator that has, as a numerator, the realized result (outflow) and, as the denominator, the resources used to achieve the result (inflows) (Bevan et al., 2010; Bouradas, 2001; Farrell, 1957; Hollingsworth, 2008; Hussey et al., 2009; Jacobs et al., 2006; Newhouse, 1992, 1994; Okunade & Murthy, 2002;

Zuckerman et al., 1994). In the case of a health-care organization, we may say that profitability is achieved by the rational allocation and the use of available resources to provide health-care services of a given quality.

The concept of hospital efficiency is defined in the seminal work of Farrell (1957) and Farrell and Fieldhouse (1962). Total efficiency which is also called X-efficiency indicates the capacity of the hospital unit to produce the maximum quantity of hospital services at the lowest cost. "X-efficiency" consists of technical efficiency and price (or allocative) efficiency. Technical efficiency shows the optimal relation between inputs (factors of production) and output. Technical efficiency is achieved when the maximum output is produced with a given amount of inputs. Allocative efficiency refers to the relation between the cost of inputs and the quantity of output. It is achieved when a given output is produced with the minimum cost. In the case that the hospital unit achieves both technical and allocative efficiency, then this unit is total efficient.

According to the relevant literature (Bates et al., 2006; Bevan et al., 2010; Chletsos, 2011; Feldstein, 1967, 2012; Hollingsworth, Dawson, & Maniadakis, 1999; Hollingsworth, 2008; Hopp & Lovejoy, 2013; Hussey et al., 2009; Jacobs et al., 2006; Kalogeropoulou, 2011; Newhouse, 1992, 1994; Palmer & Torgerson, 1999; Prior, 2006; Tsavalias, 2013; Wagstaff, 1989), efficiency may be distinguished into two main categories:

- *Technical efficiency*, associated with the least amount of inputs into every intervention that takes place during care. This technique interprets the effect of a hospital by comparing it with the productive function of a hypothetical optimal organism (Bates et al., 2006; Kalogeropoulou, 2011, p. 795; Jensen & Morrisey, 1986; Newhouse, 1970, 1992; Palmer & Torgerson, 1999; Tsavalias, 2013, p. 24; Wagstaff, 1989; Zuckerman et al., 1994).
- *Allocative efficiency*, associated with selecting a team of technically efficient care interventions to achieve the best possible improvement in outcomes. The choice is cost-effective because interventions are treated as inputs (Athanassopoulos & Gounaris, 2001; Bevan et al., 2010; Kalogeropoulou, 2011; Palmer & Torgerson, 1999; Tsavalias, 2013; Wagstaff, 1989; Zuckerman et al., 1994).

Technical and allocative efficiency together give the concept of economic efficiency, which aims to achieve the goals of the first two categories of profitability (Kalogeropoulou, 2011; Newhouse, 1970, 1992, 1994; Zuckerman et al., 1994).

Technical and allocative efficiency could be presented using the tools from the production theory. As we know, the purpose of a firm in long run period is to determine the optimal level of inputs in order to produce the optimal level of output. The isoquant curve is the geometric path of all different combinations of inputs to produce the same level of output. The isocost line shows all different combinations of inputs used in production for which the total cost is the same.

The purpose of the unit is to produce the maximum output with a given cost or to product a given output with the lowest cost. These two different cases are presented below. The first case represents the effort to maximize output with given the cost (Fig. 11.1).

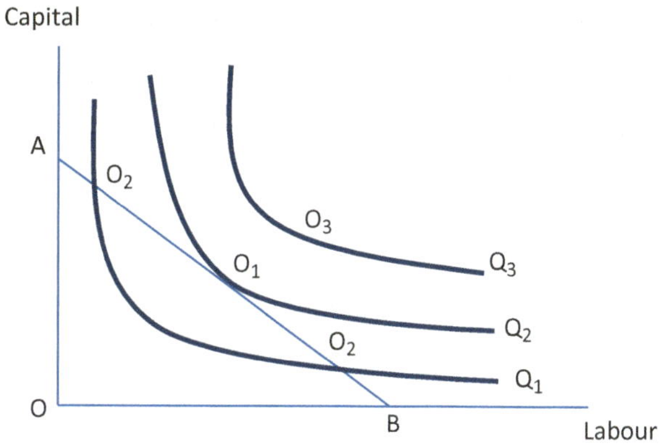

Fig. 11.1 Equilibrium point in long run period (max output with a given cost)

In the above diagram, all the points on the isoquant curve (Q_i) represent the same quantity of output produced by different combinations between labor and capital. As we move from a low isoquant curve (Q_1) to the highest isoquant curve (Q_3), the output produced increases, but the quantity of inputs is not the same. The combination O_1 is preferred than the combinations O_2 and O_3 because the output produced by the three combinations is the same, but the cost is lower. The combination O_3 cannot be achieved because it is found outside the isocost line and the cost of productions of this combination exceeds the given amount of money that the unit can spend. The optimal combination is at the point O_1. At this point, it produces the same output with a given amount of inputs and therefore a given cost.

Figure 11.2 presents the equilibrium of a productive unit in long run period when it produces a given output with the minimum cost.

As explained above, Fig. 11.2 presents the optimal decision of unit which is interested in producing a given output with the minimum cost. The equilibrium point is the point O_1 at which it produces the same output as at points O_2 and O_3 but at a lower cost. The combination O_1 is found at a lower isocost line than the combinations O_2 and O_3.

Technical, allocative, and "X-efficiency" could be shown using the isoquant curve and the isocost line in the Fig. 11.3. This figure is based on the figure presented by Farrell (1957).

As we have already mentioned, a hospital unit achieves technical or allocative efficiency when it is found on the isoquant curve or on the isocost line, respectively. Farrell measures efficiency (technical of allocative) relative to the achieved frontier. In the above diagram, the letters C, D, E, and K present different hospital units. The technical efficiency of the unit E is presented by the ratio OE/OD which is >1 and this indicates that the unit E is technically inefficient. Similarly, the allocative efficiency is given by the ratio OE/OC which is >1 and that shows that there is no allocative efficiency. Technical efficiency and allocative efficiency are achieved by

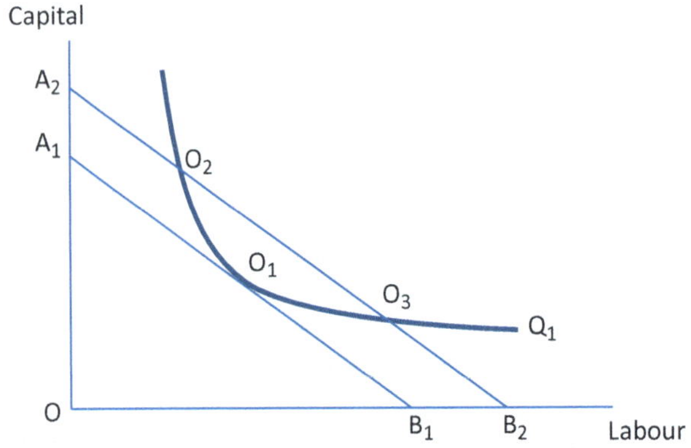

Fig. 11.2 Equilibrium point in long run period (a given output with the minimum cost)

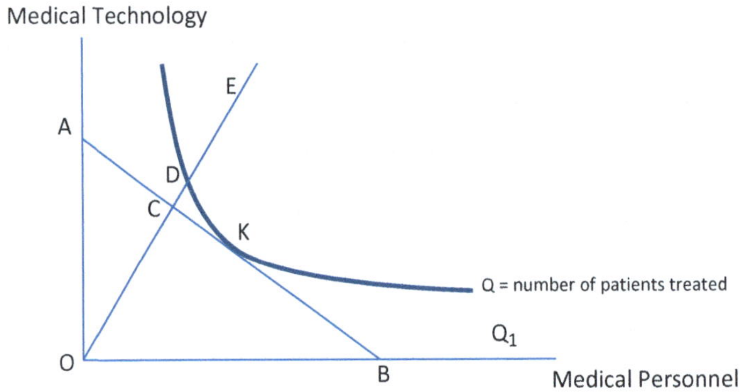

Fig. 11.3 Technical, allocative, and "X-efficiency"

the hospital unit D and C, respectively. The hospital unit K achieves both technical and allocative efficiency because technical and allocative efficiency equals to 1.

The efficiency of health-care organizations can be defined as:

- The production of the largest possible quantity/provision of health-care services, given the human and material resources available (Bates et al., 2006; Bevan et al., 2010; Helmig & Lapsley, 2001; Hollingsworth, 2008; Hussey et al., 2009; Newhouse, 1970, 1992; Polyzos, 2015; Zuckerman et al., 1994)
- The production of a given quantity/service with minimal resources (Bates et al., 2006; Bevan et al., 2010; Hollingsworth et al., 1999; Hopp & Lovejoy, 2013; Kalogeropoulou, 2011; Tsavalias, 2013) and
- The minimum cost to produce a given quantity/provide certain health-care services (Bates et al., 2006; Bevan et al., 2010; Hollingsworth, 2008; Jacobs & Rapoport, 2004; Tsavalias, 2013; Zuckerman et al., 1994).

With particular reference to the efficiency measures in the field of the health care, measures can be distinguished into the following (Feldstein, 1967, 2012; Hussey et al., 2009; Joumard, Andre, & Nicq, 2010):

- *Perspective,* which refers to who will evaluate what,
- *Inputs,* both physical (staff, equipment, etc.) and financial (expenditures),
- *Outputs,* which are the actual quantifiable results such as the number of treated people, and
- *Outcome,* which refers to the impact on society such as patients' better health condition and equal access to health-care services.

According to the relevant literature, an econometric approach to measuring efficiency in the health-care sector—the methodology of Data Envelopment Analysis (DEA)—is usually employed so as to derive outcomes and determine solutions to problems. Since there are many restrictions that dictate a hospital's functionality, this econometric approach based on mathematical and computer programming tools is used to design efficiency measures that help to ensure a hospital's successful performance.

11.3 The Determinant Factors of Hospital Efficiency

Efficiency in health-care organizations is necessary for their sustainability and for this reason, it is a major management objective. In order to facilitate the sustainable performance of these organizations, they must aim to use their resources (human and material) as efficiently as possible.

The efficiency of health-care organizations is influenced by factors that occur in their internal and external environment. As an open system, a hospital operates within a wider environment that affects and is affected by it. Essentially, a hospital is in constant interaction with its environment. For example, when communicating with its outside environment, a hospital receives inflows (such as doctors, nurses, patients, administrative staff, and materials) by performing the input function, transforming them into the internal environment by performing the function of the transformation, which in turn renders the service of this processing to the external environment, performing the function of the outflow (Bevan et al., 2010; Breyer, 1987; Wagstaff, 1989; Worthington, 2004; Zuckerman et al., 1994).

As hospitals aim to strike a balance between providing a finite set of health-care services, serving an increasing number of patients and meeting demands for higher quality health-care services, the administrations of these organizations have to apply the principles of efficiency and quality. Hence, the goal is to provide health-care services at the lowest possible cost (for example, minimize the wastage of consumables, avoid unnecessary medical examinations, control the operating costs of technology and infrastructure, ensure that treatments are proportionate for the medical condition, etc.) in terms of monetary and human sacrifice so as to achieve the best possible result without a corresponding degradation in quality.

Based on economic theory, an individual makes choices (preferences) with the ultimate goal of maximizing his/her utility (satisfaction). This means that individuals can choose between providers to achieve their goal. Providers, on the other hand, will need to seek technical efficiency, for example, to deliver the best possible result (in terms of quality and quantity) at the lowest possible cost. If there is no competition, the providers have no reason to pursue technical efficiency and this will create a problem, in terms of both the type of service offered and the quality of that service. In the field of health care, things are quite complex because of the special nature of the industry. According to the theory of Efficient Markets, establishing appropriate conditions for a healthy competitive market and having sufficient information are the basic prerequisites for improving performance in the sector (Feldstein, 1967, 2012). In the field of health care, however, these conditions cannot be met because (a) in general, patients do not have the necessary medical knowledge to make valued judgments; and (b) the quality of the health-care services is customized, so there can be no uniform assessment and this is because medical services can have differing levels of quality within the same hospital. Even among hospitals of the same type, it is likely that the levels of quality in health-care provision will differ, which will affect their operating costs and therefore their efficiency.

Indeed, no health-care organization can be perfectly efficient, which can be attributed to various factors that interact to shape the final result. Moreover, in the relevant literature (Gerdtham, Löthgren, Tambour, & Rehnberg, 1999; Grosskopf, Margaritis, & Valdmanis, 2004; Hollingsworth, 2008; Newhouse, 1970, 1992, 1994; Prior, 2006; Street & Hakkinen, 2009; Tsavalias, 2013; Wagstaff, 1989; Worthington, 2004; Zagga, 2017) it is mentioned that efficiency is being influenced, in both the short and long term, by a variety of factors. In the short term, the efficiency of a health-care organization is influenced by the degree of utilization of "work." The use of "work" can be achieved by the hospital administration in the following ways (Hussey et al., 2009; Joumard et al., 2010; Newhouse, 1970; Tsavalias, 2013; Wagstaff, 1989; Zagga, 2017):

- By adapting the input of "work" to changes in production and demand conditions
- By replacing high-paid employees with low-paid employees
- By removing nonproductive employees.

It should be noted that, according to the economic theory, the exploitation of the work is subject to the law of diminishing marginal returns. According to this law, an increase in any factor (technology, for example), while keeping other factors constant, will result in an increase in production. However, after a certain point, the additional products/services to be produced by each additional unit of the variable factor (e.g., technology) will begin to decrease.

To make it clearer, we graphically illustrate the term 'marginal efficiency,' which refers to the increase in overall efficiency a hospital can achieve by adding one unit of production factor (fixed or variable). Decreased marginal efficiency is defined as a decline in hospital efficiency when a production factor is increased by more than one unit. We present two figures (Figs. 11.4 and 11.5) which illustrates the decreasing

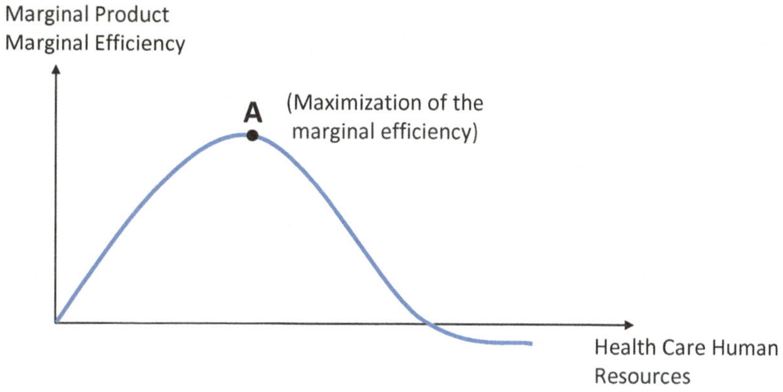

Fig. 11.4 Marginal efficiency (in terms of health-care human resources)

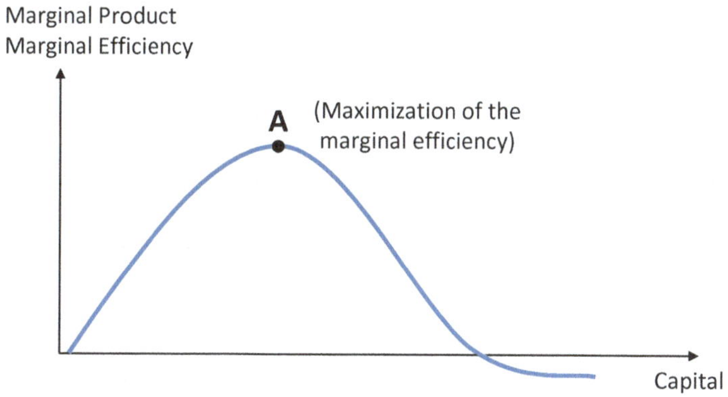

Fig. 11.5 Marginal efficiency (in terms of capital)

marginal efficiency with respect to a variable factor (labor) and a fixed factor (capital). In particular, Figs. 11.2 and 11.3 show the levels of marginal efficiency in relation to two production factors, namely labor (Fig. 11.2) and capital (Fig. 11.3).

Based on these diagrams, at point A, the marginal efficiency of the hospital is maximized. At this point, there is an optimal level of work, human resources (Fig. 11.2) and capital (for example technological equipment) (Fig. 11.3). At higher levels of employment and capital intensity, that is, beyond point A, marginal profitability decreases.

The law of diminishing marginal returns is a generalization of the reality that assumes at least one input remains constant/stable. Therefore, this particular law of managerial economics cannot be applied in the case where all inputs are increased, nor can it predict the influence of an additional input.

We will now look at the main factors that influence the efficiency of a hospital in the long run.

11.3.1 The Size of a Health-Care Unit

The size of a health-care organization can affect its efficiency either positively or negatively. Studies by several researchers such as Kontaratou (2003), Tsavalias (2013), Wagstaff (1989), and Worthington (2004) have shown that hospitals with fewer than 100 beds or more than 620 beds are generally unprofitable. Moreover, researches such as Banker, Conrad, and Strauss (1986) and Mobley and Frech (1994) suggested that the ideal size of a health-care organization is 220–260 and 200–370 beds, respectively.

Following these considerations, and bearing in mind that according to the long-term production function, efficient scale outputs are influenced by the size of the health-care organization, we can see in the diagrams how large hospitals can provide lower-cost health-care services than smaller hospital units. To see how the size of a hospital ultimately affects its efficiency, we will use the concept of the average cost. The average cost is defined as the ratio of the total cost of the health-care services rendered (quantity received by a group of consumers) and has the form of a U in the diagram (Begg, Fischer, & Dornbusch, 2005; Mansfield, 1996). Based on the trend of the average cost in relation to the quantity of health-care services rendered, we can see whether a hospital is developing positive, negative, or stable economies of scale.

Based on Fig. 11.6, the average cost increases as the size of the body increases to the point A where the lowest average cost is reached. Beyond point A, as the level of health-care production (and thus the size of the hospital) is increased, the average cost rises. The graphical depiction of the long-term average cost of a hospital is based on specific values of the productive factors (for example, the inflows into a hospital), so any change in the input factors (such as price) will result in a shift in the average cost curve.

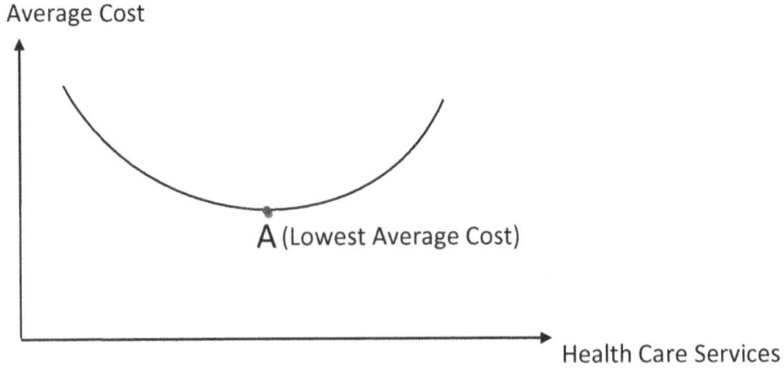

Fig. 11.6 Average cost curve

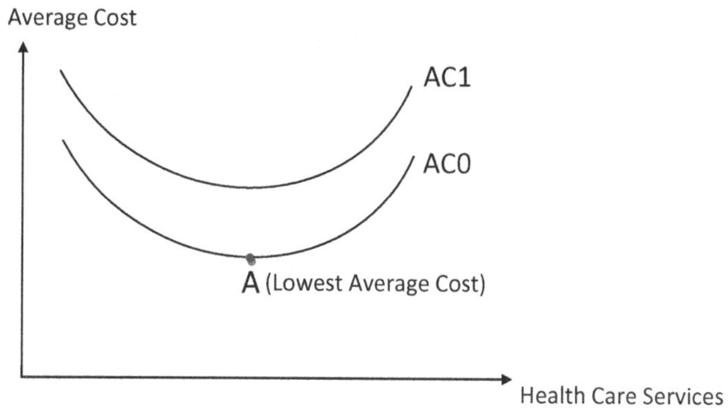

Fig. 11.7 Average cost and improvement in the level of quality of health-care services

A hospital can achieve positive economies of scale if the increase in the amount of its health-care services reduces the average cost. When the average cost increases with an increase in the amount of health-care services, then the hospital has a negative economy of scale; if it remains the same, it is said to have a stable economy of scale. The economies of scale a hospital can attain depend mainly on its use of technology and on the specialization of its human resources.

We noted in a previous chapter that, in terms of ownership, hospitals are divided into two main categories: public and private. Private hospitals are divided into profit and nonprofit institutions. Several studies (Arrow, 1963; Assaf & Matawie, 2008; Dranove, 1988; Hadley & Feder, 1985; Newhouse, 1970, 1988, 1992, 1994; Okunade & Murthy, 2002, etc.) have focused their interest on the efficiency of nonprofit hospitals, which have similar characteristics to public hospitals since both types of hospital focus on the social aspect of health-care provision as well as on the quality of health-care services. Based on the assumption that consumers are the main source of funding for hospitals, Newhouse (1970) argues that since a hospital focuses on its social purpose, it is not a priority of the hospital administration to maintain a particular range or quantity of health-care services, as it relies mainly on donations, grants, and tax privileges. Nevertheless, public and nonprofit hospitals aim to maximize the amount of health care they provide while maintaining their services at affordable prices.

In addition, in his model, Newhouse (1970) argues that any improvement in the level of quality of health-care services shifts the average cost curve upward (see Fig. 11.7) since improved quality increases the demand for health-care services, which pushes up the cost of those services.

For example, public hospitals have a broader range of health-care services and, by aiming to offer quality services to as many patients as possible while maintaining affordable prices, they are likely to accrue higher costs, making them less efficient than smaller private hospital institutions.

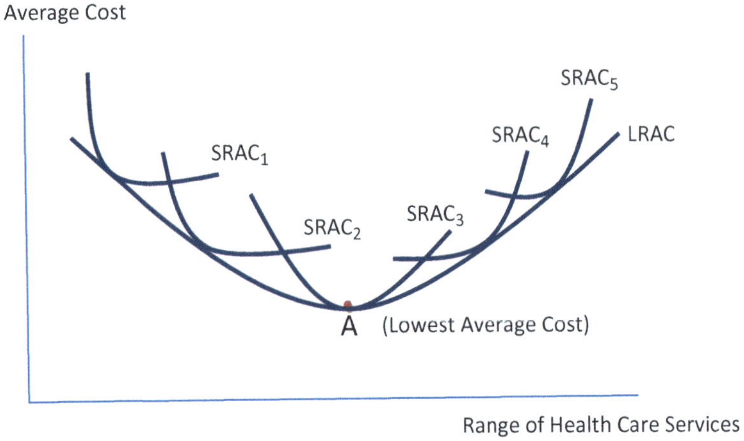

Fig. 11.8 Average cost, hospital efficiency, and the range of health-care services

11.4 The Range of Health-Care Services

It is reported in the relevant literature that increasing the size of a health-care organization is often interrelated with an increased/more diversified range of health-care services provided by the organization (Arrow, 1963; Assaf & Matawie, 2008; Dranove, 1988; Feldstein, 1967, 2012; Helmig & Lapsley, 2001; Hollingsworth, 2008; Hussey et al., 2009; Newbrander, Barnum, & Kutzin, 1992; Newhouse, 1970, 1992; Tsavalias, 2013, p. 34; Zagga, 2017, p. 52). This relationship leads to a fragmentation in the production process and hence to a reversal in the economies of scale. In general, the greater the range of health-care services a hospital provides, the lower its efficiency will be, that is, the average cost increases as the range of health-care services increases. As such, hospitals providing a small range of health services tend to exhibit a higher efficiency. If we combine the range of health-care services with the size of the health-care unit, we may see that increasing the range of health-care services increases the cost of diversification.

Figure 11.8 illustrates the long-term average cost curve in terms of range of medical services. As the range of health-care services increases beyond point A, so does the average cost. For hospitals that produce a wide range of medical care services, the question that arises is whether or not they may also achieve economies of scale. The answer to this question is that economies of scale can be achieved while increasing the range of services only if the hospital's management is able to recognize the profitable opportunities. Such economies of scale are achieved when the combined production cost of two (or more) services is lower than the production cost of each service separately (Mansfield, 1996, p. 343). Hence, the efficient performance of a hospital and the primary purpose of a hospital's efforts to maximize knowledge, abilities, and opportunities depend heavily on a capable management, and on how efficiently the available resources are used.

11.5 Ownership

The legal status affects the efficiency of health-care organizations. For example, public hospitals are exposed to a high level of state interventionism (institutional, economic, etc.) and constraints such as social and quality goals may not apply to the private sector (Arrow, 1963; Bevan et al., 2010; Czypionka, Kraus, Mayer, & Rohrling, 2014; Newhouse, 1970, 1992, 1994; Prior, 2006; Tsavalias, 2013; Worthington, 2004). In addition, private hospitals are, as a rule, relatively small organizations, administratively flexible and, as mentioned above, more efficient. On the contrary, public hospitals are complex organizations that exhibit organizational and administrative rigidity, high operating costs, and lack of incentives to improve their profitability (Newhouse, 1970, 1992; Worthington, 2004; Zagga, 2017).

11.6 The Technological Infrastructure of Health Organizations

Broadly speaking, modern technological infrastructure has a positive impact on the efficiency of hospitals, as it reduces the average service cost over the long term (Arrow, 1963; Newhouse, 1992, 1994; Okunade & Murthy, 2002; Scherer, 1993; Sullivan, 2012). For example, hospitals that use the latest biomedical equipment may have a high initial outlay, but, over time, they will recuperate their costs through the savings made from a more effective detection, diagnosis, and treatment of illnesses and a swifter rehabilitation of patients (Kontaratou, 2003, p. 53). Electronic health records (EHRs) also improve performance, reduce medical errors, and cut the cost of health care (Sullivan, 2012). Certainly, maintaining data security is a concern for health-care organizations, patients, and policy makers, but the benefits of integrated systems outweigh the risk (Trossman, 2009).

Of course, technology can affect hospital performance. According to economic theory, if the technology is effective, there will be an increase in demand for the relevant treatment by specific population groups (such as people with higher incomes). However, technology tends to reduce the number of days that patients stay in hospital, so hospitals need to find other ways of recuperating their costs. They tend to do this by increasing the cost of the technology-enhanced treatment. This cost increase will affect the efficient operation of the hospital, either negatively or positively, depending on how well the hospital is managed.

11.7 The Building Infrastructure

Another factor that affects the efficiency of a health-care institution is its infrastructure. This is because a modern building with a rational layout of its spaces and equipment creates a pleasant working environment and thus positively affects the efficiency of its employees, facilitates the decongestion of the individual nursing units, and allows the employees to be friendly, collaborative, and efficient (Hollingsworth, 2008; Hussey et al., 2009; Newbrander et al., 1992). On the contrary, obsolete buildings impair their profitability simply because they do not fully meet their current operational needs. In summary, the modernization of the building infrastructure in health-care organizations improves their efficiency because they create modern working conditions.

11.8 The Method of Payment for Health-Care Services

It is mentioned in the relevant literature that the method of payment affects the efficiency of health-care services. In particular, fee-paying health care has a positive impact on the efficiency of the hospital, as it leads to a decongestion of the system (Feldstein, 1967, 2012; Zagga, 2017). This decongestion results from the fact that, when the patient pays a fee for the health-care services provided, they use the doctor only when they have a genuine health problem, resulting in a reduced demand for the health-care units' services (Feldstein, 1967, 2012; Newhouse, 1970, 1992). On the contrary, when the patient does not contribute to the cost of the health care they receive, then they tend to use the services for more trivial (nonessential) matters. This increases the burden on the health-care unit's resources and reduces its efficiency (Tsavalias, 2013). Of course, with the latter payment method, there is a wastage of public resources and a considerable cost for the state. In one view (Arrow, 1963; Newhouse, 1970; Zagga, 2017), this is due to the central administration's incomplete developmental planning. In a fee-paying health care, which is a fully retrospective system, as the patient cannot choose its treatment, the health-care unit has no incentive to control cost (Zweifel, Breyer, and Kifmann (2009). Thus, fee-for-service payments do not provide enough incentives to control cost, while in a prospective system—in which the health-care unit is reimbursed in the beginning independently of the cost—there are incentives to decrease health-care cost.

As already mentioned, health-care systems differ across the world and therefore there are significant differences in patients' expenditures on private and public health insurance. The main difference in the health insurance cover lies in how the cost is shared between the private or public insurance organization and the patient. However, there are several externalities that affect the issue of payments and medical care service payments (Feldstein, 1967, 2012; Newhouse, 1992, 1994). Even when a person decides not to buy health insurance, whenever they use medical care services, the costs are covered indirectly by the social security contributions and taxes they pay to the state (usually deducted from their gross salary). The same applies if a person buys partial health insurance cover and cannot pay for the entire use of the medical service.

To make it clearer, each patient has their own map of indifference curves, that is, they have their own preferences. Indeed, according to rational behavior, people inevitably make choices based on cost (risk) and benefit (the expected value). They also have a specific income constraint. The goal of each patient is to maximize their utility, for example, their satisfaction with the use of health-care services. Therefore, the patient has their own utility function given by $U_p = u_p f_p$ (quantity, quality) and represents their desire to have access to enough quality health-care services in order to "get well." On the other hand, the hospital administration has its own map of indifference curves, that is, its own preferences and utility function. On its part, a hospital wants to see the quality health-care services it provides as well as its prestige increase as a function of quantity (Newhouse, 1970 cited by (Dranove, 1988, p. 49). The corresponding utility function is $U_h = u_h f_h$ (quantity, quality).

With regard to patient options and the payment method for the use of health-care services, we present two diagrams (Figs. 11.9 and 11.10) which illustrate the different patient preferences in relation to payment method. Figure 11.9 illustrates the patient's preference to pay for the use of health-care services, where we observe that the curved indifference is more vertical. In contrast, Fig. 11.10 illustrates the patient's preference for not paying for health-care services at all, where the indifference curves are more horizontal since they have access to more health-care services. If in the above figures we add the income constraint, the point of maximum utility is where the indifference curve touches the income constraint at point A, respectively, in each figure.

The budget line (CD) indicates the total cost of the patient of buying health-care services and other goods. The budget line depends on the ratio of the prices of goods and patient's income. As the patient is obliged to contribute more to the cost of buying health-care services, he considers that the price of health-care services increased and therefore he chooses to consume more from other goods and less from the health-care services.

The opposite case, the patient does not pay directly health services, is presented in Fig. 11.10. As the patient does not pay directly health-care services, he considers that the price is zero since the marginal cost of health-care services for the patient is zero.

The slope of the isoquant curve in Fig. 11.10 is more elastic than the slope of isoquant curve in Fig. 11.9. The slope of the isocost line in both figures is not the

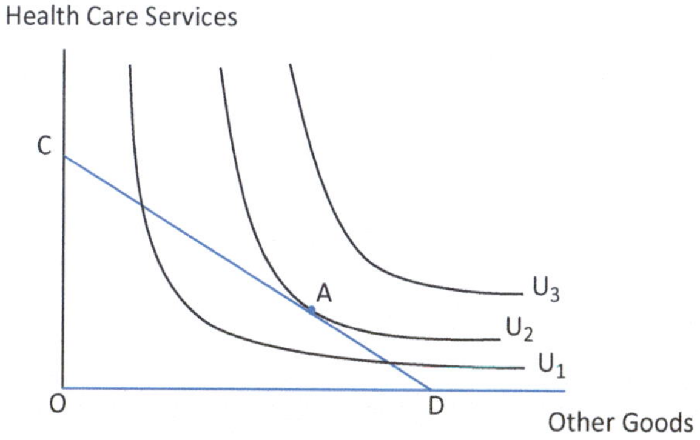

Fig. 11.9 Patient's preference to pay for the use of health-care services

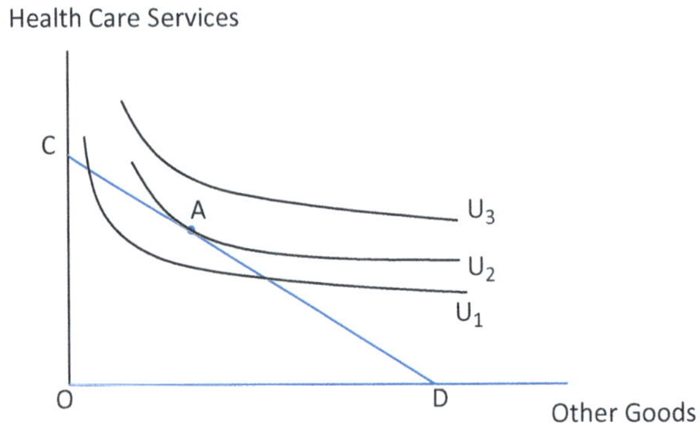

Fig. 11.10 Patient's preference for not paying for health-care services at all

same. In Fig. 11.9, as the patient is obliged to contribute more and more to the cost of buying health-care services, he considers that health care's price goes up and the isocost line becomes more elastic.

As we mentioned above, the patient considers that there is no price for health services since the marginal cost of buying health-care services is zero. Comparing the patient's preferences when he contributes to total cost with his/her preferences when there is no contribution to total cost of health-care services, we understand that patient chooses a greater amount of health-care services in the second case. Therefore, this could be influences negatively hospital efficiency.

Patients decide the optimal combination between health-care services and other goods by choosing this combination which maximizes its utility, given their income and the prices of goods. Patients' decisions are not independent on the decisions of hospital as producer of health-care services. In a model where two goods (health-care services and other goods) are produced, the equilibrium point is the point at which the highest indifference curve is tanged at the production possibilities frontier. In our case, production possibilities frontier present all different combinations between health-care services and other goods are produced given the amount of resources (Fig. 11.11).

In the above figure, the curve CD presents the production possibilities frontier for health-care services and other goods. Any combination on the production possibilities frontier indicates that there is efficiency in production in the sense that given the amount of inputs, the maximum output is produced. Combinations A and B show that there is also efficiency in consumption and these two points are Pareto equilibrium. The lines are the isocost lines and they have different slopes because the patient considers a different price for health-care services in each case. The equilibrium point A shows that patients do not contribute to the cost of health-care services, while at equilibrium B, the patients pay directly for health-care services.

Based on the Feldstein model, the overall balance between patients and hospitals is reached at the point where the hospital indifference curves intersect those of patients (Ifantopoulos, 2003).

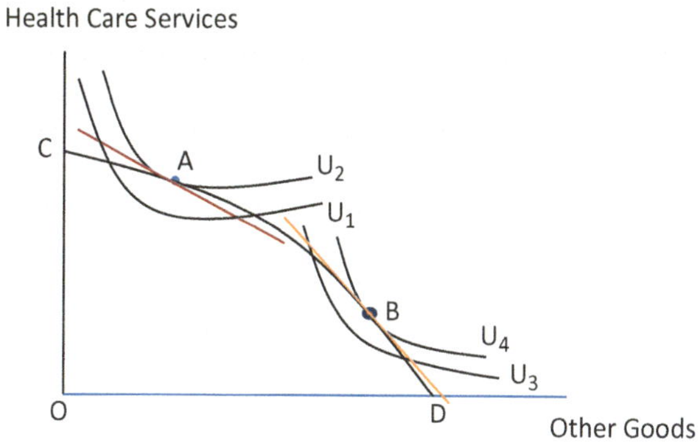

Fig. 11.11 Efficiency in production and consumption under different hospital's payments

11.9 Developmental Design

It has been mentioned above that the competitive environment of the health-care sector and the limited resources of states require health-care organizations to respond to public demands for safe, easily accessible, and high-quality health-care services (Sullivan, 2016, p. 24). But to do so, there should be a proper and valid development plan.

Development planning is a time-consuming and demanding process that should not be rushed and fragmented. This is because it is an important tool in developing a country's health-care system and in the efficiency of health-care institutions (Saiti & Mylona, 2015a, 2015b; Zagga, 2017). This designing of health-care services is conducted both *at a national level* (where each country's national health-care system is planned and the operational rules are established) and *at health-care organization level* (where modern administrative principles are applied for the organization and operation of each hospital).

It should be noted that the method of payment for health-care services, the rational distribution of credits between central and regional hospitals, the introduction of a system of incentives and the meritorious staffing of health organizations with all kinds of human resources are significant issues that need special consideration from national governments.

11.10 The Hospital Management System

Previously, we mentioned that modern hospitals (public and private) are complex organizations with their own standardization. Furthermore, the effective fulfillment of a health-care organization's goals presupposes an assessment of and improvement in the input–output relationship in the administrative sense (Feldstein, 1967, 2012; Newhouse, 1970, 1992). Despite their distinct standardization, large public health-care organizations mainly have a bureaucratic system that makes them inefficient and dependent on their central administration, compared with the private ones, with the consequence that public hospitals cannot take initiatives (independently from their central administration) in matters regarding strategy, modernization of equipment, staffing, etc. (Kontaratou, 2003). Additionally, the lack of an integrated information system, electronic patient records, a reliable statistical database, and productivity indicators have a negative effect on the performance of health-care organizations (Okunade & Murthy, 2002; Scherer, 1993; Sullivan, 2016; Trossman, 2009; Tsavalias, 2013). Within this framework, and given that hospitals are costly organizations, the existence of a competent and flexible administration is imperative. There is a need for an administration that can address the problems of the present and the challenges of the future through coordinated and continuous efforts, objectives, and controls.

11.11 The System of Incentives

Motivation is an important aspect of performance because motivated staff are generally more productive than unmotivated staff (Saiti & Mylona, 2015a, 2015b; Saiti & Papadopoulos, 2015; Sullivan, 2016). Motivation is achieved through a range of material and nonmaterial incentives that harmonize the aspirations and behavior of employees with that of the health-care organization. Financial incentives include an increase in wages that allow employees to have a better standard of living, while noneconomic incentives such as praise, facilities, and comforts in the workplace also encourage employees to work harder.

In summary, research findings such as Arrow (1963), Burgess & Wilson (1998), Chern and Wan (2000), Gerdtham et al. (1999), Grosskopf et al. (2004), Hollingsworth (2008), Hussey et al. (2009), Newhouse (1970, 1992, 1994), Street and Hakkinen (2009), Tsavalias (2013), Zagga (2017), Wagstaff (1989), and Worthington (2004), many of which are contradictory, have shown that the efficiency of health-care organizations is influenced by many factors. In its most formalized form, efficiency is the ratio of outputs generated by the inputs used, but in practice, it is difficult to assess because of the specificities and peculiarities of hospitals, which are due to the complexity of these institutions and due to the qualitative nature of inputs and outputs (Assaf & Matawie, 2008; Bevan et al., 2010; Dranove, 1988; Feldstein, 1967, 2012; Hollingsworth, 2008; Hussey et al., 2009; Newhouse, 1970, 1992, 1994; Okunade & Murthy, 2002; Zagga, 2017).

11.12 Financing and Efficiency

One of the key features of health-care policy is the relationship between the efficiency of investment in health care and equal opportunities. Active steps are needed from every government to improve the quality of the health-care system and increase the efficiency of their country's hospitals. For this to happen, the quantity and quality of hospital outputs have to be managed together (Arrow, 1963; Newhouse, 1970, 1992, 1994). Hospital financing based on efficiency can be considered at two levels, namely national and local (hospital level).

At national level, irrespective of the health-care system of the country, the government's primary objective is for hospitals to be efficient and provide a standard of health care that can maintain the population in good health. For this to happen, hospitals need to make efficient use of their resources and particularly of public funding (Gruen & Howarth, 2005). This is because the state is obliged to meet the expectations of better health and of fairer and equal access to health-care services, thus meeting the needs of the population for a more effective level of protection from their health-care system. For the state to meet the above obligation, appropriate programs need to be drawn up which, through an effective mechanism, can help to facilitate the rational allocation of available resources in order to meet public needs and implement the economic and social policies of governments.

The health-care sector is one of the most important elements of the state budget. As such, it is important to understand the decision-making processes of the public sector (Dranove, 1988; Falch & Rattso, 1999; Newhouse, 1994; Saiti & Mylona, 2015a, 2015b) and, with that knowledge, develop strategies for improving the medical care process. This may cause us to consider incentive-based methods for financing hospitals.

In many health-care systems, the funding of state hospital expenditure has a crucial impact on hospital finances. In the health-care systems of many countries, the financing of hospitals is a decentralized process, while in other countries, state hospital expenditure is determined centrally. Certainly, the role of the state can be characterized as important, as it manages budgets and, to a varying degree, distributes appropriations to hospital units. With an efficient use of time and information (Farrell, 1957; King & O'Sullivan, 2002; Newbrander et al., 1992; Nir, 2007; Reyes & Rodriguez, 2004), hospitals could be more responsive to their patients' needs. However, a key difficulty that governments have in public investment programs lies in selecting those projects that will be efficient for the country's future development.

It is evident from the above that the efficiency of hospitals is closely related to the payment structure and the appropriate management of hospital fees. As previously mentioned, hospital efficiency can be estimated by econometric analysis through the DEA method, although it is subject to several constraints such as hospital activity and various levels of technology. In Chap. 10, we talked about the issue of payments and made extensive analysis on DRG-payment systems. Efficient use of hospital resources depends on what kind of funding system that the country uses. This is because if a country uses the state budget system, then the main problem of financial management and planning is with the timing of cash inflows and expenditures, which may negatively affect the efficient operation of a hospital. In addition, it is very likely that the hospital will not be interested in applying a cost-effective production method and thus have a negative efficiency.

In the case of incentive-based financing, where funding depends heavily on efficient performance through indicators, then it is more likely that the hospital will develop the appropriate mechanisms to facilitate the creativity that will contribute significantly to the hospital's more efficient operation (Biorn et al., 2010; Czypionka et al., 2014; Donaldson & Magnussen, 1992; Farrell, 1957; Grosskopf et al., 2004; Gruen & Howarth, 2005; Hadley & Feder, 1985; Linna et al., 2006; Prior, 2006; Worthington, 2004). Of course, when talking about overall hospital efficiency, we are talking about achieving both technical efficiency (via an efficient production method) and allocative efficiency (minimizing production costs) which is certainly very difficult in practice. Indeed, even if we have a more incentivized payment method for monitoring efficiency, it is likely that the hospital will not achieve the same degree of performance for both types of efficiency. This is because, regardless of a country's health-care system, in practice, there is no perfect flow of information regarding technology or input prices, and hospitals have to operate under budget constraints due to their limited financial resources. The type and size of hospital property also play a significant role.

Regardless of the funding system, and considering that hospital units need to deal with various and multiple operational problems, then a hospital's ability to solve any financial problems efficiently could be considered as significant since it is the efficiency of performance that helps to facilitate the desired goals of a medical care system.

At the hospital level, the process is almost the same in the sense that the primary goal of the hospital is to survive through its efficient operation. And at this level, there are indicators, a comparison of inputs and outflows. A hospital's management should manage certain elements in an efficient manner to attain the desired outcome. These elements are (Pettinger, 1994, cited by Gruen & Howarth, 2005, p. 26): costs (i.e., deal efficiently with all the different types of costs), income (deal efficiently with all the different types of resources), and returns (benefits derived from achieving the desired goals). The desired goal of the hospital is to maximize efficiency, in terms of both quality and quantity.

A useful tool for dealing with efficiency at the hospital level is variance analysis. Such analysis, when applied to both production methods and prices (costs), will help hospital managers to use the budget and available resources in a more efficient manner (Gruen & Howarth, 2005). With particular reference to the analysis of efficiency variance, this includes the estimation of standard cost and quantity as well as the actual quantity (Gruen & Howarth, 2005, p. 91). Although variance analysis of hospitals deals mainly with the quantity of medical care services, it constitutes a useful tool for hospital managers, as it may help them analyze each hospital activity and with a different level of technology. Hospital management should wield its influence in order to check that appropriations for the running costs of hospitals actually reach their intended recipients.

In any case, quicker and effective decisions allow the hospital to assess its service providers more carefully, to negotiate more effectively, and thus to improve the correspondence between the hospital's needs and the provision of those services.

References

Arrow, K. J. (1963). Uncertainty and the welfare economics of medical care. *American Economic Review, 53*(5), 941–973.

Assaf, A., & Matawie, K. M. (2008). Cost efficiency modeling in health care foodservice operations. *International Journal of Hospitality Management, 27*(4), 604–613.

Athanassopoulos, A., & Gounaris, C. (2001). Assessing the technical and allocative efficiency of hospital operations in Greece and its resource allocation implications. *European Journal of Operational Research, 133*(2), 416–431.

Banker, R. D., Conrad, R. F., & Strauss, R. P. (1986). A comparative application of data envelopment analysis and translog methods: An illustrative study of hospital production. *Management Science, 32*(1), 30–34.

Bates, L. J., Mukherjee, K., & Santerre, R. E. (2006). Market structure and technical efficiency in the hospital services industry: A DEA approach. *Medical Care Research and Review, 63*(4), 499–524.

Begg, D. K. H., Fischer, S., & Dornbusch, R. (2005). *Economics*. Maidenhead: McGraw-Hill.

Bevan, G., Helderman, J. K., & Wilsford, D. (2010). Changing choices in health care: Implications for equity, efficiency and cost. *Health Economics, Policy, and Law, 5*(3), 251–267.

Biorn, G., Hagen, T. P., Iversen, T., & Magnussen, J. (2010). How different are hospitals responses to a financial reform? The impact on efficiency of activity based financing. *Health Care Management Science, 13*(1), 1–16.

Bouradas, D. (2001). *Management*. Athens, Greece: Benou Publications.

Breyer, F. (1987). The specification of a hospital cost function: A comment on the recent literature. *Journal of Health Economics, 6*(2), 147–157.

Burgess, J. F., & Wilson P. W. (1998). Variation in inefficiency among US hospitals. *INFOR, Canadian Journal of Operational Research and Information Processing 36*(3), 84–102.

Chern, J. Y., & Wan, T. H. (2000). The impact of the prospective payment systems on the technical efficiency of hospitals. *Journal of Medical Systems, 24*(3), 159–172.

Chletsos, M. (2011). *Health economics*. Athens: Pataki Publications.

Czypionka, T., Kraus, M., Mayer, S., & Rohrling, G. (2014). Efficiency ownership and financing of hospitals. The case of Austria. *Health Care Management Science, 17*(4), 331–347.

Donaldson, C., & Magnussen, J. (1992). DRGs: The road to hospital efficiency. *Health Policy, 21*(1), 47–64.

Dranove, D. (1988). Pricing by non profit institutions. *Journal of Health Economics, 7*(1), 47–57.

Falch, T., & Rattso, J. (1999). Local public choice of school spending: Disaggregating the demand function for educational services. *Economics of Education Review, 18*(3), 361–373.

Farrell, M. J. (1957). The measurement of productive efficiency. *Journal of the Royal Statistical Society, Series A, 120*(3), 253–281.

Farrell, M. J., & Fieldhouse, M. (1962). Estimating efficient production functions under increasing returns to scale. *Journal of the Royal Statistical Society, Series A, 125*, 252–267.

Feldstein, P. J. (1967). *Economic analysis for health service efficiency*. Amsterdam: North Holland.

Feldstein, P. J. (2012). *Health care economics* (7th ed.). Clifton Park: Delmar Cengage Learning.

Flatters, F., Henderson, V., & Mieszkowski, P. (1974). Public goods, efficiency and regional fiscal equalization. *Journal of Public Economics, 3*(2), 99–112.

Gerdtham, U. G., Löthgren, M., Tambour, M., & Rehnberg, M. (1999). Internal markets and health care efficiency: A multiple-output stochastic frontier analysis. *Health Economics, 8*(2), 151–164.

Grosskopf, S., Margaritis, D., & Valdmanis, V. (2004). Competitive effects on teaching hospitals. *European Journal of Operational Research, 154*(2), 515–525.

Gruen, R., & Howarth, A. (2005). *Financial management in health services*. London: Open University Press.

Hadley, J., & Feder, J. (1985). Hospital cost-shifting and care for the uninsured. *Health Affairs, 4*(3), 67–80.

Helmig, B., & Lapsley, I. (2001). On the efficiency of public welfare and private hospitals in Germany over time: A sectoral data envelopment analysis study. *Health Services Management Research, 14*(4), 263–274.

Hollingsworth, B. (2008). The measurement of efficiency and productivity of health care delivery. *Health Economics, 17*(10), 1107–1128.

Hollingsworth, B., Dawson, P., & Maniadakis, N. (1999). Efficiency measurement of health care: A review of nonparametric methods and applications. *Health Care Management Science, 2*(3), 161–172.

Hopp, W. J., & Lovejoy, W. S. (2013). *Hospital operations. Principles of high efficiency health care*. Saddle River, NJ: Pearson Education.

Hussey, D. S., de Vries, H., Romley, J., Wang, M. C., Chen, S. S., Shekelle, P. G., et al. (2009). A systematic review of health care efficiency measures. *Health Services Research, 44*(3), 784–805.

Ifantopoulos, Y. (2003). *Health economics*. Athens, Greece: Tipothito Publishing.

Jacobs, P., & Rapoport, J. (2004). *The economics of health and medical care*. Sudbury, MA: Jones and Bartlett Publishers.

Jacobs, R., Smith, P. C., & Street, A. (2006). *Measuring efficiency in health care*. Cambridge, UK: Cambridge University Press.

Jensen, G., & Morrisey, M. (1986). Medical staff specialty mix and hospital production. *Journal of Health Economics, 5*(3), 253–276.

Joumard, I., Andre, C., & Nicq, C. (2010). *Health care systems: Efficiency and institutions. Working Papers No 769, OECD Economic Department*. Paris: OECD Publishing.

Kalogeropoulou, M. (2011). Measuring the efficiency of Greek public hospitals. *Archives of Hellenic Medicine, 28*(6), 794–803.

King, R., & O'Sullivan, F. (2002). Financial management in selected community/foundation schools of the United Kingdom and charter schools of the United States. *Leadership and Policy in Schools, 1*(4), 291–316.

Kontaratou, A. N. (2003). *The art of hospital management*. Athens, Greece: Parisianou Publishing.

Linna, M., Hakkinen, U., & Magnussen, J. (2006). Comparing hospital cost efficiency between Norway and Finland. *Health Policy, 77*(3), 268–278.

Mansfield, E. (1996). *Managerial economics. Theory, applications and cases* (3rd ed.). Athens, Greece: Benos Publishing.

Mobley, L. R., & Frech, H. E. (1994). Firm growth and failure in increasingly competitive markets: Theory and application to hospital markets. *Journal of Economics and Business, 1*(1), 77–93.

Newbrander, W., Barnum, H., & Kutzin, J. (1992). *Hospital economics and financing in developing countries*. Geneva: World Health Organization.

Newhouse, J. (1970). *Toward a theory of non-profit institutions: An economic model of a hospital*. Santa Monica, CA: The RAND Corporation.

Newhouse, J. P. (1988). Has the erosion of the medical marketplace ended? *Journal of Health Politics, Policy and Law, 13*(2), 263–278.

Newhouse, J. (1992). Medical care costs: How much welfare loss? *Journal of Economic Perspectives, 6*(3), 3–21.

Newhouse, J. P. (1994). Frontier estimation: How useful a tool for health economics? *Journal of Health Economics, 13*(3), 317–322.

Nir, A. E. (2007). The effect of school –based management on schools' culture of consumption. *International Journal of Leadership in Education, 10*(4), 421–436.

Okunade, A. A., & Murthy, V. N. R. (2002). Technology as a major driver of health care costs: A cointegration analysis of the Newhouse conjecture. *Journal of Health Economics, 21*(1), 147–159.

Palmer, S., & Torgerson, D. J. (1999). Definitions of efficiency (economic notes). *The BMJ, 318*, 1136.

Pettinger, R. (1994). *Introduction to management*. London: Macmillan.

Polyzos, N. (2015). *Health care management*. Athens, Greece: Kritiki Publishing.

Prior, D. (2006). Efficiency and total quality management in health care organisations: A dynamic frontier approach. *Annals of Operational Research, 145*(1), 281–299.

Reyes, H. A., & Rodriguez, M. G. (2004). School finance: Raising questions for urban schools. *Education and Urban Society, 37*(1), 3–21.

Saiti, A., & Mylona, V. (2015a). The professional development plan of a health care workforce as a qualitative indicator of the health care system's well-being. *eJournal of Education Policy*. Retrieved from http://nau.edu/COE/eJournal/_Forms/fall2015/Saiti_Mylona

Saiti, A., & Mylona, V. (2015b). Health care human resources' planning and programming act as a necessary tool for the effectiveness and strengthening of the health care sector. *European Journal of Social Sciences Education and Research, 5*(1), 349–356.

Saiti, A., & Papadopoulos, Y. (2015). School teachers' job satisfaction and personal characteristics: A quantitative research study in Greece. *International Journal of Educational Management, 29*(1), 73–97.

Scherer, F. M. (1993). Pricing profits and technological progress in the pharmaceutical industry. *Journal of Economic Perspectives, 7*(3), 97–115.

Schermerhorn, J. R. (2010). *Introduction to management*. Asia: John Wiley & Sons.

Segal, L., & Richardson, J. (1994). Economic framework for allocative efficiency in the health care sector. *The Australian Economic Review, 27*(2), 89–98.

Skountzos, T. (2005). *Economic development. theory – practice*. Athens, Greece: Stamoulis Publishing.

Street, A., & Hakkinen, U. (2009). Health system productivity and efficiency. In P. C. Smith, E. Mossialos, I. Papanicolas, & S. Leatherman (Eds.), *Performance measurement for health system improvement experiences. Challenges and prospects* (pp. 222–248). New York: Cambridge University Press.

Sullivan, E. J. (2012). *Effective leadership and management in nursing* (8th ed.). Boston: Pearson.

Sullivan, E. J. (2016). *Effective leadership and management in nursing* (8th ed.). Athens, Greece: Giourdas Publishing.

Trossman, S. (2009). Shifting to the bedside for report. *The American Nurse, 41*(2), 7.

Tsavalias, C. (2013). *Factors that affect the efficiency of public sector hospitals and recommendations for restructuring hospitals*. PhD Thesis, Faculty of Nursing, University of Athens, Athens, Greece (in Greek).

Varabyova, Y., & Schreyogg, J. (2013). International comparisons of the technical efficiency of the hospital sector: Panel data analysis of OECD countries using parametric and non-parametric approaches. *Health Policy, 112*(1-2), 70–79.

Wagstaff, A. (1989). Estimating efficiency in the hospital sector: A comparison of three statistical cost frontier models. *Applied Economics, 21*(5), 659–672.

Worthington, A. C. (2004). Frontier efficiency measurement in health care: A review of empirical techniques and selected applications. *Medical Care Research and Review, 61*(2), 135–170.

Zagga, A. (2017). *The distribution of resources at the level of primary health care: The case of the Greek Red Cross*. Master Thesis. University of West Attica and European University of Cyprus. Athens, Greece (in Greek).

Zuckerman, S., Hadley, J., & Iezzoni, L. (1994). Measuring hospital efficiency with frontier cost function. *Journal of Health Economics, 13*(3), 335–340.

Zweifel, P., Breyer, F., & Kifmann, M. (2009). *Health economics* (2nd ed.). New York: Springer Publishing.

Index

M. Chletsos, A. Saiti, *Strategic Management and Economics in Health Care*,
https://doi.org/10.1007/978-3-030-35370-4

T

U

V

W

The manufacturer's authorised representative in the EU is Springer Nature Customer Service Centre GmbH, Europaplatz 3, 69115 Heidelberg, Germany. If you have any concerns regarding our products, please contact ProductSafety@springernature.com

Printed and bound by CPI Group (UK) Ltd, Croydon, CR0 4YY
30/09/2026
02225647-0006